Police Management and Organizational Behavior
A Contingency Approach

Roy R. Roberg
University of Nebraska at Omaha

CRIMINAL JUSTICE SERIES

West Publishing Company
St. Paul • New York • Los Angeles • San Francisco

COPYRIGHT © 1979 By WEST PUBLISHING CO.
    50 West Kellogg Boulevard
    P.O. Box 3526
    St. Paul, Minnesota 55165

All rights reserved

Printed in the United States of America

Library of Congress Cataloging in Publication Data
Roberg, Roy R
    Police management and organizational behavior.
    (The West criminal justice series)
    Includes index.
    1. Police administration. 2. Organizational behavior. I. Title. II. Series.
HV7935.R6   658'.91'3632   78-31923
ISBN 0-8299-0275-9

*To police managers
who wish to improve their work environments,
and to April,
who has definitely improved mine.*

Preface

A cursory reading of the management literature in the criminal justice field ultimately leads to the conclusion that it lags significantly behind the management literature found in other academic fields and disciplines. This book is an attempt to upgrade the state of the art of police and criminal justice management to a level equal to that generally found in business, management, and public administration. To this end, significant management research is analyzed with the emphasis placed on integrating the theory and practice of police organization and management.

An interdisciplinary approach to this subject matter is incorporated through the use of research findings from the behavioral and social sciences. While important studies from police and criminal justice management are presented, because most of the rigorous empirical research in management has taken place in the private sector, critical studies from outside the criminal justice field are also reviewed and analyzed throughout each of the chapters. Traditionally, the study of management has been divided with respect to public and private institutions. However, it is becoming increasingly clear that managerial theory and practice is a general phenomenon, and although the economic environments of the two "types" of enterprises may differ, the interrelationships and behavior of humans is similar—regardless of the public-private dichotomy. Accordingly, the focus of this book is purposely broad in scope; that is, research studies in both the public and private domain are applied to police and other criminal justice organizations with the intent of improving the quality of contemporary work environments.

It has also been customary to study the police as if they operated in a vacuum, and were apart from, rather than a part of, the administration of justice system. If the theory and practice of police management is to be properly understood, it is necessary to begin by emphasizing a general systems orientation. Such an orientation stresses the interrelated and interdependent nature of the parts or components (i.e., police, courts, and corrections) to the whole (i.e., criminal justice system). Once it is recognized that the managerial style and operating proficiency of any one of the components vitally affects each of the others, it becomes clear that for their own benefit (not to mention the benefit to the community through increased effectiveness of the criminal justice system per se), criminal justice practitioners need to manage and guide their respective organizations through a cooperative effort. In the past, by not emphasizing systems management, the criminal justice system has frequently operated in a haphazard and dysfunctional manner. Consequently, while primary attention is directed towards police organizations and their management, the organizational behavior of agencies in each of the other components is also highlighted. It is believed, therefore, that by utilizing a systems perspective, this book has a wider application to criminal justice management in general, and should prove useful in those curriculums which have developed such courses.

In the management of systems, not only are internal organizational factors of concern, but so too are those in the external environment (i.e., the community). A system that interacts with its environment in order to adapt to changing influences and conditions is therefore regarded as a open system. Because our society is dynamic and constantly changing, it is important that diverse criminal justice agencies be regarded as open systems, adapting their policies and practices to comply with environmental changes. This implies that there are no rules or principles which can be universally applied under all circumstances. However, many practicing managers still adhere to the sacredness of such "principles." Instead, the astute manager must take into account internal and external variables that are relevant to his or her particular organizational situation, and attempt to apply the most appropriate management concepts and techniques which "fit" the situation. This is known as the *contingency approach* to management, or, as it is frequently labelled, "it all depends." In other words, different management practices are required in different situations; this approach is considered the most effective for studying and predicting organizational behavior.

While contingency management is research orientated, it is also highly practical, allowing the practicing manager to apply specific actions that appear the most useful (based on available empirical evidence) for organizational and individual goal attainments. By actually integrating theory with practice, the contingency approach is of value to both the student and practitioner of criminal justice management. To increase the reader's understanding of the relationship between theory and practice, research studies conducted in natural or real life settings are presented whenever possible to supplement the text material. Furthermore, the book is written from the assumption that the reader may have only a limited knowledge of behavioral and social sciences, and is arranged to progress from general to more specific discussions on relevant research findings and their application to police and criminal justice management.

It is anticipated that the research reviewed in the book will be helpful in determining which organizational designs and management practices are the most appropriate and beneficial for specific organizational circumstances. Through the application of management actions based on sound research findings rather than tradition and intuition, the primary purpose of this book seeks to improve individual and organizational relationships and, hence, the operating efficiency and effectiveness of diverse police agencies.

I would like to express my sincere appreciation and indebtedness to several of those who provided valuable assistance in the preparation of this book. First, to Rick Mowday who rekindled my interest in the study of organizational behavior and for his help on the initial outline for the manuscript. To Fred Holbert and Harry More, Jr. who unselfishly reviewed drafts of every chapter and provided constructive comments throughout. To Vince Webb who reviewed and commented on various parts of the manuscript and who also helped provide a work environment conducive to scholarly endeavor. Furthermore, I would like to acknowledge my thanks to the authors and publishers who allowed various parts of their work to be reproduced in this volume. Finally, the excellent staff at West Publishing Co. is to be commended for their fine effort and encouragement in helping to bring this work to fruition.

Roy R. Roberg
Lincoln, Nebraska

Contents

ONE

Management's Role in the Police Organization   1

Learning Objectives   1
Individual and Organization Integration   2
The Concept of Management   6
The Police and the Criminal Justice System   10
The Contingency Approach   15
Summary   18
Discussion Questions   *18*
Annotated Bibliography   *19*

TWO

The Development of Management Theory   21

Learning Objectives   21
Classical Management Theory   22
Human Relations Theory   29
Modern Management Theory   34
Toward a Contingency Theory of Management   43
Summary   48
Discussion Questions   *49*
Annotated Bibliography   *49*

THREE

Research Methods in Management   51

Learning Objectives   51
The Concept of Theory   52
The Scientific Method   57
Research Designs   60
The Kansas City Preventive Patrol Experiment   66
Summary   76
Discussion Questions   76
Annotated Bibliography   77

FOUR

The Organization: Fundamental Characteristics   79

Learning Objectives   79
Organizations Defined   80
The "Who" of an Organization   81
The "Why" of an Organization   84
The "How" of an Organization   93
The "When" of an Organization   99
Summary   101
Discussion Questions   102
Annotated Bibliography   102

FIVE

The Individual: Behavior and Motivation   105

Learning Objectives   105
Human Behavior   106
Theories of Motivation   109
Contingency Approach to Motivation   124
Summary   125
Discussion Questions   126
Annotated Bibliography   126

SIX

Group Influences and Informal Organization   **129**

Learning Objectives   129
Concept of Group   130
Types of Groups   133
Communication Networks   134
Group Influences on Individuals   135
Conflict   139
Informal Organization   142
Summary   154
Discussion Questions   *155*
Annotated Bibliography   *155*

SEVEN

Leadership: Influencing Behavior   **157**

Learning Objectives   157
Leadership Defined   158
Trait Theory   159
Behavioral Theory   160
Contingency Theory   165
Participative Leadership   177
Summary   186
Discussion Questions   *187*
Annotated Bibliography   *188*

EIGHT

Organizational Design: Major Influences   **189**

Learning Objectives   189
Organization Classifications   191
Factors Affecting Design   194
Contingency Approach to Organization Design   203
Summary   211
Discussion Questions   *212*
Annotated Bibliography   *213*

NINE

Job Design and Performance Evaluation   **215**

Learning Objectives   215
The Design of Jobs   216
Job Design and Motivation   218
Contingency Approach to Job Design   228
Evaluating Job Performance   229
Performance Evaluation Methods   233
Who Evaluates?   242
Rewarding Performance   243
Contingency Approach to Performance Evaluation   244
Summary   245
Discussion Questions   *246*
Annotated Bibliography   *247*

TEN

Developing and Training Human Resources   **249**

Learning Objectives   249
The Developmental Process   250
Contingency Approach to Development   253
The Learning Process   253
Program Development   259
Development and Training Programs   265
Summary   276
Discussion Questions   *277*
Annotated Bibliography   *277*

ELEVEN

Planning for Organizational Change
and Development   **279**

Learning Objectives   279
The Planning Process   280
Contingency Approach to Planning   285
Change   286
Organizational Development   299
Contingency Approach to OD Interventions   307
Issues Facing OD   309
Summary   310
Discussion Questions   *311*
Annotated Bibliography   *312*

TWELVE

Police Management: Challenges of the Future   313

Learning Objectives   313
The Decline of Bureaucracy   314
Improving the Quality of Work Environments   317
Dealing with Change: The Contingency Approach   324
Concluding Comments   329
Summary   330
Discussion Questions   *331*
Annotated Bibliography   *331*

Subject Index   **333**
Name Index   **341**

Police Management and Organizational Behavior

A Contingency Approach

ONE

Management's Role in the Police Organization

LEARNING OBJECTIVES

The study of this chapter should enable you to:

- ☑ Explain the primary concern of management.
- ☑ Describe two major premises concerning individual-organization interactions.
- ☑ Describe the expectation-integration model and how it relates to the pursuit of a high quality work environment.
- ☑ Define the term management and discuss the primary features crucial to its meaning.
- ☑ Differentiate objectives from goals, and efficiency from effectiveness.
- ☑ Review the two choices that affect employees' behavior at work.
- ☑ Explain how management relates to both art and science.
- ☑ Discuss the general functions of the three major components of the criminal justice system.
- ☑ Describe the general goals of the criminal justice system, why stress and conflict arises within the system in attempting to reach such goals, and the resulting implications for criminal justice managers.
- ☑ Review the conceptual framework of the contingency approach and its application to the study of criminal justice management.

ONE

Man creates organizations to enlarge upon his own specialized talents, to protect himself, to enrich his life, and to satisfy a variety of other needs. To reach these ends, organizations are formed of people who have a common purpose and who are attracted to the group in order to satisfy their needs.[1]

From early childhood on, people band into groups. Some are social, some are utilitarian; some are formally organized, while others just develop. People form groups, or organizations, simply because human beings can get more done in a more effective way by working together.

Almost every organization, from the most simple to the most complex, needs some sort of management. This management may merely provide a sense of direction, or it may control the group as a whole. Given that most organizations are formed with a "common purpose" in order to "satisfy the needs" of their members, management has certain responsibilities to the group or organization of which it is a part. One of these involves an ability—and a desire—to respond to the needs of the organization itself and the individuals within it; in other words, to *integrate* the individual and the organization so that each party may attain its desired objectives in working toward an overall goal.

INDIVIDUAL AND ORGANIZATION INTEGRATION

With respect to the above, it would appear that the primary concern of management is to design organizations and utilize management practices in accord with individual and organizational needs. This organizing and integrating process is crucial for police and other criminal justice managers because it allows individual members to embrace the organization's goals as their own. When individual members are solidly committed to the organization and its goals, which in effect are the individual's goals also, maximum effort toward goal accomplishment is likely. To assist the practicing manager in achieving this purpose, modern management knowledge is applied through current theoretical frameworks and empirical investigations.

It should be noted that while this work stresses the managing of police organizations, the remaining agencies which collectively comprise the administration of justice system also receive some attention. In this way, the

---

1. Daniel A. Wren, *The Evaluation of Management Thought*, (New York: Ronald, 1972), p. 13.

interrelated and interdependent nature of the parts (police, courts and corrections) to the whole (criminal justice system) becomes clear; police management has a direct effect on court and correctional agencies, and vice versa. By studying police management from such a systems perspective, which shows how the parts or subsystems are related and dependent upon one another, the need for mutual understanding and cooperation among all criminal justice managers becomes apparent. It is simply not possible to study police management as distinct and separate from other types of criminal justice management.

In analyzing police management and organizational behavior, this text uses an *interdisciplinary* orientation, incorporating research findings from all of the behavioral and social sciences. In other words, prominent research studies from outside the criminal justice field are reviewed throughout the book. This is a distinctive departure from the traditional approach, which has generally ignored the significant work accomplished in other fields and disciplines. Because most of the rigorous empirical research in management and organizational behavior has taken place in the private sector, it is crucial that both the practicing police manager and the student (potential manager) be aware of such studies, which may be used to improve current working conditions in police organizations. Indeed, before any substantial reforms in police and criminal justice management can take place, the state of the art must first be upgraded to a level equal to that found in the general management literature.

When studying organizational behavior, a behavioral or social scientist should remain objective when reporting research results. Although every effort has been made to remain unbiased in the treatment of important research findings, two major premises will be advocated throughout the book.[2]

One: The quality of individual and organization interactions can be improved to the benefit of both parties. It is fairly well accepted that many employees are dissatisfied with their jobs.[3] This does not mean, of course, that every employee, or even the majority of employees, is discontent. It does mean that a significant percentage are less satisfied with their work and their relationships with the organization than they *could* be. From the organization's point of view, the performance of a number of employees is often viewed as barely adequate or as being below an acceptable level, as well as below the employees' capabilities. In other words, many workers could perform at a much higher level if they desired to do so.

One of the most serious problems in individual-organization interaction, which affects the criminal justice field as it does others, lies in the area of employee turnover. For example, the young college recruit, enthusiastic and anxious to be innovative, cannot cope with a highly tradition-bound

---

2. Both major premises were adapted from: Lyman W. Porter, Edward E. Lawler III, and J. Richard Hackman, *Behavior in Organizations* (New York: McGraw-Hill, 1975), pp. 25-27.

3. For an interesting discussion on this subject, see: Studs Terkel, *Working: People Talk About What They Do All Day and How They Feel About What They Do* (New York: Pantheon, 1974).

police agency and resigns within a short period of time. In this instance, the agency may well have been pleased that the individual departed. Such a situation could, in most instances, have been avoided from the start of the relationship, if each party had been willing to share their needs and expectations with the other.

The first premise, then, is a strong belief that the quality of interactions between the employee and the organization can be improved. Critical to this premise is the need to acknowledge that a problem exists. Once the organization and the employee realize there is a problem, positive steps can be taken to remedy it.

Two: The responsibility for improving the quality of individual and organization interactions lies with both the employee and the organization. Neither party can legitimately fix the blame or take the credit for life inside the organization, for within any organization we find a widely shared interaction process between the organization (i.e., its influential members) and its employees. If we assume premise number one to be true, then there must be a mutual give and take. Most police organizations, for instance, have not thoroughly analyzed job designs to determine which jobs might be enriched in order to improve the employee's work environment. For example, highly educated and qualified patrol officers may be inhibited from exercising their own decision-making capabilities while on the job. Allowing the officers to maximize their own job skill potential (through greater involvement in work decisions) may benefit not only the employee, but the organization as well. The employee's positive feelings, generated by increased contribution to the organization, strengthen the organization itself and are reflected in increased efficiency and reduced costs for specialists. Police organizations may also improve interactions with their employees through a systematic review of promotional and reward systems. It is questionable whether such agencies adequately reward and/or promote their employees for actions which benefit both the organization and the employee.

Throughout this book we are concerned with establishing the point that most police organizations can significantly increase the quality of interactions with their employees. On the other hand, individual employees must remember that they need to make sacrifices in order to improve the overall development and operation of the organization. In the final analysis, it is the organization which allows the individual to satisfy many needs and aspirations that could not otherwise be met. Purely self-motivated or low quality work, at the expense of a more common good, can only lead to a low quality organizational environment. Especially within the police field, which has a direct effect on society at large, selfish behavior may lead to the increased self-gratification of a specific employee or group of employees, but only while having far reaching ramifications for the organization through the loss of public support. Accordingly, while the individual employee expects the organization to provide a high-quality working environment, the employee must also expect to contribute substantially to this end.

Expectation-Integration Model

If a high-quality working environment is desired, both the individual employee and the organization must be satisfied with their relationship; they must strive to cooperate with and complement one another. An initial sharing of expectations can greatly enhance this process. In other words, what does each party expect from the other? Are their needs and goals similar? Do they feel comfortable with each other? What about the future?

If an honest and trustworthy individual-organization association can be fostered from the beginning, life inside the organization should be both rewarding and fulfilling. When the individual and the organization both strive toward *integration* (mutual sharing of expectations), relationships between them will be improved while sources of discontent will be reduced because each knows what is expected of the other. Each party is then aware of the adjustments (the "give and take") that are necessary for a mutually satisfying association. Simultaneously, many of the dysfunctions which can develop within organizations due to selfish indulgences by one party or the other should be greatly diminished.

The varying degrees to which expectations may be shared between the individual and the organization are indicated by the expectation-integration model depicted in Figure 1-1. It should be noted that the more extreme the behavior (i.e., the less either party shares expectations), the less likely a high-quality organizational environment is to develop. If either party attempts to camouflage its true intentions while using the other party to its own advantage, a poor-quality work environment is likely.

Figure 1-1

Expectation-Integration Model

Although it may not be feasible to obtain complete expectation-integration (the mid-point of Figure 1-1), each party should ultimately strive to reach this goal. Furthermore, it is crucial to understand that both conformity and deviance are found within organizations. All too frequently, police and other criminal justice organizations view strict conformity to established rules and procedures as acceptable behavior, while viewing deviation from such rules and procedures simply as a failure by the individual. One cannot deny that some individuals do in fact fail, and that a certain degree of conformity is desirable; however, so too is a certain degree of conflict. In order to achieve expectation-integration, channels of communication must be opened, allowing for constructive input of "deviant" or contrary viewpoints.

In this manner conflict can lead to positive gains for the individual and organization. While it may appear desirable for organizations to function smoothly and silently, this situation can be deceptive. Lengthy periods of quiet operation could be a sign of organizational stagnation or internal repression of legitimate concerns, which may lead to individual-organization discontent. In any case, stagnation can be a symptom of lack of organizational progress and change. Those who subvert the rules, speak out against "petty" regulations, or suggest improved methods are often crying out against stagnation and lack of timely change. Rather than categorizing such employees as recalcitrant troublemakers, the organization should react more positively and observe and listen carefully to those who may represent the cutting edge of desirable organizational change.

This book emphasizes the expectation-integration process in the belief that, by examining how expectations may be shared by both parties, a high-quality work environment will ensue. This development, in turn, should lead to more effective goal achievement for both the individual and the organization.

THE CONCEPT OF MANAGEMENT

The term *management* has almost as many meanings as there are writers in the field. In one instance, it may be used to identify all those within an organization who have supervisory powers — from the first-line supervisor through the chief executive. In another instance, management may be considered to be the process of coordinating group activity through planning, organizing, staffing, directing and controlling. Management is also perceived as involving a rapidly developing body of knowledge, moving in the direction of a recognized discipline. Admittedly, the field of management is still evolving, and yet it is already of major importance to our society—as Drucker has indicated:

The emergence of management as an essential, a distinct and a leading institution is a pivotal event in social history. Rarely, if ever, has a new basic institution, a new leading group, emerged as fast as has management since the turn of the century. Rarely in human history has a new institution proven indispensable so quickly; and even less often has a new institution arrived with so little opposition, so little disturbance, so little controversy.[4]

Management Defined

A common theme found in the literature concerning the definition of management is a concern for accomplishing organizational objectives and/

---

4. Peter F. Drucker, *The Practice of Management* (New York: Harper & Row, 1954), p. 3.

or goals. In the opening quotation of this chapter, for instance, it was suggested that organizations pursue a "common purpose" or overall goal. This should not be taken to imply, however, that individual needs and goals cannot be satisfied at the *same time*. How well individual needs are satisfied will, to a great extent, determine the overall effectiveness of the organization. This principle then, appears to be crucial to the concept of management, and should figure in any satisfactory definition of the term.

At this point, it seems appropriate to differentiate between *objectives* and *goals*. Normally, several objectives (short-range) must be accomplished before a goal (long-range) can be attained. For example, a police agency may have a goal of decreasing residential burglaries in a specific neighborhood. One objective along the path to goal achievement may be an awareness campaign whereby citizens are personally contacted and instructed about the dangers of not locking and securing their homes, etc. Another objective may be to increase patrols in the neighborhood during those hours with the highest incidence of burglaries. Achieving objectives such as these will conceivably reduce the burglary rate in the designated neighborhood.

Another feature which appears quite frequently in the literature concerning the definition of management is the idea of working with and through people (individuals or groups) in order to accomplish the organization's objectives and goals. Working *with* people describes a *mutual* participation, while working *through* people connotes a negative attitude toward the individual. In other words, if the organization cannot work with its employees, it will simply work through or, should we say, in spite of them. In relation to the expectation-integration model, this would reflect a poor-quality work environment.

Taking the above comments into consideration, management will be defined as: *the process of working with people in a humane fashion toward the accomplishment of organizational objectives and goals in as efficient and effective a manner as possible*. Several important features of this definition should be noted: First, it implies that anyone—regardless of position, status, or sex—who works with others toward organizational objectives and goals, is a manager. This acknowledges that organizational members are responsible for planning, organizing, and coordinating many of their own activities within the organization. At the same time, this does not suggest that separate managerial levels (i.e., top, middle, lower) are not necessary for the effective operation of the organization, but that such differences should be *functional* rather than *hierarchical* in nature. Second, it allows for individual-organization integration of expectations with respect to working with people; this implies cooperation by both parties. Third, it allows for some leeway in the individual-organization interaction process through the use of the phrase "as efficient and effective a manner as possible"; it does not expect or call for the impossible—only that both parties act competently in any given situation.

In our definition, when we speak of *efficiency* we are primarily concerned with the proper use of human resources, and secondarily with the uses of material resources; when we speak of *effectiveness* we are concerned with the degree to which organizational objectives and goals are attained. Each of these terms is of primary concern to the practicing manager, in that the possibility exists for an organization to be relatively efficient yet ineffective, and vice versa. It is the goal of management, of course, to maximize both the efficiency and the effectiveness of the organization.

A fourth feature of the definition deals with the concept of *humaneness,* which is infrequently mentioned with respect to management. Funk and Wagnell define humane as "having or showing kindness and tenderness; compassionate." Several synonyms listed are: benevolent, charitable, gracious, human, merciful and sympathetic. Several antonyms listed are: barbarous, cruel, fierce, inhuman, merciless and selfish.[5] Of course, this notion relates directly to the two premises mentioned at the beginning of the chapter, and is also important to the expectation-integration concept. In most police organizations, both the individual employee and the organization could associate with one another in a more humane manner. It is hoped, indeed intended, that by promoting such a definition of management, human dignity will be increased and the quality of the work environment improved.

Human Resources

While the task of management can be viewed most accurately from the perspective of coordinating and integrating all of the organization's resources (including personnel, material, money, time, etc.) toward the attainment of organizational objectives and goals, this text will emphasize the use of the most important commodity within an organization, namely, human resources. The foundation for this approach has already been laid above, with the introductory remarks and the manner in which management has been interpreted. However, there is another significant factor that has a bearing on the use of human resources—the fact that organizations typically spend 80 to 90 percent of their budget on personnel. Local police departments, for instance, expend 85 percent or more of their total operating budget on salaries.[6] What this means, then, is that the organization literally cannot afford to ignore the behavior of its employees.

Macy and Mirvis have indicated the importance to the organization of considering the behavior of its employees in terms of economic effectiveness.[7] The conceptual framework underlying their methodology emphasized that employees' behavior at work results from choices they make

5. Charles Earle Funk (ed.) *Funk & Wagnells New College Standard Dictionary* (New York: Funk & Wagnells, 1953), p. 575.

6. George D. Eastman and Esther M. Eastman (eds.) *Municipal Police Administration,* (Washington, D. C.: International City Management Association, 1971), p. 174.

7. Barry A. Macy and Phillip H. Mirvis, "A Methodology for Assessment of Quality of Work Life and Organizational Effectiveness in Behavioral-Economic Terms," *Administrative Science Quarterly,* 21, 1976, pp. 212-226.

about: (1) being available to work,[8] and (2) role performance while on the job.[9] This assumes that "employees are more likely to come to work and remain in the organization if they *obtain satisfaction* from their jobs, and that they are likely to put forth *more effort* and work *more effectively* if they expect to be *rewarded* for their *efforts and performance.* The employees' satisfaction and reward expectations are influenced by their *work environment* and the extent to which it provides valued rewards. The work environment includes the employee's jobs, supervisors, and work groups, and the organizational structure and technology (emphasis added)."[10]

In the manufacturing and assembly plant studied by Macy and Mirvis, behavioral measures were selected in relation to member participation (absenteeism, tardiness, turnover, and work stoppages and strikes) and role performance (productivity, product or service quality, grievances, accidents and job-related illnesses, etc.). During the experimental period, organizational characteristics and employees' reward expectations were altered; therefore one would expect to find changes in the employees' job-related behaviors. Sizable reductions in turnover, accidents, and grievances took place during the experiment. Although absenteeism increased, employees in the experimental groups appeared to select leave days, instead of pay bonuses, as rewards for good performance. Product quality as well as production levels also improved over the course of the experiment. This means, then, that by manipulating the *quality* of the work environment, management can influence employee performance.

As one can well imagine, such changes in employee job behavior would save the organization substantial sums of money, as well as improving product quality and quantity. Although the "products" of police agencies are more difficult to determine than those of most industrial firms (e.g., administering laws justly or providing needed social services versus number of welds made or cars assembled), the implication remains the same. Accordingly, this text will adopt the conceptual framework utilized by Macy and Mirvis in regard to the effective use of human resources: individual employees who are satisfied with their jobs are more likely to come to work and remain in the organization, as well as work more effectively, if they expect to be (and, in fact, are) rewarded for their performance.

Management: Art or Science?

A question ultimately arises in regard to management; is it is an art or a science? If one means science in the sense of the so-called "exact" sciences, such as chemistry and physics, the answer is no. The experimental controls characteristic of the natural and physical sciences, which take place in a laboratory setting where all variables except one can be held constant, are simply impossible to apply to the field of management. However, this does

---

8.   James G. March and Herbert A. Simon, *Organizations* (New York: John Wiley & Sons, 1958).

9.   Edward E. Lawler, *Motivation in Work Organizations* (Monterey, Calif.: Brooks/Cole, 1973).

10.   Macy and Mirvis, *op. cit.,* p. 213.

not mean that a manager cannot carry out valuable research through measurement of organizational variables; it does mean that when dealing with the complexity of organizational life, the controls—and therefore the results—are not as exact. In fact, the "inexact" sciences of psychology and sociology, as well as management, have been producing important empirical findings with respect to organizational behavior for many years. In this sense, which is the only sense possible in the "real world," management can certainly be referred to as a science.

What then, can be said about management as an art? Art can be defined as "the systematic application of knowledge and skill in order to achieve an objective. ... The key word in the definition of art is application. Thus management, as an activity which applies knowledge and skill to objectives, is an art as well as a science." [11] The functions of both art and science can be described in the following manner:

It is the function of the arts to accomplish concrete ends, effect results, produce situations, that would not come about without the deliberate efforts to secure them. These arts must be mastered and applied by those who deal in the concrete and for the future. The function of the sciences, on the other hand, is to explain the phenomenon, the events, effects, or situations, but explanations which we call knowledge. It has not been the aim of science to be a system of technology, and it could not be such a system. There is required in order to manipulate the concrete a vast amount of knowledge of a temporary, local, specific character, of no general value or interest, that it is not the function of a science to have or to present and only to explain to the extent that it is generally significant.[12]

To management, then, art and science are not mutually exclusive; instead, they complement each other. Astute police managers must be able to integrate what they have learned through experience (which can be interpreted as art) with what they have discovered through science. In this way, management may indeed be considered as both an art and a science.

THE POLICE
AND THE CRIMINAL JUSTICE SYSTEM

As indicated previously, the police must be studied and managed from a criminal justice system perspective. It is time that academicians and practitioners alike become concerned with the effective operation of the total system and not simply a single component of that system. This is not to imply that the effectiveness of any one component is unimportant, for each contributes to the final "product," but if the effectiveness of the total system is to be improved by any measurable degree in the foreseeable future, much

---

11. Theo Haimann and William G. Scott, *Management in the Modern Organization*, 2nd ed. (Boston: Houghton Mifflin 1974), p. 13.

12. Chester I. Barnard, *The Functions of the Executive* (Cambridge, Mass: Harvard Univ. Press, 1938), pp. 290-291.

more attention must be directed toward systems management. The following description of the functions of each criminal justice component highlights the interrelated and interdependent nature of the system.

For most Americans the goals of the criminal justice system appear obvious — the prevention and control of crime. However, such a broadly phrased statement does not tell us much about the ways that those goals may be achieved ... the criminal justice system operates to apprehend, convict, and sanction those members of the community who cannot live according to the basic rules of group existence. Additionally, the prevention and control of crime are enhanced by the deterring effect of the individual sanctions on the conduct of the general population; it is hoped that by observing the consequences of criminal behavior, others are encouraged to live according to the law.[13]

With regard to crime prevention and control, the criminal justice system is comprised of three major components or subsystems: the police, the courts (including prosecution and defense), and corrections (including probation, incarceration, and parole). Although each of the components is represented by agencies at the federal, state, and local levels of government, our focus is on the local level. Therefore, when referring to the management of police and other criminal justice organizations, this book is primarily concerned with county and municipal agencies. This does not imply that the theoretical and practical aspects of management discussed here are not appropriate or applicable to agencies at the federal and state levels, or that they may not be referred to occasionally; it simply means that the emphasis is on determining appropriate managerial concepts and techniques for local police organizations. The primary functions of the agencies which make up each of the components or subsystems are described below.

Police

Local police departments are normally considered to have three broadly defined and interactive functions. The most widely acknowledged role is that of *law enforcement;* this responsibility is mainly one of initiating criminal action against those who violate the law. The law enforcement function includes arresting offenders, preventing criminal acts, recovering stolen property, and handling civil disorders. However, the police (i.e., the patrol force) actually spend a significantly greater amount of their time maintaining order and providing social services.[14] *Order maintenance* activities include handling disputes among people who disagree over what is morally right, misconduct, or the assignment of blame in a situation; that is, the police maintain order (keep the peace) without making an arrest. *Social services* are also provided by the police; abating nuisances, traffic and crowd

---

13. George F. Cole, *The American System of Criminal Justice* (North Scituate, Mass.: Duxbury, 1975), p. 39.

14. For example, see: Roy R. Roberg, *The Changing Police Role: New Dimensions and New Issues* (San Jose, Calif.: Justice Systems Development, 1976).

control, administering first aid, and furnishing information are only a few of the many services which benefit the citizenry.[15]

Numerous studies[16] have indicated that the police actually spend less than 25% of their time working on even minimal law enforcement activities. The remainder of their time is spent on what can most appropriately be referred to as public services—keeping the peace and providing general assistance. Typical findings of police activities were reported by Wallach in a study of a Baltimore police district:

... the bulk of police activity ... does not relate to the ... crime control function. The vast majority of police activities ... do not involve crimes and most of the crime-related contacts are really after-the-fact report-taking from crime victims ... The vast majority of all resident requests sampled was related to the maintenance of order, the settling of inter-personal disputes, and the need for advice and emergency assistance. Overall, crime related calls constituted less than one-fourth of ... police service calls.[17]

Despite such findings, the police continue to be viewed primarily as "crime fighters," thus compounding the problems of police management by emphasizing incorrectly the functional aspects of the role. Bercal alludes to this problem as follows:

... to study the police in the context of a para-military organization primarily concerned with the control and prevention of crime focuses attention on but a small portion of police work. Such an orientation has encouraged police to make major policy decisions on the weight of crime statistics and to overlook, and thereby fail to take sufficiently into account, the vast majority of its activities. Conversely, emphasis on the "crime problem" and "social unrest" have hidden the majority of police work from the public's eye.[18]

In contemporary society, then, the primary functions of the police should be regarded as keeping the peace and providing needed services. The recognition of this fact, by both the public and the police, is of extreme importance. This does not imply that the police should cease dealing with criminal matters, making arrests, or investigating suspicious circumstances, or that law enforcement is not a crucial part of the total role concept—but the myth that their major function is crime fighting must be debunked. Critical assumptions relating to the entire police system depend on where

---

15. See: Paul M. Whisenard and James L. Cline, *Patrol Operations* (Englewood Cliffs, N.J.: Prentice-Hall, 1971), pp. 2-5.

16. For example, see: Elaine Cumming, Ian Cumming and Laura Edell, "Policeman as Philosopher, Guide, and Friend," *Social Problems,* 12, (Winter), 1965, pp. 276-286; Raymond Parnas, "The Police Response to the Domestic Disturbance," *Wisconsin Law Review,* (Fall), 1967, pp. 914-960; Herman Goldstein, "Police Response to Urban Crisis," *Public Administration Review,* 28, (September-October), 1968, pp. 417-418; James Q. Wilson, *Varieties of Police Behavior,* (Cambridge, Mass.: Harvard Univ. Press, 1968), pp. 18-19.

17. Irving A. Wallach, *Police Functions in a Negro Community* (McLean, Va.: Research Analysis, 1970), 1, p. 6.

18. Thomas E. Bercal, "Calls for Police Assistance," *American Behavioral Scientist,* 13, (May-August), 1970, pp. 681-690.

emphasis is placed—on law enforcement or on order maintenance and services. Such role interpretation has a direct effect on the way in which police agencies are designed, how they are managed, how policies are implemented, how officers are trained, etc. In the past, the complex nature of police work, accompanied by the high degree of discretion which must be exercised, has not generally been recognized.[19]

Because of this, police agencies have not been adequately organized and managed, and personnel have not been suitably trained to fulfill the responsibilities required by the current role. Consequently, this book emphasizes managerial practices and techniques which will allow the police organization and its members to properly prepare for their complex roles and better serve society.

Courts

Criminal courts are responsible for determining the guilt or innocence of those who are brought before them. The court process is aimed at seeking the truth and obtaining "justice" for the accused. Thus the court has as its goals: protection of individual rights, proper disposition of those convicted, and the protection of society. The foundation for the protection of individual rights is determined by federal and state constitutions and by case law. The court must make sure that the defendant is afforded due process and that no individual rights have been violated; this includes a critical review of the circumstances surrounding the case and the admissibility of evidence. If the defendant is found guilty, the court then reviews the individual's background and selects the most appropriate sentence alternative. To properly dispose of a case, both the needs of the offender and society must be considered. If a serious threat to public safety is posed, the offender must be removed from society.

Prosecution and Defense. In the administration of justice, these agencies oppose one another in an adversary relationship. That is, in a criminal trial, the prosecutor and the defense attorney attempt to produce evidence and arguments which are beneficial to their side of the case. Theoretically, the adversary system provides a fair trial for the defendant and seeks the truth in determining guilt or innocence. Besides presenting its case against the defendant, the prosecutor's office is responsible for determining what the charge is to be and whether it may be reduced through negotiation, and, in some instances, for recommending that the charge be dismissed. In short, the prosecutor is responsible for the state's case from the time of arrest through conviction and sentencing in the criminal court. The defense attorney's position is, of course, just the opposite. This office is responsible for presenting the best possible legal defense for the defendant, and attempts to make sure that the accused's rights are safeguarded. Therefore, the defense

---

19. For discussion on the complex nature of patrol work, see: Roy R. Roberg, "The Current Police Role: Some Critical Implications of Patrol Work," in *The Changing Police Role: New Dimensions and New Issues,* Roberg (ed.), (San Jose, Calif.: Justice Systems Development, 1976), pp. 87-96.

attorney is responsible for the defendant's case from initial arrest and plea bargaining, through the trial and sentencing procedures, and through the appeal process if needed.

Corrections

In the broadest sense, corrections includes probation, various types of incarceration (including jails, half-way houses, and state penitentiaries) and parole programs for both juvenile and adult offenders. This component has several critical functions: protection of society, crime deterrence, and rehabilitation. The first function is that of maintaining custody and humane treatment of offenders in order to assure that further crimes are not committed. The deprivation of liberty to those convicted of criminal acts, as well as the threat of incarceration to potential offenders, is regarded as a primary crime deterrent. The equally important function of rehabilitation—the providing of those programs and supervisory services which will assist offenders back into the mainstream of society—is also the most difficult.

Probation. Probation agencies are responsible for the supervision of offenders (probationers) who have not been committed to a correctional institution by the court, but who remain in the community subject to conditions imposed by the court. In their supervisory role, probation officers provide various social and counseling services to help individuals adjust to the community and to alleviate the types of problems which originally brought them before the court.

Incarceration. When an offender is sentenced by the court to a period of confinement, the responsibility for security and rehabilitation shifts from the court to the correctional agency. Maximum security institutions generally have a dual function: custody and treatment. That is, they protect society from the threat of harm, while providing rehabilitative services (counseling, education, training, etc.) that will assist the offenders in leading productive, noncriminal lives. Because many experts feel that only a small percentage of prison inmates require maximum security and that most can be more effectively rehabilitated under less stringent conditions, there is a movement toward the use of community-based or minimum security facilities. Such programs allow the offender to maintain normal social relationships while having access to rehabilitative services.

Parole. Parole agencies are responsible for the supervision of offenders (parolees) who have been conditionally released from a correctional institution prior to the statutory expiration of the sentence. In their supervisory role, parole officers help the ex-offender to bridge the gap between institutional confinement and life within the community; counseling services similar to those involved in probation are used to help the individual avoid further criminal activity.

In conclusion, while the primary goals of the criminal justice system may be apparent—the prevention and control of crime—it is also apparent that each of the components has differing objectives and orientations, thereby creating stress and conflict within the system. Unfortunately, the resulting apprehension—if not outright hostility—between subsystems causes the system to operate dysfunctionally. The Task Force Report on Science and Technology addresses this situation:

Police, court and corrections officials all share the objective of reducing crime. But each uses different, sometimes conflicting, methods and so focuses frequently on inconsistent subobjectives. The police role, for example, is focused on deterrence. Most modern correctional thinking, on the other hand, focuses on rehabilitation and argues that placing the offender back into society under a supervised community treatment program provides the best chance for his rehabilitation as a law-abiding citizen. But community treatment may involve some loss of deterrent effect, and the ready arrest of marginal offenders, intended to heighten deterrence, may by affixing a criminal label complicate rehabilitation. The latent conflicts between the parts may not be apparent from the viewpoint of either subsystem, but there is an obvious need to balance and rationalize them so as to achieve optimum overall effectiveness.[20]

Accordingly, the implications for criminal justice managers become clear: the manager cannot operate from an isolationist perspective; each manager must strive to understand and respect the responsibilities of fellow managers and their organizations, as well as attempt to work with them in a constructive and coordinated fashion. Only through such an approach to management will it be possible to achieve "optimum overall effectiveness" within the criminal justice system.

THE CONTINGENCY APPROACH

This book utilizes a contingency approach to the management of police organizations; this is the most contemporary and pragmatic framework for the study of organizational behavior. Contingency management is concerned with the relationship between relevant external and internal environmental variables and appropriate management concepts and techniques that lead to effective goal attainment.[21] To this end, the contingency approach considers specific organizational circumstances and attempts to apply the most appropriate organizational designs and managerial practices to particular situations. "The essence of this view is that there is *no one best way* and that there is a middle ground between 'universal principles' and 'it all depends.'"[22]

The contingency approach stems directly from a general systems scheme, in which a system is thought of as a unitary whole composed of

---

20. President's Commission on Law Enforcement and Administration of Justice, *Task Force Report: Science and Technology* (Washington, D.C.: U.S. Government Printing Office, 1967), p. 53.

21. Fred Luthans, *Introduction to Management: A Contingency Approach* (New York: McGraw-Hill, 1976), p. 29.

22. Fremont E. Kast and James E. Rosenzweig, *Organization and Management: A Systems Approach,* 2nd ed. (New York: McGraw-Hill, 1974), p. 21.

interdependent and interrelated parts or subsystems. The President's Crime Commission discusses this concept in relation to the primary criminal justice components:

The criminal justice system has three separately organized parts—the police, the courts, and corrections—and each has distinct tasks. However, these parts are by no means independent of each other. *What each one does and how it does it has a direct effect on the work of the others.* The courts must deal, and can only deal, with those whom the police arrest; the business of corrections is with those delivered to it by the courts. How successfully corrections reforms convicts determines whether they will once again become police business and influences the sentences the judges pass; police activities are subject to court scrutiny and are often determined by court decisions. And so reforming or reorganizing any part or procedure of the system changes other parts or procedures (emphasis added).[23]

The important consideration in this conceptual scheme is the recognition of the interrelatedness of the parts to one another. Munro emphasizes the relationships of a social system as follows:

The extent and activity of a social system may be observed by witnessing the events which characterize that system. These events are interrelated and interdependent so that a change in one part of the system produces a change of greater or less magnitude in other segments of the system.[24]

A change introduced into any one part of the system, such as the police —who increase their number of arrests—will also produce a corresponding change in the other parts as well, in this instance, the operations of both the courts and corrections who must deal with the increased number of arrested persons. It should be noted, however, that while this scheme takes into consideration the interrelationships among the parts of the system, it fails to consider the interactions *between* the system itself and its *external environment,* which, in the case of the criminal justice system, is the community at large. Consequently, an *open systems* conceptual scheme allows us to view the criminal justice system as it interacts with a dynamic environment, while at the same time, we take into account the interrelationships among the subsystems. Studying criminal justice organizational behavior from such a perspective is underscored by Cole:

One of the values of using systems as an organizing concept is that it not only points to the interdependence of each part of the criminal justice process, but it also allows us to focus our analysis at various levels. At a macro-level, for example, it is possible to look at various political and social influences on the criminal justice system. How does criminal justice respond to economic, political, and social forces of America? In more concrete terms, we might be interested in the way law enforcement competes

---

23. President's Commission on Law Enforcement and Administration of Justice, *The Challenge of Crime in a Free Society,* (Washington, D. C.: U.S. Government Printing Office, 1967), p. 7.

24. Jim L. Munro, "Towards a Theory of Criminal Justice Administration: A General Systems Perspective," *Public Administration Review,* 31, 1971, p. 624.

with education or defense in the allocation of public resources. At a more inclusive level it is again possible to use the concept of system to understand the impact of one subsystem of criminal justice on the work of another.[25]

By its very nature, general systems theory is broad in scope, as it relates the parts of any system to the whole. Contingency theory, on the other hand, is more *specific* and *pragmatic,* for it attempts to *apply* appropriate management concepts and techniques to specific organizational circumstances. In the past, the lack of practical application of managerial theory has been a constant source of irritation and frustration to those working in the field; contingency management comes closest to filling this void between theory and practice:

Practitioners have justifiably become baffled by the ever-increasing array of management concepts and techniques. Every concept or technique that comes along is supposedly the answer to all their problems. Yet practitioners are finding out that a particular concept or technique just does not work in their situation. The advocate [of a specific concept or technique] most often reacts by assuming that the practitioner is "copping out." It is suggested that the reasons a concept or technique does not work is that practitioners either do not understand it, or, more likely, are simply unable or unwilling to implement it properly. The disenchanted practitioner, on the other hand, points an accusing finger at the so-called experts as being entirely unrealistic. Like any such controversy, neither party is entirely right or wrong. There is certainly some truth and some misunderstanding on both parts.

The major problem in the current dilemma is that the parties are operating from different assumptions. The theorists and/or experts assume explicitly or implicitly the universality of their concepts and techniques. Practitioners, on the other hand, often assume universality of their individual style but are highly situational when it comes to applying modern management concepts and techniques. The contingency approach bridges this gap between theory and practice. The modern concepts and techniques are not wrong or necessarily unrealistic. By the same token, the practitioners are not necessarily wrong either. Many of the concepts and techniques do not work in their unique situations. What contingency management attempts to do is functionally *relate* given situational conditions to the appropriate management concepts and techniques for effective goal attainment.[26]

Due to the advantages described above, the contingency approach is regarded as the premier method for the study and prediction of police organizational behavior. This research-oriented approach enables the manager to review and select those managerial actions which appear the most appropriate in guiding the organization toward the fulfillment of its goals. Consequently, the following chapters include major management research findings, in an attempt to integrate the theory and practice of managing police organizations. Furthermore, because little empirical research has been conducted on contingency relationships within the criminal justice field, this framework should provide direction for the future development of police management in particular and criminal justice management in general.

---

25. Cole, *op. cit.,* p. 26.

26. Luthans, *op. cit.,* p. 35.

SUMMARY

The major precepts which provide the overall structure for this book have been stated in this chapter. It has been stressed that the primary task of management is to design organizations and utilize management practices in accord with individual and organizational needs; that is, to integrate the needs of both parties. It was observed that the responsibility for improving the quality of individual and organizational interactions lies with both the employee and the organization. Accordingly, an integration-expectation model was developed to suggest the importance of a mutual sharing of expectations, which should lead to the improvement of work environments. A humane definition of management has been promoted; one which acknowledges that organizational members are responsible for planning, organizing, and coordinating many of their own activities within the organization. Because human resources are the most valuable asset of any organization, this text will focus on the proper use of the people who work within police organizations. To this end, it was suggested that management is both an art and a science and that practicing managers need to integrate what they have learned through experience with what they have discovered through science.

The primary functions of each of the major components of the criminal justice system were analyzed, indicating that while their primary goals may be complementary, differing objectives and orientations create conflict which often causes hostility. This suggests that all criminal justice managers must strive to understand and respect the responsibilities of one another, and attempt to work together constructively. Consequently, the criminal justice process must be viewed from a general systems perspective, relating the parts to the whole; criminal justice managers cannot operate in a vacuum.

A contingency conceptual framework will be employed throughout the book because it is research oriented, and yet pragmatic in its approach to the study of organizational behavior. Contingency management evolved directly from a general systems scheme and examines environmental variables in an attempt to apply appropriate managerial practices to specific organizational situations. The following chapter presents a brief overview of the development of management theory and the applicability of contingency management to police organizational behavior.

DISCUSSION QUESTIONS

1. Discuss the meaning of individual-organization integration; to what extent do you think integration can occur in criminal justice agencies?

2. Why is it not possible to separate the study of police management from criminal justice management?

3. Describe the expectation-integration model and its importance to improving the quality of work environments.

4. Define the concept of management and explain what you feel to be the most important aspect of the definition.

5. Do you think management should be considered as both an art and a science; why or why not?

6. Discuss the interactive functions of the police role and why role emphasis is crucial to police management.

7. Why is the contingency approach important to the management of criminal justice systems?

ANNOTATED BIBLIOGRAPHY

Dalton, Melville. *Men Who Manage.* New York: John Wiley & Sons, 1959. This book focuses on the various activities in which managers engage, and the means they use to promote their careers; both formal and informal aspects of management are discussed.

Hall, Douglas T. *Careers in Organizations.* Pacific Palisades, Calif.: Goodyear Publishing Company, 1976. Research findings are summarized on career advancement; primary areas of concern include such topics as career choice, career stages, and methods of advancement.

House, Robert J. *Management Development: Design, Evaluation, and Implementation.* Ann Arbor, Mich.: Bureau of Industrial Relations, 1967. This anthology presents behavioral research on the effects of systematic efforts to develop managerial behavior through planned efforts; the final product represents a theory of why management development efforts fail in many situations.

McGregor, Douglas. *The Professional Manager.* New York: McGraw Hill, 1977. This book is oriented toward how a manager can think and deal with oneself—managerial role and style, managerial power, the issue of control over others, the organization of work, the problems of teamwork, and perhaps most importantly, the manner in which individual needs can and should be integrated with organizational goals.

Mintzberg, Henry. *The Nature of Managerial Work.* New York: Harper & Row, 1973. Relates behavioral research findings to a wide range of relationships which comprise the manager's "work" in contemporary organizations; significant contributions include: distinguishing characteristics of managerial work, the manager's working roles, science and the manager's job, and the future of managerial work.

TWO

The Development of Management Theory

LEARNING OBJECTIVES

The study of this chapter should enable you to:

☑ Discuss the major contributors to and general emphasis of the three principal categories of classical theory.

☑ Describe the series of experiments conducted by the Mayo researchers and explain the relevance of their findings, including the Hawthorne effect.

☑ Briefly appraise classical and human relations theory.

☑ Review the synthesizing aspects of modern management theory and the two general approaches utilized.

☑ Define the two criteria a field must meet to be classified as a behavioral science, and discuss the three levels of analysis associated with behavioral science research.

☑ Discuss the concept of general systems theory; differentiate between closed and open system models.

☑ Review the basic characteristics of open systems theory in relation to the study of criminal justice organizations.

☑ Explain what is meant by a "contingent relationship."

☑ Differentiate between contingency and general systems theory.

☑ Briefly appraise modern and contingency theory.

TWO

Although we are primarily interested in contemporary management theory and practice, it is important to understand the evolution of traditional views and the manner in which they influence current management concepts. While management practices can be traced back 5000 years,[1] systematic study and general theoretical advances in the field have been relatively recent—from the late nineteenth century to the present. Scholars from the social and behavioral sciences have contributed significantly to the development of managerial theory; numerous classification systems have also evolved, in an attempt to organize these theoretical developments. This chapter is designed to provide the reader with a basic understanding of the major theoretical advances in the field and their relation to police and criminal justice management practice. To this end, the following developmental areas will be discussed: (1) classical or traditional, (2) human relations or neo-classical, (3) modern, and (4) contingency. Figure 2-1 summarizes the primary contributions and evolution of each of the theoretical advances. It should be noted that these classifications are not mutually exclusive, but rather overlap to varying degrees and build from one another.

CLASSICAL MANAGEMENT THEORY

The first students in the field studied the anatomy of organizations and subsequently devised certain principles of management that were to be followed if the organization was to operate efficiently. Thompson has suggested three principal categories (discussed below) in the development of classical or traditional management thought: (1) scientific management, (2) bureaucracy, and (3) administrative management.[2]

Scientific Management

The systematic study of complex organizations and their management can be traced to the work of Frederick W. Taylor and his associates. Taylor began his work in the latter part of the nineteenth century and continued through the early part of the twentieth. During this time period, a major problem involved efficiency in large industrial factories. Accordingly, Taylor's work focused on methods of increasing worker productivity. He believed that workers were motivated primarily through economic rewards,

---

1. Claude S. George, Jr., *The History of Management Thought*, (Englewood Cliffs, N.J.: Prentice-Hall, Inc., 1968), p. 3.

2. James D. Thompson, *Organizations in Action: Social Science Bases of Administrative Theory*, (New York: McGraw-Hill Book Company, 1967), pp. 4-5.

and that organizations should be characterized by a distinct hierarchy of authority comprising highly specialized personnel.

Figure 2-1

Development of Major Management Theories

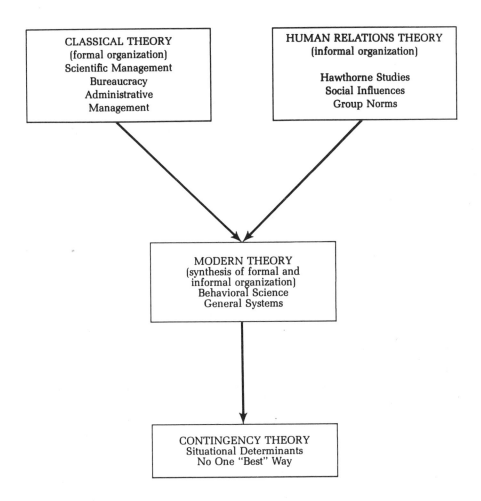

Scientific management sought to discover the best method of performing a specific task. For example, in his studies of the Midvale and Bethlehem Steel Companies in Philadelphia, Taylor determined the speed at which workers could carry loads of fifty pounds. Efforts were then made to find less tiring motions that would allow employees to carry out more work with the same degree of fatigue in a given amount of time. Taylor believed that if workers were taught the best procedures, with their pay tied to their output, they would produce the maximum amount of work physically possible, as calculated by *time and motion studies.* The worker would acquire a "friendly mental attitude toward his employers and his whole working conditions, whereas before a considerable part of his time was spent in criticism, suspiciousness, watchfulness, and sometimes in open warfare."[3]

With respect to this philosophy, the role of management changed abruptly from the earlier use of "rule-of-thumb" to a more "sophisticated" scientific approach. Taylor established the new duties of management as follows: First, develop a science for each element of an employee's work. Second, scientifically select and then train, teach, and develop the worker (in the past, workers trained themselves). Third, heartily cooperate with the employees to insure that all of the work will be done in accordance with scientific principles. Fourth, divide the work and the responsibility between management and workers. Management takes over all work for which it is better suited.[4]

Out of the scientific management approach came "the characterization of the formal organization as a blueprint according to which organizations are to be constructed and to which they ought to adhere."[5] According to Lupton:

Taylor's ideas of human motivation were primitive, and he never understood the significance of groups in organizations. Organizations were seen as disorderly aggregates of individual human beings drilled into formal order and given direction by formal structure and procedures of planning and control instituted by management.[6]

The primary criticism of Taylor's approach stems from his lack of concern for the individual within the organization, and for his over reliance on economic motives. Nevertheless, his work added greatly to the knowledge of industrial organizations and set the stage for a more comprehensive approach to management theory.

Bureaucracy

The concept of bureaucracy is generally associated with the work of Max Weber. A contemporary of Taylor, and a major contributor to modern sociology , he studied the effects of social change in Europe at the turn of the century. He saw bureaucracy as a rational means of lessening the cruelty, nepotism and subjective managerial practices which were common in earlier stages of the industrial revolution. Weber's concept of bureaucracy, therefore, cannot be fairly identified with the "red tape" syndrome often associated with the term today.

What Weber described was an "ideal type" of bureaucracy, which was not intended to perfectly reflect reality, but rather to describe how organizations should be structured and managed. His ideal model was characterized by the following:

---

3. Frederick W. Taylor, "The Principles of Scientific Management," *Scientific Management*, (New York: Harper & Row, 1947), pp. 134-144.

4. *Ibid.*, pp. 36-37.

5. Amitai Etzioni, *Modern Organizations*, (Englewood Cliffs, N.J.: Prentice-Hall, 1964), p. 20.

6. Tom Lupton, *Management and the Social Sciences: An Essay*, (The Administrative Staff College, 1966), p. 7.

1. A division of labor, based upon a "specified sphere of competence."
2. A hierarchy of authority, with each lower office under the control and supervision of a higher one.
3. A specified set of rules which are applied uniformly throughout the organization.
4. Impersonality of relationships, rational decisions can only be made objectively and without emotions.
5. Selection and promotion based on competence, not irrelevant considerations.[7]

In short, the bureaucracy was the most rational means of allowing people to attain private and social goals in a capitalistic society. Weber wrote:

> It is superior to any other form in precision, in stability, in the stringency of its discipline, and in its reliability. It thus makes possible a particularly high degree of calculability of results for the heads of the organization and for those acting in relation to it. It is finally superior both in intensive efficiency and in the scope of its operations, and is formally capable of application to all kinds of administrative tasks.[8]

The above characteristics reflect a highly formalized, impersonal, and authoritarian approach to organization and management, once again, the primary consideration was given to organizational efficiency with little or no concern for employees. It is not difficult to see the similarities between Taylor's scientific management and bureaucratization as described by Weber. The major criticism of this approach, like that of Taylor, is that employees within the bureaucracy are little more than "cogs in a machine" who have little, if any, control over their lives. Weber did, however, lay the important theoretical groundwork for much of the empirical research on complex organizations.

Administrative Management

While Taylor was concerned with lower level organizational production and Weber with the structural characteristics of organizations, during the first half of the twentieth century a third major area of study developed, which emphasized broad administrative principles applicable to higher levels within the organization. The so-called *classical principles* of organization and management were developed during this era. Henri Fayol, a French industrialist, was the first major contributor to administrative management theory. His most important work, *Industrial and General Administration*,[9] based on his experiences as a manager, was published in 1916 although it was not translated into English until 1929. Fayol realized the

---

7. H.H. Gerth and C. Wright Mills, *From Max Weber: Essays in Sociology*, (New York: Oxford Univ. Press, 1946), pp. 196-224; A. M. Henderson and Talcott Parsons (trans and ed.), *Max Weber: The Theory of Social and Economic Organizations*, (New York: MacMillan, 1947).

8. Parsons, *op cit.*, p. 337.

9. Henri Fayol, *Industrial and General Administration*, (Trans. J. A. Coubrough, Geneva: International Management Institute, 1929).

need for the development of a theory of administration: "At present, a man who is starting his career has neither theory nor methods of administration to help him, and many people remain in that condition all their lives."[10] Subsequently, Fayol defined a set of fourteen principles of efficient management which he had applied most frequently during his career. He felt that each of the principles was universal and indispensible, applicable not only to industry but to religious, military, and other organizations. Contemporary writers of this school of thought follow the same basic reasoning as Fayol. For example, Koontz and O'Donnel have stated:

When management principles can be developed, proved, and used, managerial efficiency will inevitably improve. Then the conscientious manager can become more effective by using established guidelines to help solve his problems, without engaging in original laborious research or risky trial and error."[11]

Fayol was careful to note that there was no limit to the number of principles which may be developed, or to the manner in which they may be applied. His basic principles, many of which are faithfully followed today, are listed below:

1. Division of Labor: The specialization of labor in order to increase efficiency.

2. Authority and Responsibility: Authority includes both the right to command and the power to require obedience; one cannot have authority without responsibility.

3. Discipline: Discipline is necessary for an organization to function effectively.

4. Unity of Command: An employee must receive orders from only one supervisor.

5. Unity of Management: Only one manager and one plan for all operations which have the same objective.

6. Subordination of Individual Interests to the Common Good: The interest of an employee or a group of employees must not take precedence over that of the organization.

7. Remuneration of the Staff: Compensation must be fair, and, as far as possible, be satisfactory to both the employer and the employee.

8. Centralization: Centralization of authority is always present to some degree; it is not good or bad in itself, but the problem is to find what degree is best for the organization.

9. The Hierarchy: The hierarchy, or the scalar chain, is the order of rank from the highest to the lowest levels in the organization.

10. Order: "A place for everything and everything in its place," applies to both material and human resources.

---

10. *Ibid.*, p. 17.

11. Harold Koontz and Cyril O'Donnel, 3rd ed., *Principles of Management,* (New York: McGraw-Hill, 1963), p. 9.

11. Equity: The need for fair treatment throughout the organization should be recognized.

12. Stability of Staff: An employee needs time to adjust to a new function and reach a point of satisfactory performance.

13. Initiative: The ability to conceive and execute a plan should be encouraged and developed throughout the organization.

14. Esprit de Corps: "Unity is strength"; harmony and unity among the staff must be developed.

The above principles are discussed in the first part of Fayol's book; in the second, he defines "administration" by identifying five major elements or functions. Fayol's general principles and five elements (listed below) provided the foundation for administrative management theorists:

1. Planning, which requires a forecast of events and the construction of an operating program based on that forecast.

2. Organizing, which entails the structuring of activities, materials, and personnel for accomplishing assigned tasks.

3. Commanding, which starts the organization into motion through the art of leadership.

4. Coordinating, which provides the harmony necessary to accomplish organizational goals.

5. Controlling, which consists of verifying that everything occurs in conformity with the adopted plan.

A major contribution to administrative management theory in the United States was provided by James D. Mooney and Alan C. Reiley, who in 1931 published *Onward Industry!* [12] Although they arrived at their findings independently of Fayol's work, several similarities exist. Mooney and Reiley's basic premise was that an organization must be based on certain formalized principles if it is to be efficient. In establishing their principles, they relied not only on their personal business experience but also on historical evaluations of different types of organizations—the army, church, and industry. In their model, Mooney and Reiley developed the following four principles:

1. The coordinative principle provides for a unity of action in the pursuit of a common objective.

2. The scalar principle refers to hierarchical responsibility throughout the organization, which should flow in a direct line from the highest executive in the organization to the lowest level employee.

3. The functional principle is the same as specialization; it defines duties within the scalar chain.

4. The staff principle with the line representing authority and the staff providing advice and ideas. This distinction should not lead to a divisive interpretation between line and staff, but should serve as a unifying

---

12. James D. Mooney and Alan C. Reiley, *Onward Industry!*, (New York: Harper & Row, 1931).

principle within the organization. Line and staff differentiation will be further discussed in Chapter Four.

In judging the contributions of Mooney and Reiley to the field of management, Kast and Rosenzweig have concluded: "Their ideas were related to the development of a pyramidal organizational structure with a clear delineation of authority, specialization of tasks, coordination of activities, and utilization of staff specialists. Application of their concepts led to the establishment of formal organization charts, position descriptions, and organizational manuals."[13]

Shortly after Mooney and Reiley published their work, other administrative theorists were developing their own sets of principles or functions. In 1937 Luther Gulick and Lyndall Urwick edited their classic work, *Papers on the Science of Administration*,[14] in which Gulick contributed an article which described the major functions of administration by using the acronym POSDCORB—planning, organizing, staffing, directing, coordinating, reporting, and budgeting.[15] In these papers and other works, most notably Urwick's *The Elements of Administration*,[16] the authors expanded the work of Fayol by emphasizing such principles as:

1. subscribing to the unity of command
2. departmentalizing by purpose, process, place, or clientele
3. authority commensurate with responsibility
4. utilizing the exception principle
5. limiting the span of control

Administrative theorists believe that by strictly adhering to the unity of command principle (i.e., an employee should receive orders from one superior only), the organization will operate more efficiently and effectively. Theorists stress the need for written policies in cases where an exception to this principle may occur.

Departmentalization by purpose refers to the assigning of employees with similar goals to the same organizational unit. In departmentalization by process, those employees who are engaged in a similar activity are organized together (as in a planning and research unit, for example). Departmentalization by place or geography is advantageous when the place where the work to be carried out is critical, as in a training exercise which requires special facilities. Last, it may be important to departmentalize according to the clientele served. For instance, police agencies generally have separate units that deal with traffic, juvenile, vice, and narcotic offenses.

---

13. Fremont E. Kast and James E. Rosenzweig, 2nd ed., *Organization and Management: A Systems Approach*, (New York: McGraw-Hill, 1974), p. 60.

14. Luther Gulick and Lyndall Urwick, eds., *Papers on the Science of Administration*, (New York: Institute of Public Administration, 1937).

15. Luther Gulick, "Notes on the Theory of Organization," in Luther Gulick and Lyndall Urwick, (eds.), *Papers on the Science of Administration*, p. 13.

16. Lyndall Urwick, *The Elements of Administration*, (New York: Harper & Row, Publishers, 1943).

The principle of making authority commensurate with responsibility is crucial to administrative theorists; that is, if an individual is assigned the responsibility of accomplishing a given task, he or she must also be given the authority necessary to accomplish the task. In other words, if a police detective is given the responsibility of solving a particular crime, authority must be delegated to the individual to make important decisions concerning the direction the investigation will take.

The exception principle deals with the flow of communications. In complex organizations, communications flow from one level in the hierarchy to the next, in orderly sequence; they do not skip levels. However, this procedure often results in a greatly retarded flow of communications. The exception principle allows for communications to take a circular rather than straight path. Supervisors or commanders at every level must not read every message, but only those which require their attention.

Span of control is defined as the number of subordinates who report directly to a superior. The classical view has emphasized a small span of control. In theory, at least, this permits a superior to maintain closer contact with, and control over, all subordinates. Accordingly, Urwick concluded that "no superior can supervise directly the work of more than five or, at the most, six subordinates whose work interlocks."[17] In short, the primary contributions of Gulick and Urwick were their expansion of the principles of administration and their further refinement of the works of earlier administrative theorists.

Most of the writings on management theory in the criminal justice field, especially in regard to the police, have been primarily classical in orientation. The early contributors to the police management literature, particularly O. W. Wilson[18] and V. A. Leonard,[19] emphasized bureaucratic and administrative approaches to management. Consequently, most police agencies, as well as many other criminal justice organizations, are highly rigid, bureaucratic structures which are managed by strict authoritarian practices. As the research evidence presented throughout this book will indicate, such organizational designs and management practices may not be the most efficient with respect to the contemporary environments in which police organizations operate.

HUMAN RELATIONS THEORY

As indicated previously, the "classical" writers of the early twentieth century tended to oversimplify or ignore the human aspects of organization and management. Out of this void grew the human relations movement, also known as neoclassical theory, in which the theoretical format is the same as in classical theory but the orientation is in the opposite direction. While the

---

17. *Ibid.,* pp. 52-53.

18. O. W. Wilson, *Police Administration,* (New York: McGraw-Hill, 1950). A revised 4th edition was published in 1977.

19. V. A. Leonard, *Police Organization and Management,* (Brooklyn: Foundation Press, 1951).

classical approach focused on the *formal* aspects of organization, the human relationists emphasized the *informal* organization and stressed the diverse relationships and interactions that take place within organizations. The early human relationists also introduced behavioral research methods for the study of organizational behavior.

The Hawthorne Studies

The human relations movement began with the work of Elton Mayo and his colleagues at Harvard University. A series of studies was conducted at the Hawthorne Plant of the Western Electric Company from 1927 to 1932. This series of experiments, known as the Hawthorne studies, produced some results which ran counter to the tradition emphasized by classical management theorists. The Hawthorne experiments were sparked by an earlier study of the Hawthorne company concerning *illumination,* which involved an experimental and a control group, the former working under differing illumination intensities and the latter under constant illumination intensity. The researchers believed that the different intensities of lighting would affect production in a significant manner; that is, better lighting would lead to increased output. However, the actual results were unexpected. As illumination was increased for the test group, both groups increased production. Furthermore, when illumination was decreased, productivity continued to increase. Productivity slowed only after the lighting was dimmed to the extent that the workers could not see properly. This finding suggested that variables other than physical ones may have had an influence on the increased output. At that point, Mayo and his colleagues were called in to continue the investigations. Through improved experimental designs they hoped to determine what variables were influencing the workers.

Mayo and his associates consequently undertook several sets of studies. The first involved a *relay assembly experiment* in which six telephone assemblers, in a test room separated from the other workers, were observed for a prolonged period. The researchers attempted to determine the effects on productivity of various working conditions, such as the length of the work day and of rest periods. They found that no matter how they altered the working conditions, productivity increased. They were further surprised to discover that the experimental group's productivity continued to increase even after rest breaks were abolished and the original, longer work day was reinstituted.

The researchers concluded that this continued output was the result of the changed social situation of the workers (i.e., modifications in their level of motivation and patterns of interaction), and was not related to scientific management practices (i.e., work day length and rest periods).

Another major finding of the relay assembly experiment was that of the *Hawthorne effect.* This means that the initial interest or novelty in a new situation leads to positive results, at least initially. Applying this concept to the increased productivity found in the relay room, it has been suggested that such results were simply due to the increased attention the employees received because of their participation in the research project. Further research indicated that while the Hawthorne effect did have some initial effect, social factors played a more significant role. Accordingly, social and psychological factors were thought to be major contributors to increased output and worker satisfaction.[20] Suddenly it appeared that with respect to productivity and satisfaction, human factors were more important than physical factors.

In order to further their knowledge concerning these "social factors" in industrial organizations, the Hawthorne researchers entered into a second set of studies consisting of extensive interviews, involving more than 20,000 workers over a three-year period. Initially the interviews were direct in nature, and the employees were asked specific questions about their work environment. The researchers soon discovered that this method was not very effective, for employee answers were often guarded and not very informative. This led the investigators to pursue a nondirect approach to interviewing, in which the employees were allowed to discuss subject matter which was personally important. Consequently, much relevant information concerning employee attitudes was obtained. The researchers learned that one's peers have an important effect on how one acts and performs in the work place. These interviews led to the final set of studies, which were designed to obtain more specific information on the effects of human relationships upon workers.

In the final study, known as the *bank wiring room experiment,* fourteen employees were set up as a work unit in a separate room, and observed for a period of six months. The workers were to be paid through a piecework incentive system, under which their pay would depend on the amount they produced. Given such a situation, Taylor and other classical theorists would predict that the experimental group would seek to produce the maximum amount possible in order to maximize their earnings. In actuality, the group established an output norm for a "proper day's work." In order to be socially accepted by the group, each worker had to stay within the accepted standards set by the group. Workers who overproduced were labeled as "rate busters" and those who underproduced as "chiselers." Throughout the test period, the production averages were shown to be surprisingly close to those dictated by the group. In conclusion, the researchers determined that with respect to productivity levels, social acceptance was more important than monetary rewards.

The Hawthorne studies provided significant breakthroughs toward understanding the importance of social and psychological factors in the work place. Human relationships and informal organization were now considered to be critical factors in organizational behavior and managerial practice. According to Etzioni, the following findings and conclusions were the major contributions of the Hawthorne experiments:

20. F. J. Roethlisberger and W. J. Dickson, *Management and The Worker,* (Cambridge: Harvard Univ. Press, 1939), pp. 185-186.

1. The level of production is set by social norms, not by physiological capacities.

2. Non-economic rewards and sanctions significantly affect the behavior of the workers and largely limit the effect of economic incentive plans.

3. Often workers do not act or react as individuals but as members of groups.

4. The importance of leadership for setting and enforcing group norms and the difference between informal and formal leadership. [21]

Appraisal of Classical and Human Relations Theory

Classical theories are fraught with major oversimplifications concerning complex organizations and human nature. Their primary emphasis is on the formal organization and the development of "principles" concerned with improving the efficiency of the organization, irrespective of human considerations. Accordingly, such theories have been criticized for their failure to recognize many internal factors such as informal organizational arrangements and group influences, personal motivation, and leadership styles, to name only a few. Furthermore, each of the principles developed in classical theory was to be universally applicable to management in all organizations. However, this assumption simply has not held up. For instance, current research indicates that a small span of control is more efficient in situations where employees are relatively dependent and tight supervision is desirable, while a broad span of control is more efficient in situations where employees are relatively autonomous and loose supervision is desirable. In other words, situational variables determine the appropriate span of control. As Simon[22] has indicated, we simply do not know enough about management to develop valid principles for all situations, and principles should thus be deemphasized until we do.

Most of the works in this area have been written by practitioners and based primarily on their observations and experiences—not on behavioral research. Consequently, many of the assumptions posited by the classical theorists have not withstood empirical investigation. Massie lists several erroneous assumptions implicit in classical management theories:

1. Efficiency of an undertaking is measured solely in terms of productivity. Efficiency relates to a mechanical process and the economic utilization of resources without consideration of human factors.

2. Human beings can be assumed to act rationally. The important considerations in management are only those which involve individuals and groups of individuals heading logically toward their goals.

3. Human beings prefer the security of a definite task and do not value the freedom of determining their own approaches to problems; they prefer to

21. Etzioni, *op. cit.*, pp. 34-38.

22. Herbert A. Simon, *Administrative Behavior*, 2nd Ed., (New York: MacMillan, 1959).

be directed and will not cooperate unless a pattern is planned formally for them.

4. Management involves primarily the formal and official activities of individuals.

5. Workers are motivated by economic needs, and therefore, incentives should be in terms of monetary systems.

6. People do not like to work, and, therefore, close supervision and accountability should be emphasized. Management must lead people fairly and firmly in ways that are not part of their inherent nature.

7. Simple tasks are easier to master and thus lead toward higher productivity by concentrating on a narrow scope of activity.

8. Managerial functions in varied types of activities have universal characteristics and can be performed in a given manner, regardless of the environment and qualities of the personnel involved. [23]

Human relations theorists contributed greatly to the study of human behavior in industrial settings. They pioneered the use of behavioral research methods for studying organizational behavior, and subsequently were the first to recognize the importance of human relationships in work environments. The Hawthorne experiments were crucial for later methodological advances in the scientific inquiry of complex organizations. Despite these substantial contributions, human relations theorists have not escaped criticism. In their zeal to refute the work of the classical theorists, they generally ignored the formal aspects of organization. By overemphasizing the informal aspects, human relationists failed to account for the effects of economic and structural factors on organizational behavior.

It should also be noted that both approaches viewed organizational behavior from the perspective of a closed system, and therefore failed to consider important external environmental influences. Another important criticism, leveled by Etzioni, is that neither approach "saw any basic contradiction or insolvable dilemma in the relationship between the organization's quest for rationality and the human search for happiness."[24] The classical theorists felt that the most efficient organization would also be the most satisfying, since it would maximize both productivity and pay. On the other hand, the human relationists felt that the most satisfying organization would also be the most efficient; if the employees were "happy" the organization would obtain their full cooperation and efficiency would increase. Filley, House, and Kerr note that life inside an organization is more complex than the human relations writers would have us believe:

Human relations theory began in the 1930's and became a fad after World War II, when industrial training programs in human relations were commonplace. Many of these programs were conducted with the faulty premise that a happy group is

---

23. Joseph L. Massie, "Management Theory," *Handbook of Organizations*, James G. March (ed.), (Chicago: Rand McNally, 1965), p. 405.

24. Etzioni, *op. cit.*, p. 39.

necessarily a productive one. It was not until later research showed that such training programs often had no effect at all on productivity that human relations materials began to be used more intelligently. Recent research has contributed to an understanding of the limiting factors necessary if human relations training is to have a positive effect on output.[25]

MODERN MANAGEMENT THEORY

Modern management theorists have synthesized the previous two approaches by recognizing the importance of both the formal and informal organization. In this context, individual and organizational relationships are investigated through the use of behavioral science research; furthermore, a general systems approach to the study of organizational behavior has developed. Each of these considerations is described below.

Behavioral Science Approach

The behavioral sciences (anthropology, psychology, and sociology) are relatively recent academic disciplines, but have already provided significant contributions to the study of human behavior in organizations. In separating the social from the behavioral sciences, Berelson and Steiner make the following distinction:

We do not equate the behavioral sciences with the social sciences. The latter term is usually understood to cover six disciplines: anthropology, economics, history, political science, psychology and sociology. By the behavioral sciences we mean the disciplines of anthropology, psychology and sociology—minus and plus: *Minus* such specialized sectors as physiological psychology, archeology, technical linguistics, and most of physical anthropology: *Plus* social geography, some psychiatry, and the behavioral parts of economics, political science, and law. In short, we are concerned here with the scientific research that deals directly with human behavior. [26]

In order to be classified as a behavioral science, a field must (1) deal with human behavior, and (2) study its subject matter in a "scientific" manner.[27] The scientific aim is to develop generalizations about human behavior that are supported by data collected in an objective fashion. The ultimate purpose, although it is most likely unattainable, is to understand, explain, and predict human behavior in the same sense that natural and physical scientists understand, explain, and predict the behavior of biological and physical forces.

Some of the earliest behavioral science research began with Mayo and his colleagues in the late 1920's. The behavioral approach did not come into

25. Alan C. Filley, Robert J. House and Steven Kerr, 2nd ed., *Managerial Process and Organizational Behavior*, (Glenview, Ill.: Scott, Foresman, 1976), pp. 14-15.

26. Bernard Berelson and Gary A. Steiner, *Human Behavior: An Inventory of Scientific Findings*, (New York: Harcourt, Brace and World, 1974) pp. 10-11.

27. Bernard Berelson (ed.), *The Behavioral Sciences Today*, (New York: Basic Books, 1963), pp. 2-3.

popular use, however, nor was it applied with any degree of sophistication, until the early 1950's. Behavioral research provided a means for empirically testing earlier theories as well as increasing scientific knowledge. This research has led to the support of some of the earlier theories, while others have been modified or discarded. For example, during the height of the human relations era, it was widely believed that employee satisfaction directly affected the quality and quantity of individual production. Subsequent studies in the 1950's, however, found that "there is little evidence in the available literature that employee attitudes bear any simple—or, for that matter, appreciable—relationship to performance on the job."[28] Interestingly enough, Lawler and Porter have presented some evidence that satisfaction, rather than causing positive performance, is instead caused by it[29] (further analysis of this relationship is provided in Chapter 5).

Behavioral science research has evolved into three levels of analysis: (1) *Individual*—this research is concerned with how individuals behave in organizations, and emphasizes such topics as personality, change motivation, attitudes, and leadership style. (2) *Group*—much of this research has been conducted with small experimental groups in laboratory settings, and deals with norms, patterns of interaction, conflict, emergent leadership, and problem solving. (3) *Complex Organization*—this research deals with the organization as an institutional whole; the total organization is examined in relation to other total organizations, or the design of the total system and its effects on behavior are studied. Many of the studies in this area have developed from tests of Weber's theory of bureaucracy.

Filley, House, and Kerr comment on how the development of these levels of analysis has created problems for behavioral science researchers who are studying managerial behavior in organizations:

These three levels of individual, group, and total organizational behavior, once pursued with little overlap or coordination by psychologists, social psychologists, and sociologists respectively, have now become problem centers for management writers and researchers who take a behavioral science approach. As a result, much of the provincialism that existed in management research and education before 1950 has disappeared. For example, it was once the practice to have separate bodies of literature for business administration, public administration, hospital administration, and so on. Now, with the realization that individual and organizational behavior within all institutions has much in common, management and the behavioral sciences are drawing from essentially the same body of literature. This has encouraged attention to the problems of management by people from many academic disciplines and has brought to specialists, academicians, and practicing managers alike a better understanding of their roles, while helping to remove the erroneous connotation of "theory versus practice." [30]

---

28. Arthur H. Brayfield and Walter M. Crockett, "Employee Attitudes and Employee Performance," *Psychological Bulletin*, 52, 1955, pp. 396-424.

29. Edward E. Lawler, III, and Lyman W. Porter, "The Effect of Performance on Job Satisfaction," *Industrial Relations*, 7, 1967, pp. 20-28.

30. Filley, House, and Kerr, *op. cit.*, p. 17.

Since the early 1950's, a large volume of behavioral science research on complex organizations has been conducted. One of the major problems created by this massive effort is that the findings often remain fragmented. Indik has suggested a useful framework for organizing relevant information toward the development of a theory of organizational behavior. Seven general classes of variables would be recognized: (1) organization structure, (2) organization process and function, (3) small group structure, (4) small group process and function, (5) organizationally relevant individual attitudes, perceptions, abilities, temperaments, and motivations, (6) organizationally relevant individual behaviors and (7) organizational environment.[31] Figure 2-2 depicts this framework. It should be noted that a number of specific elements (not included in the figure) make up each of the general classes of

Figure 2-2

Theoretical Framework for Organizational Behavior

Organizational Environment

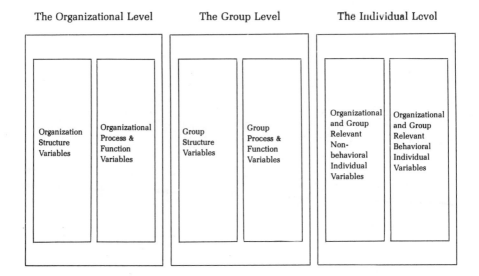

The three pairs of categories of variables are paired because it is expected that the variables at the same level of analysis are more likely to be directly and consistently related to each other. Further we expect that variables in categories closest to each other will be more likely to be related to each other. Two-way reflexive relationships will be frequently found. Finally, we expect that there will be tendencies for variables to show either positive or negative interrelationships consistently, but the amount of these relationships and sometimes the signs of those relationships will be dependent on the conditions, relations and interactions of other related variables.

Source: Bernard P. Indik, "Toward an Effective Theory of Organizational Behavior," *Personnel Administration*, 31, 4, 1968, p. 52.

31. Bernard P. Indik, "Toward an Effective Theory of Organization Behavior," *Personnel Administration*, 31, 4, 1968, p. 51.

variables. For instance, the organization structure variables would include the elements of size, span of control, number of authority levels, degree of task specialization, and so on.

Several advantages should result from such a framework. First, it allows behavioral researchers to organize the information presently available about the adequacy of measures for each of the variables. Second, it should be possible to specify more clearly what set of mutually exclusive elements should be differentiated within each of the general categories of variables; that is, different kinds of organizations may generate differentially important descriptive dimensions. Third, this systematic framework will help to organize theoretically the research findings as they accumulate. Finally, the theory that emerges should enable the manager—by understanding which variable(s) are important in certain situations—to choose the most appropriate action(s) under specific conditions.[32] This view provides the essential framework for a contingency approach to management, to be discussed in the final section of this chapter.

General Systems Approach

Following the development and increased sophistication of behavioral science research, modern management theory moved into the systems era. The primary qualities of this approach, as well as its importance to the field of management, are succinctly described by Scott and Mitchell:

The distinctive qualities of modern organization theory are its conceptual-analytical base, its reliance on empirical research data, and, above all, its synthesizing, integrating nature. These qualities are framed in a philosophy which accepts the premise that the only meaningful way to study organization is as a system.[33]

Chester I. Barnard was one of the first writers in the field to recognize the organization as a social system. In his influential work, *The Functions of the Executive*, he wrote, "...the most useful concept for the analysis of experience of cooperative systems is embodied in the definition of a formal organization as a system of consciously coordinated activities or forces of two or more persons."[34] It was evident to Barnard that the existence of the organization depended on a balance between benefits offered by the organization and the contributions and satisfactions offered by the individual. He further felt that the informal organization must be recognized, and if properly understood, would not only improve the communication process within the organization but also strengthen the feelings of individuals about themselves. With that goal in mind, he began to synthesize and integrate the formal and informal aspects of organizations.

---

32. *Ibid.*, pp. 56-57.

33. William G. Scott, and Terence R. Mitchell, *Organization Theory*, (Homewood, Ill.: Richard D. Irwin, 1972), p. 55.

34. Chester I. Barnard, *The Functions of the Executive*, (Cambridge, Mass.: Harvard Univ. Press, 1938), p. 73.

Barnard further rejected the classical concept of authority based on position within the organization. According to his "acceptance" theory of authority, authority rests with the subordinates' willingness to accept or consent to orders received from above. This depends largely on the individuals' "zone of indifference"; orders that fall within this zone will be accepted without question. However, an order which falls outside of this zone will be questioned and ultimately accepted or rejected. The width of the zone is determined by the benefits provided to the individual by the organization in relation to the sacrifices made by the individual on behalf of the organization.

Finally, Barnard emphasized the value of communication in maintaining the organization as a cooperative system. He believed that the effective executive was one who made an individual feel that he or she received more from the organization than was being given to it.

Further synthesizing the formal and informal organization was E. Wight Bakke, who developed a "fusion model,"[35] in which the informal structure interacts dynamically with the formal structure, the result being the fusion process:

When an individual and an organization come together in such a way that the individual is a participant in, and a member of, the organization and the two are mutually dependent on each other, both are reconstructed in the process. The organization to some degree remakes the individual and the individual to some degree remakes the organization.[36]

This means that both the individual and the organization contribute to, and re-define, each other's role expectations and perceptions. In any organization two basic processes are at work: the *socializing process* which allows the organization to accomplish its goals, and the *personalizing process* which allows the individual to actualize his or her needs through the organization. These processes fuse through the role of the individual who allows the organization's goals to be met. In order for the organization to operate efficiently, both processes must occur simultaneously—producing the *fusion process.* All too frequently, however, one of the processes tends to dominate the other, and the organization operates dysfunctionally.

Organization is a very human activity; it consists of people interacting with each other, but as modified and influenced by nature, material things, and, almost all ideas. The people in an organization have needs to fulfill and goals to achieve which are to a considerable extent personal in nature, and sometimes in conflict with organizational goals. Yet to achieve many, perhaps most, of these personal goals they must collaborate with other people, and the moment they do so a first step has been taken toward the creation of an organization.[37]

---

35. E. Wight Bakke, *The Fusion Process,* (New Haven, Conn.: Labor and Management Center, 1953).

36. *Ibid.,* pp. 12-13.

37. E. Wight Bakke and Chris Argyris, *Organization Structure and Dynamics,* (New Haven, Conn.: Labor and Management Center, 1954), p. 9.

One of the first in-depth analyses of systems theory was the 1963 text by Johnson, Kast, and Rosenzweig: *The Theory and Management of Systems.*[38] Since then, virtually every major work in the management field has emphasized this approach. Luthans has lucidly described the concept:

The systems approach is quite basic in concept. It simply means that all parts are interrelated and interdependent to form the whole. A system is composed of elements or subsystems that are related and dependent upon one another. When these subsystems are in interaction with one another, they form a unitary whole. Thus, by definition, almost any phenomenon can be analyzed or presented from a systems viewpoint. There are biological, physical, economic, and sociological systems, and also systems found in organization and management.[39]

Figure 2-3 illustrates the interrelated and interdependent nature of the criminal justice subsystems—depicted by the two-way directional arrows—and indicates that a change in any one subsystem will have an effect on the remaining subsystems.

Figure 2-3
Criminal Justice System

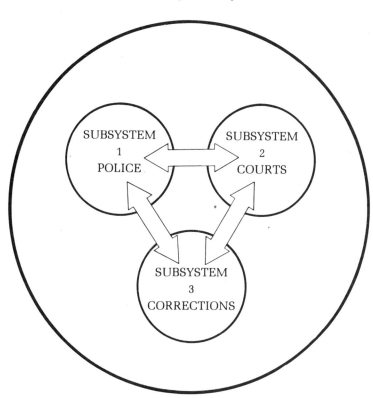

---

38. Richard A. Johnson, Fremont E. Kast, and James E. Rosenzweig, *The Theory of Management Systems,* (New York: McGraw-Hill, 1963).

39. Fred Luthans, *Introduction to Management: A Contingency Approach,* (New York: McGraw-Hill, 1976), p. 16.

It is important to note once again that systems can be viewed as either closed, or open and in interaction with their environment; the concept of closed/open, however, is not an absolute, but a relative matter. For example, all organizations are closed to a certain degree, for they simply cannot respond to all external factors. Conversely, all organizations are open to some degree, as they cannot ignore every environmental influence. Essentially, those systems which are relatively more open function more effectively because of their environmental adaptability. Katz and Kahn, two social psychologists, were the first to utilize open systems theory in analyzing complex organizations. Their 1966 work, *The Social Psychology of Organizations*,[40] remains the standard one in its field.

Figure 2-4

Open Systems Model

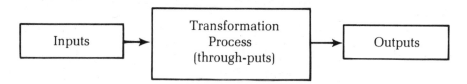

The general open systems model of organization is shown in Figure 2-4. "The open system is in continual interaction with its environment and achieves a 'steady state' or dynamic equilibrium while still retaining the capacity for work or energy transformation (throughputs). The survival of the system, in effect, would not be possible without continuous inflow, transformation and outflow."[41] As indicated previously, the classical and human relations theorists viewed organizations from a closed system perspective; they stressed internal relationships and functions while ignoring external environmental variables. The open systems model is applied to the criminal justice system in Figure 2-5, which indicates that the system's boundaries are permeable (broken lines) and are in interaction with the environment. Conversely, Figure 2-3 represented a closed systems approach; its boundaries are not permeable and are therefore closed in reference to the environment.

What follows is a brief explanation of the basic characteristics of open systems theory[42] and its implications for the study of criminal justice components as a system.

1. The importation of energy from the external environment.

2. The through-put or transformation of the energy available into product form.

---

40. Daniel Katz and Robert L. Kahn, *The Social Psychology of Organizations*, (New York: John Wiley & Sons, 1966).

41. Fremont E. Kast and James E. Rosenzweig, *Organization and Management: A Systems Approach*, 2nd ed., (New York: McGraw-Hill, 1974), p. 110.

42. The discussion on open systems theory is drawn from Katz and Kahn, *op. cit.*, pp. 19-29.

Figure 2-5

Criminal Justice as an Open System

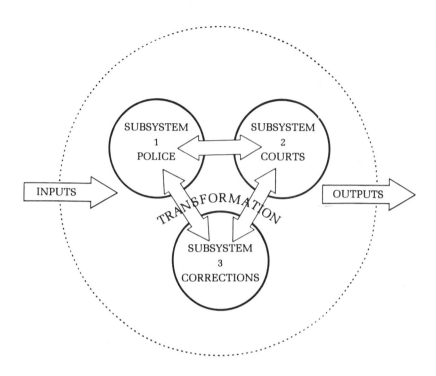

3. The output or exportation of the product back into the environment.

Each component of the criminal justice system receives energy inputs from the environment—money, personnel, material, and information. This environmental input is then transformed and used within the system, in the form of personnel (police, court and correctional), buildings, and equipment. These products are then exported back into the environment in the form of goods and services, which may be highly quantifiable, such as the number of arrests made by the police, the number of cases processed by the courts, or the number of inmates housed in a correctional facility, or which may be more intangible, such as maintaining order without making an arrest, processing all those who come before the courts in a "just" manner, or rehabilitating inmates.

4. Systems as cycles of events. The pattern of activities of the energy exchange is cyclic; the product exported into the environment provides sources of energy for the repetition of the cycle of activities.

5. Attainment of negative entropy. The entropic process is a universal law of nature under which all forms of organization move toward disorganization or death. To survive, open systems must acquire negative entropy in order not to run down. By importing more energy than it exports, the open system can store energy and therefore acquire negative entropy. All closed physical systems, on the other hand, are subject to entropy and will, over a period of time, cease to exist.

6. Processing information inputs and negative feedback. Open systems maintain a steady state (homeostasis) by processing information from the environment and adapting their behavior accordingly. The feedback of information in the open system model is shown in Figure 2-6.

Figure 2-6

Open System Model and Information Feedback

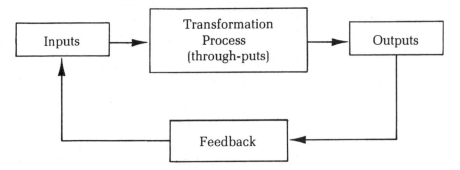

Information feedback from the environment may be either positive or negative. If the feedback is negative, the system will adapt in order to remain in harmony with its environment and maintain a steady state. With respect to the criminal justice system, environmental feedback may take the form of public opinion, political demands, complaints, or criminal and other statistics. With respect to police discretion (how shall it be applied), court sentencing procedures (flat versus indeterminate) and correctional priorities (punishment versus rehabilitation), such feedback will greatly influence the effectiveness and future orientation of the criminal justice system.

7. Differentiation. As open systems mature, functions are specialized in order to accommodate system growth.

8. Equifinality. Open systems can reach the same final state from differing initial conditions (inputs) and by a variety of methods.

From the above description, it becomes clear that open systems theory provides one major conceptual scheme which is significant to management; an analytic approach to the interactive nature of a system and its environment. If criminal justice organizations are not studied and managed from an open systems perspective, they cannot adapt well to changing environmental influences and forces (such as public opinion and community conditions), and inefficient and ineffective levels of operation will be the most likely result.

Kast and Rosenzweig have developed a useful definition of an open system as an "organized unitary whole composed of two or more interdependent parts, components, or subsystems and delineated by identifiable boundaries from its environmental suprasystem."[43] They further indicate that an open system approach "considers interrelationships among subsystems as well as interactions between the system and its suprasystem, and also provides a means of understanding synergistic aspects (the whole is greater than, or at least different from, the sum of its parts). This conceptual scheme allows us to consider organizations—individuals, small-group dynamics, and large-group phenomena—all within the constraints of an external environmental system."[44]

The above definition adds a new dimension to open systems theory: the external environment has constraining and identifiable boundaries. With respect to the system of criminal justice, the external environment consists of a local community directly affected by a particular system. This open systems model with external boundaries is depicted in Figure 2-7.

TOWARD A CONTINGENCY THEORY OF MANAGEMENT

Many internal and external environmental variables dramatically affect organizational behavior. Because these variables differ according to particular situations, the developing view in the field of management is that there is no one "best" way for structuring and managing diverse types of organizations; there simply are no universal principles that can be applied in every instance. "There are a wide variety of appropriate organizational designs, relationships between variables and subsystems, and management practices. It *all depends* on the particular circumstances in a specific situation."[45]

While both classical and human relations theorists recognized exceptions, their approaches were overwhelmingly based on the assumption of universality. Theoretical approaches to management with such built in oversimplifications and generalizations are no longer adequate. "The needed breakthrough for management theory and practice," according to Luthans, "can be found in a contingency approach," which he describes in the following manner:

A contingent relationship is a functional relationship between two or more variables. Contingency management is concerned with the relationships between relevant environmental variables and appropriate management concepts and techniques that lead to effective goal attainment."[46]

---

43. Kast and Rosenzweig, *op. cit.*, p. 20.

44. *Ibid.*, p. 20.

45. Fremont E. Kast and James E. Rosenzweig, (eds.), *Contingency Views of Organization and Management*, (Chicago: Science Research Associates, 1973), p. 307.

46. Luthans, *Introduction to Management*, op. cit., p. 29.

Figure 2-7

**Criminal Justice System With External
Environmental Boundaries**

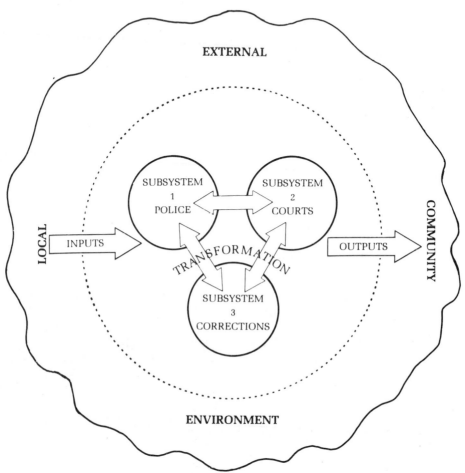

However, a "functional relationship" does not necessarily imply cause and effect. A functional relationship may be defined as "one in which it has been demonstrated that a change in one variable is accompanied by a change in the other, but the relationship is most likely based on a number of complex interactions rather than being directly causal."[47] Robbins suggests that the contingency movement began "by looking for some common characteristics that might exist in a number of situations, and that could make it possible to qualify the theory to the specifics of the situation." He adds, "If we cannot say, 'If X, then Y,' possibly we can say, 'If X, then Y, but only under conditions specified in Z.' The efforts of contingency advocates have

---

47. Donald Ary, Lucy Chester Jacobs, and Asghar Razavieh, *Introduction to Research in Education*, (New York: Holt, Rinehart and Winston, 1972), pp. 264-265.

been directed predominantly at attempts to isolate 'the Z variable,' or situational determinants."[48]

Kast and Rosenzweig further expand on the contingency approach as it relates to organizations and their management:

The contingency view of organizations and their management suggests that an organization is a system composed of subsystems and delineated by identifiable boundaries from its environmental suprasystem. The contingency view seeks to understand the *interrelationships within* and *among subsystems* as well as *between* the *organization* and its *environment* and to define patterns of relationships or configurations of variables. It emphasizes the multivariate nature of organizations and attempts to understand how organizations operate under varying conditions and in specific circumstances. Contingency views are ultimately directed toward suggesting organizational designs and managerial practices most appropriate for *specific situations* (emphasis added).[49]

In the conceptual framework underlying the contingency approach, as described above, organizational designs and managerial practices must be based on relevant external and internal environmental variables. In other words, an organization's design and managerial practices should be based on the particular situation in which the organization operates. Luthans has defined such an approach as an *If-Then* Management Contingency:

The *if* is the independent variable and the *then* is the dependent variable in this functional relationship. For example, *if* two parts of hydrogen are mixed with one part of oxygen, under the proper conditions, *then* water will be the result. In other words, water (the dependent variable) is a function of the contribution of hydrogen and oxygen (the independent variables). An if-then contingency relationship can be applied to management theory and practice. Most often, the environment serves as independent variables, and management concepts and techniques are the dependent variables in the if-then management contingency...(For example), *if* prevailing social values are oriented toward nonmaterialistic free expression and the organization employs professional personnel in a high-technology operation, *then* a very participative, open leadership style would be most effective for goal attainment. On the other hand, *if* prevailing social values are oriented toward materialism and obedience to authority and the organization employs unskilled personnel working on routine tasks, *then* a strict authoritarian leadership style would be most effective for goal attainment... Furthermore, although the environment variables are usually the independent variables and the management concepts and techniques are usually the dependent variables, the reverse can also occur. There are cases where management variables are independent and the environment variables are dependent in the management contingency relationship. For example, *if* a very participative, open leadership style is instituted by top management, then personnel will respond by exhibiting self-control and responsible social values.[50]

---

48. Stephen P. Robbins, *The Administrative Process: Integrating Theory and Practice*, (Englewood Cliffs, N.J.: Prentice-Hall, 1976), p. 41.

49. Kast and Rosenzweig, *Contingency Views*, p. ix.

50. Luthans, *Introduction to Management*, pp. 29-30.

Luthans is quick to point out that the above contingency relationships are only examples, and have not necessarily been empirically validated, as has the water example. Although the above examples are related to business organizations, they may be applied equally well to criminal justice agencies. For instance, *if* the prevailing social attitude favors a purely custodial role for a correctional agency which employs low-skilled personnel who perform repetitive or routine tasks, *then* tight leadership controls, along with a rigid hierarchial structure, would generally be the most effective for goal attainment. Conversely, *if* the prevailing social attitude is oriented toward a diverse treatment and rehabilitative role for a correctional agency which employs highly skilled personnel who perform complex tasks, *then* an open and participative leadership style, as well as a flexible organizational structure, would generally be the most effective.

It should also be noted that the contingency approach considers the need to differentiate among subunits within the same organization. The design and management of a vice unit in a police agency, for example, will not necessarily be the same as the design and management of a community relations unit (which, among other things, may employ civilian personnel). Because their specific functions are dissimilar, many internal (e.g., authority relationships) and external (e.g., public relationships) variables will also vary noticably. Under such varied circumstances, separate designs and managerial practices may be called for.

Comparing Contingency and Systems Theory

Contingency theory is closely related to general systems theory, for both recognize the importance of external environmental influences and attempt to look at the relationships of the parts to the whole. General systems theory, however, is very broad in scope, as all parts of any system are interrelated and interdependent to form the whole. In this respect, systems theory can be thought of as incorporating the contingency approach. But because systems theory is so all-encompassing, many of its concepts are highly abstract and cannot be applied to practical situations. As Kast and Rosenzweig point out, "[D]ifficulties are encountered when applying general systems theory to organizations and their management. Many of the concepts are very abstract because general systems theorists tried to develop broad concepts which are applicable to all types of systems—natural, biological, mechanical, and social. We can make use of these concepts but need to refine them for use at a practical level of organization and management practice."[51] Contingency theory attempts to refine these concepts by developing specific functional relationships between identifiable environmental variables and appropriate management practices and techniques.

---

51.   Kast and Rosenzweig, *Contingency Views*, pp. 10-11.

In the final analysis, the contingency approach is much more pragmatic than the systems approach, and can also incorporate the concepts and techniques of systems and other management theories. When using the contingency approach, comprehensiveness is not sacrificed at the expense of pragmatism. The comprehensive nature of the approach can be summarized as follows:

The contingency approach can integrate both the traditional [classical and human relations] and the systems approaches in a conceptually sound manner. Traditional theoretical approaches were micro-oriented but had trouble being inductively applied to the general practice of management. The systems approach is macro-oriented but has trouble being deductively applied to specific management situations. Like systems theory, contingency theory has macroconcerns, but unlike systems theory it can be effectively and pragmatically applied at the microlevel."[52]

Appraisal of Modern and Contingency Theory

Modern management theorists have capitalized on the deficiencies of the earlier theoretical frameworks by recognizing and synthesizing the formal with the informal organization. A multi-dimensional approach to the study of organizational behavior is now possible through the use of behavioral science research, which defines three levels of analysis: the individual, the group, and the organization as a whole. The use of behavioral science methods has allowed researchers to test the validity of the earlier theories of management as well as to add to their knowledge. Although behavioral research is still in its infancy and needs continued development in the field of management, significant empirical breakthroughs have already been made regarding organizational behavior.

Of considerable importance to modern management theory were the recognition of a general systems scheme to the study of organizations, and, most significantly, the concept of an open system continually interacting with its environment. As opposed to the closed system, the open system processes energy and information from the external environment and adapts its behavior accordingly, therefore maintaining a viable existence.

The newest and most promising approach to the field of management, and also the most pragmatic, is that of contingency theory. By recognizing that environmental variables differ according to particular organizational situations, contingency theory suggests that organizational designs and management practices must reflect these differences if they are to be effective. Through the use of behavioral science methods, this approach considers the effects of relevant environmental variables on organizational behavior, which, in turn, allows one to determine the most appropriate managerial practices and designs for a particular situation. By emphasizing contingency

---

52. Luthans, *Introduction to Management*, pp. 38-39.

management, the dynamics of police organizational behavior can be empirically studied, and practical recommendations which should substantially improve working environments and the use of human resources can be made.

SUMMARY

This chapter has been devoted to an overview of the development of the major managerial theories. Classical or traditional theorists concentrated on the formal organization and on the development of universal principles which could be applied to any type of organization, regardless of its situation. The development of classical management theory was divided into three sub-categories: scientific management, bureaucracy, and administrative management. Taylor was the first to apply a "scientific" approach to the field, emphasizing ways in which employees could become more productive workers. Weber's "ideal" bureaucracy was developed to cope with the social changes taking place in Europe at the turn of the twentieth century, and to improve upon the management practices used at that time. During the first half of the twentieth century, administrative theorists promoted what have come to be known as the classical principles of organization and management, many of which are followed today. Most of the writings and practice in police and criminal justice management have reflected the classical approach.

Human relations or neo-classical theory grew out of the failure of classical writers to recognize the human aspects of organization and management. In the late 1920's and early 1930's the Hawthorne studies produced results which were in conflict with classical theory. Through the use of experimental designs, Mayo and his associates discovered the importance of social and psychological factors in the work place. Human relationships and the informal organization were now seen as critical to the organization and its management.

While the human relations theorists criticized classical theorists for their supposedly universal principles, the human relations approach also implied universality. Modern management theory is based on the recognition of both the formal and informal organization and the importance of synthesizing the two. With the increasing sophistication of behavioral research methods, modern theorists have been able to empirically test the earlier theories and develop new directions in the field.

Modern theory also employs a general systems approach to the study of organizational behavior, which takes into consideration the external environment and relates the parts to the whole. However, because general systems theorists have tried to develop broad concepts applicable to all types of systems, this approach is highly abstract and difficult to apply to human situations. Contingency theory, on the other hand, attempts to refine these concepts by developing functional relationships between identifiable environmental variables and appropriate organizational designs and managerial practices. Although the contingency approach has by no means reached its full utility, it appears to be the most appropriate for integrating the theory and practice of police organization and management.

DISCUSSION QUESTIONS

1. Compare and contrast the theories of classicists such as Taylor, Weber, Fayol, and Gulik and Urwick.
2. Discuss the major criticisms of classical theory; to what extent do they seem valid to you?
3. Describe the implicit assumptions of both classical and human relations theory; how does modern theory differ in its approach?
4. Briefly discuss Barnard's "acceptance" theory of authority and Bakke's "fusion model."
5. Explain the significance of studying criminal justice organizations from an open systems perspective.
6. Compare and contrast general systems theory with contingency theory.
7. Discuss why the contingency approach appears the most appropriate for integrating the theory and practice of police organization and management.

ANNOTATED BIBLIOGRAPHY

George, Claude S., Jr., *The History of Management Thought*, 2nd ed., (Englewood Cliffs, N. J.: Prentice-Hall, 1972). A concise work which provides a basic framework for understanding the development of management thought by tracing the major contributions to the field.

Johnson, Richard A., Fremont E. Kast, and James E. Rosenzweig, *The Theory of Management Systems*, (New York: McGraw-Hill, 1963). One of the first textbooks in the field to offer a systems approach to the theoretical study of management.

Kast, Fremont E. and Rosenzweig, James E. (eds.), *Contingency Views of Organization and Management*, (Chicago: Science Research Associates, 1973). This anthology is meant to facilitate the understanding and development of contingency views of organizations and their management; based on systems concepts, it stresses the relevancy of theory to practice in specific situations.

Katz, Daniel and Kahn, Robert L. *The Social Psychology of Organizations*, (New York: John Wiley & Sons, 1966). This textbook was one of the first to utilize an open-systems theoretical perspective in the study of large-scale organizations. Research findings on the impact of personality and social structure are emphasized.

Koontz, Harold "The Management Theory Jungle," *Journal of the Academy of Management*, 4, (December, 1961), pp. 174-188. The various "schools" of management theory are classified in six primary groups; the major sources of differences between the groups are identified in an attempt to clarify the confusion.

Luthans, Fred *Introduction to Management: A Contingency Approach*, (New York: McGraw-Hill, 1976). This textbook uses the contingency framework to integrate the environment into management theory, and to present specific contingent relationships between the environment and management concepts and techniques in order to provide the most effective management.

Massie, Joseph L. "Management Theory" in *Handbook of Organizations*, James G. March (ed.), (Chicago: Rand McNally, 1965), pp. 387-422. This chapter concentrates on administrative management theory and presents the conceptual frameworks of the early classical writers, the most useful principles of management, and the current status of this body of knowledge.

Miner, John B. *Management Theory*, (New York: Macmillan, 1971). This brief text offers an introduction to management theory and provides a framework for viewing the field of management.

Wren, Daniel A. *The Evolution of Management Thought*, (New York: Ronald, 1972). An exhaustive study of the evolution of management thought from its earliest, informal days, to the present; examines the background of and influences on the major contributors.

THREE

Research Methods In Management

LEARNING OBJECTIVES

The study of this chapter should enable you to:

☑ Describe the concept of theory and the applicability of theory to "real life" managerial problems and settings.

☑ List several criteria which have been advanced for the valid practical application of behavioral science theory.

☑ Differentiate theory according to development (inductive and deductive), primary purpose (prescriptive and descriptive), and level of analysis (micro and macro).

☑ Describe the five criteria upon which an acceptable theory should be based.

☑ Describe the five interrelated steps of the scientific process.

☑ Define independent and dependent variables; define validity and reliability.

☑ List the three primary functions of a research design.

☑ Describe internal and external validity.

☑ Explain the usefulness of random sampling and provide an example.

☑ List the three strategies that are available to the experimental researcher and the advantages and disadvantages of each.

THREE

The previous chapter introduced several dimensions of theoretical thought concerning managerial practices and organizational behavior. Following chapters will provide additional theories which profess to explain various organizational phenomena—from motivation and leadership through organization design and organization change. In order to determine which of these theories is most likely to improve organizational conditions, one must first understand the concept of a theory as well as the processes of scientific inquiry. In other words, practicing police managers must be able to correctly interpret and utilize behavioral research as it applies to their organizational situations. Only in this manner will managers be relatively certain of implementing the most appropriate policies to meet specific organizational demands.

This chapter should enable the reader to critically analyze the theoretical developments and empirical findings reported throughout the book. To help the reader to more fully comprehend and apply the contents of this chapter to real life settings, an example of an experimental study is presented in the final section. Furthermore, because management research is relatively recent, this review should also be helpful in the evaluation of new theories.

THE CONCEPT OF THEORY

According to the psychologist Kurt Lewin, "There is nothing so practical as a good theory." Although this statement is true, many practitioners as well as students treat theoretical considerations as if they did not apply to the real world. One often hears the phrase, "It's a good theory but it doesn't work in practice." Unfortunately, many people believe this statement and subsequently close their minds to the importance and the relevance of theory. It is important to understand that an acceptable or good theory does work when applied to real life or natural settings.

The "theory versus practice" debate definitely exists in the criminal justice field and among practicing criminal justice managers. Although a spirit of scientific inquiry is growing, it has yet to become generally accepted, as can be illustrated by the manner in which many police agencies have spent the money doled out in past years by the Federal Government through the Law Enforcement Assistance Administration (LEAA), for the purpose of improving police effectiveness. Instead of using the money to establish and evaluate innovative new programs for improved services to the public, much of the money went instead for the purchase of hardware—

lights, sirens, weapons, etc. Admittedly, these objects were tangible and more readily available than the development of new programs, and less work as well, but they certainly did little to substantially improve the quality of policing. In fact, it could be argued that such purchases actually decreased the quality of police work because of increased reliance on "fire-power" as opposed to "reasonpower." The following article examines this problem in detail.

Local Crime Fighters Called Unimaginative[1]

Washington (AP)—Most state and local law enforcement officials are losers when it comes to new ideas for fighting crime, says Charles R. Work, who resigned last week after two years as deputy chief of the Law Enforcement Assistance Administration.

"The original notion was that we would be flooded with all these great ideas. And lo and behold, they didn't come at all!" said Work.

"Local law enforcement officials just won't look around for the good ideas, in part because they are as backward as they are, and in part because they are as poorly educated as they are," he said.

When Congress created the LEAA in 1968, the theory was that the federal government would put up the money to allow state and local governments to test their own new approaches particularly suited to their needs.

But Work said the LEAA is being forced to take a greater policy-making role because of "the paucity of innovative ideas" suggested by state criminal justice agencies in the annual plans they must submit to receive federal grants.

The agencies, he said, have fallen into the trap of keeping up with the Joneses. If Sheriff Shoot-em-up gets a new shotgun with LEAA money, then Chief Deadeye has to have one, too.

Work said it was easier for state and local officials to ask for money for hardware, rather than think up real innovations. Besides, he added, Congress perhaps unwittingly encouraged a heavy emphasis on hardware.

The law allows LEAA to finance an experimental program only temporarily, usually for three years. If state officials wish to continue it, they must find the money themselves.

This factor is crucial at a time when many cities are plunging into financial troubles, Work said. Buying police hardware is a one-time expense, unlike the innovations which will require local tax money when the federal largesse ends.

As the article implies, many of the agencies involved in this program have never seen the need to develop expertise in the area of theory and research. It is apparent, however, that if we are to improve the effectiveness of police and other criminal justice agencies, it will be through substantially increased interest and skill in research and evaluation. Consequently, practicing managers must become involved in research experiences by first developing a spirit of scientific inquiry.

Theory cannot supply managers with complete answers for every conceivable situation or circumstance, but it can suggest appropriate courses of action. According to Filley, House, and Kerr, "The real world, with all its

---

1. *Crime Control Digest,* 9, 481, Dec. 1, 1975, pp. 3-4.

complexities, must be ordered in a systematic fashion before we can hope to act in it or upon it. Theoretical formulation is the ordering process. Viewed in this way, theory is a goal that is valued in its own right; theories integrate and order empirical findings."[2] Consequently, theories summarize and put in order the existing knowledge in a particular area. Furthermore, theories are used to identify important *variables* (relational units of analysis, such as age, sex, edudation, organization structure, etc.) in problems being studied, as well as to suggest relationships between these variables. The Smith and Cranny model of motivation in Figure 3-1 shows how a theory, in this case, motivation, can identify important variables and suggest relationships among them. This model suggests that, in order to increase employee performance, effort must be increased; this is accomplished either through rewards or satisfaction. Of course, to establish the relevancy of a theory, such relationships must be supported empirically. The point is that theory can have very practical implications for managers, and is not necessarily irrelevant to the "real world."

Figure 3-1

Smith and Cranny Model of Motivation

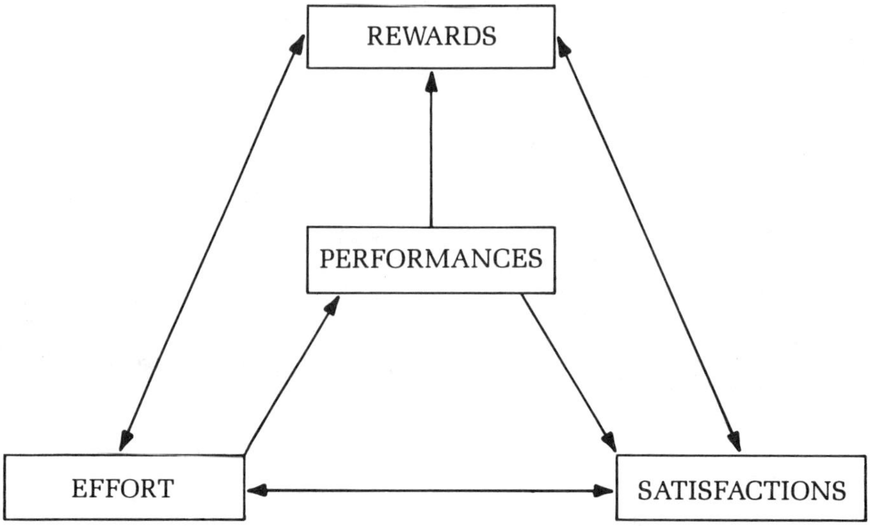

Source: Patricia Cain Smith and C.J. Cranny, "Psychology of Men at Work," *Annual Review of Psychology*, 19, 1968, p. 469.

For the practitioner, then, theory provides a description of the real world by summarizing the complexities of the environment. In a very real sense, the use of theory allows the manager to better solve problems that develop in relation to his or her particular situation. How does one go about selecting a valid theory which will be useful in improving organizational environments? According to Bennis, Beane, and Chin the criteria for the valid practical application of behavioral science theory should:

---

2. Alan C. Filley, Robert J. House, and Steven Kerr, (2nd Edition), *Managerial Process and Organizational Behavior*, (Glenville, Ill.: Scott, Foresman, and Co., 1976), p. 21.

1. Take into consideration the behavior of persons operating within specific institutional environments.

2. Account for interrelated levels (self, role, group, and large organization) within the social change context.

3. Include variables the practitioner can understand, manipulate, and evaluate.

4. Select from among variables those most appropriate to a specific local situation in terms of its values, ethics, and morality.

5. Accept the premise that groups and organizations as units are as amenable to empirical and analytical treatment as is the individual.

6. Take into account "external" social processes of change as well as interpersonal aspects of the collaborative process.[3]

Differentiation of Theory

Theory may be described and differentiated according to the following dimensions.

Development. *Inductive theory* is developed primarily to explain previous empirical observations of phenomena; it begins with empirical research and then states relationships between variables. The flow of logic is from *data to abstraction*.

Deductive theory is developed when little or no empirical observations have been made concerning the phenomena; it begins by first determining relationships between variables that should hold (i.e., if X then Y) and then deducing relationships by observing the variables. The flow of logic is from *abstraction to data*.

Whether management practices are based on inductive or deductive theory can have important consequences for the practicing manager, as the following example indicates. Police patrol strategies have long been based on the theory that visible random patrolling prevents crime by deterring potential offenders. This reasoning has been deductive in nature, although the critical variables of interest (patrol and crime deterrence) were never adequately observed. In 1974, the results of the Kansas City Preventive Patrol Experiment were released.[4] This study was inductive in nature; empirical data were collected and analyzed, then relationships between the variables of interest were established. The findings suggested that routine patrol had no significant effect on crime levels that were traditionally considered to be deterable through preventive patrol. Although the study has

---

3. Warren G. Bennis, Kenneth D. Benne and Robert Chin, (2nd Ed.), *The Planning of Change: Readings in the Applied Behavioral Sciences,* (New York: Holt, Rinehart, and Winston, 1961), taken from Filley, House, and Kerr, *Ibid.,* pp. 29-30.

4. George L. Kelling, Tony Pate, David Dieckman and Charles E. Brown, *The Kansas City Preventive Patrol Experiment: A Summary Report,* (Washington, D.C.: Police Foundation, 1974).

received some criticism,[5] as do most behavioral science studies of its scope, it was the first major test of the theory of preventive patrol.

Primary Purpose.   If the primary purpose of a theory is to prescribe what *should* occur, it is called *prescriptive* or *normative* theory. For example, organizations should reward their employees in proportion to the adequacy of their job performance; "excellent" performers should receive greater pay increases than "average" performers.

On the other hand, if a theory is meant to describe what *is* actually occurring rather than what should occur, it is referred to as *descriptive* or *positive* theory. For instance, in most police organizations all employees receive fundamentally the same pay increases yearly—whether they are average or excellent performers.

A cautionary note concerning prescriptive recommendations is in order. Our descriptive understanding of organizational behavior and managerial practice is largely superficial, and attempting to prescribe various organizational practices can thus be very perilous. Indeed, it may be dangerous if the prescription is later proven faulty. While certain research findings appear to have clear-cut implications for practice, the tentativeness of the field requires that prescription based on those findings must be applied with prudence.

This does not mean, however, that prescriptive theory is not of considerable value to the field. According to Porter, Lawler, and Hackman, "even premature prescriptions can have their place in the development of our applied-type field. This is because such prescriptions (or, more likely, an integrated set of them), when stated forcefully, often have the effect of stimulating a great deal of research. While the motivation for such research sometimes may be to prove the incorrectness of the prescriptions, it still often results in advances in knowledge."[6]

The major emphasis of this book will be descriptive—focusing on reseach which describes specific behaviors in organizations—although the reader should keep in mind that the solution to a problem in one instance may not be appropriate in another. Nevertheless, in order that we may analyze organizational behavior from both perspectives, certain relevant behavioral science prescriptions will be offered periodically, especially in the last chapter.

Level of Analysis.   Theories may take either a *micro* (specific) view, or a *macro* (overall) view. Micro theory starts with a particular unit of analysis (the individual or a specific organizational unit, such as the police officer or a patrol unit) and works upward from those parts to a theory of the whole; the individual and the groups that compose the organization are emphasized. The macro perspective, on the other hand, starts with the largest unit of analysis (the police organization) and works downward to specific elements

5.   International Association of Chiefs of Police, "Position Paper on the Kansas City Preventive Patrol Experiment," *The Police Chief,* 42, 1975, pp. 16-20, 64.

6.   Lyman W. Porter, Edward E. Lawler, and J. Richard Hackman, III, *Behavior in Organizations,* (New York: McGraw-Hill, 1975), pp. 18-19.

within, emphasizing the total organization and its relation to the environment (political, social, and economic aspects).

It should be noted that the orientation chosen to study organizations will
greatly influence, as well as restrict, the conclusions and decisions which
can be reached. For this reason, both micro and macro views will be utilized
in various parts of the book, in an attempt to provide the most comprehensive analysis of police organizational behavior and management practice.

Criteria to Evaluate Theory

Practicing managers must be able to evaluate the validity of theory
before they attempt to put it into practice. Filley, *et.al.*, suggest that a sound
or acceptable theory should meet the following criteria:

1. Internal consistency. The theory itself should contain no logical inconsistencies that could lead to contradictory conclusions or predictions. Logical consistency allows the theorist to state a chain of "if-then"
   propositions and to test them indirectly by experimenting with a small
   number of critical variables.

2. External consistency. A theory should be consistent with observations
   and measures of real life; this is known as the test of *empirical reference.*

3. Testable propositions. If a theory is not stated so that its predictions can be
   tested and verified, it may contain unintended bias or error. A theory is
   said to be *operational* when its formulation permits evaluation of its
   major propositions or predictions.

4. Generality. An acceptable theory must be generalizable in order to provide a wide range of application and extension of the field of knowledge.
   That is, it should be able to explain more than isolated, specific events. A
   theory must posit a set of relationships within a well defined class of
   events, and these relationships must explain the events that fall within
   the defined class.

5. Parsimony. A theory should be as clear and concise as possible. For
   example, if two theories both accurately predict the outcome of events
   and are equally supported by evidence, the less complex of the theories
   should be selected.[7]

THE SCIENTIFIC METHOD

As shown above, theory is used as a tool to direct empirical investigation, which either supports or does not support hypotheses. *Hypotheses* are
suggested explanations, usually in the form of a statement or proposition
about the relationship between two variables. One of the variables, termed
the *independent variable*, is the assumed "cause" or determining factor.
The remaining variable, termed the *dependent variable*, is the assumed
effect or outcome. If, for example, we were to hypothesize that college

---

7. Filley, House, and Kerr, *op.cit.*, pp. 22-23.

graduates were less authoritarian in their attitudes than non-college graduates, the independent variable would be college education, while the
dependent variable would be authoritarian attitudes. Although hypotheses
are often based on hunches or previous research, the preferable ones are
derived from theory.[8]

The scientific method can be described as "a process in which the
investigator moves inductively from his observations to hypotheses and
inductively from the hypotheses to the logical implications of the hypotheses. He deduces the consequences that would follow if a hypothesized
relationship is true. If these deduced implications are compatible with the
organized body of accepted knowledge, then they are further tested by the
gathering of empirical data. On the basis of the evidence, the hypotheses are
accepted or rejected."[9] Basically, the scientific method inovlves a systematic
process of inquiry. The interrelated steps of the scientific process are as
follows.[10]

Definition of the Problem. Scientific inquiry originates from a problem
or question in need of a solution. A question which is subject to scientific
investigation must contain one essential characteristic: it must be formulated
in such a way that observation or experimentation in the natural world can
provide an answer. Value judgments have no place in science, so implied
value judgments should be avoided when the problem is defined.

Statement of a Hypothesis. The investigator next forms the hypothesis,
which provides a tentative explanation of the problem. This process generally requires both a review of the related literature and further thought
concerning the relationships between variables.

Deductive Reasoning. After forming the hypothesis, the investigator
next deduces the implications suggested by the hypothesis (that is, what
would be observed if the hypothesis is true). For example, if college graduates are hypothesized to be less authoritarian than non-college graduates,
then one would expect to observe lower scores on authoritarian scales by
those with college degress than by those without college degrees.

Collection and Analysis of Data. Next the hypothesis (or, more precisely, its deduced implications) is tested by collecting relevant data through
observations, testing, and experimentation. In order to obtain worthwhile
research results, the reader (evaluator) must have knowledge of the errors
involved in the way a concept has been measured; validity and reliability
must be accounted for. *Validity* refers to the degree in which an instrument
measures what it purports to measure. One investigator's measure of a
concept must be compatible with those of other investigators who have used
different methods of operationalizing the same concept. *Reliability*, on the
other hand, is the degree to which a measuring device is consistent in its

---

8. M. Patricia Golden (ed.), *The Research Experience*, (Itasca, Ill.: Peacock, 1976), p. 7.

9. Donald Ary, Lucy Chester Jacobs, and Asghar Razavich, *Introduction to Research in Education*, (New York: Holt, Rinehart, and Winston, 1972), p. 10.

10. The steps included in the scientific method are drawn from Ary, Jacobs, and Razavich, *Ibid.*, pp. 10-11.

measurement. The same instrument, or different versions of an instrument, should give consistent results from one time to the next. The researcher is expected to include in his or her analysis the validity and reliability of the instruments used.

Confirming or Rejecting the Hypothesis. Once the data have been collected and analyzed, the researcher determines whether the investigation has produced evidence that supports the hypothesis. In the scientific method, one does not claim to prove a hypothesis; this would be dealing in terms of absolute truth, which is not characteristic of the approach. One merely concludes that the evidence either does or does not support the hypothesis.

Even though the various steps in this approach are conceptually separable, it should be remembered that in practice they are closely related activities which overlap rather than follow a strictly prescribed sequence. The interrelatedness of the steps pertaining to the scientific method is set forth below:

First, scientists examine the existing theories about the phenomenon they wish to investigate to determine if there is any direction they can take from another person's work on the same subject. From the other's theory or theories, the scientists may also derive their hypotheses, those testable guesses that lead to the tentative confirmation or rejection of theories. Once the research project is completed and the researchers know the results, they may return to the theories and feed the results back into them, modifying them in the process. Between the theory and the research project, there are extremely complex and important feedback mechanisms at work:

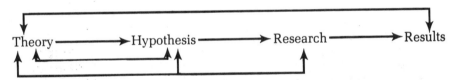

Any piece of the research process that is incorrectly (or even badly) designed will influence what the researcher can, and should, say about the theory on which the research is based. For example, the results of one study are fed back into the accumulated body of empirical knowledge that the discipline has and may be used to adjust the theory (or world view) held by members of the discipline, and in their turn to be used as ideas for further research projects which results are then fed back into the accumulated body of knowledge, and so on and on. To separate theory from the methods of research, then, is to make a false separation because the two go inextricably together.[11]

Quality of Empirical Research

According to the scientific method, the evaluator must be extremely careful when interpreting empirical findings. A healthy skepticism concerning research studies is crucial, for errors and biases may have an effect on

---

11. John F. Runcie, *Experiencing Social Research*, (Homewood, Ill.: Dorsey, 1976), p. 10.

the interpretation of the reported results. In other words, the reader must carefully evaluate the validity of the research presented as well as the manner in which it is applied. The following four evaluative questions provide direction with respect to the interpretation of research findings.

Question One: Is there a sound theoretical framework?

Does the theory or theoretical framework support the empirical results? Are theories stated prior to the start of the research, i.e., are theoretical frameworks being tested? (Again, while hypotheses are often based on prevsious research or simply on hunches, those derived from theory are preferable.)

Question Two: Is there empirical evidence available to support the theory?

A theory cannot be judged in isolation; it is or is not supported by the data collected for the study.

Question Three: What is the importance and/or implications of the research?

The results of the study should provide meaning to the practicing manager. In other words, does the research actually increase our understanding of organizational phenomena?

Question Four: What is the quality of the research itself?

Several factors should be considered in assessing the quality of research. Is the author interpreting the results correctly? Giant "leaps of faith" in interpretation are often made. For instance, in the above example concerning education and authoritarian attitudes, let us assume that college graduates did receive lower scores on a valid and reliable authoritarianism scale; does this mean that the investigator can claim higher education as the causal variable? Several other variables, such as age, I.Q., or socio-economic status, may also have been influential in determining authoritarian attitudes. Did the researcher adequately control for these and other extraneous variables?

One should also look for any logical inconsistencies, or alternative explanations of results. If the question of research quality is not addressed, the results may appear to be more significant than they actually are. If inaccurate or misinterpreted results are accepted at face value, and major managerial practices are implemented in accord with those results, such practices could have negative, long-range effects on the organizational environment. Managers have too often "jumped on the bandwagon" before all the results were in and correctly interpreted.

RESEARCH DESIGNS

A research design is meant to determine the most appropriate manner for collecting and analyzing data in relation to specific research studies. Regardless of the type of strategy selected by the investigator (manager), all research designs perform one or more basic functions, depending upon their degree of sophistication as well as on the concerns of the investigator. Black and Champion have discussed the functions of research designs as follows.[12]

Research designs provide the researcher with a blueprint for studying social questions. Without adequate drawings and plans, a homebuilder would become burdened with insurmountable problems such as where to place the foundation, what kinds and qualities of materials to use, how many workers are required, the size of the home, and so on. By the same token, a social researcher faces comparable obstacles if the study begins without some kind of research plan. To minimize research problems, several decisions should be made before beginning the project. For example, if the investigator chooses to study people directly, some possible considerations might be (1) a description of the target population, (2) the sampling methods to be used, (3) the size of the sample, (4) the data collection procedures to be used, (5) possible ways of analyzing the collected data, and (6) whether or not to use statistical tests, and if so, which one(s)?

Research designs dictate the boundaries of research activity and enable investigators to channel their energies in specific directions. Without definite research boundaries and/or objectives, a researcher's activities in a single project could be virtually endless. With clear research objectives in view, however, investigators can proceed systematically toward the achievement of certain goals.

Research designs enable the investigator to anticipate potential problems in the implementation of the study. Researchers customarily review current literature central to the topic under investigation. In the course of the review, they may learn about new or alternative approaches to their problems. At the same time they can acquire information concerning what they can reasonably expect in their own investigations. The design can provide some estimate of the cost of the research, possible measurement problems, and the optional allocation of resources such as assistants and material.

Major Research Designs

The particular design or strategy used in any investigation must be appropriate to the needs of the particular problem under study. Although there is seldom a single best plan for every situation, practicing managers and students should benefit from a comparison of the major research designs in relation to specific research goals. The major designs to be discussed are: (1) field studies, (2) experiments, (3) surveys, and (4) the use of available data.[13] Table 3-1 summarizes the usefulness of each of these designs.

---

12. James A. Black and Dean J. Champion, *Methods and Issues in Social Research*, (New York: John Wiley & Sons, 1976), pp. 76-77.

13. The four major designs and much of their discussion was drawn from Golden, *op. cit.*, pp. 15-20.

Table 3-1
Summary: Choices and Constraints In Social Research

Research Strategies	Type of "Unit in setting"	Purpose	Criteria Maximized	Primary Goal
Field study	Real groups in natural (Field) setting	Exploratory/ Descriptive	Naturalness (and insight)	To understand system character of context
Experiment Laboratory	Treatment groups in contrived (Lab) setting	Causal	Control	To extablish relationships between *variables* (internal validity)
Field	Treatment groups in natural (Field) setting	Causal	Some control/ Some naturalness	To establish relationships between *variables in context* (internal validity)
Simulation	Treatment groups in simulated/ contrived (Lab) setting	Causal/ Descriptive/ Exploratory	Some control	To establish relationships between *variables in context* (internal validity)
Survey	Sample in variable setting (Behavior is not dependent on setting)	Descriptive/ Causal/ Exploratory	Representativeness	Generalizability to other *units* and their attributes (external validity)
Available data	Sample in variable setting	Descriptive/ Causal/ Exploratory	Representativeness/ Naturalness	Generalizability to other *units* (external validity)

Source: M. Patricia Golden, (ed.), *The Research Experience*, (Itasca, Illinois: Peacock), 1976, p. 4.

Field Studies. Among the alternative research designs or strategies available, field studies come the closest to approximating real life. Because their objective is to study, in all its complexity, the behavior of real actors in actual settings (e.g. workers, supervisors, units or departments), they are usually realistic and meaningful. The investigator tries to not interfere with the ongoing behavior and to understand as fully as possible the interaction of the many variables in the particular setting.

A study of police brutality, conducted by the Center of Research on Social Organization, provides a particuarly good example of this strategy. Thirty-six people observed police-citizen encounters in the cities of Boston, Chicago, and Washington, D.C. For seven days a week, over a period of seven weeks in the summer of 1966, these observers, with police permission, sat in patrol cars and monitored booking and lockup procedures in high-crime precincts. Even in the presence of the observers, who had gained the "trust" of the police, many examples of brutality and harrassment were recorded.[14]

While such an approach makes it difficult to focus on or to isolate specific elements of the research situation, it does lend itself to openness, flexibility, and discovery. Consequently, field studies are often the preferred strategy when the purpose is to explore or to describe. However, they are seldom used where explanation is the investigator's purpose, because control of variables is difficult. Some also argue that the introduction of the

---

14. Albert J. Reiss, Jr., *Police Brutality—Answers to Key Questions*, (Warner Modular Publication, Reprint 46, July/Auugst, 1968).

observer into a natural setting is in itself disruptive, and may create an unnatural situation.

Experiments. If the primary purpose of the research is to establish relationships between variables (that is, to test a hypothesis), control is of paramount importance. Experimental designs offer the greatest degree of control, and therefore the greatest chance of establishing cause-and-effect or *causal* relationships. By manipulating the independent variable(s) of interest and by controlling statistically or holding constant other extraneous variables, the researcher can measure the change or changes which may occur in the dependent variable(s).

Frequently, an *experimental* group and a *control* group are used. In this strategy, the experimental group is exposed to the independent variable while the control group is not. Any measured change in the dependent variable within the experimental group—assuming no such change has occurred in the control group—is attributed to the independent variable. However, strict causal relationships between variables can be inferred only if all extraneous variables have been controlled. The greater the control over extraneous variables, the higher the probability that the independent variable did, in fact, cause the change in the dependent variable. Accordingly, the researcher must be aware of both the internal and external validity of any particular design.[15] *Internal validity* refers to the possibility of alternative explanations (other than those proposed) of the relationships between variables studied. In other words, did the independent variable really make the difference? *External validity* refers to the generalizability or representativeness of the findings; to what other populations and settings can the findings be generalized? The best control for external validity is *random sampling,* which assures that any initial differences between the experimental and control groups are attributable to chance alone. This particular experimental design is shown in Figure 3-2. Notice that both groups are randomly assigned and measured (or tested) on the dependent variable. The independent variable is then introduced only to the experimental group, and after a certain period of time, both groups are again measured on the dependent variable. If the independent variable had any effect, a significant difference (determined statistically) should be observed in the second measure of the experimental group.

Such a design could be highly useful to police agencies in measuring the effects of various training programs. For example, let's say a particular department was concerned with prejudicial attitudes among its officers and determined that human relations training would be useful in combating such attitudes. After the training program was properly designed, personnel would be randomly assigned to either an experimental or a control group. Prejudicial attitudes (dependent variable) would then be measured on both groups (measure 1, Figure 3-2). Following measurement, the experimental

---

15. For an excellent discussion on internal and external validity, see: Donald T. Campbell and Julian C. Stanley, *Experimental and Quasi-Experimental Designs,* (Chicago; Rand McNally, 1963).

group would be exposed to the independent variable (training) unlike the control group which would not. After the experimental group concluded the human relations training, both groups would again be measured for prejudicial attitudes (measure 2, Figure 3-2). By comparing the results of measure 1 with those of measure 2, the manager could determine whether or not the training experience had any significant effect on prejudicial attitudes.

Figure 3-2

Two Groups, Randomized Subjects, Two Measure Design

Random Assignment	Group	Measure 1 Dependent Variable	Independent Variable	Measure 2 Dependent Variable
X	Experimental	X	X	X
X	Control	X		X

Several strategies are available to the experimental researcher: (1) laboratory experiments, (2) field experiments, and (3) experimental simulations.

Laboratory Experiments. Laboratory experiments provide the most complete control by holding constant extraneous environmental and personal variables. The experimenter deliberately creates a contrived setting which lends itself to research procedures that, because they can be manipulated or controlled, are usually more precise, more accurate, more definite, and more easily quantifiable.

The very precision and control possible in such settings also provide the basis for the strongest criticisms of this strategy. Some consider laboratory experiments "artificial" and therefore meaningless. The difficulty is that, while such experiments are strong on internal validity, they are weak on external validity. Although this type of experimentation fits perfectly the needs of the physical and natural sciences, human behavior in organizations generally cannot be so neatly isolated to laboratory settings. When a laboratory design is utilized for the study of criminal justice managerial problems, generalizability back to the natural environment (organization) may not be valid.

Field Experiments. Field experiments attempt to capitalize on the advantages of both field studies and laboratory experiments. Consequently, they also present some of the difficulties of both. A field experiment introduces manipulation into real life situations; the researcher tries to gain maximum control of behavior without sacrificing the reality of the situation. Field experiments are thus more artificial than field studies and have less control than lab experiments. Because control of the environment is minimal, extraneous environmental variables can still influence the outcome. Even with these limitations, this strategy is ideal for studying police organizational behavior. Unfortunately, many organizations are unwilling to allow such research to take place for fear that normal activities may be disrupted. Or, as is often the case in the criminal justice system, the need for such research is simply not perceived. For proof that such a strategy can indeed be implemented without disrupting organizational effectiveness, see the Kansas City Preventive Patrol Experiment in the final section of this chapter.

Experimental Simulations. Like laboratory experiments, experimental simulations create a setting for the specific purpose of the research. In simulations, however, the setting is designed to represent some particular class or kind of real-life situation, as in the Curtis, Banks, and Zimbardo study on interpersonal dynamics which was conducted in a simulated prison. The researchers created a prison-like situation (using an environment which had been physically constructed to closely resemble a prison), in which the "guards" and "inmates" were initially comparable and characterized as being "psychologically healthy." The researchers then observed, for nearly a one week time period, the patterns of cognitive, emotional, and attitudinal reactions and changes that emerged; the finding supported many documented reports concering the inhumane treatment of prison inmates. Most dramatic and distressing to the investigators was the ease with which sadistic behavior could be evoked in individuals who were not "sadistic types" and the frequency with which acute emotional breakdowns could occur in persons selected precisely for their emotional stability.[16]

Studies of this type may be very helpful in determining managerial practices in organizational settings. While some degree of control is built into such studies, through manipulation of the independent variable and by selection and assignment of the subjects, still other variables are left to vary. The principal weakness of this method, as in the laboratory method, involves the generalizability to the natural environment of the results.

Surveys. A third major design available for the study of organizational behavior is the survey, which is used when the researcher wants to obtain information—usually a large amount of it—that can be generalized to a whole class of units, or actors. The survey generally requires samples that are representative of these larger populations. The two major methods of this design are the *questionnaire* and the *personal interview*. For example, with respect to the study conducted by the Center of Research on Social Organization described earlier, a survey strategy could also have been used to measure the degree of police brutality. A random sample of those arrested by the police could be interviewed and/or sent a questionnaire asking how they were treated by the police.

In this design, variables are supposed to be studied as they are in reality. Some argue that the naturally occurring interaction of factors is not altered, while others counter that the introduction of the survey instrument is reactive in itself and creates a totally unnatural situation. No manipulation of the independent variable means, of course, less control. One can

---

16. Craig Henry, W. Curtis Banks, and Philip G. Zimbardo, "Interpersonal Dynamics in a Simulated Prison," *International Journal of Criminology and Penalogy*, 1, 1973, pp. 69-97.

compensate for the absence of control at the point of data collection, however, by introducing statistical controls (that is, by holding certain variables constant) at the point of data analysis.

Although there is a tendency to associate surveys with description, they can be used in exploratory and causal research as well. It simply depends on the researcher's purpose. To engage in causal survey research, the type of statistical controls mentioned above are used. If the design is properly contemplated and planned out, most of the problems associated with survey research can be eliminated.

Available Data. Using data that is already available can provide creative opportunities for the researcher. However, the researcher has virtually no control over the original form of the data, which must be taken as they are. This strategy uses data that have been collected, usually by another researcher or organization, for other purposes or at least not for the researcher's particular purpose. Given the tremendous cost and time factors involved in collecting data, this method of *secondary analysis* should not be overlooked. Once the researcher decides on the specific source, the principles of design and analysis are little different from those of survey analysis.

THE KANSAS CITY PREVENTIVE PATROL EXPERIMENT

This final section presents a classic example of a field experiement is presented; the first ever to actually test the effectiveness of random police patrol. Because field experiments deal with natural settings, and absolute experimental control is not possible, several serious problems were encountered by the investigators. The reader should be aware of these areas of concern and how they were dealt with by the research team and the department under study.

Introduction and Major Findings*

Ever since the creation of a patrolling force in 13th century Hangchow, preventive patrol by uniformed personnel has been a primary function of policing. In 20th century America, about $2 billion is spent each year for the maintenance and operation of uniformed and often superbly equipped patrol forces. Police themselves, the general public, and elected officials have always believed that the presence or potential presence of police officers on patrol severely inhibits criminal activity.

One of the principal police spokesmen for this view was the late O.W. Wilson, former chief of the Chicago Police Department and a prominent academic theorist on police issues. As Wilson once put it, "Patrol is an indispensable service that plays a leading role in the accomplishment of the

---

*Source: George L. Kelling, Tony Pate, Duane Dieckman and Charles E. Brown, *The Kansas City Preventive Patrol Experiment: A Summary Report,* (Washington, D.C.: Police Foundation, 1974), pp. 1-10, 49.

police purpose. It is the only form of police service that directly attempts to eliminate opportunity for misconduct . . ." Wilson believed that by creating the impression police omnipresence, patrol convinced most potential offenders that opportunities for successful misconduct did not exist.

To the present day, Wilson's has been the prevailing view. While modern technology, through new methods of transportation, surveillance, and communications, has added vastly to the tools of patrol, and while there have been refinements in patrol strategies, based upon advanced probability formulas and other computerized methods, the general principle has remained the same. Today's police recruits, like virtually all those before them, learn from both teacher and textbook that patrol is the "backbone" of police work.

No less than the police themselves, the general public has been convinced that routine preventive patrol is an essential element of effective policing. As the International City Management Association has pointed out, "for the greatest number of persons, deterrence through ever-present police patrol, coupled with the prospect of speedy police action once a report is received, appears important to crime control." Thus, in the face of spiraling crime rates, the most common answer urged by public officers and citizens alike has been to increase patrol forces and get more police officers "on the street." The assumption is that increased displays of police presence are vitally necessary in the face of increased criminal activity. Recently, citizens in troubled neighborhoods have themselves resorted to civilian versions of patrol.

Challenges to preconceptions about the value of preventive police patrol were exceedingly rare until recent years. When researcher Bruce Smith, writing about patrol in 1930, noted that its effectiveness "lacks scientific demonstration," few paid serious attention.

Beginning in 1962, however, challenges to commonly held ideas about patrol began to proliferate. As reported crime began to increase dramatically, as awareness of unreported crime became more common, and as spending for police activities grew substantially, criminologists and others began questioning the relationship between patrol and crime. From this questioning a body of literature has emerged.

Much of this literature is necessarily exploratory. Earlier researchers were faced with the problem of obtaining sufficient and correct data, and then devising methodologies to interpret the data. The problems were considerable, and remain so.

Another problem facing earlier investigators was the natural reluctance of most police departments to create the necessary experimental conditions through which definitive answers concerning the worth of patrol could be obtained. Assigned the jobs of protecting society from crime, of apprehending criminals, and of carrying out numerous other services such as traffic control, emergency help in accidents and disasters, and supervision of public gatherings, police departments have been apprehensive about interrupting their customary duties to experiement with strategies or to assist in the task of evaluation.

It was in this context that the Kansas City, Missouri, Police Department, under a grant from the Police Foundation, undertook in 1972 the most comprehensive experiment ever conducted to analyze the effectiveness of routine preventive patrol.

From the outset the department and the Police Foundation evaluation team agreed that the project design would be as rigorously experimental as possible, and that while Kansas City Police Department data would be used, as wide a data base as possible, including data from external measurements, would be generated. It was further agreed that the experiment would be monitored by both department and foundation representatives to insure maintenance of experimental conditions. Under the agreement between the department and the foundation, the department committed itself to an eight-month experiment provided that reported crime did not reach "unacceptable" limits within the experimental area. If no major problems developed, the experiment would continue an additional four months.

For the purposes of measurement, a number of hypotheses were developed, of which the following were ultimately addressed:

(1) crime, as reflected by victimization surveys and reported crime data, would not vary by type of patrol;

(2) citizen perception of police service would not vary by type of patrol;

(3) citizen fear and behavior as a result of fear would not vary by type of patrol;

(4) police response time and citizen satisfaction with response time would vary by experimental area; and

(5) traffic accidents would increase in the reactive beats.

The experiment found that the three experimental patrol conditions appeared not to affect crime, service delivery and citizen feelings of security in ways the public and the police often assume they do. For example,

• as revealed in the victimization surveys, the experimental conditions had no significant effect on residence and non-residence burglaries, auto thefts, larcenies involving auto accessories, robberies, or vandalism— crimes traditionally considered to be deterrable through preventive patrol;

• in terms of rates of reporting crime to the police, few differences and no consistent patterns of differences occurred across experimental conditions;

• in terms of departmental reported crime, only one set of differences across experiemental conditions was found and this one was judged likely to have been a random occurrence.

• few significant differences and no consistent pattern of differences occurred across experimental conditions in terms of citizen attitudes toward police services;

• citizen fear of crime, overall, was not affected by experimental conditions;

- there were few differences and no consistent pattern of differences across experiemental conditions in the number and types of anti-crime protective measures used by citizens;
- in general, the attitudes of businessmen toward crime and police services were not affected by experimental conditions;
- experimental conditions did not appear to affect significantly citizen satisfaction with the police as a result of their encounters with police officers;
- experimental conditions had no significant effect on either police response time or citizen satisfaction with police response time;
- although few measures were used to assess the impact of experimental conditions on traffic accidents and injuries, no significant differences were apparent;
- about 60 percent of a police officer's time is typically noncommitted (available for calls); of this time, police officers spent approximately as much time on non-police related activities as they did on police-related patrol and;
- in general, police officers are given neither a uniform definition of preventive patrol nor any objective methods for gauging its effectiveness; while officers tend to be ambivalent in their estimates of preventive patrol's effectiveness in deterring crime, many attach great importance to preventive patrol as a police function.

Some of these findings pose a direct challenge to traditionally held beliefs. Some point only to an acute need for further research. But many point to what those in the police field have long suspected—an extensive disparity between what we want the police to do, what we often believe they do, and what they can and should do.

The immediate issue under analysis in the preventive patrol experiment was routine preventive patrol and its impact on crime and the community. But a much larger policy issue was implied: *whether urban police departments can establish and maintain experimental conditions*, and whether such departments can, for such experimentation, infringe upon that segment of time usually committed to routine preventive patrol. Both questions were answered in the *affirmative*, and in this respect the preventive patrol experiment represents a crucial first step, but just one in a series of such steps toward defining and clarifying the police function in modern society (emphasis added).

What the experiment did not address was a multitude of other patrol issues. It did not, for example, study such areas as two-officer patrol cars, team policing, generalist-specialist models, or other experiments currently underway in other departments. The findings of this experiment do not establish that the police are not important to the solution of crime or that police presence in some situations may not be helpful in reducing crime. Nor do they automatically justify reductions in the level of policing. They do not suggest that because the majority of a police officer's time is typically spent on non-crime related matters, the amount of time spent on crime is of any lesser importance.

Nor do the findings imply that the provision of public services and maintenance of order should overshadow police work on crime. While one of the three patrol conditions used in this experiment reduced police visibility in certain areas, the condition did not withdraw police availability from those areas. The findings in this regard should therefore not be interpreted to suggest that total police withdrawal from an area is an answer to crime. The reduction in routine police patrol was but one of three patrol conditions examined, and the implications must be treated with care.

It could be argued that because of its large geographical area and relatively low population density, Kansas City is not representative of the more populous urban areas of the United States. However, many of the critical problems and situations facing Kansas City are common to other large cities. For example, in terms of rates of aggravated assault, Kansas City ranks close to Detroit and San Francisco. The rate of murder and manslaughter per 100,000 persons in Kansas City is similar to that of Los Angeles, Denver and Cincinnati. And in terms of burglary, Kansas City is comparable to Boston and Birmingham. Furthermore, the experimental area itself was diverse socio-economically, and had a population density much higher than Kansas City's average, making the experiemental area far more representative and comparative than Kansas City as a whole might be. In these respects, the conclusions and implications of this study can be widely applied.

Description of the
Preventive Patrol Experiment

The impetus for an experiment in preventive patrol came from within the Kansas City Police Department in 1971. While this may be surprising to some, the fact is that by that year the Kansas City department had already experienced more than a decade of innovation and improvement in its operations and working climate and had gained a reputation as one of the nation's more progressive police departments.

Under Chief Clarence M. Kelley, the department had achieved a high degree of technological sophistication, was receptive to experimentation and change, and was peppered with young, progressive and professional officers. Short- and long-range planning had become institutionalized, and constructive debates over methods, procedures and approaches to police work were commonplace. By 1972, this department of approximately 1,300 police officers in a city of just over half a million—part of a metropolitan complex on 1.3 million—was open to new ideas and recommendations, and enjoyed the confidence of the people it served.

As part of its continuing internal discussions of policing, the department in October of 1971 established a task force of patrol officers and supervisors in each of its three patrol divisions (South, Central and Northeast), as well as in its special operations division (helicopter, traffic, tactical, etc).* The decision to establish these task forces was based on the beliefs that the ability to make competent planning decisions existed at all levels within the department and that if institutional change was to gain acceptance, those affected by it should have a voice in planning and implementaion.

The job of each task force was to isolate the critical problems facing its division and propose methods to attack those problems. All four task forces did so. The South Patrol Division Task Force identified five problem areas where greater police attention was deemed vital: burglaries, juvenile offenders, citizen fear, public education about the police role, and police-community relations.

Like the other task forces, the South task force was confronted next with developing workable remedial strategies. And here the task force met with what at first seemed an insurmountable barrier. It was evident that concentration by the South Patrol Division on the five problem areas would cut deeply into the time spent by its officers on preventive patrol.** At this point a significant thing happened. Some of the members of the South task force questioned whether routine preventive patrol was effective, what police officers did while on preventive patrol duty, and what effect police visibility had on the community's feelings of security.

Out of these discussions came the proposal to conduct an experiment which would test the true impact of routine preventive patrol. The Police Foundation agreed to fund the experiment's evaluation.

---

*The historical presentation should be viewed with care, since many episodes, concerns and problematic areas have been omitted in the interests of brevity. Chapter II of the technical report deals in greater detail with the events leading to the experiment, while Chapter IV discusses many of the technical and administrative problems experienced during that time. A comprehensive description of the experiment's development would require a volume in itself, and an analysis of the organizational dynamics involved in designing and administering the preventive patrol experiment will be published by the Kansas City Evaluation Staff at a later date.

**In this report, routine preventive patrol is defined as those patrol activities employed by the Kansas City Police Department during the approximately 35 percent of patrol duty time in which officers are not responding to calls for service, attending court or otherwise unavailable for self-initiated activites. (The 35 percent figure was a pre-experimental estimate developed by the Kansas City Police Department for use in determining officer allocation.) Information made available daily to patrol officers includes items such as who in their beats is wanted on a warrant, who is wanted for questioning by detectives, what criminals are active in their beats and type and location of crimes which have occurred during the previous 24 hours. The officers are expected to be familiar with this information and use it during their non-committed time. Accordingly, routine preventive patrol includes being guided by this information while observing from police cars, checking on premises and suspicious citizens, serving warrants, checking abandoned vehicles, and executing other self-initiated police activities. Thus routine preventive patrol in Kansas City is informed acitivty based upon information gathered from a wide variety of sources. Whether Kansas City's method of preventive patrol is typical is hard to say with exactness. Clearly, some departments place more emphasis on pedestrian checks, car checks, and field interrogating than does Kansas City (experiments on some of these activities are now taking place elsewhere). Preventive patrol as practiced in Kansas City has some unique characteristics but for the most part is typical of preventive patrol in urban areas.

As would be expected, considerable controversy surrounded the experiment, with the central question being whether long-range benefits outweighed short-term risks. The principal short-term risk was seen as the possibility that crime would increase drastically in the reactive beats; some officers felt the experiment would be tampering with citizens' lives and property.

The police officers expressing such reservations were no different from their counterparts in other departments. They tended to view patrol as one of the most important functions of policing, and in terms of time allocated, they felt that preventive patrol ranked on a par with investigating crimes and rendering assistance in emergencies. While some admitted that preventive patrol was probably less effective in preventing crime and more productive in enhancing citizen feelings of security, others insisted that the activities involved in preventive patrol (car, pedestrian and building checks) were instrumental in the capture of criminals and, through the police visibility associated with such activities, in the deterrence of crime. While there were ambiguities in these attitudes toward patrol and its effectiveness, all agreed it was a primary police function.

Within the South Patrol Division's 24-beat area, nine beats were eliminated from consideration as unrepresentative of the city's socio-economic composition. The remaining 15-beat, 32-square mile experimental area encompassed a commercial-residential mixture, with a 1970 resident population of 148,395 persons and a density of 4,542 persons per square mile (significantly greater than that for Kansas City as a whole, which in 1970 with only 1,604 persons per square mile, was 45th in the nation). Racially, the beats within this area ranged from 78 percent black to 99 percent white. Median family income of residents ranged from a low of $7,320 for one beat to a high of $15,964 for another. On the average, residents of the experimental area tended to have been in their homes from 6.6 to 10.9 years.

The 15 beats in the experimental area were computer matched on the basis of crime data, number of calls for service, ethnic composition, median income and transiency of population into five groups of three each. Within each group, one beat was designated *reactive*, one *control*, and one *proactive*. In the five reactive beats, there was no preventive patrol as such. Police vehicles assigned these beats entered them only in response to calls for service. Their noncommitted time (when not answering calls) was spent patrolling the boundaries of the reactive beats or patrolling in adjacent proactive beats. While police availability was closely maintained, police visibility was, in effect, withdrawn (except when police vehicles were seen while answering calls for service).

In the five control beats, the usual level of patrol was maintained at one car per beat. In the five proactive beats, the department increased police patrol visibility by two to three times its usual level both by the assignment of marked police vehicles to these beats and the presence of units from adjacent reactive beats.

Other than the restrictions placed upon officers in reactive beats (respond only to calls for service and patrol only the perimeter of the beat or in a adjacent proactive beat), no special instructions were given to police officers in the experimental area. Officers in control and proactive beats were to conduct preventive patrol as they normally would.

It should be noted, however, that the geographical distribution of beats (see Figure 3-3) avoided clustering reactive beats together or at an unacceptable distance from proactive beats. Such clustering could have resulted in lowered response time in the reactive beats.

Figure 3-3

**Schematic Representation
of the 15-Beat Experimental Area**

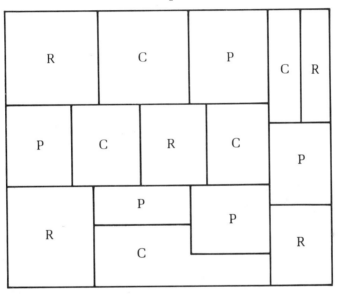

P=PROACTIVE
C=CONTROL
R=REACTIVE

It should also be noted that patrol modification in the reactive and proactive beats involved only routine preventive patrol. Specialized units, such as tactical, helicopter and K-9, operated as usual in these beats but at a level consistent with the activity level established the preceding year. This level was chosen to prevent infringement of these specialized units upon experimental results.

Finally, it should be noted that to minimize any possible risk through the elimination of routine preventive patrol in the reactive beats, crime rate data were monitored on a weekly basis. It was agreed that if a noticeable increase in crime occurred within a reactive beat, the experiment would be suspended. This situation, however, never materialized.

While the Kansas City experiment began on July 19, 1972, both department and Police Foundation monitors recognized by mid-August that experimental conditions were not being maintained, and that several problems had arisen. Chief Kelley then saw to it that these problems were rectified during a suspension of the experiment.

One problem was manpower, which in the South Patrol Division had fallen to a dangerously low level for experimental purposes. To correct this problem additional police officers were assigned to the division and an adequate manpower level restored. A second problem involved violations of the project guidelines. Additional training sessions were held, and administrative emphasis brought to bear to ensure adherence to the guidelines. A third problem was boredom among officers assigned to reactive beats. To counter this, the guidelines were modified to allow an increased level of activity by reactive-assigned officers in proactive beats. These revisions emphasized that an officer could take whatever action was deemed necessary, regardless of location, should a criminal incident be observed. The revised guidelines also stressed adherence to the spirit of the project rather than to unalterable rules.

On October 1, 1972, the experiment resumed. It continued successfully for 12 months, ending on September 30, 1973. Findings were produced in terms of the effect of experimental conditions on five categories of crimes traditionally considered to be deterrable through preventive patrol (burglary, auto theft, larceny—theft of auto accessories, robbery and vandalism) and on five other crime categories (including rape, assault, and other larcenies). Additional findings concerned the effect of experimental conditions on citizen feelings of security and satisfaction with police service, on the amount and types of anti-crime protective measures taken by citizens and businessmen, on police response time and citizen satisfaction with response time, and on injury/fatality and non-injury traffic accidents. The experiment also produced data concerning police activities during tours of duty, and police officer attitudes toward preventive patrol.

Author's Observations and Conclusions

The initial impetus behind the Kansas City preventive patrol experiment was the issue of time and staff resources. When the South Patrol Task Force began its deliberations, the concern was that any serious attempt to deal with priority problems would be confounded by the need to maintain established levels of routine patrol. Thus, in addition to testing the effect of various patrol strategies on such factors as crime, citizen fear and satisfaction, and response time, the experiment equally addressed the question of whether adequate time can be channeled to the development, testing and evaluation of new approaches to patrol.

From the beginning phases of this experiment, the evaluators formed hypotheses based upon certain assumptions. One primary assumption was that the poice, as an institutionalized mechanism of social control, are seriously limited in their ability to both prevent crime and apprehend offenders once crimes have been committed. The reasons for these limitations are many and complex. But they include the very nature of the crime problem itself, the limits a democratic society places upon its police, the limited amount of resources available for crime prevention, and complexities within the entire criminal justice system.

As a result of these limitations, many have rightly suggested that we must now begin revising our expectations as to the police role in society.

Because there are programmatic implications in the findings of this experiment, several cautionary comments are offered.

During the course of the experiment a number of preliminary findings were reported initially and subsequently reprinted in and editoralized upon in many major newspapers. A weekly news magazine carried a brief and cryptic report on the experiment, suggesting that it had produced evidence that patrol officers were unnecessary. This was subsequently picked up by a television network and given further exposure. Public response to these stories was unfortunate, but predictable. Unfamiliar with the issues of the experiment, and yet highly sensitive to these issues, some saw the study as justification for limiting or reducing the level of policing. Many saw it as a justification for two-officer cars. Others, fearing some of the conclusions drawn above, simply rejected the study out of hand.

Such implications are unfortunate. Given the distinct possibility that the police may more effectively deal with the problems of crime if they work more closely and systematically with their communities, it may be that an increase rather than a decrease in number of police is warranted. It may be that, given a different orientation and strategy, an increase in the number of police would increase chances for preventing crime. Those who drew man-power reduction conclusions from the preliminary findings assumed that if the crime prevention strategies currently being used did not work, no crime prevention strategies would work. This is not believed to be the case and such an implication is not supported by this study. Police serve a vital function in society, and their presence is of real and symbolic importance to citizens.

Nor does this study automatically lead to any conclusions about such programs as team policing, generalist-specialist models, minority recruitment, professionalization of the police or community relations programs. These are all package phrases embracing a wide variety of programs. While some recent works attempt to define the exact nature of these programs, most such terms remain ambiguous and for some, offensive.

These programs are attempting to deal with particular problems in the field of policing, including police and citizen alienation, the fragmented nature of police work, the inability to provide adequate supervision for police officers, the inability to coordinate the activities of officers in a variety of areas, the inability to adequately transmit information from officer to officer, from beat to beat, and from watch to watch, and the antiquated, quasi-military organizational structure in predominant use. These problems exist, but they were not the concern of this study.

The relevance of this study is not that it solves or even attempts to address many of these issues which admittedly are interdependent and central to the ability of the police to deal with crime. Rather, the experiment has demonstrated that the time and staff resources do exist within police departments to test solutions to these problems. The next step, therefore, will be to use that time and these findings in the development of new approaches to both patrol and polcing.

SUMMARY

Theory describes the real world by providing ways of summarizing and investigating the complexities of the environment; it allows managers to better solve problems which develop in their own particular situations. Theories can be differentiated according to their development, primary purpose, and level of analysis. The scientific method involves a systematic process of inquiry which uses five interrelated steps: definition of the problem, statement of hypotheses, deductive reasoning, collection and analysis of data, and confirming or rejecting the hypothesis. Four primary questions can help the reader to judge the quality of empirical research.

Basic research designs or strategies for accomplishing research goals that are most useful to practicing managers were also explained. The functions of research designs were discussed, as well as the four major strategies: field studies, experiments, surveys, and using available data. Several criminal justice studies were cited in order to help the reader to comprehend the nature and application of the major strategies; the strengths and weaknesses of each strategy were also noted. Although certain designs are more appropriate to the needs of particular problems under study, the quality of the research depends on how well the investigator has planned the overall content of the design. For example, although experiments offer the greatest control, they may still reflect poor quality research if the investigator has selected an improper measuring instrument or if the sample is not representative.

Finally, the Kansas City Preventive Patrol Experiment provided an example of a major social research study. The problems of implementing and conducting an experiement of this size were discussed, along with the manner in which such problems were handled. Although conducting behavioral research within criminal justice organizations poses many frustrating problems, the value of using empirical findings to improve working environments through the implementation of appropriate managerial practices cannot be overstated.

DISCUSSION QUESTIONS

1. Discuss why it is important to develop a spirit of scientific inquiry in the field of criminal justice.
2. Differentiate between inductive and deductive theory and provide an example of how managerial decisions may be affected by each.

3. Discuss the purpose of hypotheses and the association between independent and dependent variables; include an example of an hypothesis which could be used in a criminal justice research study.

4. Explain why it is crucial to develop a healthy skepticism concerning research studies.

5. Remembering that practicing managers must be careful when interpreting empirical findings, discuss the questions you would ask when evaluating research.

6. Discuss why experimental designs offer the greatest degree of control and therefore the greatest chance of establishing causal relationships.

7. Briefly describe the research design utilized in the Kansas City study, the problems encountered by the investigators, and the major results of the study.

ANNOTATED BIBLIOGRAPHY

Black, James A. and Dean J. Champion, *Methods and Issues in Social Research,* (New York: John Wiley & Sons, 1976). This book is designed to assist a broad variety of social researchers fulfill their research objectives, and is practical in orientation and elementary in presentation. Primary content includes: fundamental dimensions of social research, structuring the data-collection process, and forms of data collection.

Campbell, Donald T. and Julian C. Stanley, *Experimental and Quasi-Experimental Designs for Research,* (Chicago: Rand McNally, 1963). A concise resource book which examines the validity of 16 experimental designs against 12 common threats (internal and external) to valid inference, including: pre-experimental, true experimental, quasi-experimental, and correlational and ex post facto designs.

Golden, M. Patricia, (ed.), *The Research Experience,* (Itasca, Ill: Peacock, 1976). An anthology which includes introductions and articles and introduces the reader not only to the basic principles that influence the nature of the research process but also to the compelling personal and pragmatic considerations and constraints which somteimes alter, modify, and impede that process. It includes: choices and constraints in social research, field studies, experiments, surveys, available data, and measurement.

Runcie, John F., *Experiencing Social Research,* (Homewood, Ill.: Dorsey, 1976). A succinct introduction to research methods, which emphasizes the need to actually experience research activities and includes several aids for this purpose: why experience research?, reading articles, observations, survey, interview and social experimentation and ethnomethodology.

The following texts are excellent sources in the area of behavioral and social science methods and statistics.

Ary, Donald, Lucy Chester Jacobs, and Asgha Razavich, *Introduction to Research in Education,* (New York: Holt, Rinehart, and Winston, 1972).

Blalock, Hubert M., Jr., *Social Statistics,* (2nd Ed.), (New York: McGraw-Hill, 1972).

Hardyck, Curtis and Lewis F. Petrinovich, *Understanding Research in the Social Sciences,* (Philadelphia: Saunders, 1975).

Kerlinger, Fred. N., *Foundations of Behavioral Research*, (2nd Ed.), (New York: Holt, Rinehart, and Winston, 1973).

Miller, Delbert C., *Handbook of Research Design and Social Measurement*, (2nd Ed.), (New York: McKay, 1970).

The following materials provide excellent sources in the area of criminal justice research.

Albright, Ellen, et.al., *Criminal Justice Research: Evaluation In Criminal Justice Programs*, (Washington, D. C.: U.S. Government Printing Office, 1973).

Lewis, Joseph H., *Evaluation of Experiments in Policing: How Do you Begin?* (Washington, D. C.: Police Foundation, 1972).

Lipton, Douglas, Robert Martinson and Judith Wilks, *The Effectiveness of Correctional Treatment: A Survey of Treatment Evaluation Studies*, (New York: Praeger, 1975).

Maltz, Michael D., *Evaluation of Crime Control Programs*, (Washington, D. C.: U.S. Government Printing Office, 1972).

National Criminal Justice Reference Service, *Criminal Justice Evaluation: An Annotated Bibliography*, (Washington, D. C.: National Institute of Law Enforcement and Criminal Justice, 1975).

FOUR

The Organization: Fundamental Characteristics

LEARNING OBJECTIVES

The study of this chapter should enable you to:

☑ Explain what is meant by the interdisciplinary approach to management.

☑ Describe the five primary features or characteristics of organizations.

☑ Describe the concepts of partial inclusion, formal groups, and informal groups.

☑ Define the purpose of formal organization charts.

☑ Discuss the functions of organizational goals and the effect of multiple goals on the criminal justice process.

☑ Describe the interacting forces which influence goal setting, and the importance of making individual and organizational goal expectations compatible.

☑ Define goal displacement, means-ends inversion, and goal succession.

☑ Define differentiated functions, vertical differentiation, horizontal differentiation, and line and staff differentiation.

☑ Discuss the importance of intended rational coordination to the organization and describe several mechanisms used to achieve coordination.

☑ Define "continuity through time" and its importance to organizational members.

FOUR

What exactly is an organization? This seemingly elementary question is of vital importance to practicing managers who wish to apply appropriate managerial practices and techniques to their particular situations. In other words, before police managers can improve their work environments, they must first have some knowledge of the fundamental elements which make up organizations and guide their behavior.

ORGANIZATIONS DEFINED

People are by nature social animals; they tend to organize and work with one another. Sometimes they organize for purposes of protection and survival, at other times to achieve some common goal as well as to satisfy individual needs and desires. Because people organize for so many different reasons, how one views and defines organizations depends on one's background and academic perspective:

Each disciplinary orientation tends to focus on a particular aspect or set of features of organizations. For example, economists tend to deal with how organizations allocate resources and how decisions are made under conditions of uncertainty. Industrial engineers focus on the technological underpinning of organizational activities. Sociologists have been concerned largely with the structure of organizations and the ways in which organizations in toto cope with their external social environments. Political scientists are concerned with such issues as the exercise of power and authority in organizational settings. Psychologists, by and large, have concentrated their study on the behavior of individuals and groups within organizations.[1]

Obviously there are many ways to look at organizations and study their behavior. Among the above perspectives, none has a distinct advantage over the others. If organizational behavior is to be correctly interpreted and understood, research from many different disciplines should be utilized. Consequently, police and criminal justice management must be studied from an interdisciplinary approach.

Fundamental Characteristics

Perhaps the most appropriate way to describe the concept of organization, rather than to attempt our own definition of the term, is to review the fundamental characteristics of organizations based on representative samples of definitions set forth by scholars in the behavioral and social sciences

---

1. Lyman W. Porter, Edward E. Lawler, III, and J. Richard Hackman, *Behavior in Organizations* (New York: McGraw-Hill, 1975), p. 68.

(shown in Figure 4-1). This summary set, compiled by Porter, Lawler, and Hackman contains five primary features of organizations:

Organizations are:

1. Who—composed of individuals and groups

2. Why—in order to achieve certain goals and objectives

3. & 4. How—by means of differentiated functions that are intended to be rationally coordinated and directed

5. When—through time on a continuous basis[2]

Porter *et al.* point out that Figure 4-1 permits one to view the range of definitional attributes for each of the basic features:

Thus, for the question of composition of organizations, Barnard talks about a size as small as two or more persons, while Strother speaks of groups of two or more people and Scott uses the term "collectivities." The common element here, however, is that organizations are, first and foremost, *social* entities in which people take part and to which they react. The second fundamental feature stresses the purposeful, goal-oriented characteristics of organizations. This focuses our attention on the instrumental nature of organizations; that is, they are social instruments set up to do something. The third and fourth features concern the means by which organizations go about the process of trying to accomplish objectives. As indicated ... there are two major types of methods that are seen as essential for this: the differentiation of functions and positions, and the deliberate, conscious, intendedly rational, planful attempts to coordinate and direct the activities thus produced within the organization. Finally, some (but not all) commentators point to a fifth basic feature: as continuity through time or the activities and relationships within organizations ... These five features, taken together, supply something of an anatomical look at organizations. They are, if you will, skeletal definitions that delineate the minimal outlines of what organizations are and do. They serve to help us distinguish the types of entities we refer to as "formal organizations" (especially those in which people work) from other social groupings such as families, social classes, ethnic groups, and random gatherings of individuals.[3]

As indicated above, such a summary of definitional characteristics provides only a skeletal look at organizations, and does not tell us much about the complexities of organizational life. Accordingly, the rest of this chapter will discuss the basic features as they relate to the police and other components of the criminal justice system.

THE "WHO" OF AN ORGANIZATION

Organizations are comprised of both individuals and groups. Whether or not an individual is a member of any particular group, the influences of others working around that individual—either directly (physically present) or indirectly (psychologically present)—are strongly felt. In fact, the social nature of organizations is perhaps their primary characteristic.

---

2. *Ibid.*, p. 69.

3. *Ibid.*, pp. 69-71.

Figure 4-1

Fundamental Characteristics of Organizations
(abstracted from definitions given by behavioral and social scientists)

1. *Composition: individuals/groups*
   ... "two or more persons" (Barnard)
   ... "a number of people" (Schein)
   ... "a group or cooperative system" (Gross)
   ... "Groups of two or more people" (Strother)
   ... "at least several primary groups" (Simon)
   ... "social units" (Litterer)
   ... "social units" (Etzioni)
   ... "collectivities" (Scott)

2. *Orientation: toward goals*
   ... "devoted primarily to attainment of specific goals (Etzioni)
   ... "achievement of some common explicit purpose or goal" (Schein)
   ... "obtaining a set of objectives or goals" (Litterer)
   ... "Some kind of collective goal(s) or output(s)" (Strother)
   ... "pursuit of relatively specific objectives" (Scott)
   ... "an accepted pattern of purposes" (Gross)
   ... "toward ends that are objectives of common knowledge" (Simon)

3. & 4. *Methods:*
   3. *Differentiated functions*
      ... "differentiation of function" (Gross)
      ... "some kind of differentiation of function" (Strother)
      ... "(differentiation in) terms of authority, status, & role" (Presthus)
      ... "division of labor and function" (Schein)

   4. *Intended rational coordination*
      ... "rational coordination of activities" (Schein)
      ... "high degree of rational direction of behavior" (Simon)
      ... "conscious integration" (Gross)
      ... "consciously coordinated activities" (Barnard)
      ... "subject to criteria of rationality" (Thompson)
      ... "structured interpersonal relations" (Presthus)

5. *Continuity: through time*
   ... "more or less continuous basis" (Scott)
   ... "continuity of interaction" (Gross)

Note: Sources for these definitional characteristics, along with the general disciplinary orienta-
tion of the authors, are as follows:
   Barnard, *The Functions of the Executive*, 1938, p. 75 (Sociology/Management)
   Etzioni, *Modern Organizations*, 1964, p. xi (Sociology)
   Scott, in *Handbook of Modern Sociology*, 1964, p. 488 (Sociology)
   Thompson, *Organizations in Action*, 1967, p. 10 (Sociology)
   Gross, *Organizations and Their Managing*, 1968 p. 52 (Political Science)
   Presthus, in *Administrative Science Quarterly*, 3, 1958, p. 50 (Political Science)
   Simon, in *American Political Science Review*, 46, 1958, p. 1130 (Political Science)
   Schein, *Organizational Psychology*, 1970, p. 9 (Psychology)
   Litterer, *The Analysis of Organizations*, 1965, p. 5 (Management)
   Strother, in *The Social Science of Organizations*, 1963, p. 23, (Management)

Source: Adapted from Lyman W. Porter, Edward E. Lawler III and J. Richard Hackman,
   Behavior in Organizations, (New York: McGraw-Hill Book Co., 1975), p. 70

Individuals

Individuals bring to the organization many qualities, some of which are highly beneficial to the organization, others which are not. For instance, every member brings certain physical attributes and abilities as well as specific attitudes, prejudices, and emotions. Police organizations, because they deal with virtually all of society's members, need to establish screening procedures to eliminate those individuals whose behavior would be detrimental to the administration of justice.[4] In other words, police organizations simply cannot tolerate individuals who will not (or cannot) treat those they have contact with, whether "criminal offenders" or "ordinary citizens," in a humane and just manner.

It should be emphasized that the organization never receives the "whole" person. This means the organization must realize that individual lives are segmented; people play many different roles and belong to many different organizations and groups. Accordingly, one's total personality or psychological being is not found in any one particular organization. Furthermore, organizational membership frequently changes, often because of expectation-integration failures (see chapter 1) between the organization and the individual. Allport[5] developed the concept of *partial inclusion* to refer to this fragmented involvement of individuals in social groupings. Katz and Kahn suggest that this concept helps us to understand many of the problems of social organizations:

The organizational role stipulates behaviors which imply only a "psychological slice" of the person, yet people are not recruited to organizations on this basis; willy nilly the organization brings within its boundaries the entire person. The organizational demand on the individual to put aside some parts of himself for the sake of performing a role is literally a depersonalizing demand; in this sense the individual who joins with others to create an informal "organization within an organization" is fighting for his identity as a person.[6]

Groups

A group can be defined as any number of people who interact with one another and share to some degree norms and values regarding appropriate behavior. Within organizations there are two primary types of groups: (1) formal—those designated by the organization and (2) informal—those with membership left to the discretion of the individual. Informal groups occur naturally, without reference to the formal organization. Each type of group membership is largely responsible for the types of attitudes members form toward the organization.

---

4. For a discussion on the appropriate types of screening procedures for police personnel, see: National Advisory Commission on Criminal Justice Standards and Goals, *Police,* "Recruitment and Selection," (Washington, D. C.: U. S. Government Printing Office, 1973), p. 319-351.

5. Floyd H. Allport, *Institutional Behavior,* (Chapel Hill: N.C.: Univ. of North Carolina Press, 1933).

6. Daniel Katz and Robert L. Kahn, *The Social Psychology of Organizations,* (New York: John Wiley & Sons, 1966), p. 50.

Formal groups are specifically created by the organization in an attempt to attain the organization's goals in the most effective manner. The formal structure of the organization can be depicted by an *organization chart,* which attempts to define formal functions and relationships, as well as the flow of communication, among the designated groups within the structure. Figures 4-2 through 4-4 are examples of formal organization charts for representative police, court, and correctional agencies. Figure 4-2 depicts a medium-sized municipal police department (300 to 1200 members), Figure 4-3 depicts a superior or district court, (serving a county population in excess of 200,000), and Figure 4-4 depicts a medium-sized state penitentiary (800 to 1200 inmates). The broken lines in Figure 4-4 indicate a "functional" supervisory relationship, or "multiple supervision;" that is, the work release unit is directly responsible to both correctional and program services.

Informal groups are formed naturally, as a result of nonspecified individual interactions. Formal charts reveal very little, if any, information concerning informal relationships. Because these groups are nonspecified, it is difficult, though not impossible, to establish useful charts depicting informal relationships. Because of the tremendous influence of informal groups on individual behavior within organizations (first revealed by the Hawthorne experiments), managers must have at least an elementary understanding of the types of nonspecified groupings that may exist, as well as their possible influence. Both informal and formal groups will be discussed in greater detail in Chapter 6.

THE "WHY" OF AN ORGANIZATION

Organizations are oriented toward the attainment of goals. Many organization theorists feel that this particular characteristic is the most essential to "organized life." Etzioni, for instance, states that, "Organizations are social units which pursue specific goals; their very *raison d'etre* is the service of these goals."[7] Parsons believes that the orientation of organizations toward specific goal attainment is precisely what differentiates them from other social systems, such as audiences and crowds.[8]

With respect to organizational goals, overall functions may be described in relation to the organization. Etzioni discusses these functions as follows: (1) They provide orientation by depicting a future state of affairs which the organization strives to realize. (2) They set down guidelines for organizational activity. (3) They constitute a source of legitimacy which justifies the activities of an organization and, indeed, its very existence. (4) They serve as standards by which members of an organization and outsiders can assess the success of the organization, i.e., its effectiveness and efficiency. (5) They also serve in a similar fashion as measuring rods for the student of organizations who tries to determine how well the organization is doing.[9]

---

7. Amitai Etzioni, *Modern Organizations,* (Englewood Cliffs, N.J.: Prentice-Hall, 1964), p. 5.

8. Talcott Parsons, *Structure and Process in Modern Societies,* (Glencoe, Ill.: Free Press, 1960).

9. Etzioni, *op. cit.,* p. 5.

Figure 4-2
Medium Sized Municipal Police Department

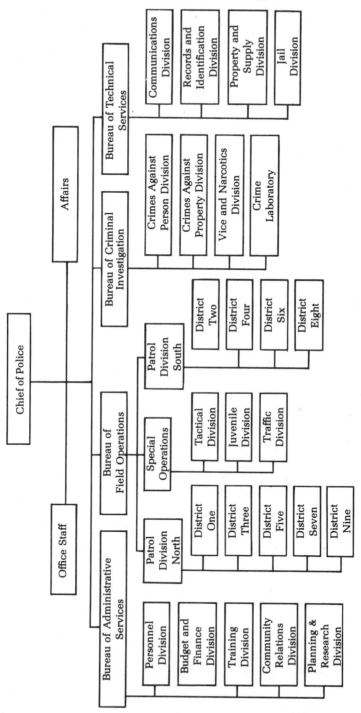

Figure 4-3
Superior/District Court of Original Jurisdiction

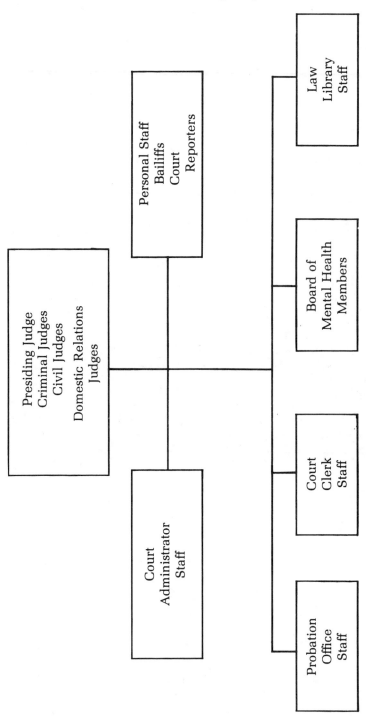

Figure 4-4
Medium Sized State Penitentiary

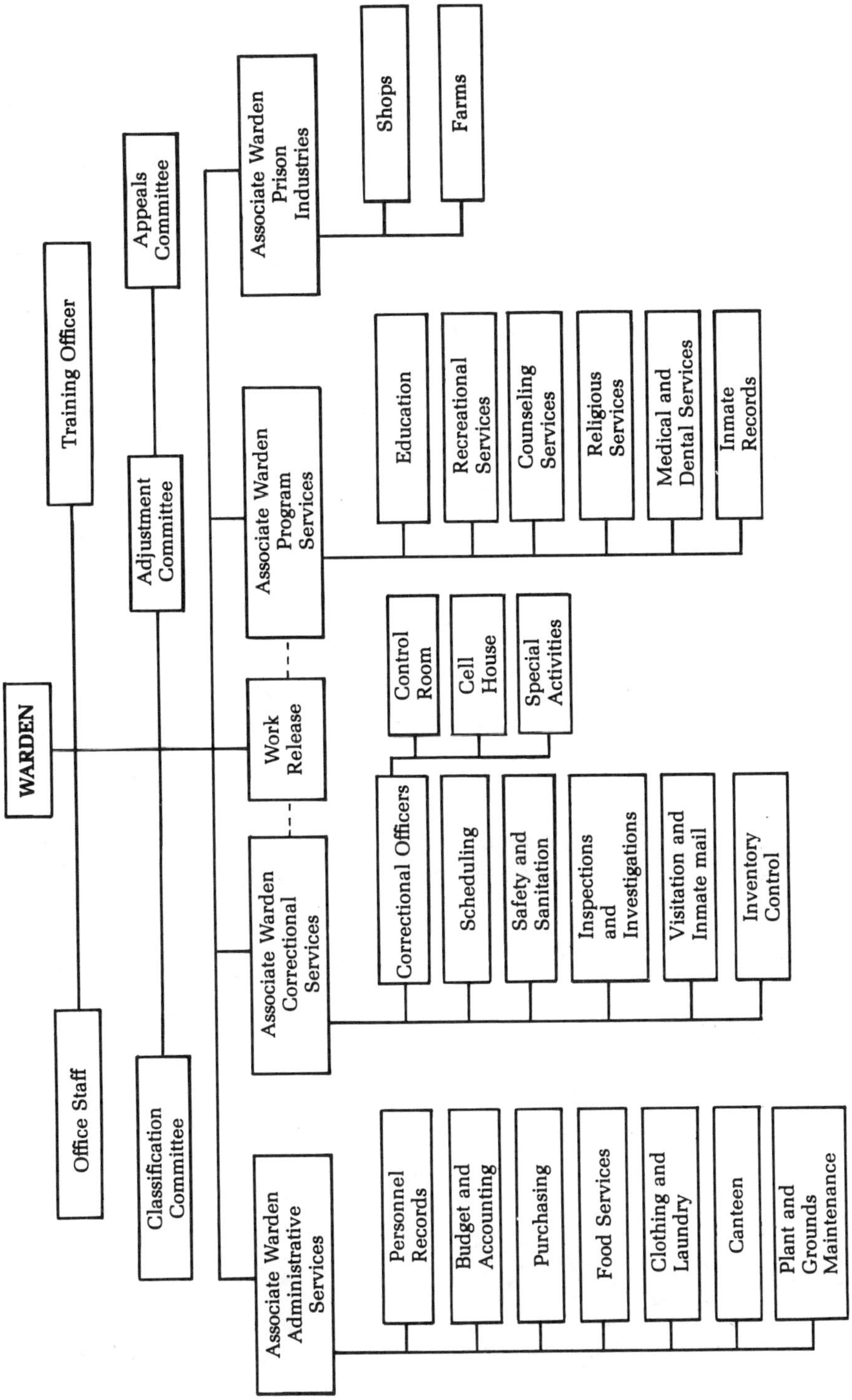

Even though organizations intend to attain specific goals, they may or may not be able to achieve them. Several objectives leading to goal attainment may be realized, without necessarily attaining the goal itself. Furthermore, most organizations, and all those within the criminal justice system, have more than a single goal. Newman discusses the intriguing effect of multiple goals on the process of criminal justice:

The tremendous complexity of the system is compounded many times over by multiple and often divergent expectations assigned to it, not only by legislatures and the general public, but by direct participants in it as well. One fact that seems very difficult to accept in analyzing criminal justice is that the system has multiple purposes, that there is not just one goal or a single objective of either the total system or of any process within it. The multiplicity of purposes, and of hopes, not only makes the system controversial, but often adds a dimension of confusion to any attempt to assess or to evaluate it. It is not unusual for persons who advocate one type of program or one objective to find themselves debating with persons interested in the same problem but with entirely different perspectives and purposes. This is the subtle and insidious issue underlying all attempts at evaluation and all proposals for reform. No matter how carefully phrased, or how effective a single crime control program is, there is bound to be opposition, equally well phrased, which seeks to achieve other, perhaps conflicting objectives. For example, today a rather strong case can be made and documented that maximum-security prisons do not rehabilitate offenders. In fact, persons who spend considerable time in prison often turn out to be worse risks when they are returned to the community than when they entered prison. Assuming strong and objective evidence of this, it could follow that imprisonment should be changed or abandoned altogether, possibly to be replaced by other forms of intervention. However, this position rests on the assumption that the primary purpose of incarceration is rehabilitation so that the prison system fails if it does not meet this goal. Another position, equally credible within historical purposes of imprisonment in our society, assumes the purpose of imprisonment to be the restraint of offenders, their incapacitation during the period of their sentences. If incapacitation is assumed as a primary goal, a case can be made that prisons are successes rather than failures, for few prisoners escape, and the community *is* protected from offenders while they are behind bars. While it might be possible by means of public opinion polls or other measurements to rank purposes of the criminal justice process, exercises in this vein would likely show that the priority given to any one goal shifts over time or differs between offense categories. Even if attempts to list and rank goals were carefully done, the most it would do would make clear the fact of multiple expectations, multiple objectives, and divergent motives for use of the criminal process.[10]

Because criminal justice organizations have multiple and frequently conflicting goal expectations, we need to understand how organizational goals are established. When viewing organizations from an open-systems perspective, we need to look at several interacting forces which may influence goal setting. First, we must be aware of *environmental influences.* Society at large imposes certain goals which legitimize the activities of the organization. In this sense, goals may also be considered as restrictions

---

10. Donald J. Newman, *Introduction to Criminal Justice,* 2nd. ed., (Phila.: Lippincott, 1978), pp. 12-13.

which limit the activities of the organization.[11] This is an important consideration, for police organizations must respond to societal needs for governmental services when establishing and setting priorities. As noted in Chapter 1, most patrol activities (as measured by citizen calls to the police) are related to keeping the peace and providing social services. Currently, then, greater emphasis should be placed on police activities other than law enforcement. For instance, the police can make a significant contribution to their communities through improved crisis intervention methods and referral practices which direct citizens (with special kinds of needs) to the proper agencies. Through proper goal emphasis, the police will be regarded as a humane and positive force within the community, a force which provides needed human services, in addition to defending and safeguarding human rights.

Second, we must be aware of *organizational influences.* The organizational system itself (i.e. influential members, especially top management) seeks certain goals, primarily for efficiency and self-perpetuation, but also to satisfy its members. Lastly, we must be aware of *individual influences,* which are generally self-enhancing (e.g., job security, pay, fringe benefits, etc.). Organizational members frequently have separate and conflicting goals. As Barnard has suggested:

Individual motive is necessarily an internal, personal, subjective thing; common purpose is necessarily an external, impersonal, objective thing even though the individual interpretation of it is subjective. The one exception to this general rule, an important one, is that the accomplishment of an organization purpose becomes itself a source of personal satisfaction and a motive for many individuals in many organizations.[12]

Compatibility of Organizational and Individual Goals

McGregor stresses management's need to make individual and organizational goal expectations compatible: "Management must seek to create conditions (an organizational environment) such that members of the organization at all levels can best achieve their own goals by directing their efforts toward the goals of the organization."[13] Without a certain degree of goal compatibility the organization cannot operate effectively, and its actual existence may be threatened. Levinson has suggested that a sort of psychological contract can be developed which helps to fulfill the goals of each party:

This process of fulfilling mutual expectations and satisfying mutual needs in the relationship between a man and his work organization was conceptualized as a

11. Herbert A. Simon, "On the Concept of Organizational Goal," *Administrative Science Quarterly,* 9, 1964, pp. 1-22.

12. Chester I. Barnard, *The Functions of the Executive,* (Cambridge, Mass.: Harvard Univ. Press, 1938), p. 85.

13. Douglas McGregor, *The Professional Manager,* (New York: McGraw-Hill, 1967), p. 13.

process of *reciprocation*. Reciprocation is the process of carrying out a psychological contract between person and company or any other institution where one works. It is a complementary process in which the individual and the organization seem to become a part of each other. The person feels that he is part of the corporation or institution and, concurrently, that he is a symbol personifying the whole organization.[14]

Recent research has confirmed that such a reciprocal process takes place. Morse, for example, reported that managers adapted to and found personal satisfaction in organizations with different structures, environments, and interpersonal relations. When organizations were appropriately designed to meet task requirements and environmental demands, members received important psychological rewards, which led to a high sense of personal competency.[15] The importance of properly designing police organizations will be the subject of Chapter 8.

Organizational Goal Setting

Cyert and March view the organizational goal-setting process as being primarily political.[16] Bargaining takes place among the various internal and external forces described above. The *interest groups* with the most power at any particular time usually have the strongest influence on goal determination. Because the membership as well as the power structure of these interest groups changes over time, the goals of the organization also shift. The demands of the various groups are frequently in conflict, so it is rarely possible to maximize the goal achievement of any specific group. Instead, the organization may attempt to "satisfy" the goals of each group and therefore maintain their participation. As Newman noted, this process is extremely complex when applied to the criminal justice system. Because many conflicting demands are made on the system, maintaining a sense of direction and perspective is often difficult.

With respect to the use of human resources, it is unrealistic to expect complete compatibility and satisfaction between individual and organizational goals. Instead, each party must be willing to make sacrifices in the best interests of all concerned, which is more likely if goal expectations are openly communicated by each party (expectation-integration).

Types of Organizational Goals

A key distinction should be made between official, operative, and operational goals. *Official* goals are publicly stated and purposely broad in nature. According to Perrow, "Official goals are the general purposes of the

---

14. Harry Levinson, *The Exceptional Executive*, (Cambridge, Mass.: Harvard Univ. Press, 1968), p. 3.

15. John J. Morse, "Organizational Characteristics and Individual Motivation," in Jay W. Lorsch and Paul R. Lawrence, eds., *Studies in Organization Design*, (Homewood, Ill.: Richard D. Irwin, 1970).

16. Richard M. Cyert and James G. March, *A Behavioral Theory of the Firm*, (Englewood Cliffs, N.J.: Prentice-Hall, 1973).

organization as put forth in the charter, annual reports, public statements by key executives and other authoritative pronouncements."[17] Official goals typically justify the activities of the organization. An organization ideally translates official goals into operative ones. *Operative* goals "designate the ends sought through the actual operating policies of the organization; they tell us what the organization is actually trying to do, regardless of what the official goals say are the aims."[18] An example of each goal is illustrated by the police agency which states its goal to be one of protecting and serving the community in a just and equal manner (official goal), while actually ignoring the "spirit of the law" in its treatment of certain ethnic neighborhoods (operative goal). A similar split between official and operative goals can be found in a penitentiary which acknowledges a goal of rehabilitation when, in reality, little if any treatment is offered, and confinement is stressed.

Goals are said to be *operational* when there is agreement on how to measure their attainment. In other words, for goals to become operational it is necessary to determine their means of achievement—usually by converting them into a concrete set of subgoals: "In the organization, the relationship between means and ends is hierarchical. Goals established at one level require certain means for their accomplishment. These means then become the subgoals for the next level, and more specific operational objectives are developed as we move down the hierarchy."[19] Through this *means-ends* chain, subgoals are specified for the functional units. These subgoals or objectives should be precisely spelled out so that the organizational units and their members know what is expected of them, and they must also be carefully integrated throughout the organization. For example, most police organizations include investigative units whose primary concern is obtaining information to solve crimes, and community relation units whose primary concern is increasing community rapport. The practicing manager should be aware that if such objectives are not integrated, conflicts between units may develop to the detriment of overall organizational goal attainment.

Individual goals may also conflict with those of the organization. One of the more popular methods for integrating individual with organizational goals is "management by objectives," or MBO, which attempts to involve all hierarchical levels in the goal-setting process. Ordione explains MBO:

The system of management by objectives can be described as a process whereby the superior and subordinate managers of an organization jointly identify its common goals, define each individual's major areas of responsibility in terms of the results expected of him and use these measures as guides for operating the unit and assessing the contributions of each of its members.[20]

---

17. Charles Perrow, "The Analysis of Goals in Complex Organizations," in *Readings on Modern Organizations,* Amatai Etzioni, ed., (Englewood Cliffs, N.J.: Prentice-Hall, 1969), p. 66.

18. *Ibid.* p. 66.

19. Fremont E. Kast and James E. Rosenzweig, *Organization and Management: A Systems Approach,* 2nd ed., (New York: McGraw-Hill Book Company, 1974), p. 163.

20. George S. Odiorne, *Management by Objectives,* (New York: Pitman, 1965), pp. 55-56.

Basically, this approach allows organizational supervisors to work with their subordinates in setting specific goals and establishing specific programs for their accomplishment—in accord with the organization's overall goals. MBO as a process of evaluation will be further discussed in Chapter 9.

Changes in Organizational Goals

Organizational as well as unit goals rarely remain unchanged over long periods of time, primarily because the organization operates in an environment which is continually changing and therefore must change its goals in order to survive. Goal changes are influenced according to changes in the composition and power of interest groups. Two major types of goal changes may occur: goal displacement and goal succession.

According to Etzioni, *displacement* takes place "when an organization displaces its goal—that is, substitutes for its legitimate goal some other goal for which it was not created, for which resources were not allocated to it, and which it is not known to serve."[21] Such a situation develops when means are distorted to ends (means-ends inversion); actions that were considered to be a means to some specific goal or end become in themselves the actual goal for the organization or the individual. This occurs easily in police agencies, which are highly bureaucratized with ridgid enforcement of rules, whenever the rules become more important than the original goals of serving the public and seeing that justice is properly administered. For example, if equal protection under the law is stated as a primary police goal, but a formal or informal quota system of enforcement is used, or arrests are based on "attitude" (such as not showing "proper respect" for the police) instead of substance, then goal displacement or means-end-inversion has occurred. Such goal changes remain hidden because they contradict the stated goals of the organization.

Goal *succession,* on the other hand, occurs when new or revised goals are intentionally substituted for existing ones; because these goals do not contradict existing goals, they are generally expressed openly. The new or revised goals are considered more beneficial to the organization, especially in its attempt to adapt to changing environmental influences. In modern police agencies, for instance, the goal of community awareness of police practices has generally replaced the "closed door," secretive orientation of the past.

Measuring Organizational Goals

Measuring organizational performance poses many problems. Criminal justice agencies have multiple goals, and therefore multiple criteria must be used in measuring performance. The organization must be evaluated from an open-systems perspective, taking into consideration both external and internal viewpoints. From an external perspective, the organization needs to know the extent to which its clientele is satisfied. In the past, for example,

---

21. Etzioni, *op. cit.,* p. 10.

goal conflicts between the police and minority sections of our communities have been apparent. The police have often felt that they "were just doing their jobs," while minority members have complained of being "over-policed" and harassed. Such conflicts must be resolved and the cooperation of minority groups enlisted, if police agencies are to perform at a desirable level.

From an internal perspective, the organization needs to know the extent to which its members are satisfied. Is there a conflict between what the organizational members feel the goal(s) should be and what the organization actually stresses? Do goal conflicts exist between operating units within the organization and/or between individual members of these units? Such conflicts can severely damage organizational-individual relationships and subsequently harm the operational effectiveness of the organization.

Overall organizational goals as well as unit and individual goals must be determined and measured. Police and other criminal justice organizations must therefore form goal statements which are honest enough to be achieveable and specific enough to be measurable. Overall organizational goals such as 'increased positive attitudes toward the police," are more difficult to measure than unit subgoals such as, "decreasing residential burglaries by 10 percent." However, through improved use of behavioral science research, the measurement of such goals is certainly within management's capability. It is beyond the scope of this chapter to explore the various techniques that can be used by organizations to assess their performance, but satisfactory and generally attainable methods include community surveys and interviews concerning organizational performance; representative community boards which participate in departmental goal setting and evaluation; organizational membership input concerning goal emphasis and operating practices and policies; individual and group performance evaluation measures; victimization surveys and other crime statistics, etc. In the past, unfortunately, the desire for accountability—both within and outside of the criminal justice system—has been noticably absent.

THE "HOW" OF AN ORGANIZATION

Because organizations are oriented toward the attainment of goals, they must contain systematic means through which goals can be reached. The third and fourth defining characteristics of organizations (see Figure 4-1) provide such means: differentiated functions and intended rational coordination.

Differentiated Functions

The concept of differentiated functions simply means that not everyone in the organization does the same thing. Also known as *division of labor* or *task specilization,* it is needed throughout the organization because tasks are too varied and too complex for a single individual to be able to perform them satisfactorily. Also, it is simply not possible for a single individual (or group of individuals, for that matter) to be in the right place at the right time to perform all organizational functions. Thus the overall organization task is differentiated so that departmental units are responsible for the performance of particular activities at particular places and times. Generally, even small organizations with only a few employees such as many of the nation's police agencies involve some degree of differentiation, which Lawrence and Lorsch define as "the state of segmentation of the organizational system into subsystems, each of which tends to develop particular attributes in relation to the requirements posed by its relevant external environments."[22]

Two primary types of organizational differentiation occur in opposite directions: vertical differentiation, representing the organization's hierarchy or differing levels of authority, and horizontal differentiation, representing different functions or activities performed at approximately equal levels of authority.

Vertical Differentiation. Vertical differentiation refers to the number of separate hierarchial levels throughout an organization and the amount of authority and responsibility within each level. In the formal organization, this hierarchy is known as the "chain of command"; the higher one's position in the hierarchy, the greater one's authority and responsibility and sphere of influence concerning organizational actions. For example, in the police agency in Figure 4-2, the top hierarchial level, the chief of police position, carries the greatest amount of authority and responsibility. Vertical differentiation also allows for the coordination and direction of specialized activities.

Porter *et. al.* recognize four major types of vertical groupings of activities with respect to relatively large organizations. [23]

Top management positions: concerned with overall goal formulation and policy decisions regarding allocation of resources.

Middle management positions: concerned with subgoal formulation and plans for implementing decisions from above and coordinating activities from below.

Lower management positions: concerned with implementing decisions made at higher levels, and coordinating and directing the work of employees at the lowest level of the organization

Rank-and-file positions: concerned with carrying out specific task activities

The police organization in Figure 4-2 can be grouped as follows: top management—Chief of Police and Asssstant Chiefs serving at the bureau level; middle management—Captains and Lieutenants serving at the division level; lower management—Sergeants (and possibly corporals) serving at the district level; rank-and-file—patrol officers and others under the supervision of lower management personnel. In smaller organizations there may be only two or perhaps three groupings. In a small police agency, for instance,

---

22. Paul R. Lawrence and Jay W. Lorsch, "Differentiation and Integration in Complex Organizations," *Administrative Science Quarterly*, 12, June, 1967, pp. 3-4.

23. Porter, Lawler, and Hackman, *op. cit.,* pp. 90-91.

with five or six full-time officers, there most likely would be only two divisions, between the chief and the patrol personnel.

Although all organizations exhibit vertical divisions, the extent to which these divisions are explicitly formalized can differ substantially. Most state and local police agencies are said to be "quasi-military" in design; there are specific role definitions for various positions as well as significant status differences between levels. Operationally, this is apparent through the ensignias and emblems attached to the uniforms worn by police personnel. In most federal law enforcement agencies, on the other hand, vertical differentiation with respect to role and fuction is not so clear. Of course, separate positions and authority levels exist within these agencies, but they are not as apparent because civilian attire is worn. In the correctional field, most correctional institutions, which tend to be quasi-military in nature, can be compared to parole and probation agencies, which tend to be civilian in nature.

Horizontal Differentiation. Organizations generally need to differentiate functions horizontally, to divide activities among individuals and groups who occupy approximately the same level of authority and responsibility. In large organizations this horizontal specialization of activities is quite apparent, and it is necessary to the effective operation of the organization. In the police agency in Figure 4-2, the horizontal dimension is indicated by the various bureaus (Administrative Services, Field Operations, etc.) at one level, and the various divisions (Personnel, Patrol, etc.) at the next. While particular bureaus or division are responsible for different functions, they share approximately equal levels of authority and responsibility.

Even in small agencies, horizontal specilization of functions often occurs. For instance, in a police department with only five or six sworn personnel, the primary function of each officer would be that of patrol, although one officer may be in charge of investigating major cases and collecting evidence (thus assuming the specialist role of detective). This kind of differentiation frequently is a result of the individual's natural interests and skills, and may even be informal in nature. If these interests and skills are recognized formally by the organization, the individual may be encouraged to attend special training classes and seminars in an attempt to increase such skills which further contribute to the organization's goals. While the employee is contributing specialized skills to the organization, he or she may, at the same time, benefit through increased job satisfaction.

Through differentiated functions, individual organization members can accomplish more than they could working alone; the benefits of this characteristic therefore are obvious. However, there are also consequences which severely limit the actions of the organization's members which may not be beneficial and should be acknowledged. Depending on the nature of differentiation, it limits the interactions of employees to those they are relatively close to physically. This may or may not contribute to organizational goal attainment or to individual needs and satisfaction. These dimensions may further contribute to a positive or negative impact on the individual's perceptions and attitudes toward the organization. The type of work activities performed, and one's attitude toward those activities, strongly affects the individual's relationship with other organizational members as well as one's motivational level to perform well on the job. Throughout the remainder of the book, we shall see just how strongly these dimensions influence individual attitudes and perceptions about life within the organization.

According to classical theory, the line represents authority over activities of the organization and is concerned with primary organizational functions (such as patrol and investigative activities); while the staff provides advice and ideas, and is concerned with activities which support the line functions (such as administrative and technical services).

The *line-staff* concept was thought to be a necessary means of integrating the knowledge and skills of highly trained specialists. However, this concept is not as simple as it might appear. The terms are difficult to define and are often used inconsistently. In some instances the terms are used in reference to functions, in others to describe organizational units, and in still others to define patterns of authority.

Traditionally, the staff's relationship with the line has been thought of as strictly advisory. In reality, however, such relationships are more intricate. Filley, House, and Kerr identify four major types of *staff authority*: staff advice, compulsory staff advice, concurrent line-staff authority, and functional authority.[24] In an advisory relationship, the line is free to seek the advice from the staff and to either accept or reject it. With respect to compulsory staff advice, the line must listen to staff advice but need not follow it. In situations where concurrent line-staff authority exists, the line and staff representative or manager must agree before action can be taken. Finally, in the case of functional staff authority, the staff is given the right to exercise authority by giving orders to various line units; this is most often used when the staff possesses some special technical competence. In a police agency, for instance, a planning and research unit may issue orders which concern an experiemental design to patrol officers, as in the Kanasas City Preventive Patrol Study, or the personnel office may issue orders which affect all line officers in matters such as college attendance while on duty.

In modern, complex organizations, staffs are becoming increasingly important. As staff roles are expanded, the once clear distinction between line and staff activities fades. This is particularly true in the case of functional staff authority cited above. Kast and Rosenzweig comment on this fading distinction:

Although many organizations, particularly business and the military, attempt to differentiate between the line and staff activities, it is our view that this distinction is becoming increasingly difficult to justify. Newer organizational forms, specifically developed to ensure the integration of activities, both in a vertical and horizontal basis, may be replacing the traditional line-staff form. While organizations with a

---

24. Alan C. Filley, Robert J. House and Steven Kerr, *Managerial Process and Organizational Behavior*, 2nd Ed., (Glenview, Ill.: Scott, Foresman, 1976), pp. 389-390.

uniform technology and operating in a stable environment may still find the differentiation of activities in terms of line and staff meaningful, organizations with dynamic technology and changing environment are finding this concept obsolete. [25]

Intended Rational Coordination

Intended rational coordination, the fourth major defining characteristic of organizations, involves "the putting together of the activities or effort of individuals in such a way that it makes sense—seems logical—to members of the organization, particularly to those who are the most influential in the allocation of resources. [26] This coordination affects only certain things that the individual does; according to the concept of partial inclusion, not all of the individual's behavior can, or should, be coordinated. Also, rational coordination may not always be completely achieved because of poor planning and other factors, nor may it be achieved to everyone's satisfaction.

Such coordination is necessary because vertical and horizontal differntiation splits the activities and functions required for organizational goal attainment. In other words, these two dimensions must be integrated if the organization is to make substantial progress toward attaining its goals. Lawrence and Lorsch define integration as "the process of achieving unity of effort among the various subsystems in the accomplishment of the organization's task." [27] There is a definite relationship between the need to differentiate functions and the requirements for integration; generally, the greater the differentiation of functions, the greater the difficulty of integration.

Organizations then, must provide mechanisms for achieving coordination. Litterer has suggested three such mechanisms: the *hierarchy*, the *administrative system*, and *voluntary activities*.[28] In hierarchical coordination, the individual at the top of the hierarchical pyramid coordinates organization activites. In simple organizations this may be sufficient, but in larger organizations hierarchical coordination is virtually impossible. A top level manager simply could not handle all of the coordination problems that would come up through the hierarchy. Furthermore, if there are many levels in the organization's structure, the individual at the top does not have enough information to properly coordinate activities at the lower levels.

A second major mechanism for coordinating activities exists in the administrative system itself. Memoranda and bulletins are two of the more obvious methods designed to help coordinate work efforts among separate operating units. To the extent that such procedures are routine, specific structural means for coordination are probably not necessary. In the case of nonroutine activities, however, specific units and committees for providing integration (see the following discussion on matrix design) may be needed.

---

25. Kast and Rosenzweigh, *op. cit.*, p. 217.

26. Porter, Lawler, and Hackman, *op. cit.*, p. 93.

27. Lawrence and Lorsch, *op. cit.*, p. 4.

28. Joseph A. Litterer, *The Analysis of Organizations*, (New York: Willey, 1965), pp. 223-232.

The third mechanism involves voluntary coordination. To a large degree, organizations depend on the willingness and the ability of individual members and groups to voluntarily combine their activities with those of other organizational members and groups. Precisely for this reason, many organizations attempt to tie individual member's identification with, and commitment to, the organization. If identification is achieved, it is believed that individuals will more readily coordinate their activities, which, in turn, will help the organization to realize its goals.

Two other important coordinating mechanisms, *subgoal specification* and *roles* should also be mentioned.[29] The more tangible and precise the subgoals of the organization can be made, and the greater their acceptance can be obtained, the more likely individual members will be able to coordinate their activities with one another. The MBO program is designed specifically for this purpose. Organizational positions or roles are established to stabilize expectations of individual behavior and therefore provide a means of coordination:

The existence of roles provides a coordinative device both for the members who occupy the positions to which the roles are attached and for other members of the organization who come into contact with them. For the occupants, the role helps define the limits of the activities to be performed by providing a basis for deciding what should be done. If others who come into contact with the occupant are aware of the occupant's role—hence of the activities expected, permitted, and prohibited—they in turn can adjust their own efforts to mesh with the occupants.[30]

Through rational coordination of activities, the organization keeps some measure of control over its environment; it is able to ensure continued existence as well as to rationally pursue specific goals. For the individual, rational coordination allows the achievement of more than could be accomplished alone. While rational coordination can benefit both the employee and the organization, it also limits the freedom of the individual. If one is to coordinate one's activities with others, one's own actions must be restricted to some degree, which can lead to individual-individual or individual-organization conflicts. According to Porter *et. al.*:

Such conflicts, while sometimes ultimately quite beneficial to both parties, may prove harmful to the individual. Though a person in effect has no choice concerning participating in some types of coordinated activities if he is to join or remain with an organization, the extent to which this characteristic will be disadvantageous for him will depend on his own needs and beliefs as well as on the way in which the organization itself handles the requirement for rational coordiantion.[31]

Matrix Organization. Recent years have seen the development of a new organizational form, which attempts to integrate and coordinate both the vertical and horizontal dimensions of the organization by using a team

29. Porter, Lawler, and Hackman, *op. cit.*, pp. 94-95.

30. *Ibid.*, p. 95.

31. *Ibid.*, p. 96.

approach to cut across intraorganizational boundaries in an attempt to solve a specific problem or task within a given time frame. In this approach, several representatives and/or specialists from throughout the organization combine their expertise. Consequently, individuals from throughout the organization, regardless of their formal status or position, are represented in the decision-making process.

According to Kast and Rosenzweig, "the pressure of accelerating technology and short lead times have made it necessary to establish some formalized managerial agency to provide overall integration of the many diverse functional activities."[32] Such "matrix" structures are also known as "systems management," "program management," "project management," and "task forces." Figure 4-5 represents a matrix structure in a police agency; divisional members from patrol, traffic, personnel, training, and community relations, are represented on one team, while the other team includes members from planning and research, community relations, records and communications, jail, and property divisions, each of whom are joined under the direction of a project manager to accomplish a specific purpose. In other words, in a matrix organization, there are multiple teams working on different projects simultaneously. Furthermore, as Figure 4-5 indicates, the members represent different status levels throughout the organization; each member is regarded as an equal participant and contributor to the task force. The matrix structure may be permanent or temporary, lasting only until various project or program objectives are completed. In either case, individuals are assigned to two or more functional units and are under multiple supervision, although this arrangement directly contradicts the classical principles of unity of command and line-staff differntiation. Such a structure permits the project or program unit to concentrate on specific tasks, but it may create superior-subordinate relationship problems for the individual, who will be responsible both to the project manager and to the functional area manager (e.g., patrol, traffic, jail, etc.). Accordingly, if such a structure is to succeed, various organizational relationships and reporting procedures must be carefully specified. Flexibility, however, is critical to the efficiency of such a structure.

THE "WHEN" OF AN ORGANIZATION

The final defining characteristic of organizations, as described in Figure 4-1, is "continuity through time." This does not mean continued existence for an unlimited amount of time, but instead involves an extension of those interrelationships and activities which are more than temporary in nature and which occur on a continued basis. This characteristic distinguishes organizations from certain other social groupings such as crowds, parties, etc. Although individual members attempt to operate the organization so as to attain continuity, there is no certainty that the organization will be able to survive for any particular length of time.

---

32. Kast and Rosenzweig, *op. cit.*, p. 231.

Figure 4-5
Police Agency With Matrix Structure

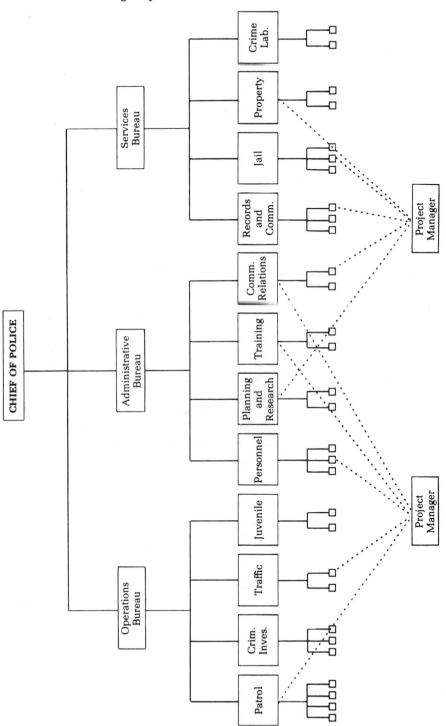

What exactly is continuous in an organization? Different theorists provide different answers; some discuss "interacting" while others suggest the "pursuit of objectives or goals." In a more comprehensive response, continuity refers to "the totality of the goal-oriented pattern of both interactions and activities that tend to recur on a more or less regular basis through time.... What is central here is the regularity in actions and relationships that seems to form some sensible thread from one time point to the next" [34] This characteristic greatly influences individuals' behavior, for they assume that the organization will be continuous, although such an assumption is more often implicit than explicit. "Nevertheless, even the fact that the individual takes for granted that there will be continuity is likely to influence his attitudes toward his job (e.g., 'it will get better'), his organization (e.g., 'this company has a good retirement plan'), his relations with others (e.g.,. 'that ought to show him next time I mean business'), and the way in which he performs his activities (e.g., 'if I work too fast, the boss may give more work'). If individuals did not hold the assumption that organizations have a degree of continuity, it is unlikely that organizations would ever be able to last for very long in the first place."[35]

SUMMARY

Organizations are composed of both individuals and groups. Groups may be either formal or informal in nature; formal relationships can be depicted by organization charts. Organizations are designed to attain specific goals, three major types of which are: official, operative, and operational. Organizations must continually change their goal orientations to reflect changes in the environment. One covert form of change is displacement, which occurs when the organization substitutes an operative goal for its official goal. On the other hand, goal succession is expressed openly and occurs when new or revised goals, which are considered more beneficial to the organization, are intentionally substituted for existing ones.

The goal orientation of organizations is crucial. Police managers must understand the necessity of goal congruence between their organization and the external environment, the community. In the past, many police-citizen problems have arisen because of differing goal expectations. The manager must continually strive to develop a process between the organization and the individual which fulfills mutual needs and goals (reciprocation). In order to accomplish this, practicing managers should have a basic understanding of individual behavior and motivation, the subject of the next chapter.

Organizations must contain systematic means for reaching their goals. Such means include differentiated functions or task specialization, and intended rational coordination. Tasks are too varied and complex for single

---

34. Porter, Lawler, and Hackman, *op. cit.*, p. 97.

35. *Ibid.*, p. 98.

individuals or groups to accomplish, so they are differentiated both horizontally and vertically. However, because differentiation splits the activities and functions required for organizational goal attainment, some form of integration or coordination is needed. Among several mechanisms for coordination, the most useful is the matrix design. The final defining characteristic of organizations is "continuity through time." Individuals assume that the organization in which they work will be relatively permanent, which has a great deal of influence on their behavior.

The reader should be aware of the fundamental elements which make up organizations, in order to understand how each of these elements can be adjusted, in varying degrees, to "fit" specific organizational circumstances. Using a contingency framework application of managerial practices and organization designs which appear to be the most appropriate for specific situations is possible.

DISCUSSION QUESTIONS

1. Why should practicing managers have some understanding of the fundamental elements that make up organizations?
2. Why is it important to study police and criminal justice management from an interdisciplinary approach?
3. Discuss several environmental influences which should be considered when establishing goals for police organizations.
4. Describe and provide an example of each of the three types of organizational goals, as well as goal displacement and succession.
5. Discuss why the measurement of goals in criminal justice organizations is so difficult; describe several methods of goal measurement which can be valuable to practicing managers.
6. Discuss the systematic means through which organizations may reach their goals, including types of differentiated functions and intended rational coordination.
7. Describe the matrix organization form and discuss the primary attributes and deficiencies associated with such a design.

ANNOTATED BIBLIOGRAPHY

Azumi, Koya and Jerald Hage, eds., *Organizational Systems*, (Lexington, Mass.: Heath, 1972). This anthology includes empirical studies on the nature of complex organizations; major topics include the environment, the social resources, the social structure, the internal control processes, and the performance and goals of organizations.

Bobitt, H. Randolph, Robert H. Breinholt, Robert H. Doktor and James P. McNaul, *Organizational Behavior: Understanding and Prediction*, (Englewood Cliffs, N.J.: Prentice-Hall, 1974). This text stresses a contemporary analysis of the fundamental characteristics of organizations, it treats the dynamics of organizations, basic concepts of organization, the individual, groups in organizations, organizations and their environments, organizations as open systems, and an attempt at integration.

Drabek, Thomas E. and J. Eugene Hass, *Understanding Complex Organizations*, (Dubuque, Ia.: Brown, 1974). A short introduction to the analysis of organizations and their behavior; discusses looking inside an organization, varieties and networks of organizations, as well as environmental variations.

Etzioni, Amitai, *Modern Organizations*, (Englewood Cliffs, N.J.: Prentice-Hall, Inc., 1964). A short analysis of modern, complex organizations, which covers organizational goals, bureaucracies, control, authority, and the social environment.

Litterer, Joseph A. *The Analysis of Organizations*, (New York: Willey, 1965). An analysis of the basic elements and interpersonal relationships of an organization, the division of work, types of coordination and control, and the individual and organizations' adaptation to change.

March, James G., ed., *Handbook of Organizations*, (Chicago: Rand McNally, 1965). A massive volume of research studies on the operation of organizations with differing tasks, including prisons.

White, William F., *Organizational Behavior*, (Homewood, Ill: Richard D. Irwin, 1969). A theoretical framework presenting such conceptual schemes as: individual and group levels of interaction, vertical, lateral and diagonal relations, and problems of the introduction of change in the organization.

The Individual: Behavior and Motivation

LEARNING OBJECTIVES

The study of this chapter should enable you to:

☑ Define the meaning of behavior: B = f(P,E).

☑ List several factors which influence individual behavior in the work place.

☑ Define perception, cognition, and motivation; discuss how each affects personal attitudes.

☑ Describe Maslow's need hierarchy and why it is popular with practicing managers.

☑ Discuss McGregor's Theory X and Theory Y assumptions and relate each theory to the need hierarchy.

☑ Describe Herzberg's motivation-hygiene theory and why it is popular with practicing managers.

☑ List the two primary concepts upon which expectancy theories of motivation are based.

☑ Discuss the three major variables which are crucial to Vroom's expectancy model of motivation.

☑ Describe the multivariate approach of the Porter-Lawler expectancy model of motivation.

☑ Discuss the potential impact of equity theory with respect to the work environment.

FIVE

The previous chapter described the fundamental characteristics of organizations; this chapter will deal with the second major variable concerning organizational behavior: the individual. In order to apply managerial practices which will lead to the attainment of organizational and individual goals, police and other criminal justice managers must have a basic understanding of the nature of human behavior and of the fundamentals of work motivation. Each of these concepts is discussed in the following sections.

HUMAN BEHAVIOR

Behavior refers to an individual's conduct, the manner in which an individual acts or reacts to certain environmental stimuli. When human behavior is discussed in research literature, one often encounters Kurt Lewin's classical formula: $B = f(P,E)$.[1] The formula states that behavior (B) is a function (f) of both the person (P) and the environment (E). The Lewin formula is undoubtedly correct in principle, but it says nothing about which external (environmental) or internal (individual) variables affect behavior. In order to isolate those variables which have an effect on behavior, a more specific approach must be used. Harold J. Leavitt suggests three related assumptions about human behavior:

1. Behavior is caused.
2. Behavior is motivated.
3. Behavior is goal-directed.[2]

The basic behavior model in Figure 5-1 shows how the three elements are interrelated. This model is applicable to all human behavior; that is, to all people, in all situations, at all times.

If Leavitt's three assumptions are valid, then behavior must be purposeful. First, there must be a goal, whether explicit or implicit. Second, behavior related to goals is caused by reacting to a stimulus. The stimulus is generated through a system of needs or desires which, if not satisfied, may cause tension or discomfort for the individual. A "feedback loop" (Figure 5-1) from goal to stimulus reveals that this process is sequential. For example, if a person is thirsty, getting a drink of water may be the behavior which results. If the goal (satisfaction of thirst) is achieved, the behavior (drinking)

---

1. Kurt Lewin, *Field Theory and Social Science*, (New York: Harper, 1951), p. 241.

2. Harold J. Leavitt, *Managerial Psychology*, 2nd ed., (Chicago: Univ. of Chicago Press, 1964), p. 12.

is terminated and the individual's attention focuses on some other activity. If the goal is not achieved, the individual may continue to drink until the need is satisfied.

Figure 5-1

Human Behavior Model

The Person

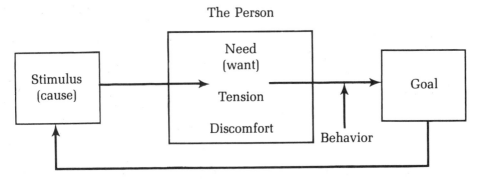

Source: Harold J. Leavitt, *Managerial Psychology*, 2nd ed., (Chicago: Univ. of Chicago Press, 1964), p. 9. Reprinted with permission.

Although this human behavior model applies to all people, actual behaviors can vary substantially. People whose perceptions or motivations differ may behave differently, even though they are receiving the same or similar stimuli. Or, because needs and desires within the individual vary, individual responses to the same stimuli may also deviate from time to time. Because of such individual differences, human behavior, even under similar circumstances, is difficult to predict.

Individual Differences

Numerous factors account for individual differences in behavior. Figure 5-2 shows some of the influences on individual behavior in a work environment. Each of these influences, and its relative importance to behavior, would vary considerably with each individual. With respect to the Personal Value System depicted in Figure 5-2, potential influences on behavior are filtered through personal attitudes by means of perception, cognition, and motivation (described below). According to Kast and Rosenzweig, "The effect of various events on behavior depends on how they are perceived by the individual. Similarly, if behavior results after a period which allows thinking or problem solving, personal attitudes play an important part in fashioning the specific response. Value systems are affected significantly by total past experience and current personal situations."[3]

Perception. Perception is the means by which stimuli affect an individual; through perception an individual selectively notices different aspects of the environment. Whether or not certain aspects of the environment are

---

3. Fremont E. Kast and James E. Rosenzweig, 2nd ed., *Organization and Management: A Systems Approach*, (New York: McGraw-Hill, 1974), pp. 251-252.

noticed depends on both the nature of the stimuli and the individual's previous experiences. In other words, people behave on the basis of what they perceive, not on what actually may be. Police interviews provide an excellent example of this process, for eyewitness perceptions of "what actually happened" are rarely consistent from witness to witness.

Figure 5-2

Influences on Behavior in a Work Environment

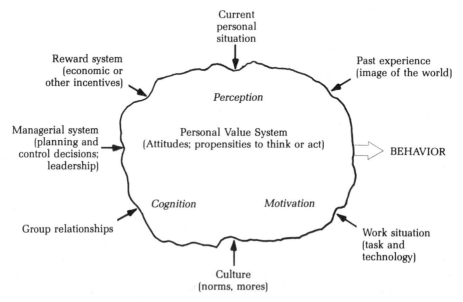

Source: Fremont E Kast and James E. Rosenzweig, 2nd ed., *Organization and Management: A Systems Approach,* (New York: McGraw-Hill, 1974), p. 251. Reprinted with permission.

In the working environment, an organization furnishes its members with more stimuli than an individual can possibly process, through memos, directives, orders, etc. Because of this, individuals select those stimuli which are supportive or satisfying to them in their particular situation within the organization. Conversely, individuals tend to ignore or misperceive stimuli which are not supportive or satisfying. Thus the same stimulus may be interpreted quite differently by individuals working in separate levels or units within the organization. For example, a member of a detective unit may not interpret an order involving the constitutional rights of arrested persons as a member of a patrol unit would. Because environmental stimuli are selectively noticed, managers may need to engage in follow-up activities to ensure that stimuli are interpreted in a consistent manner throughout the organization.

Cognition. Cognition involves the process of knowing, which includes perceiving or awareness, reasoning, and judgment or decision making. The term implies a deliberate process of acquiring knowledge, and is associated with rationality. Like perception, cognition is affected by the individual's environment, needs and desires, and past experiences. Because individuals do not perceive the environment in the same way, and do not have the same needs, desires, or personal experiences, understanding any person's cognitive processes is a difficult task. Nevertheless, the more a manager understands about an individual's cognitive system, the easier it will be to predict how an individual will react to certain organizational stimuli.

Motivation. Motivation is "what prompts a person to act in a certain way or at least develop a propensity for specific behavior. This urge to action can be touched off by an external stimulus, or it can be internally generated in individual thought processes."[4] Motivation is not a simple concept; it involves those needs and desires, tensions and discomforts which drive an individual toward the achievement of goals. It is closely related to one's cognitions:

Man's actions are guided by his cognitions—by what he thinks, believes, and anticipates. But when we ask *why* he acts at all, we are asking the question of motivation. And the motivational answer is given in terms of active, driving forces represented by such words as "wanting" and "fearing:" the individual wants power, he wants status, he fears social ostracism, he fears threats to his self-esteem. In addition, a motivation analysis specifies a goal for the achievement of which man spends his energies.[5]

Campbell, Dunnette, Lawler and Weick suggest than an individual's motivation is connected with: (1) the *direction* of behavior, or what one chooses to do when presented with a number of possible alternatives; (2) the *amplitude*, or strength, of the response (i.e., effort) once the choice is made; and (3) the *persistence* of the behavior, or how long one sticks with it.[6] In an organizational setting, the question of what motivates people to work is of primary concern to the practicing manager. Understanding the motivational process is probably the most important consideration in understanding and predicting human behavior.

THEORIES OF MOTIVATION

To understand the relationship between motivation and behavior, a number of variables (needs, wants, drives, rewards, expectancies, etc.) must be studied. Following is a discussion of the major theoretical frameworks which have greatly facilitated our understanding of the process of motivation. Motivation has been studied from two major approaches: (1) *content* theories, which attempt to identify what motivates behavior (money, status, satisfaction), and (2) *process* theories, which attempt to describe how motivation is energized or translated into behavior. Although content and process theories are not mutually exclusive, most studies have generally emphasized one approach or the other.

---

4. *Ibid.*, p. 254.

5. David Krech, Richard S. Crutchfield and Egerton L. Ballachey, *Individual in Society*, (New York: McGraw-Hill, 1962), p. 68.

6. John P. Campbell, Mavin D. Dunnette, Edward E. Lawler III, and Karl E. Weick, Jr., *Managerial Behavior, Performance, and Effectiveness*, (New York: McGraw-Hill, 1970), p. 340.

Content Theories

Traditionally, the management approach to the study of motivation has focused on a series of separate drives which motivate people to work. In Chapter 2, for instance, it was shown that Taylor and other classicial theorists viewed economic rewards as the primary motivating factor, while the human relationists stressed that good working conditions such as high salaries and job security would make employees happy and therefore productive. As noted earlier, these approaches tended to be too simplistic, and did not provide managers with a true picture of the complexity of the motivational process in working environments. Presented below are the major contributions which have led to a more sophisticated theoretical framework for the content of work motivation.

Need Hierarchy. In 1943 Abraham Maslow postulated a "heirarchy" of human needs which incorporated several levels (Figure 5-3). Basic to his theory is the concept that the satisfaction or satiation of "lower" physiological needs activates "higher" social and psychological needs.[7] This does not mean that two levels could not operate concurrently, but lower level needs take precedence. The primary basis of the theory is that once a given level of need is satisfied, it is no longer a motivating factor; the next level of need must be activated in order to motivate the individual. Maslow indentified the needs as follows:

1. Physiological needs, such as hunger, thirst, sleep, and sex.

2. Safety needs for security, such as protection against danger and deprivation.

3. Love needs for friendship, affection, affiliation, and love; need to belong.

4. Esteem needs for self-respect and the respect of others; ego or status needs.

5. Self-Actualization needs, which are at the top of the hierarchy and represent a culmination of all other needs; the need for self-fulfillment or the realization of one's potential.

Maslow's need hierarchy was not specifically directed at work motivation, but over the years it has become popular with managers, probably because of its appeal to common sense and its simplicity: learn five needs and their order. Although the theory itself is essentially non-testable, because of conceptual and measurement problems, the attempted research has not generally supported the theory and has established only two basic levels of needs: higher order and lower order.[8] In fact, as noted by Wahba and Bridwell, Maslow himself acknowledged numerous exceptions to his theory:

---

7. Abraham H. Maslow, "A Theory of Human Motivation," *Psychological Review*, 50, 1943, pp. 370-396.

8. Mahmoud A. Wahba and Lawrence G. Bridwell, "Maslow Reconsidered: A Review of Research in the Need Hierarchy Theory," in *Organizational Behavior and Industrial Psychology*, Kenneth N. Wexley and Gary A. Yukl (eds.), (New York: Oxford Univ. Press, 1975), pp. 5-11.

Notably, he pointed out that long deprivation of a given need may create a fixation for that need. Also, higher needs may emerge not after gratification, but rather after long deprivation, renunciation, or suppression of lower needs, multi-determined and multi-motivated.[9]

Accordingly, practicing managers must continually be aware of individual differences; motivation is not necessarily tied to a specific hierarchy of needs. Although there is no consistent empirical support for his theory, Maslow certainly stimulated research on motivation. Furthermore, his work involved an important implication for the practicing manager—different people have different motivations.

Figure 5-3
Maslow's Hierarchy of Needs

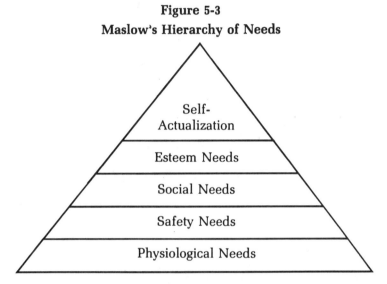

Theory X and Theory Y. Douglas McGregor, in *The Human Side of Enterprise*,[10] described several assumptions concerning human nature. While his assumptions cannot be considered a theory of motivation per se, managers should understand their significance, for depending upon one's philosophy or set of assumptions about people determines how managerial practices will be implemented as well as how the organization will be designed. In essence, McGregor distributed his assumptions along a continuum, with its extremes labeled "Theory X" and "Theory Y."

The assumptions of Theory X are:

1. The average human being inherently dislikes work and will avoid it if he can.

This assumption has deep roots. The punishment of Adam and Eve for eating the fruit of the Tree of Knowledge was to be banished from Eden into a world where they had to work for a living. The stress that management places on productivity, on

---

9. *Ibid.*, p. 6.

10. Douglas McGregor, *The Human Side of Enterprise*, (New York: McGraw-Hill, 1960).

the concept of "a fair day's work," on the evils of feather-bedding and restriction of output, on rewards for performance—while it has a logic in terms of the objectives of enterprise—reflects an underlying belief that management must counteract an inherent tendency to avoid work. The evidence for the correctness of this assumption would seem to most managers to be incontrovertible.

2. Because of their inherent dislike of work, most people must be coerced, controlled, directed and threatened with punishment if they are to work adequately toward the achievement of organizational objectives.

The dislike of work is so strong that even the promise of rewards is not generally enough to overcome it. People will accept the rewards and demand continually higher ones, but these alone woill not produce the necessary effort. Only the threat of punishment will do the trick.

3. The average human being prefers to be directed, wishes to avoid responsibility, has relatively little ambition, and wants security above all.

The assumption of the "mediocrity of the masses" is rarely expressed so bluntly. In fact, a good deal of lip service is given to the ideal of the worth of the average human being. Our political and social values demand such public expressions. Nevertheless, a great many managers will give private support to this assumption, and it is easy to see it reflected in policy and practice. Paternalism has become a nasty word, but it is by no means a defunct managerial philosophy.

The assumptions of Theory Y are:

1. Work, whether physical or mental, is as natural as play or rest.

The average human being does not inherently dislike work. Depending upon controllable conditions, work may be a source of satisfaction (and will be voluntarily performed) or a source of punishment (and will be avoided if possible).

2. External control and the threat of punishment are not the only means of bringing about effort toward organizational objectives. People will exercise self-direction and self-control when they are committed to objectives.

3. Commitment to objectives is a function of the rewards associated with their achievement.

The most significant of such rewards, e.g., the satisfaction of ego and self-actualization needs, can be direct products of effort directed toward organizational objectives.

4. The average human being learns, under proper conditions, not only to accept but to seek responsibility.

Avoidance of responsibility, lack of ambition, and emphasis on security are generally consequences of experience, not inherent human characteristics.

5. The ability to exercise a relatively high degree of imagination, ingenuity, and creativity in the solution of organizational problems is widely, not narrowly, distributed. [11]

It is easy to see why management practices and organization designs are radically different, depending on which view of human nature is accepted. Each of these theories can be related to the need hierarchy in the sense that classical management concepts and principles are based on the assumption that lower level needs are dominant in motivating people to work. Theory X assumes that people work to satisfy physiological and safety needs, primarily through financial gain; the average employee must be coerced and controlled by the threat of punishment. Theory Y, on the other hand, assumes that higher level needs are dominant. Employees are motivated by esteem and self-actualization needs, and will exercise self-direction and self-control if they are committed to their objectives. McGregor further differentiates Theory X and Theory Y:

The central principle of organization which derives from Theory X is that of direction and control through the exercise of authority—what has been called "the scalar principle." The central principle which derives from Theory Y is that of integration: the creation of conditions such that the members of the organization can achieve their own goals best by directing their efforts toward the success of the enterprise. These two principles have profoundly different implications with respect to the task of managing human resources, but the scalar principle is so firmly built into managerial attitudes that the implications of the principle of integration are not easy to perceive.[12]

Which of the two theories is valid? Depending on the situation, each theory is likely to have some validity. Each human being is a complex individual who cannot be placed at either end of the continuum, but lies somewhere in between. Still, one thing is apparent; practicing police managers have traditionally subscribed more heavily to Theory X than to Theory Y.

Likert, who has completed extensive research on diverse organizations, has concluded that a managerial system stressing Theory Y assumptions makes significantly better use of human resources and enhances both the effectiveness and efficiency of an organization.[13] While these conclusions cannot be generalized to all police and other organizations within the criminal justice system, they do apply to many of the system's agencies and/or subunits. Criminal justice managers need to be aware of individual differences, but in light of Likert's findings, they may wish to reassess their basic assumptions concerning employees. Because of the complex nature of police work environments (i.e., responsibility, decision making, etc.), there most likely is a need to move toward a Theory Y style of management.

---

11. *Ibid.*, pp.33-34, 47-48.

12. *Ibid.*, p. 49.

13. Rensis Likert, *The Human Organization*, (New York: McGraw-Hill, 1967).

Achievement Motivation. Although not specifically dealt with in Maslow's need hierarchy, the need for achievement seems crucial if needs for esteem and self-actualization are to be satisfied. McGregor's Theory Y would appear to emphasize achievement motivation. David C. McClelland,[14] John W. Atkinson,[15] and their associates have extensively researched achievement-oriented behavior:

The achievement motive is viewed as a relatively stable disposition, or potential behavior tendency, to strive for achievement or success. The motive is presumed not to operate until it is aroused by certain situational cues or incentives, which signal the individual that certain behaviors will lead to feelings of achievement (Atkinson) . . . a particular motive—achievement, affiliation, or power—is actually a label for a class of incentives, all of which produce essentially the same result. This end result is an internal experience of satisfaction such as pride in accomplishment, a sense of belonging and being warmly received by others, or the feeling of being influential and in control. These motives may be conditioned to a wide range of incentives, are learned, and have their fundamental origins in relatively early childhood experience (McClelland).[16]

In other words, practicing managers should realize that achievement motivation can be aroused by certain situational incentives that the individual believes will lead to feelings of accomplishment. To a degree, management by objectives (MBO) programs are based on this concept; objectives are set at a level that will most likely lead to task accomplishment. McClelland also suggests that achievers:

1. like situations in which they take responsibility for problem solving.

2. have a tendency to set moderate achievement goals and to take "calculated risks."

3. want concrete feedback about their performance.[17]

Obviously, findings such as McClelland's contradict the principles prescribed by the classical theorists. If individuals do not feel a sense of responsibility for their work, there is no personal sense of accomplishment and thus little motivation to do a good job. Adequate feedback on work performance also is crucial, for without it individuals do not know how well they are performing their jobs. Practicing managers must continually be aware of individual needs for responsibility and accomplishment as well as for feedback.

Motivation-Hygiene. In 1959, Frederick Herzberg and his associates extensively interviewed engineers and accountants, who were asked to

---

14. David C. McClelland, *Personality*, (New York: Dryden Press, 1951), and *The Achieving Society*, (Princeton, N.J.: Van Nostrand, 1961).

15. John W. Atkinson, "Towards Experimental Analysis of Human Motivation in Terms of Motives, Expectancies, and Incentives," in *Motives in Fantasy, Action and Society*, John W. Atkinson, ed., (Princeton, N.J.: Van Nostrand, 1958).

16. Campbell, *et. al., op. cit.*, p. 351.

17. David C. McClelland, "Business Drive and National Achievement," *Harvard Business Review*, 40, 1962, pp. 99-112.

discuss those aspects of their jobs which made them happy or unhappy.[18] The results indicated that when people are dissatisfied, their negative feelings are generally related to the environment in which they work. Conversely, when people have positive feelings toward their work, the feelings are generally related to the work itself. Herzberg used the term "motivators" for those factors which led to satisfaction, because they effectively motivated employees to greater productivity; dissatisfiers were termed "hygiene" factors because they prevented dissatisfaction but did not motivate employees to put forth extra effort.

Table 5-1 presents the two classes of work motivators postulated by Herzberg. This two-factor theory of motivation can be related to Maslow's need hierarchy; hygiene factors correspond to lower level needs, while motivators correspond to higher level needs. According to Herzberg lower level needs such as working conditions and salary are not effective motivators, and their fulfillment should not be expected to improve performance. Herzberg's theory suggests that, assuming environmental conditions are acceptable, higher level needs (such as recognition and responsibility) should be emphasized in order to motivate employees to perform more efficiently. If higher level needs are to be satisfied, the employee must be given a sense of psychological growth:

The hygiene factors are not a valid contributor to psychological growth. The substance of a task is required to achieve growth goals. Similarly, you cannot love an engineer into creativity, although by this approach you can avoid his dissatisfaction with the way you treat him. Creativity will require a potentially creative task to do.[19]

Like the need-hierarchy model, the motivation-hygiene model is popular among managers, but for different reasons. According to Herzberg's theory, money is not a motivator. As salary administration is normally one of the manager's greatest headaches, it is easy to understand why this model is so popular. Managers who accept Herzberg's model can therefore overlook the potentially troubling factor of salaries and concentrate instead on "free" motivators, such as job enrichment (which will be discussed in Chapter 9). While this may be wishful thinking on the manager's part, they should be aware of the criticisms directed at the two-factor theory.

On the basis of research stimulated by it, the Herzberg theory appears to be an oversimplification. For example, several studies have indicated that hygiene factors were as useful in motivating employees as were motivating factors.[20] Vroom, who has suggested that many conclusions could be drawn from the Herzberg findings, contends that employees are more likely to give

---

18.   Frederick Herzberg, Bernard Mausner and Barbara Snyderman, *The Motivation to Work*, (New York: Wiley, 1959).

19.   Frederick Herzberg, *Work and the Nature of Man*, (Cleveland, Ohio: World, 1966), p. 75.

20.   Donald P. Schwab, H. William DeVitt and Larry L. Cummings, "A Test of the Adequacy of the Two-Factor Theory as a Predictor of Self-Report Performance Effects," *Personnel Psychology*, Summer, 1971, pp. 293-303.

credit for satisfaction to their own achievements and blame company policies for dissatisfaction.[21] Even though the literature shows contradictory findings in regard to Herzberg's theory, he did apply and extend Maslow's need hierarchy specifically to work motivation.

Table 5-1

Motivators-Hygiene

Motivators	Hygiene
(Satisfiers)	(Dissatisfiers)
job content factors	job context factors
intrinsic factors	extrinsic factors
Achievement	Company Policy and
Recognition	Administration
Work Itself	Supervision
Responsibility	Salary
Advancement	Status
Growth	Security
	Working Conditions
	Interpersonal Relations

While problems exist in the interpretation of the content theories presented here, they have allowed managers to reevaluate the classical prescription that only lower level needs (hygiene factors) are important to work motivation. Plainly, employees are motivated by more than these needs. Furthermore, by dealing with the motivational effects of job content factors, content theories have extended the simplistic human relations approach (which focused on extrinsic factors), through the study of the motivational effects of intrinsic factors.

Process Theories

While content theories are more concerned with specifically identifying what causes behavior, process theories attempt to explain how "behavior is energized, how it is directed, how it is sustained, and how it is stopped. They first try to define the major classes of variables that are important for explaining motivated behavior. For example, a theory might talk about rewards, needs, and incentives as three general classes of variables that are important for understanding motivation. Such theories then attempt to specify how the variables interact and influence one another to produce certain kinds of behavior." [22] Process theories, then, attempt to describe the multiplicative interaction between variables in the motivation process. With respect to organizational behavior, the two most influential process theories of motivation are expectancy theory and equity theory.

---

21. Victor H. Vroom, *Work and Motivation,* (New York: Wiley, 1964).

22. Campbell, *et. al., op. cit.,* p. 341.

Expectancy Theory. The general expectancy model of human motivation is based on two primary concepts:

1. individuals have cognitive expectations about what outcomes are likely to result from their behavior, and

2. individuals have preferences among these outcomes.

The Vroom Model. The most widely acknowledged expectancy model of work motivation, developed by Victor Vroom, is expressed as follows: Motivation = Σ Valence $\times$ Expectancy.[23] According to this formula, motivation equals the sum of valence times expectancy. The three major classes of variables important to this theory are expectancy, valence, and instrumentality.

Expectancy involves the belief that a particular act will be followed by a particular outcome (if I work hard, I will receive a pay increase). The degree of belief ranges from a certainty that it will follow (1), to a certainty that it will not (0). The individual's perception of what is likely to occur is important, not the objective reality of the situation.

Valence involves the strength of an individual's preference for a particular outcome. Depending upon their desire for the outcome, individuals have either a positive (+1), neutral (0), or negative (-1) preference. Again, the perceived value of an outcome, not its objective value, is important.

Instrumentality involves the relationship as perceived by the individual, between a first level outcome and a second level outcome, each with its own valence. In a working environment, first level outcomes might include such things as pay and promotion; they have little value in themselves, but are important because of their important role in obtaining second level outcomes such as food, security, and status. Thus, individual preferences for first level outcomes (rewards) are dictated by the extent to which individuals believe that attainment of second level outcomes (needs) will occur. Figure 5-5 depicts this motivational process, which is summarized below:

Motivation is thus equal to the algebraic sum of the products of the valences of all first-level outcomes (the person's preference for each of the first-level outcomes) times the strength of the expectancy that the action will be followed by the attainment of these outcomes (the probability of attaining the respective first-level outcome). This formula helps the manager understand what motivates the *individual* worker.[24]

Although Vroom's theory is complex, it has been widely praised for its usefulness in understanding work behavior in organizations. Accordingly,

---

23.   Vroom, *Work and Motivation, op. cit.*

24.   Richard M. Hodgetts, *Management: Theory, Process, and Practice,* (Philadelphia: Saunders, 1975), p. 329.

Figure 5-4

Example of Vroom's Expectancy Model

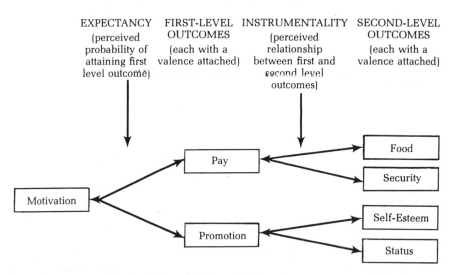

the police manager should understand the major concepts of the theory. While this theory does not provide specific solutions to motivational problems, it greatly helps in understanding the motivational process, and it does suggest general steps a manager can take to improve work effectiveness. A study of telephone company service representatives conducted by Hackman and Porter established this point.[25] With respect to worker motivation and performance, the study suggested the following:

Expectancy theory allows an investigator to identify those aspects of a performer's perceptions and evaluations which tend to enhance his motivation to work hard, and those which tend to detract from it. For example, outcomes which have high expectations and high positive valences will ... enhance a performer's motivation to work hard. Outcomes with high expectancies and high negative valences will detract from his motivation. Outcomes with relatively low expectancies or with neutral valences will have no substantial impact on the performer's motivation. By examining the expectancies and valences associated with a performer's perceived outcomes of hard work, an investigator can identify the motivational problems and opportunities which are inherent in the performance situation.

Once a diagnosis of the situation is made ... changes can be instituted to improve the performer's motivation to work hard. Such changes can involve (a) instituting new outcomes which will be valued by the performer and which will be seen by him as resulting from hard work: (b) changing the expectancies of existing outcomes so that the link between hard work and positively valued outcomes is strengthened and that between hard work and negatively valued outcomes is weakened; or (c) changing the valences of existing outcomes. The first two alternatives probably are much

---

25. J. Richard Hackman and Lyman W. Porter, "Expectancy Theory Prediction of Work Effectiveness," *Organizational Behavior and Human Performance*, 3, 1968, pp. 417-426.

more amenable to external change than is the last one; it should be much easier to change aspects of the situation so that the performer will perceive it differently than it would be to change the evaluations which a performer makes of various outcomes.[26]

While Vroom's theory has generally been accepted by researchers, it has not been as popular with practicing managers, probably because of its complexity. However, this model has several clear implications for practicing managers:

1. Because high motivation and effort should lead to task accomplishment, the manager needs to attempt to (a) set clear and understandible goals, and (b) create clear paths to these goals. Goals should be clearly stated and obstacles to their achievement should be removed to the greatest extent possible. (For further discussion, refer to the path-goal model of leadership in Chapter 7).

2. Because the performer expects particular outcomes, rewards must be related to performance. Rewards must be systematically evaluated to assure that they are given for appropriate behavior or performance. For example, one way to assure that police employees perform their duties in a just and humane manner is for managers to make rewards contingent upon such performance.

3. Because the performer attaches certain values to desirable outcomes, individual differences must be noted. In other words, individuals have different preferences for specific outcomes; this same concept, that behavior is multi-motivated, was emphasized by Maslow.

The Porter-Lawler Model. Lyman W. Porter and Edward E. Lawler[27] have extended Vroom's expectancy model by taking a *multivariate* approach to the study of the relationship between motivation and performance. Figure 5-6 illustrates the relationships among the numerous variables which must be considered in predicting behavior: effort, abilities and traits, role perceptions, and rewards and satisfaction. The relationship between performance and satisfaction is crucial to this model. Figure 5-6 treats performance as the causal or independent variable, and satisfaction as the assumed outcome or dependent variable. This proposed relationship is contrary to the human relations view that satisfaction causes performance.

Note that not only effort, but abilities and traits as well as role perceptions affect performance; that is, there may be a difference between effort and performance due to one's abilities and traits (job skills and/or knowledge) as well as to how one perceives one's role in the organization. This analysis explains how employees with low abilities and/or inaccurate role

---

26. *Ibid.*, p. 425.

27. Lyman W. Porter and Edward E. Lawler, III, *Managerial Attitudes and Performance*, (Homewood, Ill.: Irwin, 1968).

perceptions may perform poorly even though they exert a great amount of effort. While job knowledge and skills will be more thoroughly discussed in the following chapter, the concept of role perception is examined below.

Figure 5-5

Porter-Lawler Motivation Model

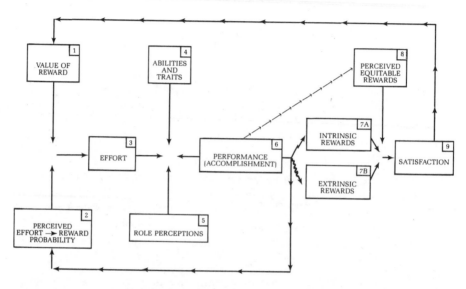

Source: Lyman W. Porter and Edward E. Lawler, III *Managerial Attitudes and Performance*, (Homewood, Ill.: Irwin, 1968),p. 165.

The various elements of role perception can be considered in terms of what Katz and Kahn describe as the *role episode*, illustrated in Figure 5-7.[28]

The role episode is based on four major concepts: (1) role expectations, which are evaluative standards applied to the behavior of any person who occupies an organizational office or position; (2) sent role, consisting of communications rooted in role expectations and which are sent by members of the role set in order to influence the focal person; (3) received role, which is the focal person's perception of the role-sendings addressed to him or her (it includes those which are "sent" to oneself); and (4) role behavior, which is the response of the focal person to the information and influence directed at him or her. "These four concepts can be thought of as constituting a sequence or role episode. The first two, role expectations and sent role, have to do with the motivations, cognitions, and behavior of the members of the role set; the latter two, received role and role behavior, have to do with the cognitions, motivations, and behavior of the focal person."[29]

---

28. Daniel Katz and Robert L. Kahn, *The Social Psychology of Organizations*, (New York: Wiley, 1966).

29. *Ibid.*, p. 182.

Figure 5-6

Model of the Role Episode

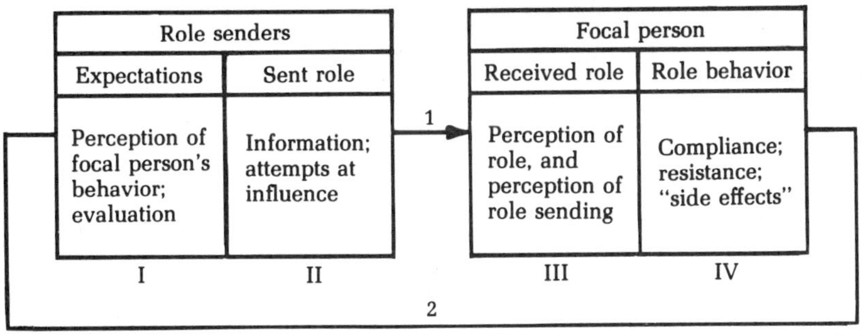

Role senders		Focal person	
Expectations	Sent role	Received role	Role behavior
Perception of focal person's behavior; evaluation	Information; attempts at influence	Perception of role, and perception of role sending	Compliance; resistance; "side effects"
I	II	III	IV

Source: Daniel Katz and Robert L. Kahn, *The Social Psychology of Organizations*, (New York: Wiley, 1966), p. 182.

Practicing managers should be aware of two primary types of conflict related to role perceptions within the organization. The first, *role conflict*, occurs when the focal person perceives two or more conflicting roles. This conflict frequently occurs in police organizations. For example, a first level manager is sent one role from the top of the hierarchy, which calls for strict control of operations; the manager's subordinates then send a separate role, which calls for minimum control and the use of wide discretion on their part. The second, *person-role* conflict, occurs when a sent role violates the focal person's value system. An individual may be sent a role which contradicts his or her personal code of ethics; for example, Frank Serpico was a member of a police department who could not accept a role which involved graft and corruption.

In addition to abilities, traits, and role perceptions, rewards are a major part of the Porter-Lawler model. Initially their model included only a single reward variable. However, after further empirical testing, the authors decided that rewards should be divided into two categories, extrinsic (those administered by the organization) and intrinsic (those administered by the individual):

It now appears that those types of needs which can be satisfied primarily by intrinsic rewards—i.e., the higher-order needs such as autonomy and self-actualization—are more likely to produce attitudes about satisfaction that are significantly related to performance than are needs—such as security and social needs—which can be satisfied primarily by extrinsic rewards. A stronger relationship for the higher-order needs is predicted because of the closer relationship between rewards and performance where higher-order needs are involved.

These two types of rewards, rather than a single reward variable, would be conceived of as intervening between *performance* and *satisfaction*. For extrinsic rewards, there would continue to be a wavy line between performance and rewards [see Figure 5-6], indicating that such rewards often are not, in fact, tied to performance. For intrinsic rewards, there would be a semi-wavy line. This is to indicate that a direct connection exists between performance and these rewards *if* the design of the job provides sufficient variety and challenge so that when a person feels he has performed well, he can reward himself. If the design of the job does not involve these characteristics, then there would be no direct connection between good performance and intrinsic rewards. Thus, the degree of connection between performance and intrinsic rewards is dependent on the make-up of the job duties.[30]

In Figure 5-6, the arrow drawn between performance and perceived equitable rewards indicates that performance is influenced by an individual's perceptions about how he or she should be rewarded. Higher levels of self-rated performance are associated with higher levels of expected equitable rewards; if rewards are below the level expected, satisfaction will be negatively affected.

The Porter-Lawler model is more comprehensive than the Vroom model, primarily because it attempts to explain the relationships among numerous variables which affect the motivational process. Consequently, this model offers a more satisfactory explanation of work motivation, but it also is more difficult to apply to management practice. Nevertheless, this model has several important implications for management. Many criminal justice managers currently believe that satisfaction leads to performance, that happy employees are good performers. However, this may not be the case. As pointed out above, the Porter-Lawler model suggests that the opposite is true, that performance *causes* satisfaction. Most of the research on the performance-satisfaction relationship supports the Porter-Lawler view. Many researchers suggest, however, that these findings are not conclusive and that more research is needed. At any rate, enough evidence has been gathered to indicate that satisfaction does not necessarily lead to performance. With these findings in mind, police and other criminal justice managers should take a second look at managerial practices based on this particular concept.

Finally, the Porter-Lawler theory addresses the importance of rewards as they are perceived by the individual. This suggests a role for performance evaluation and salary administration in increasing employee motivation and performance levels, because each of these activities has a potential influence on effort ➡ reward and performance ➡ reward outcomes. In addition, salary level and particularly salary structure, would appear to be critical determinants of perceived equity of rewards (the idea that if levels of motivation are to be maintained or increased, rewards will need to be equal to what the individual perceives they should be.)[31] This concept, known as equity theory, is included in the Porter-Lawler model, but is important enough to be considered separately below. The Porter-Lawler findings also have considerable significance concerning the manner in which jobs are designed; job activities should be challenging and provide sufficient variety for the individual to receive intrinsic rewards (accomplishment, fulfillments, etc.) for good performance. The relative effects of both performance

---

30.   Porter and Lawler, *op. cit.*, pp. 163-164.

31.   Donald P. Schwab and Larry L. Cummings, "Theories of Performance and Satisfaction: A Review," in *Management of Human Resources*, 3rd ed., Paul Rigors, Charles A. Myers, and F.T. Malm, (eds.), (New York: McGraw-Hill, 1973), pp. 283-284.

evaluation and job design on individual performance will be discussed in Chapter 9.

Equity Theory. Equity theory, as described by one of its early proponents, J. Stacy Adams,[32] predicts the effects on job performance of perceived inequity of pay. However, the theory can be expanded to include a variety of inputs (effort, skills and abilities, knowledge, etc.) and outcomes (pay, job status, fringe benefits, recognition, etc.) which might be found in work environments. According to this theory, individuals compare their own inputs and outcomes with others in similar situations. When an inequitable comparison ratio between job inputs and job outcomes (see Figure 5-8) is perceived, tension or dissonance results. The greater the perceived inequity of the two ratios, the greater the motivation to reduce the tension or dissonance. Festinger first described this concept as part of a general theory of "cognitive dissonance."[33] Individuals may pursue a number of alternatives in order to reduce this dissonance. For example, they may increase or decrease their efforts in order to make their inputs or contributions more equitable with outcomes or rewards. They may also rationalize their perceptions by deciding that inputs or outcomes are really greater (or smaller) than originally perceived, or that the outcomes being received are really of more (or less) value than previously thought. Of course, individuals may solve the problem by quitting the job altogether or by no longer associating with the comparison other.

Most of the available evidence tends to support equity theory. As with the previous theories, however, the findings cannot be considered conclusive without additional research. Research on the theory has led to some interesting findings about pay:

. . . when a person feels he is overpaid, at least initially, he tends to do more work. In this way he justifies the higher salary. However, over time he will usually reevaluate his skills and position, concluding that he is indeed worth the higher salary. Output will then drop back to its former level. This accounts for the belief of some researchers that money is a short-run motivator at best, and only one tool among many that the manager can use in the motivating process.[34]

Equity theory implies that managers need to "open-up" the reward process, in order to reduce employee misperceptions. By communicating truthfully with each individual employee, using the expectation-integration model proposed in Chapter 1, managers should be able to reduce feelings of tension and dissonance. Following the theory, practicing managers would also be wise to base their rewards, as far as possible, on objective and tangible (as opposed to subjective) criteria. It follows that employees should be allowed to participate in setting their own goals, as well as to evaluate their own performance. As a result, those individuals who fail to meet

---

32.   J. Stacy Adams, "Toward an Understanding of Inequity," *Journal of Abnormal and Social Psychology*, 67, 1963.

33.   Leon Festinger, *A Theory of Cognitive Dissonance*, (New York: Harper & Row, 1957).

34.   Hodgetts, *op. cit.*, p. 333.

specific standards would understand why their rewards are less than the rewards of those who did.

Figure 5-7

Comparison Ratios

Individual		Others

$\dfrac{\text{Inputs}}{\text{Outcomes}}$	Compare With	$\dfrac{\text{Inputs}}{\text{Outcomes}}$

Because individuals have different job inputs (skills, abilities, and knowledge), managers may need to use different performance standards and levels of rewards. Ultimately, however, the best performers must receive the greatest rewards or they will eventually lose their motivation to perform well. The practical application of this concept is critical to most criminal justice organizations. Frequently, salary increases and promotions are based more on seniority (time spent with the organization) than on actual job performance. Employees often receive yearly across-the-board salary increase regardless of their performance. Such practices clearly reduce one's motivation to be an outstanding performer. While police managers are generally forced to follow civil service salary structures, they can withhold yearly step increases from those employees who have barely performed up to standard, while granting salary increases to those who have exceeded the standard.

With respect to civil service salary structures, police managers should attempt to increase the number of salary steps for lower level personnel. In this manner, motivation for higher performance can be maintained over longer periods of time. Other factors, such as the work itself, responsibilities, and achievement, also contribute to the motivational process. Nevertheless, salary structures critically block motivation for lower level employees, especially patrol officers. In most agencies, such employees can reach their maximum pay scale within five or six years after their initial employment. When this happens, pay increases, other than cost of living adjustments, come only through promotions. This is unhealthy because only so many supervisory positions exist within an organization, and many individuals do not desire a supervisory role. Such a pay system forces outstanding performers to leave those positions which are most vital to the effective operation of the organization. There is no sound reason why a senior patrol officer who is an excellent performer should not be paid a salary equal to, or in excess of, various supervisory positions.

CONTINGENCY APPROACH TO MOTIVATION

A review of theories about motivation reveals no method which can be universally applied to motivate all individuals at all times. Because individuals have different job inputs and organizations have different work environments, numerous relevant variables must be studied and then applied. When predicting behavior in diverse police organizations, such variables as effort, skills and abilities, perceptions, achievement, satisfaction, and rewards (both extrinsic and intrinsic) must be considered.

Considerable progress has been made toward understanding individual behavior in working environments, but it is now evident that motivation is situational. Expectancy theory, especially the Porter-Lawler model, thus appears to provide the most comprehensive situational framework, a framework that is consistent with the majority of empirical research in the field and has therefore been proven successful in predicting behavior.

SUMMARY

Only through an understanding of individual differences, with respect to behavior and motivation, and the application of appropriate managerial practices, can police and other criminal justice managers achieve organizational objectives and goals. Behavior refers to the manner in which an individual acts or reacts to certain environmental stimuli; perception, cognition, and motivation all affect behavior. Because understanding the motivational process is probably the most important consideration in understanding and predicting human behavior, what motivates people to work is an important concern to the practicing manager, who needs to be familiar with both content and process motivational theories.

Content theories are important because they help managers to understand what things in the working environment motivate people. Process theories, on the other hand, help the manager understand how behavior is initiated, directed, sustained, or stopped. Although Maslow's need hierarchy and McGregor's theory X and theory Y assumptions cannot be considered theories of motivation per se, they demonstrate that behavior is multi-determined and multi-motivated, and that management practices and organization designs are based on one's philosophy about human nature. Findings by McCleland and Atkinson paved the way for a theory which explains achievement-oriented behavior, and for the idea that achievement motivation can be aroused by certain situational incentives which the individual believes will lead to feelings of accomplishment. Herzberg developed a two-factor theory of motivation, which suggested that lower level needs are not effective motivators and that higher level needs should be emphasized in order to motivate employees to perform more efficiently.

Expectancy and equity process theories have received the most adequate support from research and therefore appear to be the most useful. Vroom's basic expectancy model—motivation equals the sum of valence times expectancy—has been praised for its usefulness in explaining work behavior in organizations; this model has several important implications for practicing managers. The Porter-Lawler model extended Vroom's approach through a multivariate analysis of the relationship between motivation and performance; the model involves performance as the independent variable and satisfaction as the dependent variable. This theory also has important implications about salary levels and structures as well as job designs. According to equity theory, individuals compare their own inputs and outcomes with others in similar situations. If an inequitable comparison ratio is perceived, the individual will experience dissonance and attempt to reduce this dissonance through various alternatives. Management may reduce misperceptions by "opening up" the reward process and allowing employees to participate in setting their own goals and to take part in evaluating their own performance. Effective use of process theories should lead to high levels of employee performance and satisfaction, if such factors as skills and abilities are also present.

Finally, while considerable progress in understanding human behavior has been made, what motivates people is clearly situational. Expectancy theory brings together much of the material about motivation and provides a successful framework for predicting individual behavior in working environments.

DISCUSSION QUESTIONS

1. Discuss why the human behavior model is applicable to all people in all situations, and cite several examples of how this model applies to management practice in a criminal justice organization.

2. To what extent do you think that McGregor's Theory X and Theory Y assumptions are important to the practicing manager?

3. Contrast Maslow's need hierarchy theory with Herzberg's motivation-hygiene theory.

4. Provide several personal examples of how McClelland and Attinson's theory of achievement motivation has applied to you.

5. Discuss several clear implications for practicing managers of Vroom's expectancy model of motivation.

6. Discuss the relationship the Porter-Lawler model proposes between performance and satisfaction; what are the practical implications of this model?

7. Discuss several implications of equity theory for the reward process and salary structure of police organizations.

ANNOTATED BIBLIOGRAPHY

Adams, J. Stacy, "Toward an Understanding of Equity," *Journal of Abnormal and Social Psychology*, 67, 1963, pp. 422-436. This article describes equity theory, which makes predictions about the effects on job performance of perceived inequity of pay.

Hackman, J. Richard, and Lyman W. Porter, "Expectancy Theory Prediction of Work Effectiveness," *Organizational Behavior and Human Performance*, 3, 1968, pp. 417-426. The authors attempted to predict work effectiveness on the basis of expectancy theory predictions, and found that expectancy theory can be a useful tool in understanding behavior in "real world" settings.

Herzberg, Frederick, *Work and the Nature of Man*. (Cleveland: World, 1966). The author suggests that higher level needs should be enhanced to motivate empoloyees to perform more efficiently; the employee needs a sense of psychological growth if higher level needs are to be satisfied.

March, James G., and Herbert A. Simon, *Organizations*, (New York: Wiley, 1958). A review of the literature on organizational theory, starting with theories viewing the employee as a passive instrument, proceeding through theories concerning the motivational and attitudinal aspects of human behavior, and concluding with theories emphasizing the cognitive processes of human behavior in the organization.

Maslow, Abraham H., "A Theory of Human Motivation," *Psychological Review*, 50, 1943, pp. 370-396. The author suggests a "hierarchy" of human needs, in which the satisfaction of "lower" psychological needs activates the needs for "higher" social and psychological needs.

McGregor, Douglas, *The Human Side of Enterprise*, (New York: McGraw-Hill, 1960). This book explains the Theory X and Theory Y assumptions about human nature and human behavior; also includes chapters on Theory Y in practice and the development of managerial talent.

Porter, Lyman W., and Edward E. Lawler, III., *Managerial Attitudes and Performance*, (Homewood, Ill.: Irwin, 1968). The authors develop a conceptual model which attempts to specify some of the key variables—and their relationships involved in understanding the links between managers' attitudes and beliefs and their behavior on the job.

Vroom, Victor H., *Work and Motivation*, (New York: Wiley, 1964). In this work, the author develops the most widely acknowledged expectancy model of work motivation: motivation equals the sum of valence times expectancy:

Group Influences and Informal Organization

LEARNING OBJECTIVES

The study of this chapter should enable you to:

☑ List several characteristics of group behavior.

☑ Discuss several of the following reasons for group formation: activities, interaction, and sentiment (Homans), social elements and task objectives (Cartwright and Zander), and exchange theory.

☑ Differentiate between permanent and temporary formal groups.

☑ Describe the primary types of communication networks.

☑ Define what is meant by "discretionary stimuli."

☑ Describe the related factors that influence the degree to which group members accept stimuli from the group in forming their own views about organizational reality.

☑ Review the general mechanisms through which groups can influence the attitudes of their members.

☑ Discuss the general ways in which the group can assist members in developing their skills and role behavior.

☑ Describe each of the five informal "overlays" which coexist with the formal structure.

☑ Discuss why the Milo study is of significance to the practicing manager.

SIX

So far, this text has emphasized the impact of formal relationships and environmental influences on police organizations. The emphasis will now switch to an examination of the nature of groups, collective behavior, and the overall importance of informal relationships and influences in working environments, in short, the informal organization. Collective behavior is not the same as individual behavior discussed in the previous chapter; the infinite relationships among group members create a "life" of its own for the group. Because groups generally influence greatly the attitudes and behaviors of their members, much of a manager's success depends on how well he or she deals with group influences—both formal and informal. In order that the reader may more thoroughly understand groups and their impact on organizational behavior, this chapter discusses the dynamics of group behavior and informal organizational arrangements.

CONCEPT OF GROUP

Although there is no universal definition of what constitutes a group, numerous descriptions considerably narrow the scope of the term. For example, Schein describes a *group* as "any number of people who (1) interact with one another, (2) are psychologically aware of one another, and (3) perceive themselves to be a group."[1] All three elements of this definition are useful in understanding the nature of a group. A complex police organization, or perhaps a division within such an organization, would not be classified as a group because all members do not interact with, and are not aware of, one another. On the other hand, smaller organizational units and work groups, cliques, and other informal associations among organizational members may be classified as groups.

In order for direct or face-to-face interactions to take place, the size of a group must be relatively small. The term "interaction" refers to any type of *communication*—oral or written, as well as body and facial signals. Berelson and Steiner briefly describe the interaction process: "Usually interaction is direct communication—mainly talking and listening, often writing and reading—but it can also include gestures, glances, nods or shakes of the head, pats on the back, frowns, caresses, or slaps, or any other way in which meaning can be transmitted from one person to another and back again."[2]

---

1. Edgar H. Schein, *Organizational Psychology*, 2nd ed., (Englewood Cliffs, N.J.: Prentice-Hall, 1970), p. 81.

2. Bernard Berelson and Gary A. Steiner, *Human Behavior*, (New York: Harcourt, Brace & World, 1964), p. 326.

These types of interactions cause groups to be dynamic in nature, continually adjusting to the changing awareness, perceptions, and relationships among group members.

A group should be considered as a "dynamic whole" with properties of its own. Thus it is something more than a sum total of individuals who act in their own way; a system of relationships and expectations holds the members of a group together and gives the group a "personality" distinct from that of any particular member or members.[3] This concept that the whole is different from the sum of its parts is known as *synergy*. Groups take on the following characteristics:

1. Group members share one or more goals or objectives. These goals or objectives may not be the same for every member but every member has an objective in being a part of the group.

2. Groups develop *norms* or informal rules and standards which mold and guide the behavior of group members.

3. When a group exists for an extended period of time, structure develops which has individual members more or less permanently filling different roles.

4. When a group exists for an extended period of time, the members develop attractions for other group members, the group itself, and the things it stands for.[4]

Group Formation

Several major theories have been developed which attempt to explain why individuals either join or form groups. One of the more comprehensive theories of group formation was developed by George Homans in his classic *The Human Group.*[5] Homan's theory is based on three elements: (1) activity—the functions people perform within the group, (2) interaction—the communications they have with one another, and (3) sentiment—the feelings and attitudes of people. Each of these elements is directly related to the other; the more activities persons share in the work environment, the more likely they are to interact with one another and, consequently, to strengthen similar sentiments. Conversely, the more interactions occur between persons, the more they will share activities and sentiments, and as sentiments grow, more activities and interactions will be shared. The major element in this theory is *interaction*, which helps to explain how group members communicate, solve problems, and make decisions.

Dorwin Cartwright and Alvin Zander have divided the reasons individuals join and/or form groups into two primary categories: *social elements,*

---

3. John M. Pfiffner and Frank P. Sherwood, *Administrative Organization*, (Englewood Cliffs, N.J.: Prentice-Hall, 1960), p. 42.

4. A. Paul Hare, *Handbook of Small Group Research*, (New York: Free Press, 1962), p. 10.

5. George C. Homans, *The Human Group*, (New York: Harcourt, Brace & World, 1950), p. 43.

which involve the satisfactions a person hopes to gain from group membership, and *task objectives,* things which a person wants accomplished but are
difficult or impossible to achieve without team activity.[6]

Among the social elements, a person simply may be attracted to the
group members; most friendship cliques are developed in this manner. At
the organizational level, a person may desire to work in a particular department or unit because of friendship ties or because the people have personal-
ities that are attractive to the individual. The activity of the group also can
have an effect on group membership. For example, many police departments include individuals who volunteer their time as recreation and guidance counselors in various summer camps, youth clubs, and athletic
leagues. People join because they enjoy the activities; the attractiveness of
the members may or may not be a significant factor in determining group
membership. Finally, one of the most important social elements for group
membership is that it may help to satisfy the upper-level needs identified in
Maslow's need hierarchy. Esteem needs can be satisfied by joining a pres-
tigious group within the organization, or working within a high-status
department or unit. Group membership may also satisfy self-actualization
needs. Of course, other situational factors (self-direction, responsibility,
stimulating work, etc.) must also be present if one's potential is to be
realized.

A second category of elements involves the objectives and goals of the
group as well as the means to achieve them. Many people join because they
wish to see the group's goal—such as the forming of a union which supports
higher salaries—achieved. Once more, while the group is working toward a
certain goal, the members may receive personal satisfaction and/or
advancement. The goal of the group itself may not be as important as the fact
that the member is part of an influential or prominent group. An individual
may also join a group simply to achieve personal goals; although the group
may not accomplish its goal, the individual who thus reaches a personal goal
will continue to be attracted to the group. Lower level needs such as security
and friendship may be fulfilled in this fashion.

Finally, *exchange theory* is one of the most recent and straightforward
approaches to group formation. This theory is based upon *reward-cost outcomes* of interactions; rewards must outweigh costs if an individual is to be
attracted to a group. Rewards from such interactions fulfill needs and
desires, while costs create anxiety, embarrassment, or frustration. For example, an individual who did not like athletics would probably not volunteer as
a coach for an athletic team. In terms of exchange theory, the rewards
(fulfilled friendship and ego needs) would be outweighed by the costs
(embarrassment and frustration over a lack of knowledge and athletic ability). Exchange theory contains those elements described in the above theories, and is pragmatic in its approach.

---

6.   Dorwin Cartwright and Alvin Zander, *Group Dynamics: Research and Theory,* (New York:
Evanston, Row, & Peterson, 1953), p. 73-91.

TYPES OF GROUPS

In Chapter 4, two primary types of groups which exist within organizations were identified: formal and informal. We will now expand our discussion of these two groups and explore their relevance to the total organization.

Formal Groups

Formal groups are created and maintained by the organization in order to fill those needs and perform those tasks which are crucial for achieving organizational goals. Formal groups may be permanent or temporary, depending on the organization's need. *Permanent* formal groups include work forces such as budget and accounting units, planning and research teams, and patrol work shifts. *Temporary* formal groups include committees or task forces which are established to perform specific functions; once its function is achieved, the group is dissolved, at least until it may be of further benefit. For example, a task force may be assembled to determine how a police organization may best move from an authoritarian to a participatory style of management. Once the shift is completed, the task force is no longer needed. From this example, it is apparent that such a group may need to exist for an extended period of time, the length of which is determined by the particular project assigned by the organization.

Informal Groups

Informal groups within the organization arise naturally as a result of nonspecified individual interactions. Schein contends that informal groups are formed because of the social nature of human beings; people attempt to satisfy their needs by developing various relationships with other organizational members.[7] Practicing managers must be aware that such informal arrangements *will* develop and may even be more important to a majority of the organization's members than the formally prescribed relationships. Consequently, a manager's success or failure depends, to a large degree, on recognizing informal groups and dealing effectively with them.

The two major types of groups coexist and are often inseparable: "Every formal organization has an informal organization and every informal organization eventually evolves into some degree of formal organization."[8] As Blau and Scott point out:

It is impossible to understand the nature of a formal organization without investigating the networks of informal relations and the unofficial norms as well as the formal hierarchy of authority and the official body of rules, since the formally instituted and the informally emerging patterns are inextricably intertwined. The distinction

---

7. Schein, *op. cit.*, p. 69.

8. Fred Luthans, *Organizational Behavior,* (New York: McGraw-Hill, 1973), p. 453.

between the formal and the informal aspect of organization life is only an analytical one and should not be verified; there is only one actual organization.[9]

The final section of this chapter will deal with this complex interaction between informal and formal relationships.

COMMUNICATION NETWORKS

Communication networks, which involve how group members interact or communicate with one another, significantly affect group performance and satisfaction. Consequently, managers should be aware of the basic research conducted in this area, so that they may establish proper communication channels which allow for maximum performance and satisfaction in specific situations.

While countless communication networks exist for small groups, behavioral science studies reveal several basic patterns. The five most common structures are the *all-channel,* the *circle,* the *chain,* the *Y* and the *wheel* networks, illustrated in Figure 6-1. Each network represents a five member group, with the dots depicting individual members and the connecting lines indicating two-way communication channels. In the research design used most frequently in network studies, experimental groups are assigned a specific problem to be solved through communicating with one another. Group members are separated by partitions and arranged in one of the patterns shown in Figure 6-1. Members then pass notes (between the partitions) which contain information about the solution; the experimenter observes and measures the speed, accuracy, and frustration involved in solving the problem.

Figure 6-1
Basic Communication Networks

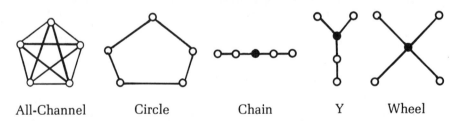

All-Channel   Circle   Chain   Y   Wheel

Although the results of the many network studies are not entirely consistent, some general conclusions have been drawn. For solving simple problems, the wheel tends to be the most efficient, followed by the Y, the chain, the circle, and the all-channel network (the least efficient). These results are most likely attributable to the nature of solving simple problems; each group member is willing to accept the decision of others in the network, and

9.   Peter M. Blau and W. Richard Scott, *Formal Organizations,* (San Francisco: Chandler, 1962), p. 6.

complete communication among all members (as in the all-channel network) is not necessary. With simple problems, complete communication may actually interfere with the problem solving process. On the other hand, complex problems are solved most efficiently by the all-channel network, followed in descending order by the circle, the chain, the Y, and the wheel (the least efficient). Thus, when dealing with complex problems, complete communication and the weighing of alternatives among network members are best.[10]

In those networks where the communication channels are the most open, or least restrictive, group members have the highest degree of satisfaction; the all-channel network, because it is least restrictive, would provide the most satisfaction to group members, followed by the circle, the chain, the Y, and the wheel. Studies have also indicated that those members who are located in the center positions of the chain, the Y, and the wheel (represented by the black dots in Figure 6-1) become recognized leaders of the group and are very satisfied, while those members at the greatest distance from the center are the least satisfied.

Because network research has remained very basic, with only three to five group members observed under laboratory conditions, generalizations must be carefully applied to groups in complex organizations. However, the above analyses provide practicing managers with three useful propositions:

1. Specific communication networks can either increase or decrease both the performance and satisfaction levels of group members.

2. Certain communication networks are beneficial to some group members while detrimental to others.

3. The choice of an appropriate communication network depends on the specific situation, and involves such issues as the complexity of the problem and the need for a team leader. Thus the best approach is the contingency approach, under which the manager applies and adapts the various communication networks to specific organizational circumstances.

GROUP INFLUENCES ON INDIVIDUALS

As first indicated by the Hawthorne studies, groups greatly affect the behavior and attitudes of individuals in organizations. Porter, Lawler, and Hackman suggest that groups control many of the stimuli which individuals encounter during their organizational activities; these "discretionary stimuli," are transmitted selectively to individual group members at the discretion of their peers.[11] Porter, *et. al.* discuss several individual characteristics

---

10. Philip B. Applewhite, *Organizational Behavior*, (Englewood Cliffs, N.J.: Prentice-Hall, 1965), p. 80.

11. Lyman W. Porter, Edward E. Lawler, III., and J. Richard Hackman, *Behavior in Organizations*, (New York: McGraw-Hill, 1975), p. 370-371.

which are affected by group-generated discretionary stimuli: (1) beliefs, (2) attitudes and values, and (3) job-relevant knowledge and skills.[12]

Beliefs

Individuals in organizations do not have a very complete or accurate view of their environment unless they obtain information from their work groups; either through direct communication or through observation, members soon discover the "social reality" of organizational life. Frequently, groups pressure members toward uniformity of beliefs about the work environment, because most groups are not very competent in handling overt disagreements among members. Such pressure is most obvious when new members, whose beliefs may be different, join the group. Such pressure often occurs in police departments when recruits report for their first tour of duty and hear the veteran officer's advice to "rookies"—"Forget what you were told in the academy, we'll show you how things really are." The more experienced officers generally inform the recruits that "divergent" views are not appreciated.

The pressure toward uniformity of beliefs can be functional for the group, as in task groups where uniformity of views is essential for completing the work. However, such pressure is dysfunctional when contrasting views of group members are automatically suppressed. Contrary beliefs, if explored, can contribute substantially to the problem-solving abilities of a group.

As noted above, group members form their views about reality on the basis of stimuli received from the group. The following related factors affect the degree to which members accept group stimuli:

1. Characteristics of the Environment: Members who do not know what beliefs are expected of them rely heavily on the group for information. In organizational settings, individuals are especially dependent upon group-supplied information for help in understanding the social environment (such as social rewards and behavior-outcome contingencies), as understanding the social environment is more difficult than understanding the physical environment.

2. Characteristics of the Receiver: If individuals feel poorly qualified to evaluate their environment, they will rely more heavily on the group for information concerning it, particularly if they are newer organizational members (although some individuals continue to rely heavily on the group).

3. Characteristics of the Group: If individuals perceive the group as being a credible source of information (competent, successful, trustworthy) they are likely to accept group-supplied data about reality. If there is uniformity among the views of group members, individuals are more likely to

---

12. The characteristics and much of the related discussion are drawn from Porter, Lawler and Hackman, *ibid.*, pp. 375-391.

accept information provided by the group, mainly because uniformity increases the perceived credibility of the group.

Attitudes and Values

Groups have a significant effect on attitude and value changes. There are three general mechanisms by which groups can, over time, influence the attitudes of their members.

1. Changing Behavior, with Attitude Changes Resulting: A group can directly influence the behavior of selected members by giving group-controlled rewards (such as acceptance and status) only to those members whose behavior the group considers desirable. As individuals begin behaving desirably, their attitudes are likely to become more consistent with their behavior. Festinger's theory of cognitive dissonance (see Chapter 5) helps to explain this tendency for behavior and attitudes to become consistent over time. If individuals experience tension or dissonance because their behavior is inconsistent with their attitudes and beliefs, and if they cannot conveniently rid themselves of this dissonance by changing their behavior, they may simply change their attitudes or values in order to make them consistent with that behavior. However, unless individuals desire the rewards controlled by the group, they are unlikely to cooperate with the group, and this method for changing attitudes and values loses its power.

2. Changing Beliefs, with Attitude Changes Resulting: Attitudes are usually based on the beliefs which individuals hold about an attitude object; consequently, the attitudes individuals associate with an object may be changed by changing their beliefs about it. Because groups powerfully influence the beliefs of their members, this mechanism can greatly affect members' attitudes and values. It is essential that (a) beliefs of the group members—whether about the environment or about their own attitudes and values—be open to change, and (b) the individuals value the group and/or see it as a source of trustworthy information. This mechanism is thus more likely to influence the attitudes and values of new and/or low-status group members than of those who are more experienced or self-confident.

3. Direct Change of Attitude: A large body of literature indicates that careful control of the positive or reinforcing stimuli available to the group (such as acceptance and status), should allow the group to "condition" the attitudes and values of its members with respect to some person, object, or concept.

Although the three mechanisms for group-generated attitude change have been discussed separately, in real-life situations they overlap to some degree. When the group *is* important to the individual, the stimuli which are supplied by it can strongly affect the person's likes and dislikes.

Job-Relevant Knowledge and Skills

The third type of group-supplied discretionary stimuli can help group members gain the knowledge and skills they need to perform their jobs or fulfill their organizational roles. Individuals learning how to behave in organizations need the group for several reasons. Trial-and-error learning of a new skill or behavior pattern is usually inefficient; in police agencies where decisions may involve life and death, it can be extremely dangerous. The help of other group members often provides the individual with short-cuts to the learning process and lessens the risks involved in the learning process. Many skills and role behaviors, such as learning to handle interpersonal conflicts in crisis situations, are impossible to master without actively involving other people. There are three general ways in which the group can assist members in developing their skills and role behaviors.

1. Direct Instruction: Direct instruction, by itself, is useful only in teaching the most simple skills and behaviors. For example, it is not enough to simply tell someone how to handle an intoxicated person or deal with a mentally unstable individual. Nevertheless, direct instruction in skill and role learning is important, especially to new members of the group or organization, and it usually is a necessary part of learning patterns. Direct instruction is an important resource of the group, and it may be provided or withheld at the group's discretion.

2. Feedback: Feedback provided by other group members serves two major functions for the individual. First, it can identify whether or not behavior is appropriate for performing one's job or role. Second, it provides reinforcement, by rewarding appropriate behavior and punishing inappropriate behavior. Both of these functions can improve a member's job skills and role behavior.

3. Modeling: By providing models, a group helps individual members to master complex roles and tasks. There are two primary methods of modeling; (a) the learner attempts to "match" the behavior of a model or b) the learner simply observes the activities of the model. In police organizations, matching takes place in training sessions which use "role playing;" the individual attempts to match the appropriate skills or behavior of a "model" by acting out the role under simulated conditions. Police agencies frequently use role playing to train employees in crisis intervention and domestic disturbance techniques. Observation is used when recruits, during their first few months on the job, are teamed with a training officer. The trainees acquire appropriate on-the-job skills as they observe the veteran officer.

In conclusion, individuals largely depend on the group for gaining the knowledge and skills needed to perform adequately. In a more complex job or role, individuals will not perform well if left to their own devices, and the more likely an individual will need to use all three methods a group can provide: direct instruction, feedback, and, modeling. The group thus has a tremendous amount of power and influence over individuals who are attempting to learn about complex new jobs or roles. In such circumstances, the capability of the group to influence the member in other areas not immediately related to the task at hand, such as beliefs, attitudes, and values, should also be great.

CONFLICT

Conflict within organizations can serve both functional and dysfunctional purposes. Traditionally, police management has perceived conflict solely as negative, and has continually attempted to avoid it, even when obviously present. According to contemporary theory, conflict is not only inevitable, but is a vital element for change, and is therefore potentially good for the organization. Coser analyses conflict best:

Groups require disharmony as well as harmony, dissociation as well as association; and conflicts within them are by no means altogether disruptive factors. Group formation is the result of both types of processes. The belief that one process tears down what the other builds up, so that what finally remains is the result of subtracting the one from the other, is based on a misconception. On the contrary, both "positive" and "negative" factors build group relations. Conflict as well as cooperation has social functions. Far from being necessarily dysfunctional, a certain degree of conflict is an essential element in group formation, and the persistence of group life.[13]

Pondy describes the conflict process within organizations as a series of dynamic episodes, each starting where the last one left off, and ending with some set of conditions which may lead to another *conflict episode*. Each episode involves four distinct stages, which are related to and modified by numerous internal and external factors: (1) latent conflict, in which conditions for conflict, such as competition for scarce organizational resources, drives for autonomy, or divergence of subunit goals, already exist; (2) perceived conflict, in which the parties, or some of them, are aware of the latent conditions for conflict; (3) felt conflict, in which at least some of the parties experience conflict emotionally, through anxiety, tenseness, frustration, and hostility; and (4) manifest conflict, in which conflict is translated into behavior ranging from open aggression (verbally or physically attacking another) to apathy (withdrawing from or ignoring the situation).[14]

Because conflict may have both functional and dysfunctional consequences, a conflict episode is judged as good or bad according to some value system. Thus a manifest conflict may result in personal costs (anxiety or frustration) and be judged undesirable by an individual. However, the same conflict might benefit the organization and be judged favorably by someone (in upper level management, perhaps) possessing a different value system. Consequently, when evaluating the results of conflict, the value system used as the frame of reference needs to be considered.[15]

---

13. Lewis Coser, *The Functions of Social Conflict*, (New York: Free Press, 1956), p. 31.

14. Louis R. Pondy, "Organizational Conflict: Concepts and Models," *Administrative Science Quarterly*, 12, 1967, p. 296-320.

15. *Ibid.*

Because conflict must be judged from a particular frame of reference, it is difficult to integrate individual, group and organizational goals. What may seem beneficial from the organization's standpoint may create conflict from group or individual perspectives, and vice versa. The expectation-intergration model (proposed in Chapter 1) may be of benefit, if all parties know what is expected of them, even though they may not agree with the expectations, choices can be debated openly and potential dysfunctional conflicts can be eliminated. Conflict thus plays a constructive and positive role within the organization, by calling attention to changes which may be needed. Without conflict, few new ideas are created, and an unchanging group or organization usually operates far below its potential level of effectiveness.

Competition

Just as conflict among individuals is unavoidable, it is also unavoidable among groups within organizations. Because the conditions for latent conflict are always present, many types of *intergroup* conflicts may arise, either between groups on the same organizational level (horizontal) or between groups on different levels (vertical). A major type of intergroup conflict involves competition among groups. A certain degree of competition, if it motivates groups to work harder or solve problems, helps an organization to reach goals. However, too much competition can cause a lack of coordination and communication among groups, which, if left unchecked, may create a hostile environment and low performance levels. In many police departments, for example, detective and patrol units compete fiercely about obtaining information and clearing or solving cases; the detectives and patrol officers often do not even talk to one another. Many cases which could be solved through mutual cooperation are not, and neither group realizes its full potential. When the safety and general welfare of the community are at stake, management cannot tolerate such dysfunctional competition.

What typically occurs when groups over-compete is that (1) each group begins to perceive other groups as a threat to its operations, (2) the perceptions of each group become more distorted, and (3) the number and significance of communications and interactions lessen.[16] Although not all intergroup or *intragroup* (within group) competition can, or should, be eliminated, practicing managers must attempt to strike a balance of competition which will help both the organization and the group achieve their goals. The tendency for groups to compete dysfunctionally can be lessened by: (1) placing greater emphasis on rewarding groups for their contribution to total organizational effectiveness, (2) promoting frequent interaction and communication on a common problem (intergroup conflict cannot be reduced simply by increasing contact among groups), (3) rotating members among groups as often as possible, to build mutual understanding of problems, and (4)

---

16. Paul M. Whisenand, *Police Supervision: Theory and Practice*, Englewood Cliffs, N.J.: Prentice-Hall, 1971), p. 64.

refraining from placing groups in situations where they compete for organizational rewards, thus emphasizing the need for "pulling-together" to maximize organizational effectiveness. [17]

One police organization used several of the above methods to strengthen the "pulling-together" concept. The results were reported in *Target*, a publication of the International City Management Association:

In early 1973, Orange City Manager Gifford Miller negotiated a wage agreement with the City of Orange Police Association. The agreement called for bonus salary increases if a reduction in the four major criminal offenses considered to be repressible (burglary, robbery, rape, and auto theft) was achieved within a specific time. During the first eight-month period, a reduction of these four crimes by three percent would be a one percent salary increase, and a reduction of six percent would be a two percent salary increase.

The following chart indicates the relationship between crime reduction and salary increase for the twenty-month period of the agreement.

Crime Reduction	Salary Increase
8%	1%
10%	2%
12%	3%

Fiscal year 1972-73 was used as the base period. All salary increases were effective immediately upon conclusion of the eight-or-twenty-month period and were permanent increases in base pay. No penalties were assessed if the crime rates increased rather than decreased. Statistical allowances were made for the effect of population increases or decreases on the crime rate. After eight months, the four major crimes had been reduced 17.6 percent, and after twenty months, by 12.6 percent. Both figures exceeded the highest goals of the program, and the police officers collected the maximum bonus pay.

The successful results of this program can be attributed to several factors. Besides the promise of higher pay and the challenge of working together to achieve a common goal, the police department benefited from a personnel organization that resulted in the formation of two specialized bureaus: a Crime Prevention Bureau, which contacted citizens and developed several successful programs for preventing crime; and a Special Enforcement Team, composed of non-uniformed officers who concentrated on the activities of crime suspects.[18]

While these results indicate that group unity and cooperation are necessary for goal achievement, unfortunately no outside evaluation (such as a victimization survey) of the results was provided. Therefore, although the findings are impressive, they must be interpreted with caution and should not be viewed as a panacea for all police departments. Indeed, if such a

---

17. *Ibid.*, p. 65.
18. International City Management Association, *Target*, 5, 2, February, 1976, p. 4.

program were not carefully monitered by management, false reporting procedures could indicate that "repressible" crimes were being reduced, when they were actually occurring at the same or even at an increased level.

INFORMAL ORGANIZATION

It is apparent that both formal and informal groups have a tremendous influence on organizational activities. While most of the discussion throughout this text has concentrated on formal organizational arrangements, our attention now turns to an in-depth analysis of informal organizational arrangements. John M. Pfiffner and Frank P. Sherwood, in *Administrative Organization*,[19] describe five informal "overlays" which coexist with the formal structure. The following discussion on informal overlays is taken from their work.

Informal Overlays*

The formal structure of an organization represents as closely as possible the deliberate intention of its framers for the processes of interaction that will take place among its members. In the typical work organization this takes the form of a definition of task specialities, and their arrangement in levels of authority with clearly defined lines of communication from one level to the next. (See Figure 6-2)

Figure 6-2

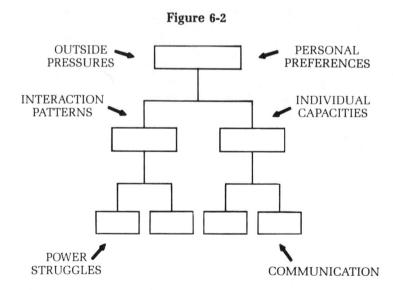

Figure 6-2. The typical job pyramid of authority and some of its interacting processes.

---

19. Pfiffner and Sherwood, *op. cit.*

* Source: John M. Pfiffner and Frank P. Sherwood, *Administrative Organization*, (Englewood Cliffs, N.J.: Prentice-Hall, Inc., 1960), pp. 18-27. Footnotes and figures have been renumbered.

It must be recognized, however, that the actual processes of interaction among the individuals represented in the formal plan cannot adequately be described solely in terms of its planned lines of interaction. Coexisting with the formal structure are myriad other ways of interacting for persons in the organization; these can be analyzed according to various theories of group behavior, but it must not be forgotten that in reality they never function so distinctively, and all are intermixed together in an organization which also follows to a large extent its formal structure.

These modifying processes must be studied one at a time; a good way to do so without forgetting their "togetherness" is to consider each as a transparent "overlay" pattern superimposed on the basic formal organizational pattern. The totality of these overlays might be so complex as to be nearly opaque, but it will still be a closer approach to reality than the bare organization chart so typically used to diagram a large group structure.

Five such overlay patterns will be considered here; many more or less might be chosen from the kinds of studies that have been made, but these five might well be considered basic:

- The sociometric network
- The system of functional contacts
- The grid of decision-making centers
- The pattern of power
- Channels of communication[20]

The idea that these processes are overlays upon the conventional job-task pyramid does not require that the latter take a subordinate position, although much of the research in organization might give this impression. The overlay approach aims to be realistic in recognizing that organizations also consist of a wide variety of contacts that involve communication, sociometry, goal centered functionalism, decision-making, and personal power. Let us consider this complex of processes one at a time.

The Job-Task Pyramid

The job-task pyramid constitutes the basis from which all departures are measured. It is the official version of the organization as the people in the organization believe that it is and should be. It would be correct to say that in most production organizations today, whether private or public, this official version of the organization-as-it-should-be reflects the view of those in the top echelons of the job-task pyramid. The actual operating organizations may differ in some respects from the formal organization; this difference can be expressed by showing the manner in which the other networks vary from the job-task hierarchy.

---

20. For much of the conceptual underpinnings of this chapter we are indebted to John T. Dorsey, Jr., "A Communication Model for Administration," *Administrative Science Quarterly*, 2, December, 1957, p. 307-324. While Dorsey would seem to view communication as the central component of administration, we would put it on a level with others dealt with here.

Job-task Hierarchy as Foundation. Variations of the other networks from the job-task hierarchy should not be taken as an indication that the latter is being undermined or has no acceptance in the organization. It is well recognized in practice that there is an operating organization that varies from the chart with the full knowledge of those in authority. Day-to-day and hour-to-hour adjustments must be made, and there is no need to revise the chart for each of these. Nevertheless, the job-task hierarchy as depicted by the organization manual does set forth the grid of official authority as viewed by those in the organization. Without it the other networks would simply not exist.[21]

Figure 6-3

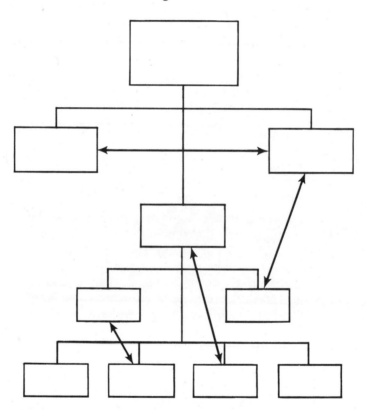

Figure 6-3. Social overlay—the special friendship in the organization. ("I'll talk to my friend George in Purchasing. He'll know what to do.")

The Sociometric Overlay (See figure 6-3)

In any organization there is a set of relationships among people which is purely social in nature; it exists because of a net feeling of attraction or

21. William Brownrigg deals with the job-task hierarchy most provocatively in *The Human Enterprise Process and Its Administration*, (Birmingham, Ala.: University of Alabama Press, 1954).

rejection. This pattern of person-to-person contacts is called sociometric because it is revealed in the kind of group testing that was given that name by its originator, J.L. Moreno. Some investigators have felt that individual attitudes lending themselves to sociometric measurement include as many as the following:

1. the *prescribed* relations, which are identical with the official or formal organization.

2. The *perceived* relations which consist of people's interpretation of the meaning of the official network.

3. The *actual* relations are those interactions which in fact take place among persons.

4. The *desired* relations are people's preferences regarding interactions they want with other persons.

5. The *rejected* relations are the relationships with other people which are not wanted.[22]

It is, however, the last two categories that are primarily sociological in nature, and it is these that will be considered sociometric here. Desired and rejected relationships are fairly easy to ascertain with statistical reliability, and are found to be very responsive to the other dynamics of the group. Ohio State studies of naval leadership have effectively utilized sociometric charts (sociograms—graphic representations of social relations) superimposed on the traditional job-task charts.[23]

The Functional Overlay (See Figure 6-4)

There is in the organization a network of functional contacts that is important to and yet different from the formal authority structure. Functional contacts occur most typically where specialized information is needed; through them the staff or other specialist, the intellectual "leader," exerts his influence upon operations without direct responsibility for the work itself. This relationship, something like that between a professional man and his client, is a phenomenon of the twentieth century, and more markedly of the mid-century period.

Frederick Taylor was so perceptive as to understand the importance of the network of functional contacts in a management institution. Taylor called these functional contacts "functional supervision;" this term upset many theorists who worshipped the concept of clear cut supervisor-subordinate authority relationships.[24]

---

22. Fred Massarik, Robert Tannenbaum, Murray Kahane, and Irving Weschler, "Sociometric Choice and Organizational Effectiveness: A Multi-Rational Approach," *Sociometry*, 16, August 1953, p. 211-238.

23. Ralph M. Stogdill, *Leadership and Structure of Personal Interaction*, (Columbus, Ohio: Ohio State University, Bureau of Business Research, Monograph No. 84, 1957), p. 10.

24. A collection of exerpts from the literature of the early scientific management movement relating to staff specialization and functionalism is contained in Albert Lepawsky, *Administration*, (New York: Alfred A. Knopf, Inc., 1949), p. 229-306.

While Taylor's original concept of multiple supervision was rejected as a theoretical instrument at the time, it is still true that most organizations exhibit a system of functional supervision. Many charts of formal authority structures, such as those of the military, also show functional contacts through such devices as broken connecting lines.

Figure 6-4

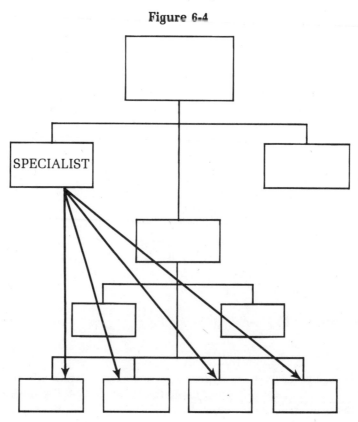

Figure 6-4. Functional overlay—the direct relationships between the specialist assistant and the operating departments. ("You'll have to see Personnel for approval to take that training course.")

The Decision Overlay (see Figure 6-5)

Simon maintains that the best way to analyze an organization is to find out where the decisions are made and by whom.[25] It can perhaps be assumed that normally in an organization the decision pattern follows the structure of the formal hierarchy, that is, the job-task pyramid.

However, the power and authority network together with the functional network, may cut across hierarchial channels. It is in this sense that they take on the configuration of a grid or network. Thus the network pattern of

---

25. Herbert A. Simon, *Administrative Behavior*, 2nd ed., (New York: The Macmillan Co., 1947), p. xix. Simon's decision model is discussed in detail in Chapter 21, Pfiffner and Sherwood, *op. cit.*

approach is helpful, not in undermining the concept of hierarchy but in conveying the picture of actual practice. It modifies the harsh overtones of hierarchy by pointing out that actual organizations permit a great many cross-contacts.

Network Influences. It might be more correct to say that there is a network of influence, not a network of decision. This, of course, depends upon one's definition of decision-making and if one insists upon there being a clear cut choice between alternatives by a person in authority, the decision-making usually follows clear hierarchial paths and channels. However, if we think in terms of a decision *process* rather than a decision *point,* the sense of interaction and influence is more appropriately conveyed. In this connection it is helpful to refer to Mary Parker Follet's concept of order giving in which she says "an order, command, is a step in a process, a moment in the movement of interweaving experience. We should guard against thinking this step a larger part of the whole process than it really is."[26]

Figure 6-5

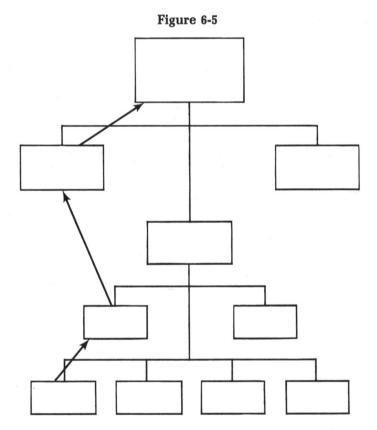

Figure 6-5. Decision overlay—flow of significant decisions in the organization. ("Don't worry about Joe. He doesn't concern himself about this. Our next step is to go topside.")

---

26. Henry C. Metcalf, and L. Urwick, eds., *Dynamic Administration: The Collected Papers of Mary Parker Follet,* (New York: Harper and Brothers, 1940), p. 49.

The Power Overlay (see Figure 6-6)

Any discussion of power as a factor in organizational dynamics rather quickly encounters difficulties in definition and terminology. Since this is a subject upon which there will be considerable discussion at a later point in this book, let it be noted here that many of these problems arise from a confusion of the terms *power* and *authority*.[27] They are not necessarily synonymous; yet there has been a tendency to look at the organization chart, note the various status levels, and to assume that power increases as one rises in the pyramid. Much of this attitude is based on old concepts of authority as they are found in jurisprudence. Within this framework there is an assumption that a rule laid down by a political superior who is ultimately sovereign can be enforced by the imposition of sanction. Translated into the terminology of management institutions, this means that authority, and hence power, rests with those at the top echelons of the job-task pyramid.

Figure 6-6

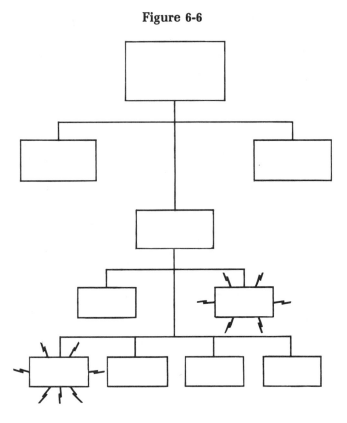

Figure 6-6. Power overlay—centers of power in the organization. ("Before you go further, you had better clear that with Jack in Production Planning.")

---

27. See Chapter 5, "Authority, Policy and Administration as Organization Factors," in Pfiffner and Sherwood, *op. cit.*

Power no longer viewed as synonymous with authority. However, there has been a considerable rebellion against this narrow view of the power factor in organization environment. Almost everyone who has had any experience in a management institution has encountered a situation where the boss's secretary, or his assistant or the executive officer, is the "person to see." For a great variety of reasons, these people may be effective decision-makers in the situation. Thus power is really personal; it is political; and it may or may not be legitimate in that it has been authorized by formal law or has achieved hierarchial legitimization. Involving a person-to-person relationship, power exists when one has the ability to influence someone to behave in a particular way or to make decisions. As a result the mapping of power centers would seldom follow the pattern of a typical hierarchy.

The important consideration from the standpoint of organizational theory is that there is a network or a grid of personal power centers, though

Figure 6-7

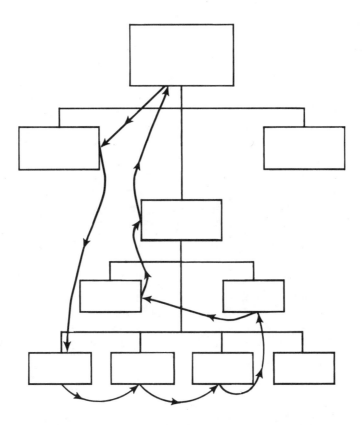

Figure 6-7. Communications overlay—the route of telephone calls on a particular matter. ("If we had to go through channels, we would never get anything done around here.")

sometimes latent and not expressed.[28] They may or may not coincide with the official structure of authority. Power is not institutionalized in the sense that one can look in the organization manual and find out where it resides. As a matter of fact, one might find it in unsuspected places. The person of comparatively low status may be a power center because he has been around so long that only he knows the intricate rules and the regulations well enough to make immediate decisions.

The Communication Overlay [See Figure 6-7]

Perhaps nowhere is the interrelationship of the various overlays more clearly to be seen than in communication. As will be observed at countless points in this book, the information process is central to organizational system. It affects control and decision-making, influence and power, interpersonal relationships, and leaderships, to name only a few facets. Dorsey, in making a case of the significance of communications, says that "power consists of the extent to which a given communication influences the generation and flow of later communications. Points in the patterned flow where this occurs . . . are positions of power . . ."[29] Furthermore, the communication net "consists physically of a complex of *decision centers* and *channels* which seek, receive, transmit, subdivide, classify, store, select, recall, recombine, and retransmit *information*."[30] This net consists not only of the technical information apparatus, but also of the human nervous systems of the people who make up the organization.

It is important to recognize that communication is itself a clearly identifiable facet of behavior. Redfield tells, for example, of the consultant who "starts his studies in the mail room, for, by plotting the lines of actual communication, he can sometimes build a more accurate organization chart than the one that hangs on the wall in the president's office."[31] Such a chart is, of course, one of communications. And it may tell a great deal more about how life is really lived in an organization than the formal authority picture. Thus an important and useful means of taking a look at an organization is to ask the question, "Who talks to whom about what?"

Answers to the question will often reveal that patterns of communication are at variance with official prescriptions. That is something the consultant mentioned in the previous paragraph frequently found. Furthermore there have been enough experiments with small groups to give great strength to the proposition that "the mere existence of a hierarchy sets up

---

28. Robert Dubin, *Human Relations in Administration: The Sociology of Organization,* (Englewood Cliffs, N.J.: Prentice-Hall, Inc., 1951), p. 173. See also Dubin, *The World of Work,* (Englewood Cliffs, N.J.: Prentice-Hall, Inc., 1958), pp. 47-54.

29. Dorsey, "A Communication Model for Administration," *Administrative Science Quarterly,* p. 310.

30. *Ibid.,* p. 317.

31. Charles Redfield, *Communication in Management,* (Chicago: University of Chicago Press, 1953), p. 7.

restraints against communication between levels."[32] Gardner has pointed out that factory production reports on productivity are sometimes rigged in order to give higher echelons the type of information which will make them happy.[33] Such blockages and distortions are certainly frequent enough to force us to recognize that the communications overlay represents an important dimension of organization analysis.

Informal Organization: An Example

A classic study conducted by Melville Dalton of the Milto Company,[34] provides an excellent example of the differences that may exist between an organization's formal chart and the informal arrangements that develop. By

Figure 6-8

Milo Formal Chart Simplified

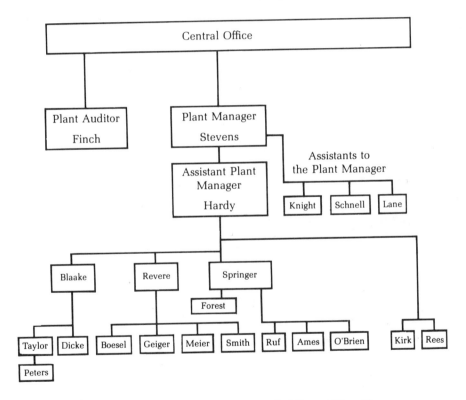

Source: Melville Dalton, *Men Who Manage*, (New York: Wiley, 1950), p. 21.

---

32. Burleigh B. Gardner and David G. More, *Human Relations in Industry*, 3rd ed., (Homewood, Ill.: Richard D. Irwin, Inc. 1955), p. 213ff.

33. Leon Festinger, "Informal Social Communication," in Dorwin Cartwright and Alvin Zander, *op cit.*, p. 201.

34. Melvin Dalton, *Men Who Manage.* [New York: Wiley, 1959].

comparing Figure 6-8 with Figure 6-9, one can readily observe the disparity between the formal and informal power and influence of the company's major executives.

Figure 6-9

Milo Informal Chart of Influence

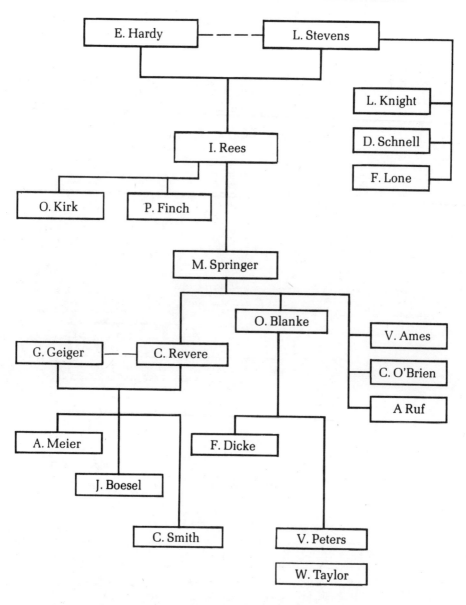

Source: Melville Dalton, *Men Who Manage*, (New York: Wiley, 1959), p. 22.

In Figure 6-9 the managers (except for Forest) of the formal chart in Figure 6-8 are reranked according to their informal power within the organization. Each individual's influence "was judged less by the response of subordinates to his officially spoken or written orders than by relative deference of associates, superiors, and subordinates to his known attitudes, wishes, and informally expressed opinion, and the concern to respect, prefer, or act on them."[35]

According to Dalton, fifteen "reliable" Milo participants evaluated the managers in Figure 6-9; all of the judges were, or had been, close associates of the people they were rating. Dalton then challenged the rankings; he based his criticisms on his experiences and conversations with executives and their subordinates of all ranks from the level of Taylor down. Dalton discusses his findings as follows:

In [Figure 6-9] the central vertical, dropping from Hardy and Stevens through Rees, Sprinter, and Blanke, ranks these officers in that order. Rectangles on the same level and horizontal [Hardy-Stevens, Geiger-Revere, Kirk-Finch] indicate that the officers therein were considered to have equal influence. At the same time each division is ranked according to the estimated power of its leader in plant affairs. That is, Springer is above Blanke, and Revere below, as least influential of the division chiefs. The department heads inside a given division are ranked in the same way but are not compared with those of other divisions.

As shown in [Figure 6-8] Peters was not a department head. But all the judges agreed that he should be put on the informal chart, and thirteen ranked him above Taylor.

There were minor disagreements on the placement of a few officers. For example, some of the judges who were line* officers objected to Rees' being regarded as more powerful than Springer. But these same officers showed such fear† of Rees that if their behavior alone were taken as a measure of Rees' influence, he should have been placed above Hardy. Two of the judges placed Peters below Taylor. These dissenters were generally foremen who apparently disliked Peters because he had been brought over from a staff organization by his powerful sponsor, Blanke. The informal chart does not of course measurably show that the executives exercised more or less than their given authority, but it does indicate that formal and actual authority differed. Scales and numbers were not used in the rankings because the judges opposed a formal device and believed it was a misleading overrefinement.[36]

Although the above study involves only a single organization, it demonstrates that differences between formal and informal arrangements do exist. Such differences also occur within all criminal justice agencies and much of a mangager's success depends upon his or her understanding of and ability to deal with informal relationships. In this respect the informal organization can greatly enhance or impede progress toward the organization's goals. If

---

35. *Ibid.*, p. 20.

* This resentment was typical of line attitudes toward staff people.

† This was frequently expressed clearly as "What he could do to you if you crossed him!"

36. *Ibid.*, p. 20-23.

handled constructively by management, the informal organization can provide several important benefits: ·

1. It blends with the formal organization to make a workable system for getting the work done.

2. It lightens the workload of formal managers and fills in some of the gaps of their abilities.

3. It gives satisfaction and stability to formal work groups.

4. It is a very useful channel of communication in the organization.

5. Its presence encourages managers to plan and to act more carefully than they would otherwise.[37]

In the final analysis, police and other criminal justice managers must make every effort to understand and work harmoniously with informal organizational arrangements. Only then can organizational members work together toward the fulfillment of organization's goals.

SUMMARY

Groups, which exert tremendous influence on their members, may be either formal or informal in nature, and are formed for a variety of reasons —some of which are social and some of which involve task accomplishment. Groups develop certain communication networks, known as the wheel, the Y, the chain, the circle, and the all-channel, which significantly affect group performance and satisfaction in specific situations. Accordingly, managers need to know which channels are the most effective in certain circumstances, thus using the contingency approach.

Because groups control many of the stimuli to which members are exposed, they affect three general individual characteristics: beliefs, attitudes and values, and job-related knowledge and skills. Individuals cannot acquire a complete view of their working environment without getting information from their work groups. Through such information, the member readily discovers the "social reality" of life in the organization. Obviously, groups largely control the individuals' perceptions about the organization; such influence may be functional or dysfunctional. Group pressure may be functional when uniformity of views is required in completing a work assignment, but is dysfunctional when contrary or divergent views, which could ultimately contribute to the problem solving abilities of the group, are suppressed. Because trial-and-error learning of skills and behavior is inefficient and even dangerous in police organizations, the help of group members through direct instruction, feedback, and modeling can provide a shortcut and lessen the dangers involved in the learning process. The individual is most dependent on the group for gaining the needed knowledge and skills for complex jobs, and in such circumstances the ability of the

---

37. Keith Davis, *Human Behavior at Work,* 4th ed., (New York: McGraw-Hill, 1972), p. 257-259.

group to influence the member in other areas not relevant to the task at hand (such as beliefs and values,) is also great.

Just as conflict is unavoidable between individuals, it also occurs between groups. The conflict process can be described as a series of dynamic episodes, each starting where the last one left off and ending with some set of conditions which may lead to another episode; the four stages are latent conflict, perceived conflict, felt conflict, and manifest conflict. Although conflict is generally assumed to be dysfunctional, it can benefit the organization by calling attention to new ideas and by preventing stagnation. A major type of intergroup conflict is competition; too much competition may lead to a lack of coordination and communication between groups, which may then lead to low performance levels. The tendency of groups to compete dysfunctionally can be lessened, especially by emphasizing "pulling-together" to maximize organizational effectiveness.

Informal organizational arrangements which develop within organizations, and coexist with the formal structure, must be recognized and dealt with. These informal arrangements can be described as transparent "overlays" imposed on the basic formal organizational pattern; they include the sociometric, the functional, the decision, the power, and the communication overlays. The Milo study illustrates that differences between formal and informal organizational structures do, in fact, exist in nature settings.

Practicing managers need to be aware of the dynamics of both formal and informal groups, their relationships with one another, and their impacts on organizational behavior. Because groups exert a great deal of influence which may be either functional or dysfunctional, police and other criminal justice managers must be able to deal effectively with groups in order to use group influence constructively.

DISCUSSION QUESTIONS

1. What are groups and why are they formed?; discuss several reasons why you might belong to a certain group in an organizational setting.

2. Contrast formal and informal groups, explain why each is important to the practicing manager.

3. Explain and give examples of those communication networks which are most appropriate for solving simple and complex problems.

4. Individual beliefs, attitudes and values, and job-relevant knowledge and skills are affected by group-generated discretionary stimuli; provide examples of how you have been affected by group stimuli in these three areas.

5. Explain the contemporary approach to organizational conflict; how can intergroup competition be lessened in a police organization?

6. Describe the research design used in the Milo study and the general findings of the study; have you observed differences in formal and informal relationships in an organization for which you have worked?

7. Discuss several ways in which the informal organization can benefit practicing managers if handled constructively.

ANNOTATED BIBLIOGRAPHY

Cartwright, Dorwin, and Alvin Zander, *Group Dynamics: Research and Theory,* (New York: Harper & Row, 1968). A collection of significant articles describing the methods and results of research on group dynamics, emphasizing: the nature of groups and group membership; the origin of group pressures to uniformity; the determinants and consequences of power and influence within groups; motivational process in groups; structural properties in groups.

Davis, Keith, *Human Behavior at Work: Organizational Behavior,* 5th ed., (New York: McGraw-Hill, 1977). The subject of this book is people at work in all kinds of organizations and how they may be motivated to work together in greater harmony; contents include: fundamentals of organizational behavior; organizational and social environments; communication and group processes; case problems and illustrations.

Hare, A. Paul, *Handbook of Small Group Research,* (New York: Free Press, 1962). A review of the literature of social interaction in small groups, which examines: small group process and structure; variables affecting the interaction process; performance characteristics.

Homans, George C. *The Human Group,* (New York: Harcourt, Brace & Co., 1950). This book provides a systematic analysis of five small groups, focusing on the activities, interactions and sentiments of group members in relation to group norms; internal and external systems; and the groups' behavior.

Pondy, Louis R., "Organizational Conflict: Concepts and Models," *Administrative Science Quarterly,* 12, 1967, pp. 296-320. Three types of conflict among subunits of formal organizations are identified and analyzed: 1) bargaining conflict among the parties to an interest-group relationship; 2) bureaucratic conflict between the parties to a superior-subordinate relationship; and 3) systems conflict among parties to a lateral or working relationship.

Schein, Edgar H., *Organizational Psychology,* (Englewood Cliffs, N.J.: Prentice-Hall, 1970). A clarification of the concepts and research of organizational psychology, emphasizing psychological problems in organizations; processes of management; groups and intergroup relationships; organizational effectiveness.

Shaw, Marvin E., *Group Dynamics: The Psychology of Small Group Behavior,* (New York: McGraw-Hill, 1976). An analysis of small group behavior with respect to group functioning in a number of environments (physical, personal, social and task), each of which is related to the other environments and each of which influences group processes.

SEVEN

Leadership: Influencing Behavior

LEARNING OBJECTIVES

The study of this chapter should enable you to:

☑ Define the concept of leadership and differentiate it from formal authority prescribed by position.

☑ Discuss the primary emphasis of trait theories of leadership.

☑ Discuss the primary focus of the behavioral approach to the study of leadership.

☑ Describe the research design and major findings of the Ohio State leadership studies (including initiating structure, consideration, and LBDQ).

☑ Explain the formula $E = f(1, f, s)$.

☑ Describe the basic approach used in Tannenbaum and Schmidt's continuum model of contingency leadership.

☑ Describe Fiedler's model of contingency leadership (including relationship and task orientation, LPC, and group situations).

☑ List each of the conditions specified by the Fiedler model and discuss the model's apparent weakness.

☑ Describe the four kinds of leader behavior included in the path-goal model of contingency leadership and discuss their implications for practicing police managers.

☑ Review the leadership case study (MacGregor) and discuss how this particular leader developed in others those values and conditions which lead to an effective participative style.

SEVEN

The previous chapter discussed the strong influence which groups have on individuals; this chapter examines the disproportionate amount of influence which group leaders have on members of their groups. Because organizational leaders have a significant impact on individual motivation and performance, police and other criminal justice managers should be familiar with research which has attempted to define effective leadership. The importance of effective leadership was stressed by Chester Barnard, the noted management theorist, who suggested that leadership is the critical factor which determines whether or not the organization will be successful.[1] The following sections review the major leadership theories and apply them to specific situations within police organizations. The final section presents a case study illustrating a particular leadership style.

LEADERSHIP DEFINED

Leadership implies that there are followers, and that a social interaction process exists between the leader and the led. This process has been defined in many ways; Keith Davis aptly describes *leadership* as, "the ability to persuade others to seek defined objectives enthusiastically. It is the human factor which binds a group together and motivates it toward goals." He adds, "Management activities such as planning, organizing, and decision making are dormant cocoons until the leader triggers the power of motivation in people and guides them toward goals."[2] Accordingly, a leader's influence and power extend beyond the limits prescribed by the organization (such as a high status position). In the past, because of the para-military design of most police organizations, leadership has often been viewed simply in terms of the formal authority of an individual's position; a person holding the rank of captain was assumed to be a leader because of the formal authority of the position. Actually, an individual may hold such a rank and yet not be a leader, because of an inability to effectively use authority and influence.

Leadership may be equated with the differential exertion of influence, an approach which Katz and Kahn treat as follows:

Thus, we would not speak of a leader in a group of people all of whom were equally effective or ineffective in influencing one another in all areas of the group's functioning. Even where one individual has more effect upon his fellows than another, we do

---

1. Chester I. Barnard, *The Functions of the Executive*, (Cambridge, Mass.: Harvard Univ. Press, 1966).

2. Keith Davis, *Human Behavior at Work*, 4th ed., (New York: McGraw-Hill, 1972), p. 100.

not ordinarily speak of his leadership if the effect derives almost entirely from his position in the social structure rather than from his special utilization of that position.[3]

Differential influence is apparent in the Milo Study cited previously. Figures 6-8 and 6-9 revealed the relative discrepancy between an individual's formal influence (authorized by position) and influence which resulted from personal attributes. In other words, some people are more able to use their authority and influence to motivate others toward accomplishing goals. For instance, an individual holding the rank of captain may gain the support of subordinates because of outstanding leadership qualities, combined with the delegated authority the position carries. Contrast this situation with that of a captain who lacks the qualities of leadership, and never fully receives the support of subordinates except through the formal authority of the position. Such an individual's influence and success are likely to be minimal, because of a lack of concern and possible resentment on the part of subordinates toward accomplishing their mission.

The reader should be familiar with those leadership characteristics and styles which research has shown to be the most effective under specific organizational circumstances. In an attempt to reveal the dimensions of effective leadership, three influential leadership theories are examined: trait, behavioral, and contingency.

TRAIT THEORY

Early research on leadership attempted to define thost traits or characteristics which distinguished leaders from those whom they led. Over the years, several investigators extensively surveyed the research on leadership traits to determine their universality. In 1940, Bird discovered that only around five percent of the listed traits, of which there were hundreds, were similar in four or more studies.[4] In 1948, Stogdill reported that only the traits of intelligence, scholarship, dependability in exercising responsibilities, social participation, and socioeconomic status consistenly separated leaders from nonleaders.[5] During this same time Jenkins, who reviewed a wide range of studies on leadership traits including those of business, professional, and military personnel, stated that, "No single trait or group of characteristics has been isolated which sets off the leader from the members of his group."[6] However, in 1971 Ghiselli compared successful with unsuccessful managers and concluded that the most important trait for successful

---

3. Daniel Katz and Robert L. Kahn, *The Social Psychology of Organizations*, (New York: Wiley, 1966), p. 301.

4. Charles Bird, *Social Psychology*, (New York: Appleton-Century-Crafts, 1940).

5. Ralph M. Stogdill, "Personel Factors Associated with Leadership: A Survey of the Literature." *Journal of Psychology*, 25, 1948, p. 35-71.

6. William O. Jenkins, "A Review of Leadership Studies with Particular Reference to Military Problems," *Psychological Bulletin*, 44, 1947, p. 74-75.

managers is supervisory ability, followed closely by the desire for occupational achievement. Intelligence, self-actualization, self-assurance and decisiveness also played moderate roles. [7]

Trait theory involves several inherent weaknesses. There is little agreement as to which traits should or should not be included, or to their relative importance. Trait theories also ignore the needs and influences of nonleaders, and fail to account for environmental variables such as task complexity. Certain traits may produce effective leadership in certain organizations and not in others. For example, an authoritarian individual may be a more successful leader in a highly bureaucratic police agency than in an agency which is less rigid. Nevertheless, the work of Ghiselli suggests that certain traits are critical to a manager's success as a leader. This approach could become increasingly important as researchers identify those traits of effective leadership which are related to specific organizational settings.

BEHAVIORAL THEORY

The behavioral approach to the study of leadership focuses on the behavioral styles or patterns of activities which characterize leaders. Instead of trying to measure traits which are not easily observed, such as intelligence, individuality, or self-assurance, this approach relies on patterns of behavior which can be directly observed and measured. The behavioral approach attempts to explain effective leadship on the basis of what leaders do, rather than on the basis of what they are.

Most of the proposed behavioral leadership dimensions can be thought of as opposite ends of a continuum, as the dichotomous styles illustrated in Figure 7-1. Those behavioral patterns on the left of the continuum represent a "scientific management" or Theory X approach, in which practically all decisions are made by the leader and communicated downward to group members; the major concern involves production and technical aspects of the job. On the other hand, those patterns on the right of the continuum represent a "human relations" or Theory Y approach, in which the suggestions and wishes of group members are considered in the decision-making process; the major concern involves the feelings and attitudes of group members.

There is a wide range of leader styles which fall between the extremes of the continuum in Figure 7-1. However, most behavioral studies have been designed to determine which of the two styles is more effective. Behavioral patterns which fall between the continuum extremes are discussed in the following section on contingency theory. The discussion here will be limited to a series of significant studies which attempted to define the major behavioral aspects of leadership styles and relate them to employee productivity and satisfaction.

---

7.   Edwin E. Ghiselli, *Exploration in Managerial Talent*, (Pacific Palisades, Calif.: Goodyear, 1971).

Figure 7-1
Dichotomous Leadership Styles

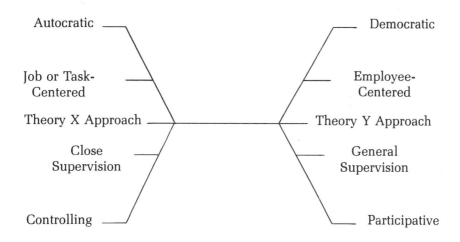

The Ohio State Studies

Perhaps the most extensive, and in many ways the most successful, inquiry into behavioral leadership was begun in 1945 by the Bureau of Business Research at Ohio State University.[8] Through a series of studies, the researchers eventually narrowed the description of leader behavior down to two major dimensions:

Initiating Structure or the leader's behavior in delineating the relationship between himself and members of the work group and in endeavoring to establish well-defined patterns of organization, channels of communication, and methods of procedure.

Consideration or behaviors indicative of friendship, mutual trust, respect, and warmth in the relationship between the leader and the members of his staff.[9]

The investigators developed the Leader Behavior Description Questionnaire (LBDQ) in order to obtain their data on leadership patterns. This instrument was designed to describe *how* a leader carries out his or her activities, and contains items relating to both initiating structure and consideration. Respondents judge the frequency with which their leader engages in each form of behavior by checking one of five descriptions—always, often, occasionally, seldom, or never—as it relates to each item of the LBDQ. Thus, consideration and initiating structure are dimensions of observed

---

8. Ralph M. Stogdill and Alvin E. Coons, eds., *Leader Behavior: Its Description and Measurement*, Research Monograph No. 88 (Columbus, Ohio: Bureau of Business Research, The Ohio State Univ., 1957).

9. Andrew W. Halpin, *The Leadership Behavior of School Superintendents*, (Chicago: Midwest Administration Center, Univ. of Chicago, 1959), p. 4.

behavior as perceived by others. Examples of items used in the LBDQ for both these dimensions are given below:[10]

Initiating Structure	Consideration
The leader assigns group members to particular tasks	The leader finds time to listen to group members
The leader asks the group members to follow standard rules and regulations	The leader is willing to make changes
The leader lets group members know what is expected of them	The leader is friendly and approachable

The findings indicated that initiating structure and consideration were separate dimensions; an individual can rank high on one without ranking low on the other. Consequently, a leader's behavior may be any combination of both dimensions, as illustrated by the four leadership quadrants in Figure 7-2.

Figure 7-2
Ohio State Leadership Quadrants

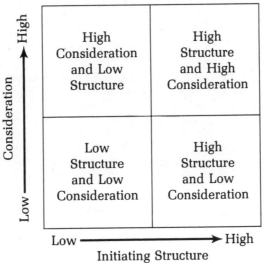

Extensive research on the quadrant design has attempted to define which behavioral pattern is most effective. Generally, the results suggest that subordinates prefer a leader who ranks high on consideration, while the leader's superiors prefer a leader who ranks high on initiating structure. This creates a dilemma for the leader, who receives separate expectations from above and below. As discussed in Chapter 5, this is the classic role conflict which frequently occurs in police organizations, in which lower and middle level managers (such as sergeants and lieutenants) are sent one role

---

10. Paul Hershey and Kenneth H. Blanchard, *Management of Organizational Behavior: Utilizing Human Resources*, 2nd ed., (Englewood Cliffs, N. J.: Prentice-Hall, 1972), pp. 73-74.

from the top of the hierarchy, emphasizing close supervision and structure, and another role from below, calling for general supervision and autonomy.

There is also some evidence that if a leader ranks simultaneously high in both structure and consideration, the differing expectations can be reconciled. However, Kerr *et. al.* point out that such an approach may oversimplify the dynamics of leader behavior:

It is true that many researchers have found a high-Consideration high-Initiating Structure combination to be related to maximal satisfaction and performance. However, argument for a high-high style of leadership overlooks several important considerations ... [I]t is known that Consideration and Structure often fail to be independent, and may in fact be negatively correlated. This may reflect "realities" of the environment being studied, or may result instead from respondent inability to consider the two dimensions separately. In either case, it is often extremely difficult for a leader to behave in such a way that his subordinates will perceive him to be simultaneously high in both Consideration and Structure ... [I]t should be pointed out that researchers have discovered a number of exceptions to the general rule that a high-high leadership style is the most effective one. Preferences for and attitudes toward Consideration and Structure have been found to vary considerably as a function of both the individual and the situation ... For those reasons it seems an oversimplification to claim that the effective leader needs "merely" to behave in a highly considerate and structuring manner.[11]

Subsequently, the effectiveness of the leader's behavior may be judged to be contingent upon various individual and situational factors; there is no single best way to determine successful leadership behavior. In effect, effective leadership is a function of the leaders, the follower(s), and the situation, or: E = f(1,f,s).[12] This formula suggests that the successful leader must be able to adapt his behavior to the particular situation.

By applying the situational approach, Kerr *et. al.* have been able to relate the Ohio State studies, to contemporary management practice.[13] In a situational model of leadership, both the leader and the situation must be classified. The LBDQ scale enables the researcher to classify leaders according to their initiating structure and consideration scores. Because sufficient data do not exist to permit predictions about leaders whose scores are "medium," a two-by-two categorization of leader behavior must be used. Thus a leader may be high in both structure and consideration, high in one and low in the other, or low in both. Such a classification is possible even though both dimensions may fail to be independent of one another. In classifying the "situation," it is both conceptually and physically impossible to define and study all the relevant variables which exist in the environment. Consequently, only those elements which are measurable and which

---

11. Steven Kerr, Chester A. Schrieshein, Charles J. Murphy, and Ralph M. Stogdill, "Toward a Contingency Theory of Leadership Based Upon the Consideration and Initiating Structure Literature," *Organizational Behavior and Human Performance*, 12, 1974, p. 63.

12. Hershey and Blanchard, *op. cit.*, p. 80.

13. This discussion was drawn from Kerr *et. al.*, *op. cit.*, p. 72-74.

exert a strong effect upon relationships between the leader behavior variables and the criteria should be selected.

Within this framework, Kerr *et. al.* attempted to distinguish those situational elements which could be made operational and which have been found by researchers to exert significant influence upon relationships between initiating structure and consideration (the independent variables) and satisfaction, morale, and performance (the dependent variables). The authors' admittedly restricted list included the following situational elements:

Subordinate considerations: Expertise, experience, competence, knowledge of job, hierarchical level of occupied position, expectations concerning leader behavior, perceived organizational independence, and psychological aspects.

Supervisor considerations: Similarity of attitudes and behavior to those of higher management, and upward influence.

Task considerations: Degree of time urgency, amount of physical danger, permissible error rate, presence of external stress, degree of autonomy, degree of job scope, importance and meaningfulness of work, and degree of ambiguity.

The authors identified two general propositions which are useful in trying to develop a unified approach to much of the initiating structure-consideration literature. The first: the more subordinates depend on the leaders for valued or needed services, the higher the positive relationship between leader behavior measures and subordinate satisfaction and performance. Some practical managerial considerations in relation to this proposition are:

1. Rigid bureaucratic rules and regulations in police agencies can reduce subordinates' structuring information needs almost to zero. In such cases, attempts by the leader to impose structure would be viewed by subordinates as unnecessary.

2. To the extent that the task itself is intrinsically satisfying to subordinates (as in the form of a challenging and autonomous work assignment like a critical investigation), their dependency on the leader for extrinsic satisfaction (through consideration) is reduced, and their need for externally-imposed structure is also reduced. At the same time, subordinates are less likely to view such structure as dissatisfying, since it focuses attention on a task which is already intrinsically satisfying.

3. To the extent that tasks which are highly structured are less likely to prove intrinsically satisfying (as in the form of a highly regulated work assignment like traffic direction and control), subordinates who perform such tasks are more likely to respond to extrinsic satisfiers. Under such circumstances, leader consideration can be effective.

The second proposition: the more the leader is able to provide subordinates with valued, needed, or expected services, the higher the positive relationship between leader behavior measures and subordinate satisfaction and performance. Some practical considerations for management are:

1. When supervisors (such as corporals and sergeants) are perceived by subordinates to have high upward influence, subordinates will view

supervisors as able to provide organizational rewards. Under these conditions, a leader's consideration will be positively associated with subordinate satisfaction. When higher-level management (such as lieutenants and captains) appears to exhibit and encourage high consideration, lower-level consideration will be positively associated with subordinate satisfaction.

2. To the extent that leader behavior reflects subordinate expectations concerning structure and consideration, it will be positively associated with both subordinate satisfaction and performance. Thus if a patrol officer expects an immediate superior to lead in a structured (or considerate) manner, both satisfaction and performance levels will be relatively high. If, however, the officer expects to be directed in one way but is directed in another, satisfaction and performance levels will be considerably lower than they might be.

CONTINGENCY THEORY

It should not be surprising that leadership research has not produced a specific trait, group of traits, or a single leadership style which is the most effective under all organizational conditions. As with other organizational characteristics, the contingency approach is highly applicable to effective leadership. By analyzing critical environmental variables with respect to a particular situation, the contingency approach allows one to choose an appropriate leadership style for a specific situation. Discussed below are three highly regarded contingency models of leadership, which should be valuable to practicing managers.

Continuum Model

Robert Tannenbaum and Warran H. Schmidt, in "How to Choose a Leadership Pattern," provided one of the better known discussions of contingency leadership.[14] The authors developed a continuum of possible leadership styles based on the degree of authority exercised by a manager with respect to the amount of freedom exercised by subordinates. As the leadership continuum in Figure 7-3 indicates, the behaviorial styles range from the two dichotomous extremes illustrated in Figure 7-1 (boss-centered or autocratic, and subordinate centered or democratic) to the various combinations in between.

Tannenbaum and Schmidt suggested three factors which should be considered when determining the most effective leadership style for a particular situation: forces in the manager (assumed leader), forces in the subordinates (or followers), and forces in the situation.[15]

---

14. Robert Tannenbaum and Warren H. Schmidt, "How to Choose a Leadership Pattern," *Harvard Business Review*, (March-April), 1958, p. 95-101.

15. Discussion of the three forces drawn from Tannenbaum and Schmidt, *ibid.*, pp. 99-100.

Figure 7-3
Continuum of Leadership Behavior

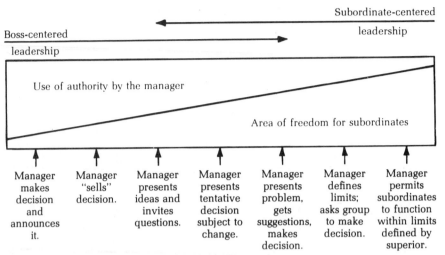

Source: Robert Tannenbaum and Warren H. Schmidt, "How to Choose a Leadership Pattern,"
Harvard Business Review, March-April, 1958, p. 96.

Forces In The Manager. A manager's behavior is greatly influenced by
many forces operating within his own personality. Previous experience,
background, and knowledge will affect the manner in which a manager
perceives how a particular situation should be handled. Among the internal
forces which influence the type of leadership style are:

1. Value System: How strongly does the manager feel that individuals
   should share in making the decisions which affect them? What does the
   manager feel are his responsibilities, and how should they be
   implemented?

2. Confidence in Subordinates: How much does the manager trust other
   people generally, and in the group's membership in particular? In dealing with a particular group, a manager is likely to consider the members'
   knowledge and competence concerning the problem, but a manager is
   also influenced by his basic assumptions about human nature. A manager
   with Theory X views is less likely to have confidence in group members
   and will therefore exert tighter controls than a leader with Theory Y
   views.

3. Managerial Inclinations: Some managers function more comfortably and
   naturally with a highly directive, authoritarian style, while others are
   more comfortable when using a more participative manner.

4. Feeling of Security in an Uncertain Situation: The manager who releases
   control over the decision-making process reduces the predictability of the
   outcome. Depending upon the particular organizational circumstances, a
   manager may feel relatively secure or insecure. The more insecure the
   feeling, the greater the tendency to structure the style and control the

decisions. Because municipal police chiefs are political appointees with uncertain tenure, this may account for one of the reasons why many of these agencies tend to be tightly structured and controlled.

Forces in the Subordinates. Before deciding how to lead a certain group, a manager should consider a number of forces affecting the behavior of subordinates. The manager should remember that each employee is influenced by many personality variables. In addition, subordinates have expectations about how the leader should act in relation to them. A manager who understands these forces is more able to determine which kind of behavior will enable the group members to act most efficiently.

Tannenbaum and Schmidt suggested that, if the following conditions exist, there is a greater need for democratic or participative leadership (those styles on the right side of the continuum):

1. Group members have high needs for independence. (people differ greatly in the amount of direction they desire.)

2. Group members are ready to assume responsibility for decision-making. (Some see additional responsibility as a tribute to their ability; others see it as "passing the buck.")

3. They have a relatively high tolerance for ambiguity. (Some prefer to have clear-cut directives given to them; others prefer more freedom.)

4. They are interested in the problem and feel that it is important (ego involvement).

5. They understand and identify with the goals of the organization.

6. They have the knowledge and experience to deal with the problem.

7. They have learned to expect to share in decision-making. (Persons who come to expect strong leadership and are then suddenly confronted with the request to share more freely in decision-making are often upset by this new experience. On the other hand, persons who have enjoyed a considerable amount of freedom resent leaders who begin to make all the decisions themselves.)

When these conditions do not exist, a manager is more likely to use his or her own authority and to move in the direction of an autocratic or boss-centered style. This does not mean that the above conditions cannot be acquired by group members if they are not already present; an insightful leader can help employees acquire these types of values. The case study on "MacGregor" (in the final section of the chapter) reveals such a leadership style.

Forces In The Situation. In addition to forces in the leader and other group members, certain characteristics of the general situation also affect leadership style. Some of the more critical environmental factors include the type of organization, the effectiveness of the work group, the nature of the problem, and the pressure of time for decision-making.

1. Type of Organization: Many types of criminal justice organizations exist, even within the police, court, and correctional subsystems. They may

vary in their style of operation, structural design, or in the type of individuals which they include. Consequently, the type of organization will most likely have a strong influence on the choice of leadership style. For instance, a correctional agency which emphasizes reform and rehabilitative programs would most likely be more comfortable with a democratic, participative leadership orientation than would an agency which is primarily concerned with custody and rigid following of the rules.

It is also possible that the amount of group participation is influenced by the size of the work group, their geographical distribution, and the degree of secrecy required to attain organizational goals. Wide geographical distribution may severely limit participative decision-making, even though it is otherwise desirable. Similarly, a large work group or the need for confidentiality (as in a narcotics or internal affairs unit) may force the leader to exercise more control than would otherwise be necessary.

2. Group Effectiveness: When deciding how much decision-making power can be allowed a group, a manager needs to know how effectively its members work together. A group can usually handle increased participation in decision-making if: (1) it has functioned together for some time; (2) its members have similar backgrounds and interests, thus lessening communication problems; and (3) its members have confidence in their problem-solving abilities.

3. Type of Problem: The nature of the problem may help determine how much authority should be given to the group members. If the group lacks the information, experience, or knowledge needed to solve the problem, the leader could do members a disservice by assigning the problem to them. The key question is, "Have I heard the ideas of everyone who has the knowledge necessary to make a significant contribution to the solution of this problem?"

4. The Pressure of Time: The more a leader is pressured into making immediate decisions, the harder it is to involve other people. In criminal justice organizations which are in a constant state of "crisis," managers often use a high degree of their authority and delegate little to group members. Conversely, when there is less pressure for time, there is a greater likelihood that group members will be brought in on the decision-making process.

Tannenbaum and Schmidt suggest that these principal forces determine leadership behavior in relation to group members. In each particular case, managers should adapt their behavior to effectively attain their immediate objectives within the limits facing them; that is, leadership style should match the situation.

In a republication of their original article, the authors updated their thoughts on leadership behavior.[16] In contemporary organizations, Tannenbaum and Schmidt acknowledge that the principal forces (manager, subordinates, situation) are more *interdependent* than was originally stated. For instance, they now recognize that the manager does not act alone, but must share power and influence with group members; the balance in the relationship between the manager and group members is achieved through an interaction process. "We did not attempt to deal with unions, other forms of joint worker action, or with individual worker's expressions of resistance. Today, we would recognize much more clearly the power available to all parties, and the factors that underlie the interrelated decisions or whether to use it."[17] The authors used the terms "manager" and "subordinate" in their original discussion, but eventually felt uncomfortable with "subordinate" because of its "demeaning, dependency-laden connotations," and prefer instead the term "nonmanager," which makes the terminological difference functional rather than hierarchical.

Finally, in their original discussion on situational forces, Tannenbaum and Schmidt identified only organizational phenomena. Subsequently, they recognized a need to include forces lying outside the organization and to explore the interdependence between the organization and its external environment. By recognizing environmental forces, the authors changed their original view of leadership behavior from a closed to an open system perspective. With respect to a contingency framework, all organizational characteristics should be viewed from an open-systems perspective. Figure 7-4 presents the interdependent forces which should be considered in selecting an effective leadership style.

Figure 7-4

Considerations in Selecting a Leadership Style

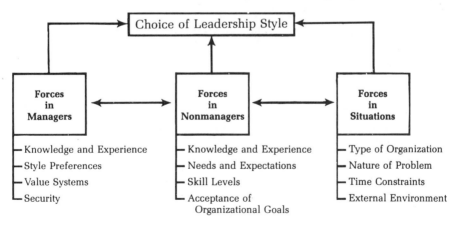

---

16. Robert Tannenbaum and Warren H. Schmidt, "How to Choose a Leadership Pattern," *Harvard Business Review*, (May-June), 1973, p. 162-180.

17. *Ibid* ., p. 168.

Fiedler Model

Fred E. Fiedler and his associates have developed a theory of leadership effectiveness which cites the specific circumstances under which certain leadership styles are the most effective.[18] The Fiedler model is unique because it predicts that a leader's effectiveness can be improved by "engineering" or fitting the job to the leader's style. Such an approach is, of course, the opposite of the Tannenbaum and Schmidt model described above.

To classify leadership styles, Fiedler and his colleagues developed a questionnaire (containing a set of adjectives used to describe one's least preferred co-worker) which proposes to measure a manager's leadership style. Fiedler suggests that a leader who describes his or her *least preferred co-worker* (LPC) in a favorable manner (high LPC) tends to be considerate, permissive, and employee centered. Conversely, a leader who describes his or her least preferred co-worker in an unfavorable way (low LPC) tends to be controlling, structuring, and task or job-centered.

According to this theory, three variables influence the favorability of a situation for the leader and determine whether considerate or structuring leader styles are more appropriate:

1. Leader-member relations: the degree to which the leader is liked, respected, and trusted by group members.

2. Task structure: the degree to which job assignments are structured and programmed in a step-by-step basis.

3. Position power: the degree of formal authority possessed by the leader based on position in the organization.

Figure 7-5 illustrates the results of a number of studies on group performance and leadership style. Leadership styles, as measured by the LPC, are shown on the vertical axis; situational variables are shown along the horizontal axis; and the dotted line indicates the correlations between leadership style and group performance. The bell-shaped curve suggests that *either* leadership style can be effective, depending on the favorableness of the situation. In other words, when the situation is either favorable or unfavorable to the leader (leader-member relations, task structure, and leader position power are either very high or very low), a structuring, task-oriented leader will be effective. In situations which are in between (moderately favorable or unfavorable, either because the task is relatively unstructured or because the leader is not well accepted, even though position power is high and the task is structured), a more considerate, employee-centered leader will be effective.

Fiedler further elaborates on these findings:

---

18. Fred E. Fiedler, "Engineer the Job to Fit the Manager," *Harvard Business Review,* 43, (Sept.-Oct.), 1965, pp. 115-122; *A Theory of Leadership Effectiveness,* (New York: McGraw-Hill 1967; "Style or Circumstance: The Leadership Enigma," *Psychology Today,* March, 1969, pp. 38-43.

In the very favorable conditions in which the leader has power, informal backing, and a relatively well-structured task, the group is ready to be directed, and the group members expect to be told what to do ... In the relatively unfavorable situation, we would again expect that the task-oriented leader will be more effective than will the considerate leader who is concerned with interpersonal relations [the group will not function well without the active control of the leader] ... In situations which are only moderately favorable or which are moderately unfavorable for the leader, a considerate, relationship-oriented attitude seems to be most effective. Under these conditions, in which the accepted leader faces an unambiguous, nebulous task, or one in which the task is structured but the leader is not well accepted, considerate, relationship-oriented leadership style is more likely to result in effective team performance.[19]

Figure 7-5

How the Style of Effective Leadership Varies with the Situation

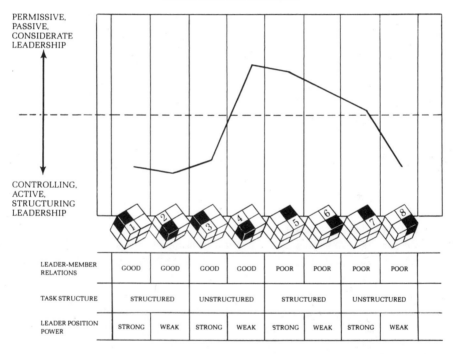

LEADER-MEMBER RELATIONS	GOOD	GOOD	GOOD	GOOD	POOR	POOR	POOR	POOR
TASK STRUCTURE	STRUCTURED		UNSTRUCTURED		STRUCTURED		UNSTRUCTURED	
LEADER POSITION POWER	STRONG	WEAK	STRONG	WEAK	STRONG	WEAK	STRONG	WEAK

Source: Fred E. Fiedler, "Engineer the Job to Fit the Manager," *Harvard Business Review*, 43, (Sept.-Oct.), 1965, p. 118.

In short, which style of leadership is effective depends on a combination of situational forces. For example, in a police communication center in which leader-member relations are good, the tasks are structured, and leader power is strong—factors which apply to condition 1—the most effective leadership style is task-or job-oriented. On the other hand, in a patrol unit which uses team policing, in which leader-member relations are good,

---

19. Fiedler, *A Theory of Leadership Effectiveness*, p. 147.

the tasks are unstructured (a feature of team policing), and leader power is weak (participative decision-making is also a feature)—factors which apply to condition 4—the most effective leadership style is employee- or relationship-oriented.

Fiedler's model predicts that a leader's performance can be improved by fitting the job to the leader, because it is easier to change a leader's work environment than it is to change personality or leadership style. For instance, condition 4 (leader-member relations good, tasks unstructured, leader power weak) calls for a considerate, participative leadership style. If a leader feels uncomfortable with this style, additional position power may be provided (changing the situation to condition 3), or the leader may be transferred to a job involving structured tasks (changing the situation to condition 2). In either case, the leader would be in a situation suited to a more autocratic style. Of course, many other alternatives exist in which the situation may be changed to fit the leader's style.

The Fiedler model suggests that effective leadership performance depends as much on the *organization* as it does the leader. "This means," Fiedler explains, "that we must learn not only how to train men to be leaders, but how to build organizations in which specific types of leaders can perform well."[20] The practical application of this approach depends on the organization's particular circumstances (is it within the organization's power, is it practical, and so on) and overall willingness to allow work changes to take place. If organizational-individual relationships have been developed cooperatively and openly, and if organizational circumstances permit it, any problems which arise should be able to be worked out to the mutual benefit of both parties. Nevertheless, this approach appears to suffer from a major weakness in that it does not call for any self-improvement or change on the leader's part; the leader can simply blame the job situation for any deficiencies or problems which are encountered. Also, many police agencies are too small to allow for many situational changes. Even so, if organizational circumstances permit, this approach may increase leadership effectiveness in police and other criminal justice organizations.

The work of Fiedler and his associates has been challenged on methodological and empirical grounds. The sample sizes are said to be too small, and the statistical tests used on the data have been criticized as inappropriate and invalid.[21] The measure of leadership style, the LPC, has also been criticized as not being reliable; the same individual may obtain substantially different LPC scores on different days.[22] However, Chemers and Skrzypek have recently tested the model by using an experimental research design

---

20. Fiedler, "Style or Circumstance: The Leadership Enigma," p. 43.

21. For example, see: George Graen, Kenneth M. Alvares, and James B. Orris, "Contingency Model of Leadership Effectiveness: Antecedent and Evidential Results," *Psychological Bulletin*, 74, 1970, p. 285-296; Ahmed S. Ashour, "The Contingency Model of Leadership Effectiveness: An Evaluation," *Organizational Behavior and Human Performance*, 9, 1973, p. 330-368.

22. Terrence Mitchell, Anthony Biglan, Gerald Oncken, and Frederick Fiedler, "The Contingency Model: Criticisms and Suggestions," *Academy of Management Journal*, 13, (Sept., 1970), pp. 253-267.

with large sample sizes and appropriate statistical analyses. Their results support the predictive ability of the model.[23] Although more research on the model's validity is needed, it remains a significant contribution toward the development of a contingency theory of leadership effectiveness.

Path-Goal Model

A third major contingency approach emerging from the study of leader effectiveness is the path-goal model of leadership, originally developed by M.G. Evans[24] but recently extended by Robert J. House[25] and Terrence R. Mitchell.[26] According to this model, a leader is effective because of his or her impact on subordinates' motivation, ability to perform, and satisfactions. The model is called path-goal because its primary concern is how the leader influences subordinate's perceptions of their work goals, personal goals, and paths to goal attainment. The model suggests that a leader's behavior motivates subordinates toward attaining goals by *clarifying* the paths to those goals.

The path-goal model is based on the expectancy theory of motivation, according to which individuals will be motivated to work hard if they perceive that their efforts will lead to various outcomes or performance (expectancy), which will in turn lead to desired outcomes or rewards (valences). While this model is still in its infancy, House and Mitchell explain:

The initial theoretical work by Evans asserts that leaders will be effective by making rewards available to subordinates and by making these rewards contingent on the subordinate's accomplishment of specific goals. Evans argued that one of the strategic functions of the leader is to clarify for subordinates the kind of behavior that leads to goal accomplishment and valued rewards. This function might be referred to as path clarification. Evans also argued that the leader increases the rewards available to subordinates by being supportive toward subordinates, i.e., by being concerned about their status, welfare and comfort. Leader supportiveness is in itself a reward that the leader has at his or her disposal, and the judicious use of this reward increases the motivation of subordinates.

Evans studied the relationship between the behavior of leaders and the subordinates' expectations that effort leads to rewards and also studied the resulting impact on ratings of the subordinates' performance. He found that when subordinates viewed leaders as being supportive (considerate of their needs) and when these

---

23. Martin M. Chemers and George J. Skrzypek, "Experimental Test of the Contingency Model of Leadership Effectiveness," *Journal of Personality and Social Psychology*, 24, 1972, p. 172-177.

24. Martin G. Evans, "The Effects of Supervisory Behavior on the Path-Goal Relationship," *Organizational Behavior and Human Performance*, 5, 1970, p. 277-298.

25. Robert J. House, "A Path-Goal Theory of Leader Effectiveness," *Administrative Science Quarterly*, 16, 1971, p. 321-338.

26. Robert J. House and Terrence R. Mitchell, "Path-Goal Theory of Leadership," in *Organizational Behavior and Industrial Psychology*, Kenneth N. Wexley and Gary A. Yukl (eds.), (New York: Oxford Univ. Press, 1975), p 177-186. The discussion of the path-goal model is drawn from this article.

superiors provided directions and guidance to the subordinates, there was a positive relationship between leader behavior and subordinates' performance ratings.

However, leader behavior was only related to subordinates' performance when the leader's behavior also was related to the subordinates' expectations that their effort would result in desired rewards. Thus, Evan's findings suggest that the major impact of a leader on the performance of subordinates is clarifying the path to desired rewards and making such rewards contingent on effective performance.[27]

The theory was developed to explain the effects of four specific kinds of leader behavior on (1) the job satisfaction of subordinates, (2) their acceptance of the leader, and (3) their expectations that effort will result in effective performance, which is the path to personal rewards. The four kinds of leader behavior are:

1. Directive leadership, which is characterized by a leader who lets subordinates know what is expected of them, maintains definite standards of performance, and asks that subordinates follow standard rules and regulations.

2. Supportive leadership, which is characterized by a friendly and approachable leader who displays concern for the well-being and needs of subordinates, and treats members as equals.

3. Participative leadership, which is characterized by a leader who consults with subordinates, asks for their suggestions, and seriously considers their input before making a decision.

4. Achievement-oriented leadership, which is characterized by a leader who sets challenging goals, expects subordinates to perform at their highest level, continuously seeks improved performance, and shows a high degree of confidence that members will assume responsibility, put forth effort, and accomplish challenging goals.

According to House and Mitchell, a number of studies suggest that the same leader can use different styles in various situations. For example, a leader may be directive toward group members in some instances, and be supportive or participative in others. This approach contrasts with the Fiedler model, which does not allow for a combination of leadership styles (by definition, a leader high on the LPC scale is task-oriented while a leader low on the scale is relationship-oriented).

The path-goal model involves two general propositions. The first: leader behavior is acceptable and satisfying to subordinates when they see such behavior as either an immediate source of satisfaction or as instrumental to future satisfaction.

The second: the leader's behavior will be motivational (will increase subordinate effort) when (1) it makes satisfaction of subordinates' needs contingent on effective performance, and (2) such behavior complements the environment of subordinates by providing coaching, guidance, support, and rewards which are necessary for effective performance.

---

27. *Ibid.*, p. 178.

These two propositions suggest that the leader's primary functions are to increase subordinates' motivation to perform, their satisfaction with the job, and their acceptance of the leader. According to previous research on the expectancy theory of motivation, the specific functions of the leader should consist of:

1. Recognizing and/or arousing subordinates' needs for outcomes over which the leader has some control.

2. Increasing personal rewards to subordinates for work-goal attainment.

3. Making the path to those rewards easier to travel, by coaching and direction.

4. Reducing frustrating barriers.

5. Increasing the opportunities for personal satisfaction contingent on effective performance.

How the leader determines which behavior will be most appropriate for performing the above functions depends on two factors: (a) subordinate characteristics, such as degree of authoritarianism, abilities, etc; and (b) environmental factors such as the task itself, formal authority system, and work groups. Because the model is still tentative, additional situational factors not yet identified may eventually help determine the effects of leader behavior.

House and Mitchell report that the model has been tested in a limited number of studies, and that the results provide considerable empirical support for their ideas. The results and their implications for practicing police managers are presented below.

Directive Leadership: This leadership style has been found to be positively related to the satisfaction and the expectancies of subordinates who work on ambiguous tasks, and to be negatively related to the satisfaction and the expectancies of subordinates who work on clear tasks. These findings have been supported in studies of seven organizations and are consistent with the predictions of the model. Apparently, when task demands are ambiguous, or when the organization procedures, rules, and policies are not clear, a leader who uses the direct style complements the tasks and the organization by providing the necessary guidance and psychological structure for group members. Such a situation might exist when a new officer is first assigned to patrol duty and is not familiar with certain aspects of the job, or when an individual is transferred to a job with different role responsibilities, (from patrol to a juvenile unit, for example). However, when task demands are clear to members, leader directiveness is felt to be a hindrance.

Supportive Leadership: The model hypothesizes that this leadership style will positively affect the satisfaction of subordinates who work on tasks which are stressful, frustrating, or dissatisfying (such as vice and narcotics control can be). This hypothesis has been tested in ten samples of employees; in only one of the studies was it disconfirmed. Despite some inconsistency in the research on supportive leadership, the evidence suggests that managers should be aware of the need for supportive leadership under such conditions.

Achievement-oriented Leadership: The model hypothesizes that this leadership style will cause subordinates to strive for higher standards of performance and to have more confidence in their ability to meet challenging goals. One recent unpublished study, which partially tested this hypothesis among white collar employees in service organizations, found that for subordinates performing ambiguous, non-repetitive tasks, the subordinates' confidence in their efforts depended on the leader's level of achievement orientation. Such a situation is likely to be found in medium- and large-size police agencies serving diverse populations, in which a high degree of discretion is applied and tasks are seldom repetitive.

Participative Leadership: After reviewing a number of recent studies, Mitchell concluded that this leadership style affects subordinate attitudes and performance in at least four ways.[28] First, through participation in decision-making, subordinates learn about what leads to what in the organization. From a path-goal point of view, this knowledge should lead to a greater clarity of the paths to various goals. Second, if subordinates participate in decisions about various goals, they generally select goals which they value highly. Therefore, participation should increase the integration between organizational and individual goals. Third, participation increases the members' control over what happens to them on the job. If their motivation is higher (as it should be according to the preceding two points), then having greater autonomy and ability to carry out their intentions should lead to increased effort and performance. Finally, under a participative style, pressure for high performance should come from sources other than just the leader or the organization. Because the decisions made are in some part their own, members tend to become more ego-involved. Their peers also know what is expected, and social pressure has a greater impact. Motivation to perform well is thus derived from a variety of internal and social factors as well as from formal external ones.

A number of studies have supported the idea that participation is motivational. Several studies have also suggested that subordinates who prefer autonomy and self-control respond more favorably to participative leadership, in terms of both satisfaction and performance, than do subordinates who do not have such preferences.[29] Furthermore, some evidence supports the following hypotheses:

1. When subordinates are highly ego-involved in a decision or a task, and the decision or task demands are ambiguous, participative leadership will have a positive effect on the satisfaction and motivation of the

28. Terrence R. Mitchell, "Motivation and Participation: An Integration," *Academy of Management Journal*, 16, 1973, p. 660-679.

29. See: Arnold S. Tannenbaum and Floyd H. Allport, "Personality Structure and Group Structure: An Interpretive Study of Their Relationship Through an Event-Structure Hypothesis," *Journal of Abnormal and Social Psychology*, 53, 1956, p. 272-280; and Victor H. Vroom, "Some Personality Determinants of the Effects of Participation," *Journal of Abnormal and Social Psychology*, 59, 1959, p. 322-327.

subordinate, regardless of the subordinate's predisposition toward self-control, authoritarianism, or need for autonomy.

2. When subordinates are not ego-involved in their tasks and the task demands are clear, subordinates who are not authoritarian and who have high needs for autonomy and self-control, will respond favorably to participative leadership, and their opposite personality types will respond less favorably.

In other words, in tasks or decisions which are ego-involving and relatively ambiguous, such as research and planning, employees (regardless of their personality characteristics) are more satisfied under participative leaders than non-participative leaders. However, in tasks or decisions which are less ego-involving and relatively clear, such as traffic enforcement, the amount of authoritarianism of subordinates affect the relationship between leadership style and satisfaction. Specifically, low-authoritarian subordinates are more satisfied under participative leaders than under non-participative leaders.

House and Mitchell's model is useful in understanding the effect of leadership behavior on subordinate satisfaction and motivation. The path-goal approach goes one step further than those approaches which attempt to match certain types of leaders with certain types of situations, such as the Fiedler model. The path-goal model not only suggests what type of style may be most effective in a given situation; it also attempts to explain *why* that type is most effective. If, in fact, a leader can apply different behavioral styles in different situations, the path-goal model could prove to be highly useful to police and other criminal justice agencies.

PARTICIPATIVE LEADERSHIP

Effective leadership is a function of the leader, the follower(s), and the situation. Therefore, as the contingency models suggest, there can be no single best leadership style for every situation. Nevertheless, it is often assumed that a Theory Y approach, (a participative or democratic style) is better than a Theory X approach (an authoritarian or autocratic style). Although each of the contingency models disproved this assumption, the nature of the managerial function has been tempered by general societal changes concerning organizations identified with the establishment. According to Tannenbaum and Schmidt:

Today's manager is more likely to deal with employees who resent being treated as subordinates, who may be highly critical of any organizational system, who expect to be consulted and to exert influence, and who often stand on the edge of alienation from the institution that needs their loyalty and commitment.[30]

With respect to this general employee view of organizations, Tannenbaum and Schmidt made several critical changes when they republished their

---

30. Tannenbaum and Schmidt, "How to Choose a Leadership Pattern," (May-June), 1973, *op. cit.*, p. 166.

article on the continuum model; one of the most important was their change in terminology for rank-and-file employees, from "subordinate" to "nonmanager", the difference is functional rather than hierarchical. In accord with Tannenbaum and Schmidt, this approach has been utilized throughout the text, as our definition of management provided in Chapter 1 implies that differences among employees are functional rather than hierarchical in nature.

With these thoughts, the following behavioral case study shows, not only how one individual uses a participative style of leadership, but also how he develops within others those values and conditions which lead to an effective participative style. Again, it must be stressed that this particular leadership style is not always appropriate, however, it is believed that most police organizations could benefit from this style of leadership to a far greater degree than they presently do.

MacGregor*

No question about it—some managers are better organized than others, but how often have you run into a really well organized manager—I mean *really* well organized? Not too often, I bet! In the course of my work I run into hundreds of managers a year, yet I can think of only one who managed to be super-organized—to the point where he had time to play an enormous amount of golf. As further proof of his organization, consider this: About two years after I ran into MacGregor, which incidentally is not his real name, he was promoted to the post of chief of operations at the corporate level—a fact I discovered when I saw his face looking out at me from the financial section of my newspaper above the announcement of his new executive assignment.

My encounter with MacGregor came about during the course of a study of the extent to which operating managers actually *use* participative management techniques in their dealings with subordinates. The problem with an inquiry of this nature is that nearly every manager either says he uses a participative approach (because isn't that what every good manager does?) or maybe honestly believes that this is his preferred *modus operandi;* in any event, what I was interested in was information about behavior, not about beliefs (pious or otherwise). So I had to develop an indirect approach for use with the managers being interviewed and follow it up with some questions directed at the subordinates they supervised. Accordingly, I developed a questionnaire that I used in interviewing more than 100 managers in ten major U.S. and Canadian firms. The first item on the questionnaire asked whether the interviewee held regular meetings with his subordinates; if so, how often; and what was the nature of the matters discussed. Finally, it tried to determine whether subordinates were offered the opportunity to initiate discussion and actively participate in the decision-making process or were merely afforded the opportunity to hear about decisions the boss had made.

---

* Source: Arthur Elliott Carlisle, "MacGregor," *Organizational Dynamics*, 5, Summer, 1976, pp. 50-56, 59-60.

MacGregor, who at the time was manager of one of the largest refineries in the country, was the last of more than 100 managers I interviewed in the course of the study. Although the interview had been scheduled in advance, the exact time had been left open; I was to call MacGregor at his office early in the week that I would be in the vicinity and set up a specific date and time.

Here's how that phone call went: The switchboard operator answered with the name of the refinery. When I asked for MacGregor's office, a male voice almost instantly said, "Hello," I then asked for MacGregor, whereupon the voice responded, "This is he." I should have recognized at once that this was no ordinary manager; he answered his own phone instantly, as though he had been waiting for it to ring. To my question about when it would be convenient for me to come see him, he replied, "Anytime." I said, "Would today be all right?" His response was, "Today, tomorrow, or Wednesday would be O.K.; or you could come Thursday, except don't come between 10:00 a.m. and noon; or you could come Friday or next week—anytime." I replied feebly, "I just want to fit in with your plans." Then he said, "You are just not getting the message; it makes no difference to me when you come. I have nothing on the books except to play golf and see you. Come in anytime—I don't have to be notified in advance, so I'll be seeing you one of these days," and he then hung up. I was dumbfounded. Here was a highly placed executive with apparently nothing to do except play golf and talk to visitors.

I took MacGregor at his word and drove over immediately to see him without any further announcement of my visit. MacGregor's office, in a small building at one corner of the refinery, adjoined that of his secretary—who, when I arrived, was knitting busily and, without dropping a stitch, said to me, "You must be Mr. Carlisle; he's in there," indicating MacGregor's office with a glance at a connecting door.

MacGregor's office was large and had a big window overlooking the refinery, a conference table with eight chairs arranged around it (one of which, at the head, was more comfortable and imposing than the rest), an engineer's file cabinet with a series of wide drawers, two easy chairs, a sofa, a coffee table with a phone on it, and a desk. The desk had been shoved all the way into a corner; there was no way a chair could be slipped in behind it, and it was covered with technical journals. A lamp stood on the desk, but its plug was not connected to an outlet. There was no phone on the desk. MacGregor, a tall, slender man with a tanned face, stood by the window peering absently into space. He turned slowly when I entered his office and said, "You must be Carlisle. The head office told me you wanted to talk to me about the way we run things here. Sit down on the sofa and fire away."

MacGregor's Modus Operandi.

"Do you hold regular meetings with your subordinates?" I asked.

"Yes, I do," he replied.

"How often?" I asked.

"Once a week, on Thursdays between 10:00 a.m. and noon: that's why I couldn't see you then," was his response.

"What sorts of things do you discuss?" I queried, following my interview guide.

"My subordinates tell me about the decisions they've made during the past week," he explained.

"Then you believe in participative decision-making," I commented.

"No—as a matter of fact, I don't," said MacGregor.

"Then why hold the meetings?" I asked. "Why not just tell your people about the operating decisions you've made and let them know how to carry them out?"

"Oh, I don't make their decisions for them and I just don't believe in participating in the decisions they should be making, either; we hold the weekly meetings so that I can keep informed on what they're doing and how. The meeting also gives me a chance to appraise their technical and managerial abilities," he explained. "I used to make all the operating decisions myself; but I quit doing that a few years ago when I discovered my golf game was going to hell because I didn't have enough time to practice. Now that I've quit making other people's decisions, my game is back where it should be."

"You don't make operating decisions any more?" I asked in astonishment.

"No," he replied. Sensing my incredulity, he added, "Obviously, you don't believe me. Why not ask one of my subordinates? Which one do you want to talk to?"

"I haven't any idea; I don't even know how many subordinates you have, let alone their names. You choose one," I suggested.

"No, I wouldn't do that—for two reasons. First, I don't make decisions, and second, when my subordinate confirms that I don't make decisions, you'll say that it's a put-up job, so here is a list of my eight immediate subordinates, the people who report directly to me. Choose one name from it and I'll call him and you can talk to him," said MacGregor.

"OK—Johnson, then. I'll talk to him if he's free," I said.

"I'm sure he's able to talk to you. I'll call him and tell him you're on the way over." Reaching for the phone, he determined that Johnson wasn't doing anything either, and would be happy to have someone to talk to.

Subordinate's View of MacGregor. I walked over to Johnson's unit and found him to be in his early thirties. After a couple minutes of casual conversation, I discovered that MacGregor and all eight of his subordinates were chemical engineers. Johnson said, "Suppose MacGregor gave you that bit about his not making decisions, didn't he? That man is a gas."

"It isn't true, though, is it? He does make decisions, doesn't he?" I asked.

"No, he doesn't; everything he told you is true. He simply decided not to get involved in decisions that his subordinates are being paid to make. So he stopped making them, and they tell me he plays a lot of golf in the time he saves," said Johnson.

Then I asked Johnson whether he tried to get MacGregor to make a decision and his response was:

"Only once. I had been on the job for only about a week when I ran into an operating problem I couldn't solve, so I phoned MacGregor. He answered the phone with that sleepy 'Hello' of his. I told him who I was and that I had a problem. His response was instantaneous: 'Good, that's what you're being paid to do, solve problems,' and then he hung up. I was dumbfounded. I didn't really know any of the people I was working with, so because I didn't think I had any other alternative, I called him back, got the same sleepy 'Hello,' and again identified myself. He replied sharply, 'I thought I told you that you were paid to solve problems? Do you think that I should do your job as well as my own?' When I insisted on seeing him about my problem, he answered, 'I don't know how you expect me to help you. You have a technical problem and I don't go into the refinery any more; I used to, but my shirts kept getting dirty from the visits and my wife doesn't like washing all the grime out of them, so I pretty much stick in my office. Ask one of the other men. They're all in touch with what goes on out there.'

"I didn't know which one to consult, so I insisted again on seeing him. He finally agreed—grudgingly—to see me right away, so I went over to his office and there he was in his characteristic looking-out-the-window posture. When I sat down, he started the dirty-shirt routine—but when he saw that I was determined to involve him in my problems, he sat down on the sofa in front of his coffee table and, pen in hand, prepared to write on a pad of paper. He asked me to state precisely what the problem was and he wrote down exactly what I said. Then he asked what the conditions for its solution were. I replied that I didn't know what he meant by that question. His response was, 'If you don't know what conditions have to be satisfied for a solution to be reached, how do you know when you've solved the problem?' I told him I'd never thought of approaching a problem that way and he replied, 'Then you'd better start. I'll work through this one with you *this* time, but don't expect me to do your problem solving for you because that's *your* job, not mine.'

I stumbled through the conditions that would have to be satisfied by the solution. Then he asked me what alternative approaches I could think of. I gave him the first one I could think of—let's call it X—and he wrote it down and asked me what would happen if I did X. I replied with my answer—let's call it A. Then he asked me how A compared with the conditions I had established for the solution of the problem. I replied that it did not meet them. MacGregor told me that I'd have to think of another. I came up with Y, which I said would yield B, and this still fell short of the solution conditions. After more prodding from MacGregor, I came up with Z, which I said would have C as a result; although this clearly came a lot closer to the conditions I had established for the solution than any of the others I'd suggested, it still did not satisfy all of them. MacGregor then asked me if I could combine any of the approaches I'd suggested. I replied I could do X and Z and then saw that the resultant A plus C would indeed satisfy all the solution conditions I had set up previously. When I thanked MacGregor, he replied, 'What for? Get the hell out of my office; you could have done that bit of problem solving perfectly well without wasting my time. Next time you really can't solve a problem on your own, ask the Thursday man and tell me about it at the Thursday meeting.'

I asked Johnson about Mr. MacGregor's reference to the Thursday man.

"He's the guy who runs the Thursday meeting when MacGregor is away from the plant. I'm the Thursday man now. My predecessor left here about two months ago."

"Where did he go? Did he quit the company?" I asked.

"God, no. He got a refinery of his own. That's what happens to a lot of Thursday men. After the kind of experience we get coping with everyone's problems and MacGregor's refusal to do what he perceives as his subordinates' work, we don't need an operating superior any more and we're ready for our own refineries. Incidentally, most of the people at our level have adopted MacGregor's managerial method in dealing with the foremen who report to us and we are reaping the same kinds of benefits that he does. The foremen are a lot more self-reliant, and we don't have to do their work for them."

I went back to see MacGregor. His secretary was still knitting. The garment she was working on was considerably more advanced than it was on my first visit. She motioned me into MacGregor's office with her head, again not dropping a stitch. MacGregor was in his traditional office posture, looking vacantly out of the window. He turned and asked, "Well, now do you believe that I don't make any decisions?"

I said, "No, that could have been just a fluke." He suggested I see another subordinate and asked me to pick another name from the list. I picked Peterson who, when phoned to see whether he was available, said that he had nothing to do. So I went to Peterson's office.

Peterson was in his late twenties. He asked me what I thought of MacGregor. I said I found him most unusual. Peterson replied, "Yes, he's a gas." Peterson's story paralleled Johnson's. MacGregor refused to make decisions related to the work of his subordinates. When Peterson got into a situation he could not deal with, he said he called one of the other supervisors, usually Johnson, and together they worked it out. At the Thursday meetings, he reported on the decision and gave credit to his helper. "If I hadn't," he added, "I probably wouldn't get help from that quarter again."

In reply to a query on what the Thursday meetings were like, he said, "Well, we all sit around that big conference table in MacGregor's office. He sits at the head like a thinned-down Buddha, and we go around the table talking about the decisions we've made, and if we got help, who helped us. The other guys occasionally make comments—especially if the particular decision being discussed was like one they had had to make themselves at some point or if it had some direct effect on their own operations." MacGregor had said very little at these past few meetings, according to Peterson, but he did pass on any new developments that he heard about at the head office.

Head-Office Assessment of MacGregor. By the time I had finished with Johnson and Peterson, it was time for lunch. I decided I'd go downtown and stop at the head office to try to find out their assessment of MacGregor and his operation. I visited the operations chief for the corporation. I had wanted to thank him for his willingness to go along with my study, anyway. When I told him I had met MacGregor, his immediate response was, "Isn't he a gas?" I muttered something about having heard that comment before and asked him about the efficiency of MacGregor's operation in comparison with that of other refineries in the corporation. His response was instantaneous. "Oh, MacGregor has by far the most efficient producing unit."

"Is that because he has the newest equipment?" I asked.

"No, as a matter of fact he has the oldest in the corporation. His was the first refinery we built."

"Does MacGregor have a lot of turnover among his subordinates?"

"A great deal," he replied.

Thinking I had found a chink in the MacGregor armor, I asked, "What happens to them; can't they take his system?"

"On the contrary," said the operations chief, "Most of them go on to assignments as refinery managers. After all, under MacGregor's method of supervision, they are used to working on their own."

More Pointers on MacGregor's Style of Managing. "How do they run their own operations—like MacGregor's?" I asked.

"You guessed it. More and more of our operations are using his system."

I went back to the refinery with a few last questions for MacGregor. His secretary had made considerable progress on her knitting and her boss had resumed his position by the refinery window.

"I understand you were downtown. What did they tell you about this place?"

"You know damn well what they said—that you have the most efficient operation in the corporation."

"Yup, it's true," he replied, with no pretense at false modesty. "Periodically, I get chances to go to work for another major oil company—but I've gotten things so well organized here that I really don't want to take on a job like the one I faced when I cam here five years ago. I guess I'll hang on here until something better comes up."

"Let me ask you a couple of questions about the Thursday meeting," I continued. "First of all, I understand that when you are away, the 'Thursday man' takes over. How do you choose the individual to fill this slot?"

"Oh, that's simple. I just pick the man who is most often referred to as the one my subordinates turn to for help in dealing with their problems. Then I try him out in this assignment when I'm off. It's good training and, if he proves he can handle it, I know I have someone to propose for any vacancies that may occur at the refinery manager level. The head-office people always contact me for candidates. As a matter of fact, the Thursday-man assignment is sought after. My subordinates compete with each other in helping anyone with a problem because they know they'll get credit for their help at the Thursday meeting. You know, another development has been that jobs on the staff of this refinery are highly prized by young people who want to get ahead in the corporation; when junior management positions open up here, there are always so many candidates that I often have a tough time making a choice."

"Sounds logical," I said. "Now let me focus a bit more on your role as refinery manager. You say you don't make decisions. Suppose a subordinate told you at a Thursday meeting about a decision he'd made and you were convinced that it was a mistake. What would you do about it?"

"How much would the mistake cost me?"

"Oh, I don't know," I answered.

"Can't tell you, then. It would depend on how much it would cost."

"Say, $3,000," I suggested.

"That's easy; I'd let him make it," said MacGregor. I sensed I'd hit the upper limit before MacGregor either would have moved in himself or, more likely, would have suggested that the subordinate discuss it with the Thurs-day man and then report back to him on their joint decision.

"When was the last time you let a subordinate make a mistake of that magnitude?" I asked skeptically.

"About four weeks ago," said MacGregor.

"You let someone who works for you make such a serious mistake? Why did you do that?"

"Three reasons," said MacGregor. "First, I was only 99.44 percent sure that it would be a mistake and if it hadn't turned out to be one, I'd have felt pretty foolish. Second, I thought that making a mistake like this would be such a tremendous learning experience for him that he'd never make another like that again. I felt it would do him more good than signing him up for some of the management-development courses that are available. Third, this is a profit center. It was early in the budget year and I felt that we could afford it."

"What was the result?" I asked.

"It *was* a mistake—and I heard about it in short order from the controller downtown by phone." (I realized suddenly during the whole time I had been in the office, neither MacGregor's phone nor his secretary's had rung.)

"The controller said, 'MacGregor, how could you let a stupid mistake like that last one slip through?' "

"What did you say?"

"Well, I figured a good attack is the best defense. I asked him which refinery in the corporation was the most efficient. He replied, 'You know yours is. That has nothing to do with it.' I told him that it had everything to do with it. I added that my people learn from their mistakes and until the rest of the plants in the organization started operating at the same degree of efficiency as this one, I wasn't going to waste my time talking to clerks. Then I hung up."

"What happened?"

"Well, relations were a bit strained for a while—but they know I'm probably the best refinery manager in the business and I can get another job anytime, so it blew over pretty quickly," he said, not without a degree of self-satisfaction.

Uniqueness of MacGregor. MacGregor was unique among the managers I interviewed in the course of my study. Presumably his approach was a distinct possibility for each of the refinery managers I talked to, and certainly with adaptations it could have been used by many of the 100 executives I interviewed—but it wasn't. He had taken management by objectives to its logical limits by concentrating his efforts on formulating and negotiating objectives and had divorced himself from direct involvement in solving problems his subordinates came upon in carrying out their responsibilities.

MacGregor's frequency of regularly scheduled meetings with his subordinates was typical of the managers interviewed in the study; 10 percent met less frequently and about 5 percent more often. But his focus on discussion of completed decisions was unique. Slightly less than three-quarters of the executives with whom I talked saw the purpose of their meetings as a combination of information communication and problem solving; the balance were split evenly between a primary focus on communication of information and a primary emphasis on problem solving. Interestingly, the majority of those who emphasized problem solving were refinery executives.

When describing the degree of reliance they placed on the contributions made by subordinates in the determination of final decisions, half of the managers felt that it was considerable, a quarter that it was heavy, and the balance that it was either not too significant or that it varied with the individuals involved. Only MacGregor left the actual decision making (except in rare circumstances) to the subordinates themselves.

All of the managers, except MacGregor, either stated explicitly or made it clear during the course of the interviews that all important decisions arrived at in these meetings were made by themselves. They received suggestions, considered their sources, and either compared the proffered solutions with solutions they have developed on their own, or considered them carefully before reaching a final solution. In using this approach to group decision making, the managers were obviously manifesting their deeply held convictions that one of the key responsibilities of an upper-level executive is to act as chief decision maker for those who report to him. They believed that, after all, the superior is ultimately responsible for the quality of the decisions made in his organization and the only way to carry out this task is to become directly involved in the decision-making process itself.

Most of the managers I have encountered—both organizational superiors and outside managers involved in the studies I've conducted or the consulting assignments I've carried out—pride themselves on the extent to which they invite their subordinates to participate in organizational decision making; but their perceptions of this process and its organizational impact often differ sharply from those of the subordinates involved. For many of the latter, the participative management routine is just that—a routine acted out by the boss because it evidences his espousal of a technique that is supposed to increase the likelihood that subordinates will accept and commit themselves to decisions; he may even believe the decisions were jointly determined. However, most participative management is seen by lower-level participants as, at worst, a manipulative device and at best an opportunity for them to avoid decision-making responsibility and assure that if a wrong solution is reached, the boss himself was a party to the decision.

MacGregor avoided this trap by refusing to give managers reporting to him the opportunity to second-guess the solution he would be most likely to choose. Although he allowed himself some margin in case emergency action on his part should become inevitable, he made it clear that he wanted to hear about problems only after they had been solved and about decisions only after they had been made.

SUMMARY

This chapter has emphasized Davis's definition of leadership: "the ability to persuade others to seek objectives enthusiastically." The ability to lead thus requires more than simply holding a particular rank within an agency. Police and other criminal justice organizations must pay careful attention to what constitutes effective leadership, because the quality of leadership often determines whether or not an organization will successfully attain its goals.

Early leadership research concentrated on defining the traits or characteristics possessed by leaders. The findings were contradictory; some studies found that certain traits consistently differentiated leaders (successful managers) from nonleaders (unsuccessful managers), while other studies failed to isolate any trait differences between leaders and nonleaders. Although trait theory was only the starting point for leadership research, it may become increasingly important as attempts are made to identify effective leadership traits related to specific organizational settings.

In a second approach to the study of effective leadership, the behavior patterns or styles of leaders are directly observed. The Ohio State studies are perhaps the most extensive inquiry into behavioral leadership. The Leader Behavior Description Questionnaire (LBDQ) was developed to measure leadership patterns; findings indicated that subordinates preferred one type of leader (considerate) while the leader's superiors preferred another type (structure), thus creating a role conflict. Some evidence suggested that a leader who ranks simultaneously high on both dimensions could resolve this conflict. It was pointed out, however, that this style over-simplifies the dynamics of leader behavior; it was concluded that no single behavioral style is effective, regardless of the situation. Effective leadership depends on various individual and organizational factors: the leader, the follower(s), and the situation. Using these situational factors, Kerr *et.al.* developed two general propositions which significantly influence the relationships between initiating structure and consideration and employee satisfaction, morale, and performance.

The contingency approach to leader effectiveness suggests that there must be a "fit" between the leader's traits and behavior, on the one hand, and the particular situation, on the other. Compared with the other theories discussed, contingency theory appears to be the most useful for predicting appropriate leadership behaviors within diverse police organizations. The Tannenbaum and Schmidt continuum model depicts various leadership styles based on the amount of authority exercised by managers over nonmanagers. By considering numerous environmental factors, the leader can determine which of the continuum styles will be the most effective in the situation at hand. The Fiedler model, which determines leader style on the basis of one's least preferred coworker (LPC), predicts that a leader's effectiveness can be improved by "engineering" the situation to fit a particular style; leader performance depends as much on the organization as it does on the leader. The third major contingency model is based on the expectancy theory of motivation. According to House's path-goal model, leader behavior can improve group member performance when the behavior clarifies and/or clears the path to desired rewards, and makes such rewards contingent on effective performance.

Finally, a case study presented a particular leadership style (participative). Although this style is not the most efficient under all conditions, it could be useful to practicing police managers in many situations, especially because of societal changes in attitude concerning organizations identified with the establishment.

DISCUSSION QUESTIONS

1. All managers are leaders; agree or disagree with this statement and provide a supporting example.

2. Discuss the strengths and weaknesses of the trait approach to leadership.

3. Define the two propositions, identified by Keir *et. al.*, which are useful in synthesizing the initiating structure-consideration literature, and discuss several implications for police management with respect to each.

4. Describe the three interdependent forces which the Tannenbaum and Schmidt contingency leadership model suggests should be considered when selecting a leadership style.

5. Discuss the unique approach of the Fiedler contingency model of leadership and how it may be used in a police organization.

6. Describe the path-goal model of contingency leadership and how it suggests that a leader's behavior is motivating; do you agree or disagree? Why?

7. With respect to the leadership case study on MacGregor, explain why you feel such a leadership style would or would not be helpful in police organizations; give specific examples where appropriate.

ANNOTATED BIBLIOGRAPHY

Cribben, James J., *Effective Managerial Leadership*, (New York: American Management Association, 1972). This book presents an overview of the major theories of leadership and interprets these theories for practicing managers.

Fiedler, Fred E., *A Theory of Leadership Effectiveness*, (New York: McGraw-Hill, 1967). The first comprehensive contingency model for leadership which attempts to specify the conditions under which a particular leadership style is the most conducive to group effectiveness; the research indicated that the job should be engineered to fit the leader.

Ghiselli, Edwin E., *Exploration in Managerial Talent*, (Pacific Palisades, Calif.: Goodyear, 1971). One of the recent works on the trait approach to the study of effective leadership; findings in many different organizations suggested that several attributes (supervisory ability, occupational achievement, intelligence, etc.) are significantly related to both a manager's level and ratings of performance.

House, Robert J., "A Path-Goal Theory of Leader Effectiveness," *Administrative Science Quarterly*, 16, 1971, p. 321-338. This contingency model is based on the expectancy theory of motivation and suggests that a leader's behavior is motivating to the degree that it increases group member goal attainments by clarifying paths to those goals.

Kerr, Steven, Chester A. Schriesheim, Charles J. Murphy and Ralph M. Stogdill, "Toward a Contingency Theory of Leadership Based Upon the Consideration and Initiating Structure Literature," *Organizational Behavior and Human Performance*, 12, 1974, p. 62-82. This article reviews the literature involving the leader dimensions of initiating structure and consideration and develops several situational propositions of leader effectiveness, thus taking into account situational variables which the Ohio State Leadership Studies failed to do.

Stogdill, Ralph M., and Alvin E. Coons, eds., *Leader Behavior: Its Description and Measurement*, Research Monograph No. 88, (Columbus, Ohio: Bureau of Business Research, The Ohio State Univ., 1957). The most comprehensive of the behavioral leadership studies; the research developed two separate and distinct dimensions of leader behavior: initiating structure and consideration.

Tannenbaum, Robert, and Warren H. Schmidt, "How to Choose a Leadership Pattern," *Harvard Business Review*, (May-June), 1973, p. 162-180. The authors identify a continuum of possible leadership styles based on the degree of authority exercised by a manager with respect to the amount of freedom exercised by non-managers; the selection of the most effective style is contingent on three variables: forces in the leader, the followers, and the situation.

EIGHT

Organizational Design: Major Influences

LEARNING OBJECTIVES

The study of this chapter should enable you to:

☑ Review the relationships among organizational members which are consistent with the classical pyramidal design.

☑ Describe several different organizational classifications and discuss how various criminal justice agencies may fall within each classification scheme.

☑ Describe three different types of police agencies, based on policing styles (Wilson), and four types of correctional agencies, based on change strategies (Duffee).

☑ Describe the research design of the Burns-Stalker study and differentiate between mechanistic and organic managerial systems.

☑ Describe the research design of the Woodward studies (including complexity of technologies) and their general conclusions.

☑ Explain the relevance of considering the mean level and degree of dispersion of employee skill and ability levels when determining an organization's design.

☑ Explain the relevance of considering the needs and personality traits of employees when determining an organization's design.

☑ Define the concepts of centralization and decentralization and give an example of each.

☑ Differentiate between tall and flat organizational hierarchies.

☑ Define at least eight organizational characteristics which may be used to distinguish between organic and mechanistic systems.

EIGHT

The last chapter dealt with leadership styles and their effect on individual and group behavior; this chapter examines the major influences which have an effect on the design of police organizations, and how these agencies may be structured to meet the needs of both the organization and its membership. In terms of *organizational design,* we are concerned with the particular arrangements and relationships of the formal structural factors or components which make up the organization.

The need for objective and scientific analysis of organization design within the criminal justice field has largely been ignored. It has generally been assumed, for instance, that a para-military or multi-leveled hierarchical structure is satisfactory for most police agencies. This classical pyramidal design is shown in Figure 8-1; the relationships of organizational members are presumed to follow this structure. As a result:

1. Nearly all contacts take the form of orders going *down,* and reports of results going *up* the pyramid.

2. Each subordinate must receive instructions and orders from only one boss.

3. Important decisions are made at the top of the pyramid.

4. Superiors have a limited "span of control," that is, they supervise only a limited number of individuals.

5. Individuals at any level (except at the top and bottom) have contact only with their boss above them and their subordinates below them.[1]

In the discussion which follows, it will be shown that many of the simplistic, classical prescriptions which have been applied to police organization design are clearly inadequate. According to Lawrence and Lorsch:

During the past few years there has been evident a new trend in the study of organizational phenomena. Underlying this new approach is the idea that the internal functioning of organizations mut be consistent with the demands of the organization task, technology, or external environment, and the needs of its members if the organization is to be effective. Rather than searching for the panacea of the one best way to organize under all conditions, investigators have more and more tended to examine the functioning of organizations in relation to the needs of their particular members and the external pressures facing them. Basically, this approach seems to be leading to the development of a "contingency" theory of organization with the

---

1. Leonard R. Sayles and George Strauss; *Human Behavior in Organizations,* (Englewood Cliffs, New Jersey: Prentice-Hall, 1966), p. 349.

appropriate internal states and processes of the organization contingent upon external requirements and members needs.[2]

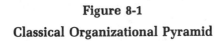

Figure 8-1
Classical Organizational Pyramid

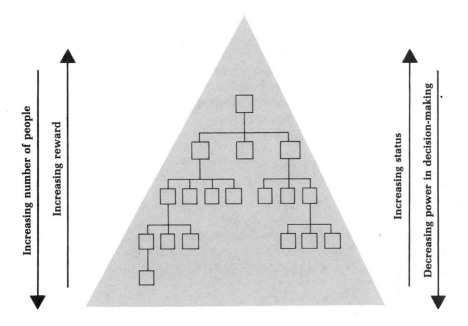

Source: Leonard R. Sayles and George Strauss, *Human Behavior in Organizations,* (Englewood Cliffs, New Jersey: Prentice-Hall, 1966), p. 349.

This chapter will present the major classification schemes of organizations, factors which affect the designs of organizations, and, finally, the contingency approach as applied to organization design.

ORGANIZATION CLASSIFICATIONS

There are really no right or wrong ways to classify organizations. However, one of the most salient schemes (related to much of the discussion in Chapter 4) has been suggested by Parsons, who states that "organizations may in the first instance be classified in terms of the *type of goal or function* about which they are organized."[3] Parsons describes four major types of organizations:

---

2. Jay W. Lorsch and Paul R. Lawrence, *Studies in Organization Design,* (Homewood, Ill.: Irwin, and Dorsey Press, 1970), p. 1.

3. Talcott Parsons, *Structure and Process in Modern Societies,* (New York: Free Press, 1960), p. 45.

1. Organizations oriented to economic production primarily include business firms which engage in the production—understood in the full economic sense as "adding value"—of goods and services. Although their basic function is economic, there may be other goals which the organization must realize if it is to be well integrated in the society.

2. Organizations oriented to political goals are directed toward the attainment of valued goals and to the creation and distribution of power in the society. These include most governmental organizations.

3. Integrative organizations are concerned with the adjustment of conflicts and the direction of motivation to the fulfillment of institutionalized expectations. This would include the court system and legal profession [as well as the police and correctional systems].

4. Pattern-maintenance organizations whose principle functions are cultural, educational, and expressive. Primary examples include schools and churches.[4]

A major problem in classifying organizations is that of overlap. For example, criminal justice agencies, because of their multiple goals, may have characteristics of both the second and third categories above rather than falling strictly within the limits of the third.

With respect to two other influential means of classifying organizations, criminal justice organizations may again overlap or fall within more than a single category. Etzioni classified organizations according to the kinds of power brought to bear on lower echelon personnel. This use of power can result in three *compliance patterns*, which provide a basis for differentiating three kinds of organizations:

1. Coercive organizations which use force as a primary control method. These organizations tend to alienate the coerced lower level members; examples include custodial mental hospitals, and most prisons and correctional institutions.

2. Utilitarian organizations use salaries as a means of control; lower-level members have calculative involvement. Examples would include most business and governmental organizations.

3. Normative organizations use moral control to influence members who are willingly involved and highly motivated. Examples include churches, voluntary associations, and many political parties.[5]

Blau and Scott have suggested four types of organizations, based on *who benefits* from them:

1. Mutual-benefit organizations of which the prime beneficiary is the membership. Examples include labor unions, private country clubs and most professional associations.

2. Business concerns of which the owners are the prime beneficiaries.

3. Service organizations of which the clients are the prime beneficiary. Examples include universities, hospitals, delinquent reformatories and most social agencies.

---

4. *Ibid.,* pp. 45-47.

5. Amatai Etzioni, *A Comparative Analysis of Complex Organizations,* (New York: The Free Press, 1961), pp. 23-67.

4. Commonwealth organizations of which the public at large is the prime beneficiary. Examples include law enforcement agencies, penal institutions, post office and state hospitals.[6]

Organizations can obviously be classified in a number of ways, but the practicing manager must remember that the fundamental basis for each classification scheme will vitally affect the design of the organization. Under Parsons' scheme, for example, the organization's primary function(s) in society is a factor which will help shape its design. In other words, even though not all police agencies are alike, they are all concerned with preserving the peace and assisting citizens, as opposed to manufacturing automobiles or selling insurance. However, among criminal justice organizations differences exist with respect to goal emphasis and operational techniques.

Police departments, for instance, have different styles of operation. James Q. Wilson, after observing eight communities, noted three distinct styles of policing: watchmen, service, and legalistic.[7] The *watchman* style of police organization emphasizes an order-maintenance approach to policing; officers use the law "more as a means of maintaining order than regulating conduct, and judge the requirements of order differently depending on the character of the group in which the infraction occurs." Officers also judge "the seriousness of infractions less by what the law says about them than by their immediate and personal consequences."[8] Many minor or misdemeanant violations are thus ignored. At the opposite end of the organization style continuum is the *legalistic* approach, under which police officers are encouraged to see every situation from a legal point of view. The police act as if there were "a single standard of community conduct—that which the law prescribes." Many traffic citations are issued and misdemeanant violations result in arrest, "even when the public order has not been breached."[9] Members of the *service* style organization, on the other hand, view all situations seriously (unlike the watchman style), but do not apply formal sanctions or make arrests as frequently as would happen under the legalistic style; "This style is often found in homogeneous, middle-class communities in which there is a high level of apparent agreement among citizens of the need for and definition of public order but in which there is no administrative demand for a legalistic style."[10]

The point of this discussion is that the *style* of policing emphasized by each particular agency will most likely require a different type of organization design. The watchman style organization, for instance, requires broad discretion by its members, and would therefore need a more flexible and less structured design than would the legalistic style organization.

---

6. Peter M. Blau and Richard Scott, *Formal Organizations: A Comparative Approach*, (San Francisco: Changler Publishing Company, 1962).

7. James Q. Wilson, *Varieties of Police Behavior*, (New York: Atheneum, 1974).

8. *Ibid.*, pp. 140-141.

9. *Ibid.*, pp. 172.

10. *Ibid.*, pp. 200.

Correctional agencies may be differentiated by using a continuum similar to that used with police agencies. Duffee has categorized prisons into four typologies based on *change strategies:* [11]

1. Restraint, in which no change strategy is involved. Correction is viewed as a "warehousing" of inmates; the primary goal is retribution where the offender is sent off to prison as a punishment for wrongdoing.

2. Reform, in which the change strategy is one of compliance; people are "molded" into different behavior reactions according to a well established set of rules with rewards and punishments freely administered. Correction is viewed as general deterrence, the primary goal is to deter the offender as well as others from committing future crimes.

3. Rehabilitation, in which the change strategy is one of identification; people change through a manipulation of intrapersonal and interpersonal relationships. The inmates are allowed considerable freedom to express themselves and develop their feelngs within the institution. The primary goal of correction is viewed as rehabilitation.

4. Reintegration, in which the change strategy is internalization; people change as they discover and test alternate behavior patterns congruent with their values and beliefs. This approach does not correspond to traditional legislative and judicial goals because it treats criminal deviance as an interactive process that requires changes in both the individual and the system of criminal justice, and also in the external community. The inmate's view of themselves is recognized and respected, and alternate means of achieving goals are presented and tested as substitutes for previous criminal methods.

Regardless of which strategy seems most appropriate, the last two approaches require a more flexible organization design than the first two. Consequently, when analyzing the designs of criminal justice organizations, one must realize that functional emphases and operational techniques may vary. In other words, separate organizational characteristics must be taken into account, and no single "best design" exists for police, court, or correctional agencies.

FACTORS AFFECTING DESIGN

This section discusses relevant external and internal influences which need to be considered when designing criminal justice organizations. With respect to the external environment, two classic studies are reviewed which indicate the significant impact of environmental conditions (stability/instability) on an organization's structure. With respect to internal factors, several employee characteristics are analyzed in regard to their affect on the proper design of police agencies.

---

11.   David Duffee, *Correctional Policy and Prison Organization,* (New York: Sage Publications, 1975), pp. 72-74.

External Influences

Burns-Stalker Study. In the early 1960's, Tom Burns and G. M. Stalker attempted to determine what type of design and management practices were appropriate for different environmental conditions.[12] The investigators, using in-depth interviews, comprehensively studied a number of manufacturing firms in Scotland and England. Several of these firms, accustomed to stable technology and organizational environments, were attempting to move into a field (electronics) with a rapidly changing technology and environment. The investigators hypothesized that different managerial systems would be used, depending on whether or not a firm was operating in a stable environment or a rapidly changing, unstable environment. The findings led the researchers to differentiate between two types of managerial systems: *mechanistic*, which appeared most appropriate to stable environments, and *organic*, which appeared most appropriate to unstable, constantly changing environments.

The mechanistic system was characterized by a rigidly defined organization structure, with hierarchical control, authority, and communication. Methods, duties, and powers attached to each functional role are precisely determined. Interactions within the management system tend to be vertical in nature; that is, between superior and subordinate. "Management, often visualized as the complex hierarchy familiar to organizational charts, operates a simple control system, with information flowing up through a succession of filters, and decisions and instructions flowing downward through a succession of amplifiers."[13]

By contrast, the organic managerial system was characterized by a relatively flexible organization structure. Such a system is adaptable to unstable conditions in which problems arise that cannot be distributed among specialized roles within a clearly defined hierarchy. "Jobs lose much of their formal definition in terms of methods, duties, and powers, which have to be redefined continually by interaction with others participating in a task. Interaction runs laterally as much as vertically. Communication between people of different tasks tend to resemble lateral consultation rather than vertical command."[14]

From these descriptions, it is apparent that the mechanistic system tends to follow classical theory, more specifically, a "bureaucracy," (as discussed in Chapter 2). The organic system, on the other hand, tends to follow human relations theory, as it stresses less formal relationships and structures. Burns and Stalker carefully noted that neither design is superior to the other under all circumstances. Although the organic style may appear the most desirable, the authors insist that the nature of the environment must be taken into

---

12. Tom Burns and G. M. Stalker, *The Management of Innovation,* (London: Tavistock, 1961).
13. *Ibid.,* p. 5.
14. *Ibid.,* pp. 5-6.

account; although the organic system appears superior in a changing environment, "nothing in our experience justifies the assumption that mechanistic systems should be superseded by organic in conditions of stability."[15]

Woodward Studies. The studies reported by Joan Woodward focused on the relationship between technology and organization design.[16] Woodward and her associates extensively researched the formal structures and operating procedures of 100 industrial firms in southeast England; research methods included case studies, surveys, and longitudinal analyses. The firms were classified as being one of three types, according to the complexity of their technologies: (1) unit or small batch (production of single items—the least complex); (2) mass production or large batch (assembly lines); and (3) continuous process production (chemicals—the most complex). Results indicated a strong relationship among technology, structure, and organizational success.

The findings revealed that organizational characteristics of successful firms in each production category tended to "cluster around the medians" for that particular category, while the same characteristics for less successful firms clustered at the extremes of the range. For example, successful firms in each category tended to display a certain number of vertical levels of management, or a certain span of control size for first-line supervisors, while the less successful firms tended to have either too many or too few levels of management, and too large or too small a span of control for their type of technology. Table 8-1 illustrates the pattern for span of control size in the "above average" and the "below average" firms.

According to the figures in Table 8-1, a first line-supervisor in a successful unit firm was responsible for 23 subordinates; in a successful mass firm for 49 subordinates; and in a successful process firm for 13 subordinates. Such results clearly indicate that environmental influences must be considered before proper organizational characteristics and overall design can be determined. The findings strongly refute the concept of universality of managerial principles advocated by the administrative theorists. As the reader may recall, one such theorist (Urwick) had concluded that, with respect to the span of control, ". . . no superior can supervise directly the work of more than five or, at the most, six subordinates whose work interlocks."

The Woodward team also found that the operational procedures of the firms varied according to type of technology. Woodward uses the organic-mechanistic differentiation of Burns and Stalker to explain this:

There was a tendency for organic management systems to predominate in the production categories at the extremes of the technical scale, while mechanistic systems predominated in the middle ranges. Clear-cut definition of duties and responsibilities was characteristic of firms in the middle ranges [mass or large-batch], while flexible organization with a high degree of delegation both of authority and with

---

15. *Ibid.*, p. 125.

16. Joan Woodward, *Management and Technology*, (London: H.M. Stationary Office, 1958); *Industrial Organization: Theory and Practice*, (London: Oxford Univ. Press, 1965).

permissive and participating management, was characteristic of firms at the extremes [unit or small-batch and continuous]. [17]

Additionally, those firms which were most successful tended not to deviate from the above pattern. Those firms at the extremes, which used a flexible, human relations approach, were more successful than those firms which followed a highly rigid, classical management style. Conversely, mass-production firms which emphasized a mechanistic style were more successful than those using an organic style.

Table 8-1

Average Span of Control of First-Line Supervisors
Analyzed by Business Success

| Production system | Number of people controlled: | | | | | | | | | | | |
	Less than 10	11 to 20	21 to 30	31 to 40	41 to 50	51 to 60	61 to 70	71 to 80	81 to 90	Un-classi-fied	Median	Total
Unit and small batch:												
All firms	1	6	8	4	3	1	—	—	—	1	23	24
'Above average' in success	—	—	4	1	—	—	—	—	—	—		5
'Below average' in success	1	1	—	—	2	1	—	—	—	—		5
Large batch and mass:												
All firms	—	1	2	5	9	4	5	1	3	1	49	31
'Above average' in success	—	—	—	—	3	2	—	—	—	—		5
'Below average' in success	—	1	1	1	—	—	—	1	2	—		6
Process:												
All firms	6	12	5	2	—	—	—	—	—	—	13	25
'Above average' in success	1	5	—	—	—	—	—	—	—	—		6
'Below average' in success	1	—	1	2	—	—	—	—	—	—		4

Source: Joan Woodward, *Industrial Organization: Theory and Practice,* (London: Oxford Univ. Press,), p. 69.

The Woodward findings support the conclusions drawn by Burns and Stalker. Both studies have been influential in the development of contingency theory; one writer suggests that the Woodward study is "as important to the contingency approach to management as the Hawthorne study is to the behaviorial approach to management. It was a pioneering effort that could be considered the beginning of contingency management."[18] Although both studies involved industrial organizations,

---

17. *Ibid., Industrial Organization*, p. 64.

18. Fred Luthans, *Introduction to Management: A Contingency Approach,* (New York: McGraw-Hill, 1976), p. 42.

the characteristics of the external environment are crucial to the design of any organization, whether private or public. To provide one example:

Surely, a federal agency set up in the 1960's to deal with some aspect of modern urban problems faces a more turbulent and changing environment than, say, a unit created many years ago to deal with problems that have gradually receded or at least stabilized over time. This difference, in turn, can be assumed to have an effect on the basic outlines of the agency's structure and operating design. The point is that the dimensions of environmental simplicity-complexity and stability-change can affect all comparisons of organization design, regardless of whether the system is producing a product for profit or a service for the general welfare.[19]

The above studies have important implications for police managers and their organizations. Because police agencies operate in unstable, constantly changing environments (made up of changing community demands and needs, changing laws and ordinances, and changing political influences), highly rigid, para-military structures do not allow the flexibility needed in order to adapt to these changing conditions. It appears that these agencies must become more flexible (organic) in their designs if they are to adapt to the shifting demands of their external environments and adequately serve the needs of their communities. An organization with a highly mechanistic structure cannot adequately function in an unstable and dynamic environment.

Internal Influences

The previous discussion involved the effects of external factors on organization design. The organization's human resources also greatly affect design. Two employee characteristics are most important: (1) skills and abilities, and (2) needs and personality traits.[20]

Skills and Abilities. With respect to the skills and abilities of the human resources within an organization, two dimensions are critical to design: *mean level* and *degree of dispersion.* Porter, Lawler, and Hackman discuss the mean (or average) level of skill in an organization:

If any organization is composed of employees who have a very high mean level of skill—as evidenced, say, by experience in jobs requiring a high degree of skill and by considerable amounts of appropriate formal education—then it is presumed that the nature of the structural-operational features of the organization should take cognizance of this. To be more specific, if employees tend to be especially skilled and well educated, it is likely that a high degree of formal specification and standardization of activities, and the imposition of close and severe controls, would result in an inefficient use of human resources, both from the organization's standpoint and from the individual's standpoint. Resulting behavior could be presumed to be characterized

19. Lyman W. Porter, Edward E. Lawlor, III, and J. Richard Hackman, *Behavior in Organizations,* (New York: McGraw-Hill, 1975), p. 231.

20. *Ibid.* pp. 242-245.

by performance much lower than potentially possible, frustration, and perhaps overt expressions of resentment against the organization.[21]

The authors add, "many organizations that . . . employ individuals with high skill levels fail to take this factor into account and are designed as if their employees constitute a low level of human resources when actually their potential is much greater." [22] This appears to be the case in many police organizations today. Because of their traditional hierarhical designs, such organizations stifle the performance of members who may have high skill levels. An example of this situation is provided by the experience of a former student, who had been a member of a police agency with just such a structure. In one incident, this individual was the first officer to arrive on the scene of a traffic accident in which one of the cars had overturned and pinned the driver inside. The officer could not free the accident victim from the car. Not knowing the extent of the injuries, and fearing that the car might catch fire and explode, the officer immediately radioed for an ambulance and a fire truck to help free the victim. The firemen, after some effort, removed the victim from the car and the ambulance took the victim to the hosital. Instead of receiving praise for his efforts, the officer was later repri-manded by the department for not going through channels and receiving permission from his immediate superior (sergeant) to call for the ambulance and fire truck. Such a judicious following of rules could have cost the traffic victim his life. This officer would most likely be hesitant about applying innovative or even "common sense" solutions to future non-routine situations.

An organization could inappropriately design its structure by making the opposite mistake and judging the skills of the employees as high, when in fact they are low. However, because of the para-military designs of most police agencies, this does not seem likely. Also, some theorists argue that it is better for organizations to expect too much rather than too little from their employees because "self-fulfilling prophesies" will occur, and individuals will strive to meet the levels of performance expected of them.[23]

The degree of dispersion (or distribution) of the mean level of skills and abilities throughout the organization is also important. For example, two organizations might have employees with the same average amount of expe-rience, skills, and abilities, but one of them may assign these individuals throughout the organization while the other may concentrate them in only one or two units. In such a situation, "for both organizations to adopt the same kind of structural-operational features of design would appear to be inappropriate. The enterprise with the greater dispersal of high skill and experience levels might be more likely to take advantage of them in a more

21. *Ibid.,* p. 243.

22. *Ibid.,* p. 243.

23. For example, see: R. E. Miles, "Human Relations or Human Resources," *Harvard Business Review,* 43, 1965, pp. 148-163.

organic rather than mechanistic structure. On the other hand, the organization with a narrow dispersal might well adopt an organic form for the unit containing most of the people with high-level abilities and skills, but a more mechanistic form for the majority of units in the organization."[24]

Needs and Personality Traits. Individuals who work for criminal justice organizations differ in needs and personality traits as well as in their capabilities. As mentioned above, this characteristic may significantly influence the effectiveness of the organization's design. Not all individuals need or desire a highly flexible, organic managerial style. The reverse is also true; many individuals do not want to be a part of a highly structured, mechanistic style of operation. Acording to Porter *et. al.:*

[I]t is not just a matter of how individuals differ in their needs, say, for achievement or affiliation. It is also a matter of how they differ in their characteristic modes of behaving and in their own views of themselves. These kinds of regularities, commonly referred to as personality traits, also have an impact on the effectiveness of different types of organization design for the person and for the organization. We can hypothesize that if individuals have strong needs for independence and self-actualization and have relatively high self-confidence, they will prefer organic-type organizations and will do better in them. Individuals who have less of these traits can be presumed to fare better in a relatively more highly structured organization.[25]

Several comprehensive studies have indicated that college graduates possess the traits described by Porter *et. al.* to a greater extent than do individuals without college backgrounds.[26] In one such study, Feldman and Newcomb inspected hundreds of research reports, intensively examined many of them, and often conducted their own analyses beyond those of the original investigators. The studies reviewed were both cross-sectional (measuring certain characteristics of students at different class levels) and longitudinal (measuring the same students over a period of time). The investigators summarized their findings as follows:

Declining "authoritarianism," dogmatism, and prejudice, together with decreasing conservative attitudes toward public issues and growing sensitivity to aesthetic experiences, are particularly prominent forms of change—as inferred from freshman—senior differences. These add up to something like increasing openness to multiple aspects of the contemporary world, paralleling wider ranges of contact and experience. Somewhat less consistently, but nevertheless evident are increasing intellectual interests and capacities, and declining commitment to religion, especially in its more orthodox forms. Certain kinds of personal changes—particularly

---

24.   Porter, *et.al., op. cit.,* pp. 243-244.

25.   *Ibid.,* p. 244.

26.   For two excellent treatises on this subject, which incorporate longitudinal data, see: James W. Trent and Leland L. Medsker, *Beyond High School,* (San Francisco: Jossey-Bass, 1968); and Alexander W. Astin, *Four Critical Years: Effects of College on Beliefs, Attitudes and Knowledge,* (San Francisco: Jossey-Bass, 1978).

toward greater independence, self-confidence, and readiness to express impulses—
are the rule rather than the exception.[27]

Such findings suggest that many individuals with college backgrounds
would prefer organic-type organizations and would perform better in them.
This trend toward greater openness, independence, and self-confidence is
not shared by every college graduate (keeping individual differences in
mind), but higher education appears to be one of the critical variables
contributing to those traits.

Numerous studies on police attitudes have supported the Feldman-
Newcomb findings.[28] In one of the better controlled studies, Guller surveyed police officers of varying rank in the New York City Police Department, hypothesized that police officers who were college seniors would
show lower levels of authoritarianism (more open belief systems) than
police officers who were freshmen of similar age and socio-economic background, with similar amounts of work experience.[29]

The findings indicated a relationship between the amount of college
experience and authoritarianism; police officers who had been in college
longer (seniors) were significantly less authoritarian than those who had just
begun college (freshmen). Guller also reported that, because his subjects
had widely varied majors, the college major of the subjects made little
difference in level of authoritarianism.

A study by Roberg on higher education, police attitudes, and job performance of 118 patrol officers of the Lincoln, Nebraska Police Department,
supports the Guller findings.[30] This study used four control variables: (1) age,
(2) seniority (work experience), (3) college major (including criminal justice,
education, business, sociology, psychology, humanities, and agriculture),
and (4) student status (pre-service: education completed prior to entering
police work; in-service: education started and continued after entering
police work; and continuing: education started prior to and continued after
entering police work). The results indicated that the higher the educational
level of patrol personnel, the more open the belief systems (less authoritarian). The control variables had little or no impact on this attitude change

---

27. Kenneth A. Feldman and Theodore M. Newcomb, *The Impact of College on Students,*
(San Francisco: Jossey-Bass, Inc., 1969), p. 326.

28. For example, see Alexander B. Smith, Bernard Locke, and William F. Walker, "Authoritarianism in College and Non-College Oriented Police," *Journal of Criminal Law, Criminology,
and Police Science,* 58, 1967, pp. 128-132; Alexander B. Smith, Bernard Locke, and Abe Fenster,
"Authoritarianism in Policemen who are College Graduates and Non-College Police," *Journal
of Criminal Law, Criminology, and Police Science,* 61, 1970, pp. 313-315; L. Craig Parker, Jr.,
Martin Donnelly, David Gewitz, Joan Marcus and Victor Kowalewski, "Higher Education: Its
Impact on Police Attitudes," *The Police Chief,* 43, 1976, pp. 33-35.

29. Irvin B. Guller, "Higher Education and Policemen: Attitudinal Differences Between
Freshman and Senior Police College Students," *Journal of Criminal Law, Criminology and
Police Science,* 63, 1972, p. 396-401.

30. Roy R. Roberg, "An Analysis of the Relationships Among Higher Education, Belief Systems, and Job Performance of Patrol Officers," *Journal of Police Science and Administration,* 6,
1978, pp. 336-344.

process. This finding is significant with respect to both the choice of major and student status, for it has long been argued that certain majors should be encouraged for individuals planning a career in the police field, or that pre-service students "untainted" by police work are more susceptible to change than continuing or in-service students. These findings do not support such arguments. It should be noted, however, that all of the study participants with a college background had either graduated from or were attending a land grant institution which emphasized an interdisciplinary curriculum. Thus, the role played by a broadly based education in relation to open belief systems appears crucial.

The investigator further discovered a relationship between belief systems and job performance. Although previous studies have indicated a relationship between higher education and police performance, they have not adequately explicated the nature of the relationship.[31] The Roberg study indicated that increased levels of education led to relatively open belief systems, which in turn led to increased job performance. The researcher concluded that those patrol officers with higher levels of education had more open belief systems and performed in a more satisfactory manner than those patrol officers with less education. Accordingly, those patrol officers with college degrees had the most open belief systems *and* the highest levels of job performance.

Because most police activities are interpersonal and non-enforcement in nature, these results appear to have important implications for the complex nature of the police role. The comprehensive job performance evaluations used in the study, combined with the fact that less authoritarian patrol officers were generally rated higher in their performance, suggests that officers with open belief systems were more likely to handle the myriad situations they encountered in a more satisfactory manner. It would also follow that such officers are also likely to exhibit a more flexible, less authoritarian attitude toward those with whom they have contact.

Although the above results can only be generalized to those patrol officers within the particular department under investigation, such findings may have significance for other police agencies. In order to deal with all of society's citizens in a humane and just manner, police personnel must be able to take a rational and non-prejudicial approach to each situation they encounter, something which is difficult for an individual with a relatively closed or authoritarian belief system. When situations are mishandled in an authoritarian or prejudicial way, the agency involved, and indeed, the entire criminal justice system, lose community support.

---

31. See: Raymond P. Witte, "The Dumb Cop," *The Police Chief,* 36, 1969, pp. 37-38; David Patrick Geary, "College Educated Cops—Three Years Later," *The Police Chief,* 37, 1970, pp. 59-61; Roy R. Roberg, *An Analysis of the Relationship Between Performance and Educational Levels of Police Officers in a Selected Police Organization,* Master's Thesis, Washington State University, 1970; Bernard Cohen and Jan M. Chaiken, *Police Background Characteristics and Performance,* (New York: The New York City Rand Institute, 1972); James C. Finnigan, "A Study of Relationships Between College Education and Police Performance in Baltimore, Maryland," *The Police Chief,* 43, 1976, pp. 60-62.

It is important to note that the agency under investigation was relatively organic; task forces were used in decision-making, and a team policing or decentralized style of patrol was used. These same results may not be applicable to organizations which are highly mechanistic. In those departments which use authoritarian managerial styles, college educated personnel may become increasingly dogmatic (or closed-minded), with a corresponding decrease in job performance. Additional research is needed on organizational variables, but the preliminary results suggest that higher education may influence *both* internal design factors concerning needs and personality traits (independence, and self-confidence) as well as skills and abilities (job performance). Consequently, as more college graduates are employed in police agencies and throughout the entire criminal justice system, practicing managers must carefully monitor the rising mean levels of education within their organizations, especially with respect to their dispersion or distribution among individual departments or units. Traditional, mechanistic managerial styles may become increasingly dysfunctional to the use of human resources in police and other criminal justice agencies.

CONTINGENCY APPROACH TO ORGANIZATION DESIGN

Considering the above studies, there apparently is no one "best" way to design organizations for effective goal attainment. As the contingency view emphasizes, the "patterns of relationships among organizational variables" must be understood if police organization designs and working environments are to be improved. The remainder of this chapter focuses on the contingent relationship between the characteristics of centralization-decentralization and flat-tall hierarchies and organization design, and finally on the overall design of police organizations, using either mechanistic or organic managerial systems.

Centralization and Decentralization

There is much confusion in management literature about the precise meanings of centralization and decentralization. *Decentralization* is most commonly referred to as either (1) the dispersion of decision-making throughout an organization, or (2) the geographical dispersion of an organization's operations. According to Robbins, "The latter interpretation is incorrect, for the concepts of centralization/decentralization are meant to reflect the degree of authority [decision-making] that is delegated to lower levels in the organization. The error is caused by the fact that organizations that are geographically dispersed are usually decentralized in nature."[32] Thus, the *dispersion* of *authority* is critical to decentralization, which does not refer to geographic dispersion.

---

32. Stephen P. Robbins, *The Administrative Process: Integrating Theory and Practice*, (Englewood Cliffs, N.J.: Prentice-Hall, 1976), p. 245.

In decentralized organizations, individuals at lower levels have more decision-making authority than they do in centralized organizations. However, the amount and type of decisions allowed lower level personnel is a matter of degree. Even in highly centralized organizations, top management usually cannot control every decision made at the lower levels. Conversely, in decontralized organizations, top management ultimately has some control over decisions made at the lower levels. Centralization and decentralization should not be regarded as opposite extremes, but as different ends of one continuum. It is almost impossible to find an organization which is completely centralized or decentralized. For instance, certain police activities tend to be more effective when centralized (such as records and communications), while other activities tend to be more effective when decentralized (field operations such as patrol.)

Advantages and Disadvantages. In modern management literature, decentralization has been so highly praised that it would appear to be the single best way. Centralization, on the other hand, has been left with a negative connotation. As one writer observed:

In recent years, decentralization has become the golden calf of management philosophy. It has been lauded by such terms as "more democratic," "a step toward world peace," "greater freedom of spirit," and "less authoritarian." The implicit assumption is that centralization reflects the opposite of these worthy qualities.[33]

The truth lies somewhere between these extremes, for both approaches have some advantages. Decentralization allows for lower level participation in decision-making, which has been shown to increase employee motivation. Stieglitz states that it also leads to quicker and better decisions, managerial development, fewer levels of organization, and the freeing of supervisors to concentrate on broader responsibilities.[34] On the other hand, Flippo maintains that centralization leads to uniformity of policy and action, lessens the risk of errors by subordinates who lack information or skill, uses the skills of central specialists, and over-all enables closer control of operations.[35]

In order to establish the conditions in which one approach is superior to the other, several researchers have attempted to define the situational determinants for decentralization and centralization. Chandler discovered a relationship among environment, technology, and decentralization.[36] His findings indicated that industries with rapidly changing environments and complex technologies (such as electronics) tended to decentralize their operations, while industries with stable environments and routine technologies (such as steel) tended to centralize theirs. Other researchers have found a

33. Henry H. Albers, *Principles of Management,* 3rd ed., (New York: Wiley, 1969), p. 186.

34. Harold Stieglitz, *Organizational Planning,* (New York: National Industrial Conference Board, 1962).

35. Edwin B. Flippo, *Management: A Behavioral Approach,* 2nd ed., (Boston: Allyn and Bacon 1970).

36. Alfred Chandler, *Strategy and Structure,* (Cambridge, Mass.: MIT Press, 1962).

relationship among uncertainty, task complexity, and organization size (large) and decentralization (see Table 8-2).

As mentioned previously, police organizations have some activities that are centralized and others that are decentralized; however, the research indicates that situational influences (shown in Table 8-2) should be considered when determining the proper degree of centralization or decentralization. Patrol operations, for instance, because of their uncertain environment, complex tasks and diverse clientele, are likely to be more successful under a decentralized, democratic style of management than under a centalized, authoritarian style.

Tall and Flat Hierarchies

The concept of flat and tall hierarchies refers to the total spans of control and levels of management within an organization.

Table 8-2
Situational Factors Influencing Decentralization

Situational Factors Degree of Decentralization	Tendency Toward Centralization	Tendency Toward Decentralization
Uncertainty; rate of change; task complexity. (Chandler, Lawrence and Lorsch, Burns and Stalker, Hall)	Low Uncertainty	High Uncertainty
Differentiation of clientele; diversity. (Dill, Chandler)	Little Differentiation	Much Differentiation
Organizational size. (Dale, Child, Woodward, Pugh et.al., Hall)	Small Size	Large Size

Source: Adapted from Gary Dessler, *Organization and Management: A Contingency Approach,* (Englewood Cliffs, N.J.: Prentice-Hall, 1976), p. 112.

The size of the span of control is usually related to the number of managerial levels. Tall hierarchies usually have small or narrow spans of control with many levels of management, allowing for close supervision and control of employees and operations (a mechanistic system). Flat hierarchies tend to have large or wide spans of control with few levels of management, allowing for greater employee autonomy and less control of operations (an organic system).

The differences between tall and flat hierarchies are shown in Figure 8-2. These simplified organizational charts reveal that the tall structure has a narrow span of control (two) while the flat structure has a wider span (five); the tall structure also has more managerial levels (four) than the flat structure (two). The tall hierarchy obviously allows for the tighter controls and discipline of employees advocated by classical theorists.

Advantages and Disadvantages. As with decentralization, the virtues of a flat organizational hierarchy have been praised in the current literature, while the tall hierarchy has generally been dismissed as obsolete. This is understandable if one associates the tall structure with the concepts advocated by the administrative theorists, who wished to regulate and control employees as if they were robots. The tall structure has developed a bad reputation in the criminal justice field, where it has been faithfully applied for many years. However, tall structures have certain advantages over flat structures, as noted by Luthans:

> One behavioral implication that is often overlooked in analyzing flat versus tall structures is the opportunity that tall structures offer for more personal contact between superior and subordinate. This contact is generally assumed to be negative and conflicting, but it need not be. In a tall structure, the superior may create a positive rapport with his subordinate that may not be possible in a flat structure.

Figure 8-2
Tall and Flat Organizational Hierarchies

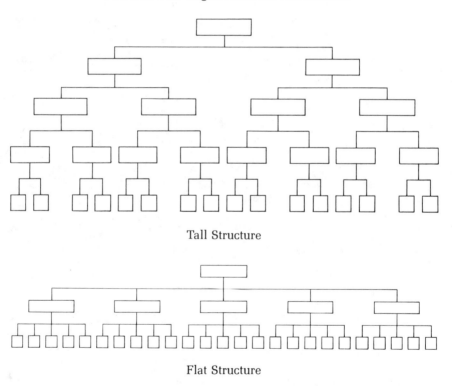

Tall Structure

Flat Structure

Another consideration besides personal contact are the levels of communication in the two structures. In the flat structure there are fewer levels, which means that both downward and upward communication is simplified. There should be less distortion and inaccuracy. The red tape and endless communication channels associated with bureaucratic tall structures are not present in flat structures. On the other hand, the increased equality that exists between subordinates in a flat structure may lead to communication problems. If no status or authority differentials are structurally created, a heavy burden is placed upon horizontal communications . . . the horizontal communication system is notably deficient in all types of organizations. The problem may be compounded in flat organizations where more dependence is placed on this type of communication, but it is not structurally facilitated. Also, coordination may be seriously impaired by a flat structure for the same reason.[37]

Most of the advantages of flat structures are associated with decentralization. In his pioneering study of decentralization at the Sears Roebuck Company, Worthy concluded that "flatter, less complex structures, with a maximum of administrative decentralization, tend to create a potential for improved attitudes, more effective supervision, and greater individual responsibility and initiative among employees."[38] This broad generalization, however, has not been fully supported by other studies. Also, "It must be remembered that flat structures only encourage decentralization and individual responsibility and initiative. The supervisor of a small span does not always keep close control and never decentralize, nor does the supervisor of a large span always create an atmosphere of self-control and decentralization. The degree of centralization or its reverse depends on the overall management and organizational philosophy and policies and on individual leadership style and personality."[39]

A study by Porter and Lawler demonstrates the importance of the situation in determining the appropriateness of tall or flat strucutres.[40] In their study of over 1500 managers, the researchers attempted to determine the nature of the relationship between tall and flat hierarchies and manager satisfaction. Although their findings did not reveal any clear superiority of flat over tall structures, Porter and Lawler did discover that in companies with less than 5000 employees, managerial satisfaction was greater when flat hierarchies were used. Conversely, in companies with more than 5000 employees, manager satisfaction was greater when tall hierarchies were used. Of special interest with respect to the discussion on motivation in Chapter 5, the researchers found that tall structures were associated with lower level satisfactions (security and social needs), while flat structures were associated with upper level satisfactions (esteem and self-actualization). Such research needs to be conducted in police and other criminal justice agencies of various sizes. If the results show that employees have strong lower level needs, a case may be made for tall structures in large criminal justice organizations. Otherwise, flat structures may offer more to criminal justice agencies and their personnel. Because of the increasing number of highly educated people (who tend to have strong upper level satisfaction needs) entering police work, this may be particularly true of police organizations.

---

37. Fred Luthans, *Organizational Behavior*, (New York: McGraw-Hill, 1973), p. 149.

38. James C. Worthy, "Organization Structure and Employee Morale," *American Sociological Review*, 15, 1950, p. 179.

39. Luthans, *Organizational Behavior*, pp. 149-150.

40. Lyman W. Porter and Edward E. Lawler, III, "The Effects of Tall Versus Flat Organization Structures on Managerial Job Satisfaction," *Personnel Psychology*, 17, 1964, pp. 135-148.

Mechanistic and Organic Systems

Table 8-3 summarizes the major characteristics of organizations and their influences upon organizational designs as they apply to the Burns-Stalker concept of mechanistic and organic managerial systems. The mechanistic system is characterized by permanent, structured positions, while the organic system has "less structuring, more frequent change of positions and roles, and more dynamic interplay among the various functions.[41] The organic system is thus more flexible and adaptive than is the mechanistic system.

Table 8-3

Organizational Characteristics of
Organic and Mechanistic Structures

	Types of Organization Structure	
Organizational Characteristics Index	Organic	Mechanistic
Span of control	Wide	Narrow
Number of levels of authority	Few	Many
Degree of centralization in decision making	Low	High
Proportion of persons in one unit having opportunity to interact with persons in other units	High	Low
Quantity of formal rules	Low	High
Specificity of job goals	Low	High
Specificity of required activities	Low	High
Content of communications	Advice and information	Instructions and decisions
Range of compensation	Narrow	Wide
Range of skill levels	Narrow	Wide
Knowledge-based authority	High	Low
Position-based authority	Low	High

Source: Adapted from Ralph M. Hower and Jay W. Lorsch, "Organizational Inputs," in John A. Seiler, (ed.), *Systems Analysis in Organizational Behavior*, (Homewood, Ill.: Irwin, and the Dorsey Press, 1967), p. 168. (This table is an adaptation of one prepared by Paul R. Lawrence and Jay W. Lorsch in an unpublished "Working Paper on Scientific Transfer and Organizational Structure," 1963. The latter, in turn, draws heavily on criteria suggested by W. Evans, "Indices of the Hierarchical Structure of Industrial Organizations," *Management Science*, 9, 1963, pp. 468-77, Burns and Stalker, *op. cit.,* and Woodward, *op. cit.,* as well as those suggested by R. H. Hall, "Intraorganizational Structure Variables," *Administrative Science Quarterly*, 9, 1962, pp. 295-308).

Kast and Rosenzweig, influenced by the dichotomy of mechanistic versus organic systems and closed versus open systems, have developed a summary which provides a fundamental basis for the contingency

---

41. Fremont E. Kast and James E. Rosenzweig, *Organization and Management: A Systems Approach,* 2nd ed., (New York: McGraw-Hill, 1974), p. 240

approach.[42] In Table 8-4, they combine the major contingency themes under two classifications: closed/stable/mechanistic and open/adaptive/organic systems. Those authors whose views are expressed in Tables 8-3 and 8-4 point out that a strict duality does not exist, but that organizations have characteristics which fit somewhere between the extremes of the two classifications. Kast and Rosenzweig warn:

Concepts about these relationships have not been "proven" via substantial empirical research. In fact, it is doubtful whether or not they can ever be proven conclusively. Organizations and their environments are much too dynamic to allow us to set forth "laws" about relationships. Rather, we can only expect to identify tentative patterns of relationships among organizational variables.

Table 8-4

Common Themes In Contingency Views
Characteristics of Organizational Systems

Author	Closed/Stable/Mechanistic	Open/Adaptive/Organic
James D. Thompson	Closed system Certain, deterministic, rational	Open system Uncertain, indeterministic, natural
Harold J. Leavitt	Power concentration Combination of relatively independent parts or components	Power equalization Multivariate systems of interacting variables: task, structural, technical, and human variables
Henry P. Knowles and Borje O. Saxberg	Pessimistic View (Man as Robot) System emphasizes competition and relies upon imposed organization controls	Optimistic View (Man as Pilot) System emphasizes cooperation and relies upon individual self-control
Herbert A. Simon	One goal, one criterion Decision-making strategy to achieve a goal	Multiple goals, multiple criteria Decision-making strategy to satisfy a *set* of constraints.
Charles Perrow	Routine technology Analyzable search procedures, few exceptions, programmable decisions	Nonroutine technology Unanalyzable search procedures, numerous exceptions, nonprogrammable decisions
Raymond G. Hunt	Performance	Problem solving
Jay W. Lorsch	Certain, homogeneous	Uncertain, diverse
D.S. Pugh, D.J. Hickson and C.R. Hinings	Full bureaucracy: stuctured, concentrated authority, impersonal control	Implicitly structured organizations: unstructured, dispersed authority, line control
Fred E. Fiedler	Leadership style: task oriented, low tolerance for ambiguity	Leadership style: relationship oriented, high tolerance for ambiguity
George F.F. Lombard	Undimensional Dualism (right-wrong) Closed, rationalistic decision processes	Multidimensional Relativism (multiple values; "It all depends") Open, contingent, satisficing, heuristic decision processes

Source: Adapted from Fremont E. Kast and James E. Rosenzweig, (eds.), *Contingency Views of Organization and Management,* (Chicago: Science Research Associates, 1973), pp. 311-312.

---

42. Fremont E. Kast and James E. Rosenzweig, (eds.), *Contingency Views of Organization and Management,* (Chicago: Science Research Associates, Inc., 1973), pp. 305-320.

However, this initial step of identifying patterns of relationships can be of major importance ... For example, the research literature suggests that there are significant differences among correctional institutions which could be better understood by using a contingency view. Those institutions that have *confinement* of inmates as a primary goal tend to exhibit characteristics set forth under "closed/stable/mechanistic." Those organizations which emphasize the goal of *rehabilitation* of participants tend to exhibit characteristics set forth under "open/adaptive/organic." The maximum security prison is very closed, highly structured, and exercises tight control (externally imposed) over inmates. The rehabilitation oriented correctional institution is more open to society (for example, work-release programs), has a more flexible structure and tries to develop self-control with each participant.[43]

In order to guard against sweeping generalizations in classification schemes, French and Bell suggest that the question of which system is better should be posed in terms of contingencies, such as:

1. Under what conditions is the organic system superior to the mechanistic, or vice versa? Or,

2. What is the most effective mix of organic and mechanistic characteristics for a given organization or unit and its current circumstance?[44]

In answering question number one above, Porter *et. al.* have considered several national studies, and have subsequently reduced the contingency approach to the following:

Organic, low-structured, non-bureaucratic-type designs are most effective when:

Individuals have relatively high skills, widely distributed.

Individuals have high self-esteem and strong needs for achievement, autonomy, and self-actualization.

The technology is rapidly changing, non-routine, and involves many non-programmable tasks.

Mechanistic, high structured, more bureaucratic-like designs are most effective when:

Individuals are relatively inexperienced and unskilled.

Individuals have strong needs for security and stability.

The technology is relatively stable and involves standardized materials and programmable tasks.

The environment is fairly calm and relatively simple.[45]

The authors defend these basic generalizations by taking a practical view:

Lest anyone be tempted to conclude that these involve invidious comparisons, let him be reminded that not all employees are highly skilled and experienced, not all individuals want high degrees of freedom and autonomy in work situations, not all

---

43. Kast and Rosenzweig, *Organization and Management*, p. 509.

44. Wendell L. French and Cecil H. Bell, Jr., *Organization Development*, (Englewood Cliffs, N.J.: Prentice-Hall, 1973), p. 188.

45. Porter, *et. al., op. cit.*, p. 272.

technology involves highly intricate tasks, etc. The trend over time may well be in this direction, but at present there is still so much variation across organizational situations on all these dimensions that sophisticated analysis continues to be required for achieving appropriate designs.[46]

While the above statement is correct, because of environmental instability, the complexity of tasks, and the type of individuals who are entering the field, organic designs appear to offer more potential for effectiveness to police organizations than do mechanistic designs.

The statement above that "there is still much variation across organizational situations" relates to the second question posed by French and Bell. Because many police organizations are relatively complex, it is unlikely that any one type of design is going to be effective for all parts of the organization. Consequently, multiple or mix structures will be necessary in many, if not most, police agencies. The above organic-mechanistic generalizations, as well as the themes summarized in Table 8-4, should be valuable in determining the most appropriate designs for specific organizational situations. Because neither the organic nor the mechanistic system is superior under all circumstances, practicing managers must carefully study the pattern of relationships among relevant external and internal variables and decide which system and/or mix of systems would be most effective under current conditions.

SUMMARY

According to the contingency approach to organization design, different types of organizations require different types of designs. For example, under Parson's classification scheme an organization's primary function(s) in society is a factor which will help determine its design. However, organizations which have similar functions may differ substantially in their approaches to goal achievement and in their operational techniques. Wilson emphasized this point with his analysis of three distinct styles of policing (watchman, service and legalistic); Duffee classified prisons, using four primary typologies (restraint, reform, rehabilitation, and reintegration). Separate organizational characteristics must be considered in order to properly design any organization, and no single "best design" exists for police and other criminal justice organizations.

Relevant external and internal influences affect organization design. The Burns-Stalker study led to the differentiation between two distinct types of managerial systems: the mechanistic, best suited to stable environments; and the organic, most appropriate for unstable environments. The Woodward studies emphasized that technology was an important influence on organization design; they also strongly supported the conclusions of Burns and Stalker. While these studies involved industrial firms, their conclusions are meaningful for criminal justice agencies. The internal factors critical to the design of organizations included two primary employee characteristics:

---

46. *Ibid.*, pp. 272-273.

skills and abilities, and needs and personality traits. The first characteristic included two dimensions: mean level and degree of disperson; the second characteristic included individuals' needs for independence and self-actualization, as well as their degree of self-confidence. It was suggested that higher education may influence both internal design factors; as mean educational levels increase within criminal justice organizations, the traditional mechanistic style may not be the most effective with respect to human resource utilization.

In regard to centralization-decentralization and tall-flat hierarchies, each concept has certain advantages and disadvantages, depending on environmental circumstances. Centralization appeared to be more effective in organizations with stable environments and routine technologies, while decentralization appeared to be the most effective in organizations with constantly changing environments and complex technologies. Similarly, the advantages of tall structures seemed to coincide with those of centralization and the advantages of flat structures seemed to coincide with those of decentralization. Furthermore, these structural arrangements only create the atmosphere for increased effectiveness; overall managerial philosophy and leadership styles actually determine the degree of success.

A summary table has combined the major contingency themes in two classifications: closed/stable/mechanistic and open/adaptive/organic. The contingency approach does not view either the mechanistic or organic system as superior, but is concerned with the conditions under which either system would be most effective. Ultimately, multiple or mix structures may be needed if police organizations are to effectively attain goals.

DISCUSSION QUESTIONS

1. Discuss the importance of recognizing separate organizational characteristics when studying criminal justice agencies; provide an example of how these characteristics may affect the organization's design.

2. Explain the significance of the Burns-Stalker and Woodward studies when applied to police organizations.

3. Discuss "self-fulfilling prophesies" and how they may apply to the traditional para-military designs of police organizations.

4. Discuss the significance which rising mean levels of education among police personnel may have on organizational design.

5. Discuss the advantages of both centralization and decentralization and provide several examples of situational factors in police organizations which influence the proper degree of centralization-decentralization.

6. Discuss, in general terms, under what conditions organic and mechanistic designs tend to be the most effective, and relate these to the design of contemporary police organizations.

7. Explain why multiple or mix structures are necessary in many, if not most, police agencies.

ANNOTATED BIBLIOGRAPHY

Blau, Peter M., and Richard Scott, *Formal Organizations: A Comparative Analysis*, (San Francisco: Chandler, 1962). A survey of the theory and research on formal organizations, comparing various types of organizations with respect to their work group structures, processes of communication, hierarchy and peer relations, managerial control, and relations to the larger social context.

Burns, Tom, and G. M. Stalker, *The Management of Innovation*, (London: Tavistock, 1961). A study of several manufacturing firms which attempted to determine what type of organization design and management practices were appropriate for different environmental conditions; findings suggested that mechanistic systems appeared most appropriate for stable conditions while organic systems appeared most appropriate for changing conditions.

Hall, Richard H., *Organizations: Structure and Process*, (Englewood Cliffs, N.J.: Prentice-Hall, 1972). Emphasizes research on the structural features of organizations, especially in relation to size, formality and complexity.

Parsons, Talcott, *Structure and Process in Modern Societies*, (New York: Free Press, 1960). Sees the primary reference for analyzing the structure of an organization as its value pattern in the situation in which it operates; organizations are classified according to the type of goal or function they perform in society.

Reiss, Albert J., and David J. Bordua, "Environment and Organization: A Perspective on the Police," in *The Police: Six Sociological Essays*, David J. Bordua, ed., (New York: Wiley, 1967). A perspective on the metropolitan police which emphasizes the influence of the external environment on police organization and operations.

Thompson, James D., *Organizations in Action*, (New York: McGraw-Hill, 1967). This concise work analyzes how organizations monitor and respond to their environments; contents include: strategies for studying organizations, organizational design, technology and structure, organizational rationality and structure, and the assessment of organizations.

Woodward, Joan, *Industrial Organization: Theory and Practice*, (London: Oxford Univ. Press, 1965). A comprehensive analysis of studies on the formal structures and operating procedures of 100 industrial firms in southeast England; the findings indicated a strong relationship between technology, structure, and organizational success.

NINE

Job Design and Performance Evaluation

LEARNING OBJECTIVES

The study of this chapter should enable you to:

☑ Define the primary concerns of job design.

☑ Discuss why individual needs and goals as well as skill and ability levels must be considered if jobs are to be properly designed.

☑ Differentiate between job enlargement and job enrichment.

☑ Describe the Job Characteristics Model of work motivation (including the core job dimensions, psychological states, and personal and work outcomes), and why this model is unique.

☑ Describe the four sequential steps to the process of job enrichment.

☑ Define construct validity, measurement deficiency, and measurement contamination.

☑ Differentiate between variable and constant errors and between intraindividual and interindividual errors.

☑ Explain how the IACP graphic rating scale eliminates many of the ambiguities associated with this type of evaluation.

☑ Review the three basic aspects of MBO which affect its success.

☑ Review several implications of linking rewards to performance.

NINE

The preceding chapter indicated that the structural design of organizations has a strong impact on the individuals who work within them. This chapter deals with two related issues: the design of jobs and the evaluation of job performance. Once an organization's structure has been determined, how jobs are designed and performance evaluated becomes important. With respect to both of these issues, this chapter will concentrate on the principal considerations which affect organizational behavior and which must be dealt with effectively by police managers.

THE DESIGN OF JOBS

Job or *work design* involves appropriately developing and structuring work activities of the organization's membership in order to meet both organizational and individual needs. Proper job and task design leads to increased work effort and productivity. Job design is thus one of the greatest influences on the work motivation of employees.

Individual Differences

The traditional criterion used in evaluating and designing jobs is worker efficiency. According to this approach, developed by Frederick Taylor and the scientific management movement, increased worker efficiency— through highly simplified and routinized jobs—leads to increased organizational effectiveness and productivity. When jobs are "scientifically" developed, however, the job's impact on the individual who must perform it is overlooked. The Hawthorne studies have indicated the importance of considering the human aspects of organization and management. By ignoring the human element in work design, scientific managers failed to consider that some people are highly dissatisfied in jobs over which they have virtually no control, are tightly structured and repetitive, and which provide little challenge. Such worker dissatisfactions lead to behavior which hurts the organization's effectiveness, through low morale, absenteeism, and high turnover.

Human factors, such as employee satisfaction and adjustment to work, must be considered along with technological factors if work efficiency is to be improved; individual needs and goals must be considered as much as the employee's ability levels. According to one source, most industrial and business organizations (and many police organizations, as well) fail to consider individual needs and goals with respect to work design or how employees respond to their jobs:

Both the adherents of the traditional scientific management approach to job design and the more recent evangelists of job enlargement have tended to deny either the existence of differences among employees in job-relevant needs and goals, or the importance of these needs and goals in determining how a person reacts to his work. This is not to suggest, however, that those who persist in the scientific management tradition and those who advocate job enlargement make even approximately similar assumptions about the needs and goals which characterize "typical" employees in organizations. The point is only that advocates of both sides of the fence have implicitly (and occasionally even explicitly) denied the existence and the importance of what might be called the "second" class of individual differences.[1]

Since these differences are frequently ignored, proponents of the two views have conducted their studies of job design on groups having characteristics that are congruent with the researchers' notions about individuals and work.[2] For example, Taylor's work originally involved very menial, unchallenging jobs and low skilled workers. When his approach to job design was applied to more challenging work and capable employees, the results indicated that scientific management was not desirable in all situations. Conversely, many of the successful job enlargement studies (those which show higher satisfaction and productivity and lower absenteeism and turnover) have been conducted in professional organizations which employ highly educated and skilled personnel who would be responsive to job enlargement in the first place. As Hulin and Blood point out in their review of the literature on this subject, there are a large number of studies in which the results are ambiguous.[3] They concluded that enlarged jobs are not universally better than simple jobs. Individual differences among employees are an important concern to the organization. If a good match is to be made between employees and their work, personal needs and goals as well as individual skills and abilities must be considered.

Expanding Jobs

In attempting to better fit jobs to the individual employees, thus leading to improved motivation and satisfaction, the major concern has been with the expansion of jobs. Expansion can take two general approaches: *job enlargement* and *job enrichment*. The former involves expanding a job horizontally, while the latter involves vertical expansion. A job may be expanded by allowing an employee to take responsibility for the tasks of others who are at the same (horizontal) level in the organization. Conversely, a job may be expanded by allowing an employee to assume responsibility for some of the tasks normally assigned to those who hold a higher (vertical) position in the organization. Efforts to expand or load jobs both horizontally and vertically, are also called job enrichment.

---

1. Lyman W. Porter, Edward E. Lawler, III, and J. Richard Hackman, *Behavior in Organizations*, (New York: McGraw-Hill, 1975), p. 287.

2. *Ibid.*

3. Charles L. Hulin and Milton R. Blood, "Job Enlargement, Individual Differences, and Worker Responses," *Psychological Bulletin*, 69, 1968, pp. 41-55.

Job enlargement and job enrichment may be differentiated as follows:

... by merely giving a person a greater variety of activities to do, we are horizontally expanding his job. Enrichment, on the other hand, would require that he do increased planning and evaluating of his work, usually with less supervision and more self-evaluation. From the standpoint of increasing the internal rewards from a job, job enrichment offers greater potential. (One worker commented recently, concerning job enlargement, "You call this a more challenging job? Before, I had one lousy task to perform. Through expansion, now I have five lousy tasks to do.") However, job enrichment is successful only when it increases responsibility, increases the employee's freedom and independence, organizes tasks so as to allow him to do a complete activity, and provides feedback to allow him to correct his own performance.[4]

JOB DESIGN AND MOTIVATION

To date, the most influential theory about expanding jobs has been the Herzberg motivation-hygiene theory.[5] This two-factor theory suggests that only factors which are intrinsic to the job itself (achievement, recognition, responsibility, advancement, and personal growth, all labeled as "motivators") can produce employee motivation to perform. On the other hand, dissatisfiers or "hygiene factors" (company policies, supervision, salary, working conditions) are extrinsic and therefore not capable of motivating and improving performance. According to Herzberg's theory, a job will increase worker motivation and performance only if the "motivators" are built into the job itself.

Although the previous discussion of this theory (see Chapter 5) indicated that it is an oversimplification, it has led to some interesting studies concerning the redesign of jobs. The most significant involved a series of generally successful job expansion studies conducted throughout the American Telephone and Telegraph system, based on principles suggested by the two-factor theory.[6] It has also been recently suggested that the performance of patrol officers could be improved through using the two-factor theory and job redesign, as opposed to trying to change the individual put into the job through higher education.[7] This latter suggestion has primarily taken the form of team policing, which emphasizes broader formal discretionary powers and allows officers responsibility for all police-related functions in an assigned area or "beat."

---

4. Stephen P. Robbins, *The Administrative Process: Integrating Theory and Practice*, (Englewood Cliffs, N.J.: Prentice-Hall, 1976), p. 263.

5. Frederick Herzberg, "One More Time: How Do You Motivate Employees," *Harvard Business Review*, 46, 1968, pp. 53-62; William J. Paul, Jr., Keith B. Robertson, and Frederick Herzberg, "Job Enrichment Pays Off," *Harvard Business Review*, 47, 1969, pp. 61-78.

6. Robert N. Ford, *Motivation Through the Work Itself*, (New York: American Management Association, 1969).

7. Thomas J. Baker, "Designing the Job to Motivate," *FBI Law Enforcement Bulletin*, 45, November 1976, pp. 3-7.

With respect to job design, the motivation-hygiene theory has been criticized because it fails to account for individual differences in how people react to the expansion of jobs. In the AT&T studies based on the theory, it was assumed that the motivating factors (such as achievement, recognition, and responsibility) could motivate *all* employees; the same assumption applies to the team policing concept. This is not supported by the evidence so far presented, and it also conflicts with the contingency approach. In addition, "the theory in its present form does not specify how the presence or absence of motivating factors can be measured for existing jobs ... this increases the difficulty of testing the theory in on-going organizations. It also limits the degree to which the theory can be used to diagnose jobs prior to planned change, or to evaluate the effects of work redesign activities after changes have been carried out."[8]

Because of these problems with the Herzberg theory as applied to work design, an alternative model was developed by J. Richard Hackman and Greg R. Oldham. Their unique Job Characteristics Model considers individual differences and actually provides the means for diagnosing existing jobs.

Job Characteristics Model

The model specifies the conditions under which individuals become internally motivated to perform effectively on their jobs. The model was tested for 658 employees who worked on 62 different jobs (including blue collar, white collar, and professional work) in seven organizations; the results support its validity.[9] Figure 9-1 presents the basic job characteristics model. At the most general level, five "core" job dimensions prompt three "psychological states" which, in turn, lead to a number of beneficial personal and work outcomes. The links between the job dimensions and the psychological states, as well as between the psychological states and the outcomes, are moderated by individual growth and need strength.

Behavioral scientists have discovered that the following psychological states are critical in determining a person's motivation and satisfaction on the job:

1. Experienced Meaningfulness of the Work: The degree to which individuals experience the job as meaningful, valuable, and worthwhile.

2. Experienced Responsibility for Work Outcome: The degree to which individuals feel personally responsible for the results of the work they do.

3. Knowledge of Results: The degree to which individuals know and understand, on a continuous basis, how effectively they perform.

---

8. J. Richard Hackman and Greg R. Oldham, "Motivation Through the Design of Work: Test of a Theory," *Organizational Behavior and Human Performance*, 16, 1976, p. 252.

9. *Ibid.*, pp. 251-279. The discussion of the job characteristics model is drawn from this article (especially pp. 255-259), and Hackman, Oldham, Robert Janson and Kenneth Purdy, *A New Strategy for Job Enrichment*, Technical Report, No. 3, (New Haven: Yale Univ., Department of Administrative Services, 1974), (especially pp. 3-6, 8-11).

When these three conditions are present, individuals feel good about themselves when they perform well. These good feelings prompt the individuals to continue to do well, in order that they can continue to earn these positive feelings. If one of the three psychological states is lacking, motivation will drop markedly. For example, if individuals feel responsible for work outcomes in a meaningful task, but do not find out how well they are doing, they will not be internally motivated. The relationship between the three psychological states and on-the-job outcomes is illustrated in Figure 9-1. When all three are high, then internal work motivation, work quality, and job satisfaction are high, while absenteeism and turnover are low.

Figure 9-1
Job Characteristics Model of Work Motivation

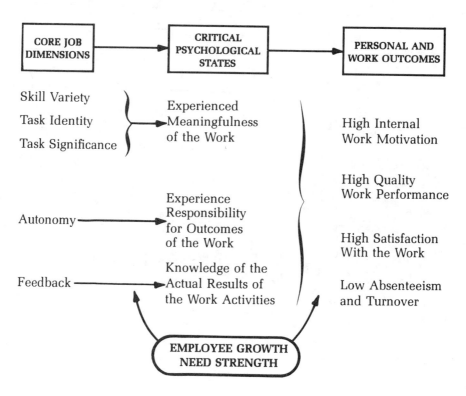

Source: J. Richard Hackman and Greg R. Oldham, "Motivation Through the Design of Work: Test of a Theory," *Organizational Behavior and Human Performance*, 16, 1976, p. 256.

Once the above variables have been identified, one has to identify the characteristics of the job which will elicit the three psychological states. The model identifies five "core" job dimensions, described below, which provide the basis for objectively measuring jobs, and for giving them higher potential for motivating people.

Toward Meaningful Work. Three of the five core dimensions contribute to the job's meaningfulness for the worker:

1. Skill Variety: The degree to which a job requires a variety of different activities in carrying out the work, which involve a number of different skills and talents.

2. Task Identity: The degree to which the job requires completion of a "whole" and identifiable piece of work; doing a job from beginning to end with a visible outcome.

3. Task Significance: The degree to which the job affects the lives or work of other people, whether in the immediate organization or in the external environment.

Each of these three job dimensions represents an important route to experienced meaningfulness. If the job ranks high in all three, the worker will experience his or her job as very meaningful. It is not necessary, however, for a job to rank high in all three dimensions. If the job ranks low in any one dimension, some drop in overall experienced meaningfulness will occur; however, even when two dimensions rank low the worker may find the job meaningful, if the third ranks high enough.

Toward Personal Responsibility. The fourth core dimension, autonomy, leads a worker to experience increased responsibility in the job.

4. Autonomy: The degree to which the job allows the individual freedom, independence, and discretion in scheduling the work and in determining the procedures to be used in carrying it out.

Toward Knowledge of Results. The final core dimension is feedback.

5. Feedback: The degree to which carrying out required work activities results in the individual obtaining direct and clear information about the effectiveness of his or her performance.

Summary: The Overall "Motivational Potential" of a Job. Figure 9-1 shows how the five core dimensions combine to affect the psychological states critical in determining whether or not an employee will be internally motivated to work effectively. By using the Job Diagnostic Survey (JDS), an instrument (whose content is reported elsewhere) designed by the authors to specifically measure each of the model's characteristics, a Motivating Potential Score (MPS) can be computed for any job.[10] The MPS provides a summary index of the degree to which objective characteristics of the job will prompt high internal motivation. According to the theory above, a job high in motivating potential must be high on at least one (and hopefully more) of the three dimensions which lead to experienced meaningfulness, and high in autonomy and feedback as well.

---

10. Properties of the JDS (including description of item content and format, and reliabilities of each measure) are described in Hackman and Oldham, "Development of the Job Diagnostic Survey," *Journal of Applied Psychology*, 60, 1975, pp. 159-170.

MPS is computed by combining scores as measured on the five dimensions:

$$\text{Motivating Potential Score (MPS)} = \left[\frac{\text{Skill Variety} + \text{Task Identity} + \text{Task Significance}}{3} \right] \times \text{Autonomy} \times \text{Feedback}$$

As the formula indicates, a near-zero score of a job on either autonomy or feedback will reduce the overall MPS to near-zero, while a near-zero score on one of the three job dimensions which contribute to experienced meaningfulness cannot by itself do so.

Diagnosing the Job

The Job Diagnostic Survey is used by employees, supervisors, and outside observers in assessing the target job and employees' reaction to it. The instruments measure the following:

1. The objective characteristics of the job itself, including both an overall indication of the "motivating potential" (MPS) of the job as it exists, and the score of the job on each of the five core dimensions.

2. The motivation, satisfaction, and work performance of employees on the job. In addition to satisfaction with the work itself, the JDS measures how people feel about other aspects of the work setting, such as pay, supervision, and relationships with co-workers.

3. The growth need strength of the employees. Because previous research has indicated that employees who have strong growth needs are more likely to respond to job enrichment than employees with weak growth needs, it is important to know at the outset just what kinds of satisfactions motivate (and do not motivate) employees. This makes it possible to identify where changes should begin and which persons need help in adapting to the enriched job.

Job Enrichment Implementation

Once the job has been diagnosed using the above methods, what approach to job enrichment should be used? Four other questions provide the answer:

Step 1. Are Motivation and Satisfaction Central to the Problem? Sometimes organizations undertake job enrichment to improve the work motivation and satisfaction of employees, when the real problem lies elsewhere. For example, work performance of the patrol division is highly dependent on the communications division; if dispatching and other vital functions provided to patrol are faulty, low performance could result. Under such circumstances, it would be more appropriate to focus attention on improving the operations of the communications division (where the problem is located), than to implement job enrichment techniques. Consequently, the first step is to determine whether or not employee motivation and satisfaction are problematic, by examining employee scores in these areas on the Job Diagnostic Survey. If employee motivation and satisfaction are low, the change agent (or manager) should continue on to Step 2; if motivation and satisfaction are high, then the change agent should identify the real problem.

Step 2. Is the Job Low in Motivating Potential? To answer this question, the change agent should compare the Motivating Potential Score of the target job to the MPS scores of other jobs, to determine whether or not the job itself is a probable cause of the motivational problems discovered in Step 1. If the job is low on the MPS, the change agent should continue to Step 3; if it scores high, attention should then be directed to other possible reasons for the motivational difficulties (the pay system, the nature of supervision, and so on).

Step 3. What Specific Aspects of the Job are Causing the Difficulty? At this point the change agent should examine the job in each of the five core dimensions, to determine the specific strengths and weaknesses of the job as currently structured; which dimensions score low on MPS? Plans are then made for improving those dimensions. For example, if a job scores reasonably high in feedback and autonomy, but one or more of the core dimensions which contribute to experienced meaningfulness (skill variety, task identity, or task significance) scores low, then these latter three dimensions should be strengthened.

Step 4. How "Ready" Are the Employees for Change? Once a need for improvement in the job is established, and the troublesome aspects of the job have been identified, then the change agent should consider the specific steps which will be taken to enrich the job. The growth needs of the employees should be considered, because employees high on growth needs usually respond more readily to job enrichment than employees with little need for growth. The JDS provides a direct measure of the growth need strength of the employees, and can be helpful in planning how to introduce the changes (cautiously or dramatically) and in deciding who should first have their jobs changed.

Finally, Hackman *et. al.* comment:

We believe that job enrichment is moving beyond the stage where it can be considered "yet another management fad." Instead, it represents a potentially powerful strategy for change which can help organizations achieve their goals for higher quality work—and at the same time further the equally legitimate needs of contemporary employees for a more meaningful work experience.

The diagnostic tools and implementing concepts we have presented are useful in deciding on and designing basic changes in the jobs themselves. They do not address the broader issues of who plans the changes, how they are carried out, and how they are followed up. The way these broader questions are dealt with, we believe, may determine whether job enrichment will grow up—or whether it will die an early and unfortunate death, like so many other fledgling behavioral science approaches to organizational change.[11]

Although job design and work motivation are as crucial to criminal justice agencies as they are to business and industrial firms, little empirical research has been conducted. Presented below is one of the first studies of this nature in the criminal justice field, involving job enlargement and correctional personnel. While this study does not test the validity of the job characteristics model described above, it does measure many of the same dimensions. Although the study was conducted in a penitentiary, the focus of the investigation is relevant to police organizations. Because many police departments are attempting to expand patrol jobs through job enlargement or enrichment, similar studies should be conducted in such agencies, to determine whether or not levels of motivation, satisfaction, and performance are actually increased.

Job Enlargement: An Example*

The research was carried out in the Division of Corrections of a Midwestern state. The subjects were 104 participants in a division-sponsored training program and occupied a variety of jobs such as prison guard, youth counselor, and correctional officer. Data was collected prior to the beginning of the program with the explanation the responses were anonymous and that the research was unrelated to the remainder of the program. Seventy-eight percent of the subjects were males. The average age of the subjects was 41.1 years. The average length of employment with the division was 7.1 years.

Instruments and Measures. An enlarged job has been operationally defined as a set of tasks exhibiting the following four characteristics: skill variety—the job provides the opportunity to utilize a variety of skills; autonomy—the job provides the worker with a feeling of personal responsibility for his work; task identity—the job involves performing a sufficiently whole piece of work so that the worker feels that he has accomplished something of consequence; and feedback—the job provides meaningful feedback to the worker about what he has or has not accomplished. Included in the questionnaire completed by the subjects were four scales aimed at measuring the degree to which the subject's job was seen by him to exhibit these salient task characteristics. The development, scoring, reliability, and validity of these scales are reported elsewhere.[12] A few sample items and the dimensions they were instrumental in measuring were as follows:

11. Hackman, Oldham, Janson, and Purdy, *op cit.,* pp. 27-28.

* Source: Arthur P. Brief, Jim Munro and Ramon J. Aldag, "Correctional Employees' Reactions to Job Characteristics: A Data Based Argument for Job Enlargement," *Journal of Criminal Justice,* 4, 1976, pp. 225-229. Footnotes have been modified and some deletions have been made.

12. J. Richard Hackman and Edward E. Lawlor, III, "Employee Reactions to Job Characteristics," *Journal of Applied Psychology,* 55, 1971, pp. 259-286.

- *How much variety is there in the job?* That is, to what extent does a person have to do many things on the job, using a variety of skills and talents? (Skill variety)
- *In general, how significant or important is the job?* That is, are the results of work on the job likely to significantly affect the lives or well-being of other people? (Task significance)
- *How much autonomy is there in the job?* That is, to what extent does a person decide on his own how to go about doing the job? (Autonomy)

Contained within the questionnaire was a scale designed to tap the subject's desire for the fulfillment of higher order needs. The scale was drawn from the Yale Job Inventory.[13] Higher order needs as used in this study include such needs as self-actualization and achievement. Previous investigations have shown that individuals with strong higher-order need strength respond more positively to enlarged jobs than do those individuals with weak higher-order need strength. Higher-order need strength was measured by asking respondents to indicate the extent to which they preferred one or the other of a pair of jobs. In each case, one of the jobs was relevant to fulfillment of needs for achievement, recognition, or growth, while the other job had as key elements such factors as pay, security, supervision, or working conditions. For example, a few job pairs for which respondents indicated relative preferences were:

A job where the pay is good.	A job where there is considerable opportunity to be creative and innovative.
A job where you are often required to make important decisions.	A job with many pleasant people to work with.
A job which provides constant opportunities for you to learn new and interesting things.	A job with a supervisor who respects you and treats you fairly.

The extent to which respondents showed preference for jobs offering opportunity to satisfy needs for factors such as achievement or growth was used to attain a measure of higher-order need strength.

Also drawn from the Yale Job Inventory were three measures of a worker's affective reactions to his job: level of internal work motivation, degree of job involvement, and general job satisfaction. Typical items from these scales, each with a seven-point response format, include:

- Generally speaking, I am very satisfied with this job. (General satisfaction)
- The most important things that happen to me involve my work on this job. (Job involvement)
- I feel bad and unhappy when I discover I have not done well on this job. (Internal work motivation)

---

13. J. Richard Hackman, *Scoring Key for Yale Job Inventory,* (New Haven: Yale Univ., Department of Administrative Services, 1974).

One additional dependent variable, satisfaction with work itself, was tapped. That measure was taken from the Job Descriptive Index and is composed of eighteen items concerning work itself. [14] For each item, the respondent indicates that he agrees, disagrees, or cannot decide if the item describes the type of work he does. Typical items are:

_____ Frustrating

_____ Satisfying

_____ Boring

_____ Challenging

Results

Relationships between the Task Characteristics and Employee Affective Reactions. As indicated in Table 9-1, each of the salient task characteristics is significantly related to each of the affective reactions measured, with the exception of task identity to level of internal work motivation. Thus, it is clearly demonstrated that the degree to which the subject's jobs are enlarged is positively associated with higher levels of motivation, involvement, and satisfaction.

Table 9-1

Relationships Between Task Characteristics and Employee Reactions

	Task Characteristics			
Employee Reactions	**Variety**	**Autonomy**	**Task Identity**	**Feedback**
Level of internal motivation	.26*	.32*	.06*	.37*
Job involvement	.35*	.34*	.20*	.40*
General job satisfaction	.31*	.51*	.34*	.37*
Satisfaction with the work itself	.37*	.51*	.39*	.35*

* $p < .05; N = 104$.

Higher Order Need Strength. Table 9-2 depicts the differences in reactions between those subjects whose higher-order need strength scores fell into the top third of the distribution and those subjects whose scores fell into the bottom third of the distribution. All differences are in the predicted direction except for the relationships between feedback and level of internal work motivation, and between feedback and general job satisfaction. Therefore, it appears that subjects with strong higher-order need strength do respond more positively to the degree to which the job is enlarged than do subjects with weak higher-order need strength.

---

14. Patricia Cain Smith, Lorne M. Kendall, and Charles L. Hulin, *The Measure of Satisfaction in Work and Retirement*, (Chicago: Rand McNally, 1969).

Discussion

The above findings indicate that the results of job enlargement studies conducted in industrial settings generalize to the corrections institution. Correctional personnel respond more positively to a job that offers them skill variety, autonomy, task identity, and feedback than they do to a job that is perceived as dull and monotonous. From an administrative perspective, this more favorable response may ultimately translate into reduced rates of absenteeism and turnover, and into enhanced levels of job performance.

Table 9-2

Moderating Effects of Higher-Order Need Strength

Dependent Variable	Variety		Autonomy		Task Identity		Feedback	
	High Strength	Low Strength	High Strength	Low Strength	High Strength	Low Strength	High Strength	Low Strength
Level of internal Work motivation	.47*	.22	.32	.15	.07	-.06	.44*	.46*
General job satisfaction	.47*	.35*	.53*	.35*	.40*	.33	.36*	.36*
Job involvement	.42*	.27	.39*	.12	.36*	.15	.52*	.30
Satisfaction with the work itself	.63*	.20	.62*	.36*	.40*	.35*	.52*	.18

* $p < .05$; N=104.

The results further indicate that an employee's desire for the fulfillment of higher-order needs influences his reactions to his job. The correctional employee who is searching for such job outcomes as recognition, achievement, and advancement is particularly sensitive to attempts to job enlargement. In fact, one might anticipate an institution whose staff is composed of a preponderance of individuals striving for the fulfillment of higher-order needs to experience exceedingly low levels of morale *unless* employees are offered enlarged jobs.

In addition to the personnel and managerial arguments for job enlargement, a strong case can be made on the basis of theoretical considerations affecting institutional programming. The first of these considerations is in the nature of the relationship existing between custodial and rehabilitative personnel. For many years authorities in the field of corrections have been pointing out the ill effects that arise from viewing custody and treatment as two different and unrelated functions.[15] Certainly the preponderance of evidence favors viewing all personnel as treatment personnel. One management response to accomplish this end might be to redefine the structure of tasks within the organization that the enlarged jobs would encompass both functions.

---

15. President's Commission on Law Enforcement and Administration of Justice, *Task Force Report: Corrections,* (Washington, D. C.:Government Printing Office, 1967), see Chapter 5.

Another consideration buttressing the argument for job enlargement is that of general systems theory. Whether or not the administrator recognizes it as such, the correctional institution is an open system from both a managerial and programmatic point of view. Enlarging the jobs of correctional personnel would be one method of assisting the institution in conforming to environmental reality.

The data support the position that job enlargement enhances motivation and satisfaction. In this particular case, a good personnel practice also makes excellent program sense by recognizing the openness of the correctional institution and by overcoming the therapy-custody dichotomy in staffing.

CONTINGENCY APPROACH TO JOB DESIGN

The discussion of the job characteristics model and the above study emphasize the need to understand something about both the individual characteristics of the employee and the nature of the job being performed, if a good fit is to be made between the employee and the job, and organizational effectiveness thus improved.

With respect to the contingency approach and job design, the impact of the overall structure of the organization should be mentioned. As Porter, Lawler, and Hackman have noted, "the way an organization is structured appears to set functional limits on the latitude it has in determining how jobs may be designed."[16] According to the Burns-Stalker dichotomy between mechanistic and organic systems (discussed in the previous chapter), the former type of structure tends to be "tall," with a strong centralization of authority and control, while the latter tends to be "flat," with authority and control decentralized. Concerning these generalizations, Porter *et. al.* comment on work design and organizational structure:

Mechanistic systems could not, for example, enlarge jobs in what has been called a "vertical" direction without disrupting the rational coordination of the organization. The reason is that ... workers are given authority and responsibility to make a maximum number of their *own* decisions about how they do their work, the pace they set, and (to a limited extent) the goals they establish for their performance. In a mechanistic system these kinds of decisions are clearly the responsibility and perogative of management. Employees are the doers and in no sense the decision makers or the planners.

"Horizontal" enlargement of jobs might be attempted in mechanistic organizations, since horizontal job enlargement is restricted to expanding the scope of the job content—e.g., by giving the employees added duties which would increase the variety of their work. But even horizontal enlargement would ... have to come through the chain of command ... It would appear that mechanistic organizations would tend to reinforce jobs designed according to the principles of scientific management, i.e., highly simplified with little decision making required of employees. Thus, to some extent any move to enlarge jobs, either horizontally or vertically, might

---

16. Porter, Lawler, and Hackman, *op cit.,* p. 307.

be expected to be resisted by such organizations. [This is precisely the problem in attempting to implement the results in the above study on correctional personnal.]

It would appear that organic systems would tend to reinforce jobs which are enlarged in both the horizontal and vertical directions. Such organizations should have the capability to design jobs in a number of different ways throughout the system without introducing organizational chaos. In addition, organic organizations should be much more able to adjust job designs to individual needs on either a temporary or semipermanent basis that would be the case for mechanistic organizations.[17]

In conclusion, the overall structure of the organization, and individual characteristics and job dimensions, must be considered when redesigning work.

EVALUATING JOB PERFORMANCE

Because of the way criminal justice organizations are structured and their jobs are designed, individual performance must be evaluated. Both the organization and the individual must have some idea of how well tasks are being performed and goals and objectives are being realized. Much of the evaluation in organizations is informal, coming from peers, but also from those in "superior" and "subordinate" positions within the organization's hierarchy. However, criminal justice agencies should develop formal evaluation procedures based on valid criteria, in order to determine the effects of agency personnel on the public they serve, as well as to supplement the organization's planning, development and training, and reward systems.

Developing a
Valid Evaluation System

While most medium and large-sized police agencies have some formal method of evaluating performance, they have seldom examined the validity and reliability of the method used. An invalid and unreliable evaluation system very easily leads to low employee morale, motivation, and job satisfaction, which can severely limit the operational effectiveness of the organization. Construct validity is the first step in developing an effective evaluation system.[18]

Construct Validity

A construct involves a mental image of something, such as intelligence, original thinking, or organizational effectiveness. Construct validity is concerned with the relationship between the definition of the construct and some measure of it; the object of construct validation is to make the measure match as closely as possible the definition of the construct; as illustrated in

---

17. *Ibid.,* p. 308.

18. Much of the discussion in this and the following section is drawn from L. L. Cummings and Donald P. Schwab, *Performance in Organizations: Determinants and Appraisals,* (Glenview, Ill.: Scott, Foresman, 1973), pp. 70-100.

Figure 9-2. The upper circle of the diagram represents some construct, while the lower circle represents a measure of that construct. The object is to create complete overlap between the circles. While it is virtually impossible in the behavioral and social sciences to make the measure conform exactly to the construct, more overlap means more accurate measurement.

Complete overlap may not occur for two general reasons. First, all elements of the construct might not be measured. This situation, depicted by the area with vertical lines in Figure 9-2, is termed *measurement deficiency*. Performance evaluation measures may be deficient in a number of ways; measures of employee productivity which accounted for quantity of output

Figure 9-2

Deficiency and Contamination in Construct Validity

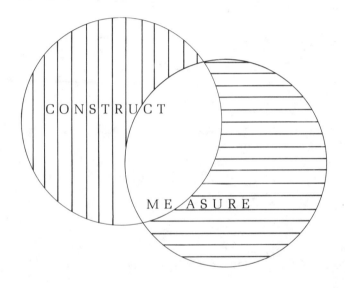

Source: L. L. Cummings and Donald P. Schwab, *Performance in Organizations*, (Glenview, Ill.: Scott, Foresman, 1973), p. 72.

but not quality would be viewed as deficient for example. Measurement deficiency occurs in police agencies which directly measure only the number of arrests made (quantity) and do not consider the number of convictions obtained (quality) from those arrests.

The measure may not overlap totally with the construct because the measure may cover elements not in the construct. This situation, depicted by the area with the horizontal lines in Figure 9-2, is termed *measurement contamination*. Contamination occurs frequently in performance evaluation; for example, a measure can tap the rater's personal likes or dislikes for the employee being evaluated.

Although the construct validity problem is easily understood conceptually, it is difficult to apply operationally. Two approaches which can be used to solve this problem are discussed below. The first emphasizes the role of judgment in developing an evaluation method with high construct validity. The second approach, related to the first, emphasizes the reduction of errors in the evaluation measure used.

Judgmental Approach

The construct validity of any specific evaluation technique can be increased through a development procedure based on: (1) job analysis, (2) successful task performance definition, and (3) performance measure development.

Job Analysis: In any evaluation system, the job which the employees to be evaluated perform is first analyzed; this step will be further analyzed in the following chapter. Regardless of the procedures used, job analysis has two major objectives. The first involves the outcomes of the tasks, and is concerned with the questions: What are the goals of the activity? What level of performance must be attained in these goals? The second objective involves the questions: What behaviors does an employee on this job have to engage in to attain the desired goals? What is the relative importance of each of these behaviors?

Definition of Success: Information about outcomes and employee behaviors helps determine which components account for job success; what job outcomes differentiate between successful and unsuccessful job performance (what are the elements of the job-success construct)? Second, the elements identified must be weighted in terms of their importance to overall job success. Generally, these weightings are judgmental, based on the philosophy and goals of the organization. For example, in the last chapter it was noted that criminal justice agencies have separate "styles" and goal emphases; watchman, service, and legalistic styles have been observed in the police subsystem, while restraint, reform, rehabilitation and reintegration typologies have been specified within the correctional subsystem. The point is simply that each type of agency would most likely assign different weights to those elements which combine to produce job success.

Development of Measures: The final step in the process involves the development of the instrument which measures the elements of success identified above. Specific procedures will be reviewed in the next section, but regardless of the procedure used, this step should be closely connected with the one above. Items should be designed for each element identified in the construct, in order to reduce deficiency and contamination in the final overall measure. The weightings of these items should also correspond closely with the weights previously assigned to the construct elements.

Error Reduction Approaches

In the second approach to increasing construct validity, those types of errors which may be present in evaluation measures and reduce construct validity are identified and eliminated. Two common types, variable and constant errors, exist.

Variable Errors: Two types of variable errors occur in evaluations; the first involves *disagreement between raters* and the second involves *disagreement over time.* Two or more evaluators may not agree on the assessed performance of a group of employees for several reasons, and removal of these conditions will facilitate construct validity. For instance, the instrument designed for performance evaluation may use ambiguous standards (constructs), leading to evaluation disagreement and low validity. Another reason has to do with the evaluators themselves. Disagreements are likely if they do not see the same behavior in the individual to be assessed; a first level supervisor (sergeant) who has close contact with an employee may evaluate him differently than a higher ranking official (lieutenant) who has less contact.

Only individuals who are very familiar with the employee's work behaviors should assess their performance. Subsequently, this suggests the need to have evaluation accomplished by immediate supervisors, or even peers, because lack of knowledge about the individuals evaluated is a serious source of error. A further source of error is lack of motivation on the evaluator's part. Poor motivation often stems from a failure to understand the importance of the evaluation procedure. This suggests the need to engage in some training activities before implementing an evaluation program. The organization must be certain that the raters understand and accept the purpose of the program and are thoroughly familiar with the specific evaluation techniques to be used.

In the second approach to measuring for potential variable error, evaluations taken from one rater at two points in time, are compared. However, measurement by one evaluator over a period of time is generally less satisfactory than measurement by different evaluators at approximately the same time. One would expect some change in an employee's performance over time; this is obviously not variable error. Thus, other things being equal, disagreement over time will overstate variable error, to the extent that real performance changes take place. Also, when a person makes several evaluations over a period of time, his or her memory may lead to fairly consistent results, therefore overstating agreement.

In short, because of the stated limitations in measuring disagreement at different points in time, a comparison by different evaluators at approximately the same time is to be preferred. However, when it is difficult or impossible to use two raters who are knowledgeable about an employee's performance, a measure of disagreement over time may be the only available approach; subsequently, such data must be interpreted with caution.

Constant Errors: While variable errors involve forms of disagreements, constant errors involve an unreal *similarity between scores.* This similarity may show up in the scores assigned to an individual performer (*intraindividual* error), or in scores assigned to a number of performers (*interindividual* errors). In intraindividual or *halo* error, an evaluator rates a performer as good or bad on all characteristics, based on knowledge of only one characteristic. A supervisor would make a halo error if he or she rated an employee high on all characteristics simply because the employee was known to be outstanding in one characteristic, such as initiative. Therefore, any evaluation which contains similar ratings across all characteristics should be suspected of containing halo error.

An evaluator may make interindividual errors by giving falsely similar evaluations across individuals. This can take three forms: *leniency* error, in which the evaluator rates everyone too high; *strictness* error, in which the evaluator rates everyone too low; and *central tendency* error, where everyone may be given average ratings.

Although certain types of constant error occur with certain types of evaluation techniques, the rater may contribute to these errors regardless of the evaluation technique used. Indeed, Taft has suggested that the evaluator's motivation to do a good job is probably the most important factor in obtaining error-free evaluations.[19] This indicates that the organization must give special consideration to the manner in which evaluators are approached with the responsibility for assessing performance.

In order to develop high degrees of construct validity in performance evaluation measures, both approaches discussed above should be utilized. The first focuses on the need to employ job analysis, to define successful task performance, and to develop an evaluative measure based on the definition of success. The second emphasizes the identification and elimination of constant and variable errors. Once the problems inherent in developing a valid evaluation system have been dealt with, specific types of performance measures can be described.

PERFORMANCE EVALUATION METHODS

The most important determinant of the validity and effectiveness of any evaluation procedure is likely to be the type of measure used. A few of the more popular methods currently used in police agencies, and the major problems or concerns of each, are discussed below.

Graphic Rating Scale

The graphic rating scale is by far the most frequently used method of evaluation. Graphic scales provide a list of behavioral characteristics or standards (such as quality of work, cooperation, and effectiveness) and a range of degrees for each (such as low, average, and high). The rater, generally a supervisor, simply places a check on the evaluation form next to the word or phrase which best describes the employee with respect to each standard or characteristic. An overall evaluation of the individual's performance is often computed by summing the individual item scores.

Graphic scales use three major dimensions, all of which involve the degree to which: (1) the meaning of the response categories is defined; (2) the person interpreting the ratings (for example, a first line supervisor or higher

---

19. Ronald Taft, "The Ability to Judge People," *Psychological Bulletin*, 52, 1955, pp. 1-23.

official) can tell what response was intended by the rater; and (3) the rated performance dimension is defined for the rater.[20]

If the rater is to make determinations of individual performers which are useful, the response categories must be marked off in meaningful units of some type. Whether these units are descriptions of different behaviors or numerical values or both, they leave much to the interpretation of the rater. Numerical values are generally more useful when specific descriptive statements accompany them. The second major dimension involves the degree to which the person interpreting the evaluation can determine what response was intended; the conditions affecting the scaling descriptions apply to the reader of the ratings as well as to the rater. The third dimension involves how well the performance characteristic being rated is defined for the rater. For example, if only the term "work quality" is used, many different interpretations may result. Accordingly, if the raters do not have similar interpretations of each item to be rated, the validity of the evaluations will be low and the ratings will not be meaningful.

The possible ambiguities in this type of performance evaluation lead to a number of serious limitations. First, the scaling method allows for halo error as well as for the interindividual errors of leniency, strictness, and central tendency. Additionally, this method makes it easy for raters to bias their evaluation for or against a performer. Finally, graphic rating scales frequently focus on employees' personality characteristics instead of concrete behavior, with which performance evaluation is actually concerned.

Research suggests that nonbehaviorally related feedback leads to defensiveness and rigidity on the part of the person being evaluated. For instance, simply telling people that they are low in work quality does not explain how they can change and improve a particular behavior. Such an approach only suggests that the behavior is not acceptable, and people do not react well to this type of feedback. If evaluation methods are not related to behavior, it is difficult to set future goals and objectives, which reduces the motivational potential of the procedure. The motivational potential is further reduced because it is difficult to tie rewards to specific behaviors.

Figure 9-3 exemplifies a graphic rating scale for police personnel. Recommended by the International Association of Chiefs of Police (IACP), the scale provides for the semi-annual rating of both sworn and civilian police personnel with the rank of captain and below. According to the IACP, this rating system accounts for the most recent trends in performance evaluation:

1. It avoids the confusion caused by multiplicity of purposes. This system has only one definite objective in mind—to inform the employee of his or her standing, with intent to improve performance or to sustain performance which is already superior.

2. It eliminates summary or numerical ratings; it is impossible to categorize an employee as "Excellent," "Above Average," "Average," and so forth.

---

20. Robert M. Guion, *Personnel Testing*, (New York: McGraw-Hill Book Company, 1965).

Figure 9-3

IACP Performance Evaluation Report

PERFORMANCE EVALUATION REPORT	USE INK OR TYPEWRITER FOR FINAL MARKINGS		

EMPLOYEE NAME (Last) (First) (Init.)	EMPLOYEE NO.	DIVISION	DISTRICT OR SECTION
CLASS TITLE	EMPLOYEE STATUS	ASSIGNMENT	DUE DATE:

SECTION A	1 2 3 4	5	FACTOR CHECK LIST — Immediate Supervisor Must Check Each Factor in the Appropriate Column	DOES NOT APPLY	SECTION B — Record job STRENGTHS, superior performance incidents, progress achieved, or checks in Col. 4.

Column headers for Section A (diagonal): NOT SATISFACTORY, SOME IMPROVEMENT NEEDED, MEETS STANDARDS, EXCEEDS STANDARDS

Factor Check List:
1. Observance of Work Hours
2. Attendance
3. Grooming & Dress
4. Compliance with Rules
5. Safety Practices
6. Public Contacts
7. Suspect Contacts
8. Employee Contacts
9. Knowledge of Work
10. Work Judgments
11. Planning and Organizing
12. Job Skill Level
13. Quality of Work
14. Volume of Acceptable Work
15. Meeting Deadlines
16. Accepts Responsibility
17. Accepts Direction
18. Accepts Change
19. Effectiveness Under Stress
20. Appearance of Work Station
21. Operation & Care of Equip.
22. Work Coordination
23. Initiative
24. (ADDITIONAL FACTORS)
25.
26.
27.
28.
29.

SECTION C — Record specific GOALS or IMPROVEMENT PROGRAMS to be undertaken during next evaluation period.

SECTION D — Describe STANDARD performance. (Optional for most factors checked in Col. 3; MANDATORY for some factors — see instructions.)

SECTION E — Record specific work performance DEFICIENCIES or job behavior requiring improvement or correction. (Explain checks in Col. 1 and 2.)

FOR EMPLOYEES who SUPERVISE OTHERS
30. Planning & Organizing
31. Scheduling & Coordinating
32. Training & Instructing
33. Effectiveness
34. Evaluating Subordinates
35. Judgments & Decisions
36. Leadership
37. Operational Economy
38. Supervisory Control
39. (ADDITIONAL FACTORS)
40.
41.

□ I DO

RATER: I certify this report represents my best judgment. □ I DO NOT recommend this employee be granted permanent status. (For final probationary reports only.)

(RATER'S SIGNATURE)   (TITLE)   (DATE)

REVIEWER: (IF NONE, SO INDICATE)
(REVIEWER'S SIGNATURE)   (TITLE)   (DATE)

EMPLOYEE: I certify that this report has been discussed with me. I understand my signature does not necessarily indicate agreement. □ I wish to discuss this report with the reviewer.

Comment:

(EMPLOYEE'S SIGNATURE)   (DATE)

CHECKS IN COLS. 1 AND 2 MUST BE EXPLAINED IN SECTION E

Source: International Association of Chiefs of Police, *Guide to Performance Evaluation*, (Gathersburg, Maryland: IACP, 1971), p. 19.

3. Factor definitions or standards, rather than intangible qualities, are provided to help form opinions about performance.

4. Ample provision is made for explanatory comments.

5. An employee interview is a major feature.

6. Explanatory material is part of the package to be given to raters at the beginning of each rating period.[21]

If this system is properly utilized, many of the ambiguities associated with this type of evaluation may be eliminated. By requiring the listing of specific job behavior strengths, performance deficiencies, and goals for improvement, all of which are discussed with the employee during the evaluation interview, the motivational potential can be maintained or increased (see Figure 9-3, sections B, C, and E). Also, by defining the factors or behavior characteristics to be evaluated, each rater should have a similar understanding of the items to be rated (assuming proper training has taken place). A sampling of the factor definitions used in this system is provided by Table 9-3.

Employee Comparisons

A second popular method of evaluating employee performance involves comparison techniques. An alternative to the traditional graphic rating scale, comparison methods attempt to minimize halo and inter-individual errors. The three widely used procedures, known as ranking, paired comparison, and forced distribution, are all characterized by two features: (1) they evaluate individual performers by comparing one against the other on the dimension of interest; and (2) this comparison is generally made on one global overall dimension of job performance.

Ranking. In the simple rank-order procedure, the rater merely orders the employees from the highest performer in the group to the lowest performer on a given dimension. In a more complex variation, known as the alternative ranking method, the rater first selects the very best performer in the group and then the very worst performer. The evaluator then selects the second best and second worst performer, alternating between the best and poorest employees until the evaluations are completed.

Paired Comparison. Another common alternative to the rank-order procedure is the paired comparison method, in which the rater compares each employee with every other employee, one at a time. An employee's performance or standing in the final ranking is determined by the number of times he has been chosen over the other employees.

Figure 9-4 illustrates how this technique is used when four employees are to be rated. The circled letters indicate who the rater considers the better performer in each pair; the highest ranked employee would be C, followed

---

21. International Association of Chiefs of Police, *Guide to Performance Evaluation*, (Gaithersburg, Maryland: IACP, 1972), pp. 3-4.

Table 9-3
IACP Factor Definition Examples

No.	Factor	Definition
6	Public Contacts	Refers to all public contact made through personal or telephone conversation, correspondence, and day-to-day appearances before the public. Does the employee's exposure to the public eye and ear reflect credit on the department and promote a good public image? Is the employee courteous and discreet in his public contacts and behavior? Is he aware of the necessity to present a consistently good appearance on the public?
7	Suspect Contacts	As with public contacts, this factor may not apply to some employees and yet may be extremely significant in the cases of other employees. Is the employee too harsh or too timid with suspects or prisoners? Is his attitude or behavior toward suspects or prisoners detrimental to security, a good image, or investigative efficiency?
8	Employee Contacts	Reflects only those contacts which either improve or reduce the effectiveness of the employees involved. It does not apply to an employee's personal popularity or lack of it. Does he mind his own business, but at the same time have a proper concern for the problems of other employees whose jobs touch his? Is he a disruptive influence? Does he bother or embarrass others with his personal problems? Is he a positive influence on the morale of others?
13	Quality of Work	The degree of excellence of the work performed over the entire rating period is measured here. In rating this factor, attention should be paid to the consequences of poor quality work. Is the employee's work effective, accurate, thorough, and acceptable? Must the work be redone, thus reducing the potential volume of acceptable work which could have been produced? Do errors in the employee's work affect the efforts of others? Does poor work too often reflect adversely upon the department? Are reports clear, concise and accurate?
18	Accepts Change	Use this factor to evaluate the traits of adaptability and flexibility. Does the employee accept change willingly? Does he slow down progress or cause inefficiencies by resistance to change? Does he adapt satisfactorily to new work surroundings, new equipment, new procedures, new supervisors?
23	Initiative	Refers to initiation of action by the employee. While initiative shows up in the form of suggestions and constructive criticism, it is most obvious when the employee originates investigations or acts to produce more efficient, productive or economical methods and procedures. Does he take opportunities to exercise initiative or must he be prodded into action? Is he alert to operating efficiency and cost-cutting? Is he inventive? Does he offer practical constructive criticism?

Source: International Association of Chiefs of Police, *Guide to Performance Evaluation*, (Gaithersburg, Maryland: IACP, 1972), pp. 13-16.

by employees A, B, and D. The formula for calculating the number of comparisons to be made in N(N-1)/2, where N is the number of employees to be ranked. Thus if there are 10 employees to be ranked, there will be 45 pairs: 10 x 9 = 90 ÷ 2 = 45.

Figure 9-4

**Paired Comparison Evaluation Method
with Four Employees**

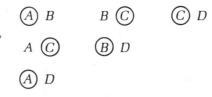

Source: L. L. Cummings and Donald P. Schwab, *Performance in Organizations*, (Glenview, Ill.: Scott, Foresman, 1973), p. 83.

Ranking methods avoid the interindividual errors of leniency, strictness, or central tendency, because the evaluator must rank employees from high to low. Also, ranking techniques make it easier to obtain adequate agreement between different raters; alternative ranking, and especially paired comparisons, are best.

A major criticism of these ranking methods is that the ranking is usually done on some global measure, and such evaluations are unrealistic. Problems develop because two or more evaluators may not define overall effectiveness in exactly the same manner. On the other hand, if more than one dimension is being ranked, halo error may affect an individual's ranking. Another weakness of the ranking systems results from the lack of comparability of evaluations across groups or locations. For example, it is difficult to compare employees in separate patrol units because the highest-ranking performer in one unit may be only average in the other unit. If, however, the evaluators adequately know employees in both units, the rankings can then be meaningfully combined. More accurate employee evaluations can result from periodically transfering supervisors to different units and comparing evaluations on the same employees.

A final limitation increases the difficulty of using ranking procedures for feedback and developmental purposes. Little concrete information for improving performance is provided when only a single global dimension is evaluated. Additionally, revealing the comparisons to individual employees often results in dysfunctional, highly personal discussions concerning the relative merits of various individuals. Thus ranking procedures may severely limit employee motivation while preventing opportunities for specific suggestions concerning improvement and overall development.

Forced Distribution. This comparative method forces the rater to assign a certain percentage of employees to specific categories on each dimension evaluated. The categories typically represent a normal curve; the evaluator rates 10% of the employees highest on an item, 20% above average, 40% average, 20% below average, and 10% lowest.

By including comparisons based on several performance factors rather than on a single global dimension, this procedure eliminates one of the major criticisms directed at ranking methods. Furthermore, by forcing the distribution to follow a normal curve, such interindividual errors as leniency and strictness are controlled. A problem persists, however, because the performers as a group may not conform to the distribution. In a particular group, a greater percentage of its performers could belong at the high end of the curve than the 10% would normally allow. This is most common when small groups like planning and research or personnel units are being evaluated; thus when small groups are involved, a more suitable distribution scheme should be developed. Such a scheme, for example, could compare employees with respect to the top one-third, middle one-third, and bottom one-third.

Management by Objectives

In recent years, the management by objectives (MBO) approach has provided an alternative to rating scales and comparison methods of measuring employee performance. This approach is becoming fashionable in the police field, but while the potential benefits of MBO are substantial, the weaknesses of this method should be carefully considered before it is put into practice.

MBO is based on mutual agreement between superiors and subordinates concerning specific performance objectives and how achievement of those objectives is to be measured. Cummings and Schwab suggest that this concept involves a four-step process:

The first step involves defining goals for the employee to accomplish during some specified future time period. These goals may be initially proposed by the subordinate with resulting approval by the superior with resulting discussion and acceptance by the subordinate. Advocates of the method stress the need for subordinate participation, regardless of who initiates the process . . . Advocates also stress the need to specify goals as quantitatively as possible. In a sales job, for example, specific goals might be set with respect to sales volume, new accounts, customers called on, and so on. A personnel manager may set goals with respect to selection instruments validated, number of employees retrained, and so on. Goal statements may be set for methods or for means of accomplishment as well as for desired outcomes.

The second step consists of the subordinate's carrying out the objectives established. In some respects MBO may make the task easier since the goals to be achieved have presumable been clearly stated in the previous step.

The third step involves an evaluation of the performance against the goals initially established. This step is often begun by a self-appraisal. The subordinate writes a report describing how well he has met his objectives. This appraisal is discussed with the superior. Reasons for goals not being met are analyzed and discussed.

The final step consists of establishing new goals for the subsequent time period. Thus the process repeats itself.[22]

The advantages of evaluating employees in terms of mutually set measures include greater ego involvement, increased motivation, and increased planning behavior, all of which have an effect upon performance.[23]

Tosi and Carroll suggest that three basic aspects of MBO affect its success: goals and goal setting; participation and involvement of subordinates; and feedback and performance evaluation. The authors describe each of these aspects as follows:

Goals and goal setting. A number of studies have clearly demonstrated that when an individual or group has a specific goal, there is higher performance than when the goals are general, or have not been set. Generally, high performance can be associated with higher individual or group goals. A number of studies also suggest that performance improvement occurs when an individual is successful in achieving past goals. When there is previous goal success, the individual is more likely to set higher goals in future periods, and he is more likely to attain them.

Participation. There have been a number of diverse findings about the relationship of participation in decision-making and productivity. These apparently contradictory findings have been resolved by concluding that if the subordinate perceives the participation to be legitimate, it will have positive effects on productivity. In additon, participation does seem to have an effect on the degree of acceptance of decisions reached mutually. There is also evidence that involvement and participation are positively correlated with the level of job satisfaction.

Feedback. Both laboratory and field research have demonstrated that relatively clear, unambiguous feedback increases problem solving capacities of groups and improves the performance of individuals. Positive attitudes, increased confidence in decisions, and greater certainties of superior's expectations were found to be related to communications which clarified roles and role expectancies with more and better information . . . Positive actions are more likely to be taken by subordinates when feedback is viewed as supportive and is objectively based.[24]

The MBO system is consistent with this text's emphasis on individual differences. Individualized goals are especially appealing when related to an evaluation procedure with high construct validity. Ironically, this is also one of the major problems of MBO in police organizations. Because most police jobs are complex, especially patrol work with its large degree of discretion, it is difficult to develop objective performance measures. For example, it is hard to objectively measure social service and order maintenance activities of patrol officers; it may be simple enough to add up the number of arrests made by an officer over a specific period of time (or even the number of convictions obtained), but how does one objectively measure the amount of good an officer may do without making an arrest? Indeed, an officer who makes few arrests is most likely performing more efficiently than

---

22. Cummings and Schwab, *op. cit.,* pp. 95-96.

23. Henry L. Tosi and Stephen J. Carroll, "Management by Objectives," *Personnel Administration,* 33, 1970, p. 44.

24. *Ibid.,* p. 45.

an officer who makes many, as problems can frequently be ameliorated without the use of arrest. For this reason, Tosi, Rizzo, and Carroll have written that MBO "is deemed most appropriate in situations where activities tend to be recurring or repetitious, where change toward new or improved conditions is sought."[25] This does not mean that MBO cannot be used in complex job situations, but valid objectives for measuring performance must be carefully developed. For instance, methods could be devised which credit patrol officers for their performance in defusing potentially hazardous situations without the use of arrest.

Individualization may also create a problem with respect to the equitable distribution of rewards. Because goals are set according to their difficulty, two employees may be working toward goals which require substantially different levels of competency. Are they to be rewarded equally, even though one accomplishes a far more difficult set of goals? What if one employee accomplishes a relatively simple set of goals, while the other fails to reach the more difficult set? Such a system would not motivate the more highly skilled individual. Tying rewards directly to MBO may encourage employees to set easily attainable goals, thus stifling problem solving and innovation within the organization.

Some further limitations of MBO were discovered by Raia, in a two-part study of the Purex Corporation covering a four-year period.[26] In the initial study, the investigator found that participants felt the program had increased awareness of the company's goals and had improved communications and understanding. The follow-up study, however, indicated that the participants perceived the program as a weak motivator for the improvement of performance. They also felt that MBO increased paperwork, over-emphasized production (quantity, not quality), failed to involve all levels of management, and was used as a whip.

The above criticisms indicate that the MBO is not a panacea for evaluating performance; it has strengths and weaknesses like any other method. Kerr suggests that the following features of MBO are valuable: conscious emphasis on goal-setting, frequent feedback and interaction between superior and subordinate, and opportunities for participation. The following features should be discarded: linking MBO to the compensation system, using MBO to measure performance "objectively," over-emphasis on paperwork, and pre-packaged programs and expensive consultants. Finally, to improve the use of MBO, Kerr would incorporate group goal-setting and group evaluation of performance.[27]

---

25. Henry L. Tosi, John R. Rizzo, and Stephen J. Carroll, "Setting Goals in Management by Objectives," *California Management Review*, 12, 1970, p. 70.

26. Anthony P. Raia, "Goal Setting and Self-Control," *Journal of Management Studies*, 11, 1965, pp. 24-53; and Raia, "A Second Look at Management Goals and Controls," *California Management Review*, 8, Summer 1966, pp. 49-58.

27. Steven Kerr, "Some Modifications in MBO as an OD Strategy," presentation, Academy of Management Proceedings, 1972 National Meeting.

WHO EVALUATES?

Evidence suggests that regardless of the method used, the individual doing the evaluation—superior, peer or subordinate, or self—has a vital impact on the effectiveness of the performance evaluation system.

Supervisory Evaluation

In police agencies, the performer's immediate supervisor is usually responsible for carrying out evaluations. This arrangement is rarely questioned, and evaluation is perceived as an important part of a supervisor's job. According to research on supervisory ratings, an average of several evaluations made by competent raters is more valuable than a single rating.[28] An employee would most likely receive a more valid rating if he or she had worked for (and was evaluated by) three or four supervisors over a period of time. An important consideration is that the supervisors being used as evaluators be in a position to rate the employee's performance competently.

This may have special significance for police evaluations of probationary employees. Frequently, a single supervisor decides whether or not the employee has performed at a satisfactory level and can be "promoted" from probationary to permanent status. From both the employee's and the organization's standpoint, it would be advantageous to rotate the probationary employee among several supervisors, in order to obtain a more valid, unbiased opinion of the employee's performance. In this way, the critical decision about retaining the employee becomes more meaningful.

Peer and Subordinate Evaluations

Ratings by peers have been found to be facilitated by two considerations: (1) a high level of interpersonal trust and sharing among peers, coupled with a noncompetitive reward system, and (2) where information about the person's performance is uniquely available to peers. Peer evaluations may be appropriate when the supervisor is unable to effectively observe subordinate behavior. They can also help to discover communication and coordination problems among work team members, and to further delineate mutual expectations.[29]

Peer evaluations are not appropriate for organizations which have highly competitive reward systems; conflicts arise between evaluating peers highly and maintaining one's own chances of a large salary increase, or between evaluating peers poorly and maintaining their friendship. Peer evaluations are thus invalid, and even disruptive, in such organizations. Evaluations by peers could be used efficiently for gathering information not

---

28. John B. Miner, "Management Appraisal: A Capsule Review and Current References," *Business Horizons*, 11, 1968, pp. 83-96.

29. Cummings and Schwab, *op. cit.*, pp. 104-105.

tied to the reward system, and, if used anonymously, many of the personal conflicts mentioned could be avoided.

Most criminal justice organizations can benefit from ratings by subordinates of their superiors, especially anonymous evaluations used as part of the development process for managers. However, there are several problems in such an approach. Studies have indicated that some subordinates perceive it as illegitimate, while others fear that they may be reprimanded for an unfavorable but honest evaluation. Also, it has been shown that subordinates may base their evaluations on how well their superiors meet their personal needs, and not on the extent to which the supervisor contributes to the organization's goals.[30] Nevertheless, subordinate evaluations are helpful when used in developing managers, who see how they are viewed by others and how they may need to change their behavior.

Self-Evaluation

Evidence indicates that employees like to know where they stand and are constantly evaluating themselves. This approach has several positive aspects, including: (1) more satisfying and constructive evaluation interviews, (2) less defensiveness by performers, with respect to both the evaluation interviews and the overall performance evaluation process, and (3) improved job performance.[31] However, the usefulness of participation depends on a number of factors, including the interviewee's self-esteem, authoritarianism, and the need for independence.[32]

A major problem with respect to the validity of self-evaluations involves the low agreement between self and supervisory evaluations; subordinates tend to evaluate their own performance more favorably than do their superiors. However, two recent studies concluded that self-evaluations display less central tendency and fewer halo errors than superior evaluations.[33] Another potential defect involves the attaining of goals; employees often get carried away with attempting to reach goals, and feel that any means are justified in order to accomplish the goals. By using self-evaluation primarily as a development technique, and by not tying salary increases or promotions to this approach, these problems can usually be avoided.

REWARDING PERFORMANCE

While the effectiveness of any evaluation procedure is based largely on the type of measure used, and on who conducts the evaluation, how rewards

---

30. R. S. Barrett, *Performance Rating*, (Chicago: Science Research Associates, 1966).

31. Cummings and Schwab, *op. cit.*, p. 106.

32. Joseph M. Hilleory and Kenneth N. Wexley, "Participation Effects in Appraisal Interviews Conducted in a Training Situation," *Journal of Applied Psychology*, 59, 1974, pp. 168-171.

33. Herbert G. Heneman, III, "Comparison of Self and Superior Ratings of Managerial Performance," *Journal of Applied Psychology*, 59, 1974, pp. 638-642; Richard H. Klimoski and Manuel London, "Role of the Rater in Performance Appraisals," *Journal of Applied Psycholoyg*, 59, 1974, pp. 455-451.

are tied to successful performance is also of major significance when attempting to increase employee performance and motiviational levels. Although it is important to link rewards to performance, this does not necessarily lead to an argument for an incentive-based system. While incentive systems are sometimes appropriate, work in police organizations is usually not easily connected to piece-rate or group-rate payment methods. However, because it does not make much sense to pay salaries without obtaining some motivational return, police agencies should allocate a portion of their wage-increase budget for merit compensation.

The reward-performance issue is much broader in scope than a discussion on monetary compensation would imply. Because people experience a wide variety of rewards for work, it is in the organization's best interests to link as many other rewards to performance as it controls, such as promotions, status, and work assignments. Rewards should also include such informal outcomes as the selective use of managerial recognition and praise.

Based on the discussion in this section and on the expectancy and equity theories of motivation presented in Chapter 5, several implications of linking rewards to performance can be suggested: (1) the reward process should be open to the extent that it reduces employee misperceptions; (2) rewards should be equal to the level of performance achieved; (3) to the greatest extent possible, rewards should be based on objective rather than subjective criteria; (4) moderately difficult goals should be set; (5) employees should be allowed to participate in setting their own goals as well as to evaluate their own performance; and (6) adequate job performance feedback must be provided. Research indicates that if the performance evaluation system interacts effectively with the compensation system, the motivation and performance levels of employees should be high.

CONTINGENCY APPROACH
TO PERFORMANCE EVALUATION

While there has not been as much research conducted on the contingency aspects of performance evaluation as on other organization variables (such as structure and leadership), it does appear that the organizational climate will strongly affect the major factors in evaluation systems. Accounting for the primary differences with respect to the organizational systems discussed in the last chapter (closed, stable, mechanistic and open, adaptive, organic), and for the factors which contribute to effective performance evaluation, the proposed contingency views in Table 9-4 can be applied to police organizations. An organization which uses several different performance measures and evaluators will most likely obtain more valid and meaningful information upon which to base rewards and make other decisions.

Table 9-4

Contingency Views of Preformance Evaluation

Performance Factors	Organizational Characteristics	
	Mechanistic Structure	Organic Structure
Performance Characteristics	Many, precisely defined characteristics; emphasis on how work is carried out	Few, broadly defined characteristics; emphasis on goals accomplished
Method of Performance Evaluation	Emphasis on use of graphic rating scales	Emphasis on use of MBO and/or a combination of methods (rating scales, comparisons, etc.)
Goal Setting	By the organization	Mutual: between the organization and the performer
Use of Feedback	Infrequent, non-behavioral orientation	Frequent, behavioral orientation
Who Evaluates	Emphasis on immediate supervisor or superior	Emphasis on both performer and supervisor and/or combinations (peer, subordinate, etc.)
Use of Rewards	Based on seniority	Based on merit

SUMMARY

How jobs are designed and performance evaluated significantly affects employee behavior and the overall efficiency and effectiveness of the organization. While jobs can be expanded either horizontally (enlarged) or vertically (enriched), individual differences (in needs and goals and skill and ability levels) must be considered if a proper match is to be made between an employee and his or her work. The job characteristics model takes individual differences into account, and provides the means for diagnosing jobs (in ongoing organizations) for their motivational content. In general terms, five "core" job dimensions promote three "psychological states", which in turn lead to a number of beneficial personal and work outcomes. Once the job has been diagnosed, job expansion can help police and other criminal justice organizations achieve their goals for higher quality work, as well as provide employees with more meaningful work. A study involving job enlargement and correctional personnel indicated that job enlargement increased the motivation and satisfaction of correctional employees, particularly those employees who had a strong desire for fulfilling higher order needs. Similar studies need to be carried out in the police field, in order to determine whether or not expanded jobs would lead to similar results with respect to motivation and satisfaction, as well as increased performance.

Performance evaluation is necessary because both the organization and the individual must have some idea of how well tasks are being performed and goals are being met. In order to accurately determine these, the method(s) used must be valid and reliable. While most medium and large-sized police organizations have some type of formal evaluation system, they have seldom considered whether or not they are actually measuring what they wish to measure; this involves construct validity, or the relationship between the measure and construct. Construct validity may be affected by both measurement deficiency and measurement contamination; both judgmental and error reduction approaches should be used to increase construct validity.

The validity and effectiveness of the evaluation system is greatly influenced by the specific method employed. The graphic rating scale is the most frequently used method in police agencies, although it is subject to a number of limitations such as halo and interindividual errors, as well as non-behaviorally related feedback. Comparison methods attempt to minimize halo and interindividual errors, but tend to rate employees on only one global dimension; they also are difficult to use for constructive feedback and developmental purposes. MBO individualizes the evaluation process through the participation of both the performer and the supervisor, and focuses on relatively specific performance behaviors. However, it is difficult to use MBO in developing objective performance measures for many police jobs because of their complexity, and it cannot be used effectively with departmental compensation systems.

Evaluations are normally conducted by the immediate superior of the performer. While this procedure is rarely questioned, its validity is increased by averaging several evaluations made by competent raters. Evaluations by a performer's peers have been found useful for gathering information and discovering communication and coordination problems among work team members; they are not appropriate, however, when tied to highly competitive reward systems. Subordinate evaluations of superiors appear to be the most useful for feedback and developmental purposes. Self-evaluations are the most useful for the purpose of development.

Finally, the contingency approach to job design and performance evaluation was presented. Mechanistic systems might be expected to resist any approach to expanding jobs (although the horizontal direction might be attempted), while organic systems would tend to reinforce jobs which are expanded both horizontally and vertically. The organizational climate will also have a strong influence on the evaluation system(s) used. The more traditional methods are used in the mechanistic structures, while organic structures are more willing to innovate by using more contemporary methods and/or a combination of several methods connected to performance evaluation.

DISCUSSION QUESTIONS

1. Discuss the traditional approach to job design and its major weaknesses.

2. Contrast job enlargement with job enrichment and discuss how each could apply to a particular job in which you have worked.

3. Contrast Herzberg's motivation-hygiene theory of job design with the Job Characteristics Model of work motivation.

4. Review the research design of the job enlargement study conducted in the correctional agency, and discuss the general results of the study.

5. Discuss why it is important that police and other criminal justice agencies develop formal evaluation procedures based on valid criteria.

6. Discuss the major advantages and disadvantages of the following performance evaluation methods: graphic rating scales, employee comparisons (including ranking, paired, and forced distribution), and MBO; which method do you feel would be the most advantageous in a police organization? Why?

7. Discuss under what circumstances supervisory, peer and subordinate, and self-evaluations appear to be the most appropriate.

ANNOTATED BIBLIOGRAPHY

Cummings, L.L., and Donald P. Schwab, *Performance in Organizations: Determinants and Appraisal,* (Glenview, Illinois: Scott, Foresman and Company, 1973). This concise book is aimed at improving organizational productivity and performance; it suggests that this can best be accomplished by manipulating the major behavioral determinants of performance, by utilizing accurate concepts and techniques of appraisal, and by designing performance utilization and evaluation systems to fit specific environments.

Ford, Robert N., "Job Enrichment Lessons from AT&T," *Harvard Business Review.* The results of 19 formal field experiments from 1965 to 1968 at AT&T are reported; jobs were designed so that each employee could identify with some meaningful unit of production or could serve a specific set of clients or customers. Furthermore, the research suggested that "nesting" several enriched jobs may be the next step, after the enrichment of single jobs, in the proper utilization of human resources.

Hackman, J. Richard, and Greg R. Oldham, "Motivation through the Design of Work: Test of a Theory," *Organizational Behavior and Human Performance,* 16, 1976, pp. 250-279. The proposed Job Characteristics Model specifies the conditions under which individuals will become internally motivated to perform effectively on their jobs; support for the validity of the model was indicated through tests on 62 different jobs in seven organizations.

Landy, Frank J., and Carl V. Goodin, "Performance Appraisal," in *Police Personnel Administration,* O. Glenn Stahl and Richard S. Staugenberger, eds., (Washington, D.C.: Police Foundation, 1974), pp. 165-184. This article reviews the evolution of the evaluation process in police work and identifies the common philosophies accompanying performance measurement; it also identifies the current trends in this area and points out the pitfalls to be avoided in administering a performance appraisal plan.

McConkie, Mark L., *Management by Objectives: A Corrections Perspective,* (Washington, D.C.: Government Printing Office, 1975). This report is one of the few "how-to" manuals which deals with MBO in corrections; it describes in step-by-step fashion how MBO can be effectively implemented in correctional settings.

Miner, John B., "Management Appraisal: A Capsule Review and Current References," *Business Horizons*, 11, 1968, pp 83-96. Much of the current research on the management-appraisal process is reviewed in this article; many of the potential influences which can affect the quality of managerial evaluations (such as characteristics of the rater, number of raters used, and characteristics being rated) are discussed along with some feasible solutions.

Paul, William J., Jr., Keith B. Robertson, and Frederick Herzberg, "Job Enrichment Pays Off," *Harvard Business Review*, March-April, 1969, pp. 61-78. The effects of job enrichment on employee performance and job satisfaction in five field studies are examined; the feasibility of job enrichment in different situations and the implications of job enrichment for management are also discussed.

Tosi, Henry L., and Stephen J. Carroll, "Management by Objectives," *Personnel Administration*, 33, 1970, pp. 44-48. A general overview of the MBO process is presented; the basic elements of MBO, the relationship of MBO to employee motivation and compensation, and the overall strengths and weaknesses of this approach are discussed.

TEN

Developing and Training Human Resources

LEARNING OBJECTIVES

The study of this chapter should enable you to:

☑ Explain what is meant by the developmental process.

☑ List two prominent reasons why many police agencies still do not adequately train and retrain their employees.

☑ Define learning, discuss several implications of the learning process with respect to individual behavior.

☑ Define the following terms and concepts: S-R, Law of Effect, respondant and operant behavior, B Mod and OB Mod, cognitive and Gestalt.

☑ Review the contributions of the following individuals to learning theory: Edward Thorndike, B.F. Skinner, and Edward Tolman.

☑ Differentiate between behavioral and Gestalt-field theories of learning and between the andragogical and pedagogical teaching philosophies (include their assumptions about the characteristics of learners and technological implications).

☑ List each of the components of the program development model.

☑ Define what is meant by a training objective, and list the three things that a useful objective must do.

☑ Differentiate between recruit, in-service, and management and supervisory training.

☑ Describe the three basic categories of management and supervisory training.

TEN

Most of the material reviewed to this point will be of little use to practicing managers unless the organization's human resources are properly developed. While police organizations have generally recognized their need in this area, they have failed to provide little more than "lip service" to adequate development and training programs. Because of the tremendous impact which police agencies and their personnel have on the everyday lives of citizens, this is indeed alarming.

Although it was suggested in Chapter 7 that leadership may be the catalyst which determines whether or not an organization is successful, without the proper development of individual skills, knowledge, and abilities, the effects of leader behavior can only be negligible. Accordingly, this chapter examines those aspects of human resource development which must be dealth with by the practicing manager in order to maximize the full potential of organizational members. Those aspects include the developmental process, learning-teaching theories, a program development model, and primary types of police developmental programs.

THE DEVELOPMENTAL PROCESS

In today's multi-faceted and rapidly changing society, criminal justice organizations must be able to develop within their employees the skills and abilities necessary to perform their jobs and satisfy society's demands on them. Nowhere is this developmental need more apparent than within the criminal justice system. Because the demands placed on criminal justice personnel are becoming increasingly sophisticated, continual development of human resources is critical. The skill and ability levels which are required to adequately perform a particular job today may be inadequate tomorrow. Because of an increasing and justified emphasis on human rights, criminal justice personnel, at all levels, must understand their role in a democratic society. Consequently, there is an ongoing need for specific job training for new and in-service employees who must keep abreast of new developments and specialized techniques.

The *developmental process* refers to those learning experiences, provided by the organization to its members, which lead to behavioral changes intended to further the organization's goals and those of its members. *Human resource development* has been defined as "a teaching activity planned and initiated by the organization":

The word "planned" is not meant to imply negativistic things about manipulation or efforts toward eliciting conformity behavior, nor does it necessarily mean the planning must be done by the management hierarchy—in fact, it is usually delegated. Its aim is to further the goals of the organization by enhancing the managerial inputs which are in the form of abilities, skills, motives, and attitudes of individuals . . . Although the development effort must have something to do with the organizational goals, the particular goals under consideration need not be restricted to narrow economic aims. Personal development for personal development's sake may indeed be a conscious objective of the organization.[1]

The developmental process should be regarded positively, in terms of individual-organization integration. If properly designed, a developmental program will benefit both the organization and its individual members through increased goal accomplishment.

Training and Education

Through training and education, organizations attempt to provide their employees with the skills and abilities needed to effectively perform their work. Traditionally, training and education have been differentiated in terms of their orientations; one writer suggests that a "simplified distinction might be to designate *training* as the process of instructing the individual how to do the job and providing him with basic information about the job, and *education* as the process of providing the individual with a body of knowledge on which he may base his decisions when performing his job."[2] The current literature suggests, however, that this once clear distinction is becoming hazy; training is acquiring a much broader meaning. According to Bass and Vaughn:

Now, it [training] refers to activities ranging from the acquistion of simple motor skills to the development and change of complex socio-emotional attitudes. Nevertheless, for many persons the word *training* still has the unfavorable implication of "narrow education" . . . Yet, by whatever name it is called—orientation, development, education, or simply training—under its aegis formal and informal programs of company's activities exist today whose purpose is not only to promote employee learning of job-related skills, knoweldge, and attitudes but to increase employees' worth or serviceability to the company as well as to themselves."[3]

State of the Art

Police managers generally agree about the importance of developing and training their personnel. However, many agencies still do not adequately train or retrain their employees. Undoubtedly, there are many

---

1. John P. Campbell, Marvin D. Dunnette, Edward E. Lawler, III, and Karl E. Weick, Jr., *Managerial Behavior, Performance, and Effectiveness,* (New York: McGraw-Hill, 1970), p. 234.

2. Thomas F. Adams, Gerald Buck and Don Hallstrom, *Criminal Justice Organization and Management,* (Pacific Palisades, Calif.: Goodyear, 1974), p. 145.

3. Bernard M. Bass and James A. Vaughn, *Training in Industry: The Management of Learning,* (Belmont, Calif.: Wadsworth Publishing Company, Inc., 1966), p. 73.

reasons why this is the case, but two are most prominent: (1) the failure to recognize the complexity of police roles in a democratic society, especially that of patrol, and (2) the traditional treatment of the training function as a low priority when allocating resources. If police roles are viewed as simple and non-challenging, there is little perceived need for training, and little money will be allocated for such purposes. Of course, nothing could be further from the truth; police roles are complex and the need for development and training is immense. Practicing managers must make these needs known to the general public, and then bring their development programs up to the standards required by the various role functions.

Although both the quantity and the quality of police training have increased in recent years, the 1973 National Advisory Commission on Police reported that:

No state required any basic training for its police personnel until 1959. By 1970, 33 states had passed some form of basic police training standards, but only one state specified the minimum 400 hours recommended by this report and by the President's Commission on Law Enforcement and Administration of Justice. Seventeen states have no basic training standards. Many states that do require training permit agencies to wait as long as 12 or 18 months after police are hired before it is given. In Germany, by contrast, a police officer undergoes 2 years of training before he is ever assigned to field duty.[4]

This suggests that the police field could do much more to meet its developmental and training needs. The other components of the criminal justice system also need to improve their developmental and training programs, as the following examples illustrate:

The National Council on Crime and Delinquency's training study of correctional systems throughout the United States revealed that over half of the responding agencies had no training programs at all (this included probation and parole systems as well as correctional institutions).[5]

Within the legal profession it has been a long standing assumption that any licensed lawyer is capable of handling any type of case, consequently, little, if any, training is provided for specialist functions, i.e., defense attorney, prosecutor, judge, etc. The National Advisory Commission on Courts has challenged this tradition and makes numerous recommendations for the training needs in these areas.[6]

In conclusion, training should be viewed as an investment in the organization's most valuable asset—human resources. Not only will the organization and the individual benefit from a sound developmental program, but so

---

4. National Advisory Commission on Criminal Justice Standards and Goals, *Police,* (Washington, D.C.: Government Printing Office, 1973), p. 380.

5. Herman Piven and Abraham Alcabes, "Educational Training and Manpower in Corrections and Law Enforcement," *Source Book II, In-Service Training,* (Washington, D.C.: Department of Health, Education, and Welfare, 1966), p. 3,139.

6. National Advisory Commission on Criminal Justice Standards and Goals, *Courts,* (Washington, D.C.: Government Printing Office, 1973).

too will the general public, through better treatment by and increased performance of criminal justice personnel.

CONTINGENCY APPROACH TO DEVELOPMENT

The remainder of this chapter discusses various methods and techniques of developing and training human resources in police organizations, which also have implications for the court and correctional subsystems. The discussion should encourage practicing managers to use a developmental program which "fits" their agencies' specific needs. The relevancy of the contingency approach is once again apparent, for no single program design will be effective for every police agency; pertinent organizational and individual variables must be considered before a proper developmental program can be designed and implemented.

The primary determinant in molding human behavior is learning. Therefore, one must first acquire a basic understanding of the learning process and of teaching methods. Actually, the development of a teaching philosophy is a critical step in establishing an effective training program. Unfortunately, this step is totally ignored by many police agencies when they establish their curriculum.

THE LEARNING PROCESS

Learning is most often defined as a relatively permanent change in behavior which occurs as a result of practice or experience. With respect to the study of individual behavior in organizations, and more specifically, to the training experience, learning would seem to include the following:

1. Knowing something intellectually or conceptually one never knew before.

2. Being able to do something one couldn't do before—behavior or skill.

3. Combining two knowns into a new understanding of a skill, piece of knowledge, concept, or behavior.

4. Being able to use or apply a new combination of skills, knowledge, concept or behavior.

5. Being able to understand and/or apply that which one knows—either skill, knowledge, or behavior.[7]

Because a department's theoretical orientation greatly influences the manner in which organizational personnel are trained, practicing managers should a have basic understanding of learning theories and their use in the developmental process. Two of the most prominent theoretical perspectives on the learning process are discussed below.

---

7. Leslie E. This and Gordon L. Lippitt, "Learning Theories and Training," *Training and Development Journal*, 20, April, 1966, p. 3.

Theories of Learning

Twentieth-century learning theories may be classified into two broad families: Stimulus-Response (S-R) theories of the behavioristic family, and Cognitive theories of the Gestalt-field family.[8] The two theoretical orientations are contrasting, and thus view learning from opposite ends of a continuum.

Behavioral Theories. In general terms, behavioral theories explain behavioral changes in terms of environmental *stimuli* and specific acts of behavior referred to as *responses.* Consequently, the S-R abbreviation is used:

Some relationships involve antecedent stimuli and subsequent responses, and are termed S-R theories; others deal with coinciding stimuli and responses, where behavior changes are ascribed to the contiguity of S and R. Many students of learning believe that what is "learned" in such cases are the connections between various stimuli and accompanying responses. From this viewpoint, responses which have occurred frequently and recently will have a tendency to recur if the same stimulus is again encountered; the concept of reinforcement [any object which will increase or maintain the strength of a response] is not crucial to this explanation.

Other behavioralists, however, view reinforcers as an essential component of the learning process. They would redefine learning as a relatively permanent change in behavior which occurs as a result of reinforced practice.[9]

One of the early researchers, Edward L. Thorndike, maintained that learning was a trial-and-error process; if a learner must respond appropriately to a stimulus, numerous response patterns are attempted, and the one which works will be repeated while the others are neglected. From his basic research on reinforcement, Thorndike proposed what he called the *Law of Effect,* which stated the now famous *pleasure-pain principle* associated with his name. According to this law, if a connection between a stimulus and response is satisfying, its strength is increased, and conversely, if the response is dissatisfying, its strength is reduced. Empirical studies have supported this law. Reinforcement increases the strength of a response and increases its probability of being repeated.

B. F. Skinner, a contemporary behaviorist, has identified two types of behavior: *respondent* and *operant.* Respondent behavior occurs when a reinforcing stimulus elicits a response. In operant behavior "the reinforcing stimulus occurs not simultaneously with or preceding the response but following the response."[10] Therefore, operant behavior is emitted by the organism and not elicited by a prior stimulus. Bigge explains:

In operant conditioning, an organism must first make the desired response and then a "reward" is provided. The reward reinforces the response—makes it more likely to

---

8.   Morris L. Bigge, *Learning Theories for Teachers,* (New York: Harper & Row, 1971), p. 12.

9.   Alan C. Filley, Robert J. House, and Steven Kerr, *Managerial Process and Organizational Behavior,* 2nd ed., (Glenview, Ill.: Scott, Foresman, 1976), p. 73.

10.   Bigge, *op. cit.,* p. 97.

recur. The response is instrumental in bringing about its reinforcement. The essence of learning is not stimulus substitution but response modification. In learning, there is a feedback from the reinforcing stimulus to the previous response. To illustrate, in the training of pets, a desired response is reinforced after it occurs—a dog is fed after it "speaks," and this increases the likelihood of its "speaking" in the future.

Note that in operant conditioning the stimulus producing the response in the first place is not centrally involved in the learning process. The original response is the result of a stimulus, but the nature of this stimulation is irrelevant to operant conditioning. . . . Emphasis is on reinforcing agents, not on original causitive factors.[11]

Consequently, the emphasis with respect to learning involves correlating a response with a reinforcing stimulus, thus, Skinner has introduced an R-S model into the learning process. This emphasis is the basis for programmed instruction, in which a correct response is reinforced while incorrect responses are ignored.

Combining the R-S model with Thorndike's Law of Effect produces a technique for predicting and controlling organizational behavior known as *behavior modification,* or B Mod. Essentially, behavior modification controls behavior through the systematic use of reinforcement; behavior which is desired is positively reinforced and behavior which is not desired is negatively reinforced or ignored. According to the Law of Effect, the behavior which is positively reinforced will be repeated, while the behavior which is negatively reinforced or simply ignored will eventually be eliminated. With respect to Skinner's operant conditioning, the individual must emit or perform the correct response before being reinforced.

This technique is primarily designed to change or modify undesirable behavior into behavior which is considered desirable. Of course, a critical question arises, "Desirable to whom?" A potential problem with behavior modification involves the possibility for its misuse and the consequent stifling of "deviant" viewpoints or non-conforming behavior. As emphasized previously in this text, if "contrary" opinions and behavior are arbitrarily stamped out, the organization may become stagnant and no longer function as effectively as it might if timely changes had been introduced. Practicing managers should be aware of this potential problem, for the stifling of contrary views and innovative ideas has continually plagued and stagnated police organizations.

An advocate of this method explains its use:

There seems to be potentially unlimited applicability of the behavior modification technique to the management of human resources. To emphasize this approach, the term organizational behavior modification, or more simply OB Mod, is used. The most obvious application of OB Mod is in the training of workers to use certain methods, to perform certain tasks, or to increase their knowledge in a particular area. As a training technique, OB Mod can be used on the new employee, the experienced employee who needs retraining, and especially the disadvantaged, hard-core unemployed individual. For example, in the last case, a plan might be developed whereby

---

11. *Ibid.,* pp. 97-98.

trainees are given points or monetary credits for certain types of desirable responses (attendance, promptness, or performance). If the hard-core trainee is absent, tardy, or performing poorly, he is given no points or has some points taken away. The new behavior attained during the training period will then be transferred to the regular job.[12]

The author does point out that people may be troubled by the manipulative aspects of this technique. "To answer this type of criticism," he explains, "it must be remembered that behavioral control, like any other type of management control, should not become an end in itself. Rather OB Mod should be thought of and used as a management technique to adapt human behavior positively to organizational goal attainment."[13]

Many police agencies have manipulated, wittingly or unwittingly, the behavior of their employees toward maintenance of the status quo, which has led to the stagnation and inefficient operation of these organizations. To be sure, behavior modification manipulates behavior, and raises strong ethical questions about the direction and magnitude of the behavior being manipulated. Consequently, if B Mod is used as a management technique, individual needs and values must be carefully considered. Because of the strong ethical concerns raised by it, B Mod is most useful when applied to those behavioral responses which are basic to the proper operation of the organization, such as good attendance and promptness.

Gestalt-field Theories. The second major family of contemporary learning theories originated in Germany during the early part of the twentieth century. These gestalt or cognitive theorists believe that learning is not a simple matter of stimulus and response; they maintain that learning is *cognitive,* (it emphasizes knowledge and understanding) and involves one's total personality. To them, the process of learning is much more complex than the S-R theories seem to recognize. They note that learning may occur simply by thinking about a problem, and that it does not occur by establishing, step-by-step, a series of S-R connections. They examine the phenomenon of insight, either long-term or instantaneous. To them, the whole is more than the sum of its parts.

Gestalt is a German noun for which there is no English equivalent, so the term has been carried over to English psychological literature; the nearest English translation is "configuration" or "pattern."

For Gestalt field theorists, learning is a process of gaining or changing insights, outlooks, or thought patterns. In thinking about the learning processes of students, these theorists prefer the terms *person* to *organism, psychological environment* to *physical* or *biological environment,* and *interaction* to either *action* or *reaction.* Such preference is not merely a whim; there is a conviction that the concepts *person, psychological environment,* and *interaction* are highly advantageous for teachers in

---

12. Fred Luthans, *Organizational Behavior,* (New York: McGraw-Hill, 1973), p. 522.
13. *Ibid.,* p. 523.

describing learning processes. They enable a teacher to see a person, his environment, and his interaction with his environment all occurring at once; this is the meaning of *field.*

Consequently, whereas a behavioristic teacher desires to change the behaviors of his students in a significant way, a Gestalt-field oriented teacher aspires to help students change their understandings of significant problems and situations.[14]

One of the most influential cognitive theorists was Edward C. Tolman, who maintained that learning consisted of a relationship between cognitive environmental cues and expectations. To Tolman, learning involved cognitive changes which resulted from individual experiences and perceptions of the environment: "Thus learned behavior is not merely the automatic, blind emission of responses that have been associated with particular stimuli and reward patterns of the past. Rather, learned behavior always involves implicit and explicit goals and also hypotheses and expectations about how to achieve them. Thus learning is purposive and rationally directed."[15]

In short, Gestalt theorists place far greater emphasis than behavioral theorists upon analytical processes such as reasoning and problem solving. Also, while behavioral theories imply that humans are mechanical and nonpurposeful, Gestalt theories assume that humans are purposeful, and allow room for insight. (This emphasis on purposiveness, goals, and expectations was the basis for one of the more important theories of motivation discussed in Chapter 5, expectancy theory.)

The particular theoretical orientation used in a police agency's development and training program will have a significant impact on its trainees. In general terms it appears that Gestalt theories are more effective for problem-solving kinds of learning (such as conflict resolution and working with people under stress), while behavioral theories are more appropriate for the learning of mechanical tasks and behaviors (the use of equipment, shift responsibilities, and the like). Unfortunately, many police agencies rely primarily on behavioristic techniques to train their personnel, although most of the functions they must perform require a high degree of problem-solving ability. This is particularly true of the patrol force, which handles order maintenance and social service responsibilities. Practicing managers must review, and in many instances, reverse this situation.

Andragogy and Pedagogy: Contrasting Teaching Philosophies

Police development and training programs are generally oriented toward a one-way transfer of knowledge (usually in the form of facts), from the instructor to the trainee. The instructor takes the active role by lecturing to the trainees, who placidly take notes and "absorb" the presented material. The major concern involves "absolute solutions" to issues based on the

---

14. Bigge, *op. cit.,* pp. 12-13.

15. Philip G. Zimbardo and Floyd L. Ruch, *Psychology and Life,* 9th ed., (Chicago: Scott, Foresman, 1975), p. 110.

memorized materials, as opposed to careful analysis of the numerous dimensions and alternative decisions which characterize most of the issues confronting the police. Consequently, trainees are frequently unprepared to adequately handle the complicated situations which often arise in their jobs.

The techniques described above are those of the traditional teaching philosophy known as *pedagogy,* or, the art and science of teaching children. An alternative teaching philosophy, which not only stresses analytical and conceptual skills but also promotes the mutual involvement of students and instructors in the learning process, is known as *andragogy* or, the art and science of helping adults learn. Malcolm Knowles, the innovator of this concept, writes:

> But I believe that andragogy means more than just helping adults learn; I believe it means helping human beings learn, and that it therefore has implications for the education of children and youth. For I believe that the process of maturing toward adulthood begins early in a child's life and that as he matures he takes on more and more of the characteristics of the adult on which andragogy is based.[16]

While Knowles does not necessarily suggest any fundamental differences between the way adults and children learn, he believes that there are significant differences between adult and child learning which emerge in the learning process as maturation takes place. Accordingly, andragogy is based on at least four assumptions about the characteristics of adult learners, as opposed to the assumptions about child learners on which traditional pedagogy is based: (1) the learner's self-concept moves from that of a dependent personality toward that of a self-directing human being; (2) the learner accumulates a growing reservoir of experience which becomes an increasing resource for learning; (3) learner's readiness to learn becomes oriented increasingly to the developmental tasks of his or her social roles; and (4) the learner's time perspective changes from one of postponed application of knowledge to immediate application and, accordingly, his or her orientation toward learning shifts from subject-centeredness to problem-centeredness.[17]

With respect to andragogical assumptions, the above four *technological* implications concerning program development should be differentiated from those of the pedagogical model. First, the learning climate (psychological as well as social) should be cooperative and non-threatening; students and teachers should see themselves as joint inquirers. Second, the learning-teaching transaction is seen as a mutual responsibility of both the learners and the teacher. The teacher's role is that of resource person and facilitator; the teacher is recognized more as a catalyst to learning than as an instructor. Mutual planning, self-diagnosis of needs, and the mutual assessment of the learning experience are emphasized, because adults are more motivated to learn those things which they need to learn. Third, there is a

---

16. Malcolm S. Knowles, *The Modern Practice of Adult Education: Andragogy Versus Pedagogy,* (New York: Association, 1970), pp. 38-39.

17. *Ibid.,* p. 39.

shift away from transmittal techniques (such as pure lecture, assigned read-ings, and canned audio-visual presentations) and toward more participatory techniques which can tap the experiences of the learners (such as group discussion, simulation exercises, role playing, field projects, seminars, coun-seling, and group therapy). Finally, the orientation to learning is problem-centered and focuses on the practical concerns of the learners. Early in the session there may be a diagnostic exercise in which the participants identify the specific problems they want to be able to deal with more effectively.

Andragogy thus incorporates a Gestalt-field theoretical orientation, while pedagogy is more oriented toward behaviorism. Consequently, although andragogy has been seldom used in police development and train-ing programs,[18] the use of such a teaching style would be advantageous where analytical processes are emphasized.

PROGRAM DEVELOPMENT

Frequently, practicing managers have difficulty in defining what they want their training to accomplish and how it should be carried out. In many agencies which provide some type of formalized program, training has been concerned primarily with how many hours of instruction are provided, and how many courses are offered. Program development has therefore con-sisted largely of determining which courses should be offered first, which courses should be offered last, and then "filling" the rest of the program with the remaining hours in the best possible way.

Such make-shift training programs will not fit the needs of either the individual or the organization, and will probably provide little more than the satisfaction that "all our personnel have completed X number of hours of training." A program like this also assumes a definite starting and ending point; once the training has met its objectives, the program is considered completed. However, if program development is approached from a systems perspective, the training function should be thought of as a continual proc-ess, and some provision should be made for feeding back information throughout every stage in the program.

Figure 10-1 depicts a systems model for the development of a training program. Using such a model can help to improve and modify the training program in order to meet changing organizational needs and demands. Consequently, the program model depicted uses the contingency approach; any development and training activity may be adapted to a particular situation.

As mentioned above, each of the component parts of this model should be viewed as a continuous activity which does not just begin with the determination of training needs and end with the formal evaluation of the

---

18. The andragogical teaching philosophy, is, however, becoming recognized in police train-ing; for example, see: George E. Shagory and Henry N. Deneault, "Police Training in Manage-rial Budgeting: An Application of Andragogy," *Journal of Police Science and Administration*, 3, 1975, pp. 327-331.

program. However, in order to adequately describe the developmental processes of a training program, each component must be considered separately. Some of the activities crucial to each of the components are discussed below.

Figure 10-1

Program Development Model

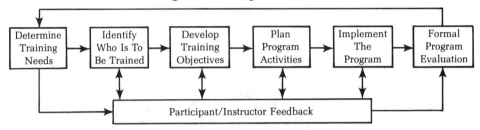

*Determining Training Needs:*The initial phase of the model is also one of the most difficult. Basically, this aspect involves analyzing job tasks and identifying those behaviors which lead to task accomplishment and thus to successful overall job performance. This can be handled by breaking down a particular job into specific tasks and determining how to train employees to perform each task in such a way that the transfer of these tasks to the whole job will occur smoothly.

Typically, police training programs have not been based on careful analysis of the type of behavior required for effective job performance. This does not mean, however, that comprehensive job analysis cannot be conducted within the field. While it is beyond the scope of this chapter to describe the various techniques available for this purpose, some of the more obvious methods include observational techniques, questionnaire approaches, community surveys, and job performance analysis procedures.

This first developmental step requires considerable time and effort, but it is less costly to properly analyze job requirements (and to base behavioral training on them) than to use training programs which may be based on incorrect criteria. For example, most training concerning police patrol is oriented to the law enforcement function, although such activity actually takes up a small amount of a patrol officer's time. One training specialist describes the gap between current training programs and actual job performance as follows:

We have come to the realization that, what we do in training nationally has minimal relevancy to what the policeman does on the street. There are indications through the use of computers that only about 20 percent of a policeman's time is spent in responding to criminal-type calls, the rest of his time is spent generally dealing with people. So the training programs that we have established teach a man how to behave for the 20 percent of the time that he has to operate in a crime situation; and 80 percent of his time we scarcely touch as far as training is concerned.[19]

---

19. American Bar Association, *Standards Relating to the Urban Police Function*, (New York: American Bar Assoc., 1973), p. 205, note 296.

Identifying Who Is To Be Trained: After the type of behavior required for effective job performance has been identified, the organization should decide who is to be trained. The organization must be able to determine if the individual performer is satisfactorily carrying out those behaviors identified above in such a way that leads to effective job performance. This diagnosis is usually conducted by the employee's supervisor, primarily through the performance evaluation process. However, performance evaluation sessions are notoriously poor places in which to discuss training needs, because of employee defensiveness with respect to their performance. A better approach may involve supervisor-employee sessions which are concerned only with the discussion of individual training needs. Another approach, used successfully by many business organizations, is to assign a staff specialist the responsibility for the development and training needs of personnel.

Another factor involves the employees' motivation to learn the behavior being taught. Although some learning can occur even though a person is not motivated to learn, more learning will obviously take place if the person is motivated. With respect to the expectancy model of motivation, if employees can make a connection between learning a new behavior and being better able to obtain desired rewards from the job, they will be motivated. The organization should thus regard development and training as a two-way or mutual decision-making process involving the individual and the organization. If the organization makes a one-way decision without considering individual needs, the connection between behavior and rewards cannot be made.

Also, unless the organization actually rewards individuals for demonstrating the new job behavior, the behavior will quickly disappear. The key organizational member, who can provide such rewards on a day-to-day basis, is the employee's immediate superior. The organization must adequately sanction and reward the behavior learned in training if that behavior is to be sustained.

Developing Training Objectives: A *training objective* can be defined as the description of a training intent to bring about behavioral changes which lead to task accomplishment and successful overall job performance. The proper design of appropriate learning activities and the measurement of whether or not they have met some determined need depend on clearly stated objectives. Robert Mager, author of *Preparing Instructional Objectives,* suggests that a useful objective must do three things: (1) identify the expected behavioral change, (2) define the important conditions under which the change is to occur, and (3) define the related criteria for measuring the change requirement.[20]

A stated objective is not clear enough to be useful until it indicates how the understanding is to be measured; the objective should identify and define the desired behavior as well as specify the criteria of acceptable

---

20. Robert F. Mager, *Preparing Instructional Objectives,* (Palo Alto, Calif.: Fearon, 1962).

performance. For example, a performance objective, such as stopping a traffic violator or intervening in a family disturbance, must be followed by a description of the minimum level of acceptable demonstrated ability, against which the training program can be evaluated.

Performance objectives have been used in a number of police training programs. The Metropolitan Police Department in Washington, D. C. has based its entire recruit training program upon terminal performance objectives; Project STAR (Systems Training and Recruitment) in California seeks to identify specific performance objectives universal in police work and then to design pre-packaged training guidelines which will best teach these objectives. It should be noted that the use of performance objectives has been criticized on some grounds, especially because they may fail to consider adequately the "soft" aspects of training such as social understanding, but there is general agreement that performance objectives are usually beneficial: " [They] can guide course content toward the development of desired skills and away from the non-performance-oriented course content which has become common in a large number of training programs."[21]

Planning Program Activities: Once the program's objectives have been identified, the program must be planned so as to accomplish these objectives, which requires the proper sequencing of learning activities and the determination of appropriate instructional techniques. According to Wasserman and Couper:

Trainers must recognize that some subjects are better taught before others, that some skills require proficiency in other skills before the new skills can be learned. The more advanced training systems utilizing terminal performance objectives have been based upon these concepts and a recognition that a logical course structure and formal course interrelationship can maximize the learning process. In this sense, patrol-car utilization precedes patrol activities; interviewing skills come before advanced investigative techniques.

The sequencing of subjects is important not only to the learning of specific skills but also to more general subjects. For example, discussion of community dynamics and neighborhood structures can have an important influence upon how the patrol technique is perceived and utilized. Likewise, it seems appropriate for recruits to consider the whole issue of force as a means of dealing with conflict before actual firearms practice begins.

Major concerns of sequencing must be dealt with first in the overall program-design stage, answering questions such as what is a part of the course orientation, what is a basic unit of instruction, and what is more advanced material. Then more detailed and specific inter-relations can be dealt with. While sequencing in this manner is a complicated process, it is far more effective than simply placing a subject in a time slot because there happens to be available time.[22]

21. Robert Wasserman and David Couper, "Training and Education," in *Police Personnel Administration,* O. Glenn Stahl and Richard A. Staufenberger, eds., (Washington, D.C.: Police Foundation, 1974), p. 142.

22. *Ibid.,* pp. 143-145.

The selection of appropriate instructional techniques is related to the discussion in the preceding section of theories of learning and teaching philosophies. Cognitive theories and the andragogical teaching method appear to be the most effective for the major portion of police training, which pertains to activities involving reasoning and problem-solving. However, such training involves a certain amount of mechanical learning activities, such as the memorization of specific statutes, court interpretations, or standard operating procedures. For such activities, pedagogical methods are likely to be the most effective. In other words, more than one theoretical orientation is probably necessary for the adequate training of police personnel.

Implementing The Program: Implementing the program requires the use of the activities planned during the earlier components of the model. This includes such things as establishing a learning climate to meet the needs of the trainees, managing the learning activities and instructional efforts, collecting evaluative information, and making appropriate decisions as situations warrant them. If the other components have been adequately addressed, implementing the program should be relatively trouble-free.

Formal Program Evaluation: The importance of program evaluation cannot be overemphasized; however, this component has often been abused or ignored in police training programs. Evaluation is critical if trainers are to know how effective their programs have been. Managers have been reluctant to allocate resources to the training function, partly because the results provided through training are often difficult to evaluate. Bass and Vaughn have suggested:

Most management decisions involving the outlay of fairly large sums of money are based on the results a company can expect to achieve. Unfortunately, the evaluation of training has progressed very slowly; consequently, it is often difficult to determine the effects of training in general (particularly when it involves the development of complex skills and attitudes) and virtually impossible in most cases to attach valid, meaningful, dollars-and-cents values to these effects.[23]

If the program has been properly planned and adapted to individual and organizational needs, the evaluation will provide the manager with sufficient data to adequately support the development and training function in the organization's budget.

The formal evaluation component involves measuring the effects of the training experience, and asks the question: Is behavioral change the result of the training experience? Experimental designs (discussed in Chapter 3) offer the greatest degree of control and therefore the greatest chance of establishing causal relationships between variables; in the formal evaluation, between the training activity (independent variable) and the behavioral change (dependent variable).

Arthur MacKinney describes the various types of experimental designs which may be used to reduce the ambiguity in evaluating the results of

---

23. Bass and Vaughn, *op. cit.*, p. 74.

training programs.[24] At the lowest level of the scale, the most ambiguous procedure is the use of an after criterion measure only. This plan is obviously simple in its approach; unfortunately, nothing in the criterion behavior can be attributed to the effects of the training. The next step up the scale would be an approach which measures the trainees both before and after the training program. This at least demonstrates whether or not some change had taken place. However, any observed changes cannot be attributed solely to the training program, because other things going on in the organization at the same time could have caused the changes in the trainees. What is needed, of course, is a second group of employees or a control group, who are also given before and after measures but who do *not* receive any training. Such a group is influenced by all the forces in the organizational environment which affect the experimental or training group, except for the training itself. Consequently, this design reduces ambiguity in the results and significantly increases the likelihood that the training program was the cause of any behavioral changes observed in the experimental group and not in the control group. MacKinney stresses that this last approach—which includes both an experimental and a control group, both of which are measured before and after—is the only worthwhile design for obtaining evaluative training results, even if such a study requires outside assistance.

Although MacKinney is right, many police and other criminal justice agencies are not prepared at this time to implement the controlled experimental design. The practicing manager should therefore be aware that there are a number of what Campbell and Stanley refer to as "quasi" experimental designs, which may have to suffice as a compromise to the control group design.[25] Although such designs are not as stringently controlled, they are more valuable than no attempt at evaluation, and they may provide a crucial first step toward developing a spirit of scientific inquiry.

One "quasi" experimental design which could be useful in evaluating training results is known as the "time series experiment." Criterion information on one group of individuals is collected at several points in time, including several time periods before and after the training program; criterion measures obtained before the introduction of training and those obtained after are then compared. Figure 10-2 depicts this design, illustrating three measures taken before training and three measures taken after training.

In order for an effect to be demonstrated, the training program must produce an abrupt change in the criterion behavior curve over the trial periods which does not occur at *any other point* in time; such a change is

24. Arthur C. MacKinney, "Progressive Levels in the Evaluation of Training Programs," *Personnel,* 34, 1957, pp. 72-77.

25. For a detailed discussion on "quasi" experimental designs, see: Donald T. Campbell and Julian C. Stanley, *Experimental and Quasi-Experimental Design for Research,* (Chicago: Rand McNally, 1963), pp. 34-64.

depicted by the curve in Figure 10-2. This curve indicates that some behavior, such as pistol shooting, was consistently low for three successive measures prior to training. After training, the shooting scores were consistently higher for three successive measures. Such results would strongly support the effectiveness of the training program with respect to this activity.

Figure 10-2

One-Group Time Series Design

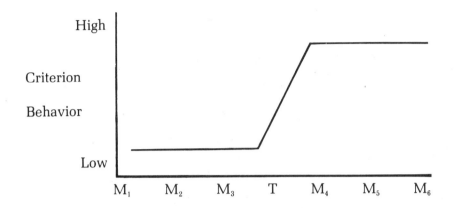

The one-group design is similar to the simple before and after approach, except it provides more information about whether or not the observed change after the training program represents a typical or atypical change in the criterion behavior curve. The practicing manager should remember, however, that without a control group (thus the design is "quasi" experimental), one cannot be sure whether the training program or something in the environment produced the change.

Participant/Instructor Feedback: A systems approach to program development considers training a continuous and self-correcting process. As the two-way directional arrows in Figure 10-1 indicate, this allows for the use of evaluative findings to strengthen the developmental process, adjusting for needed changes throughout the process, and providing information for the training needs of future programs. Accordingly, the information obtained from participants and instructors is fed back to each component and is used to modify and adjust each component's activities to changing program needs, even before any formal evaluation is conducted.

DEVELOPMENT AND TRAINING PROGRAMS

This final section describes and analyzes the primary types of police developmental programs: recruit or preparatory, in-service, and management and supervisory training. Although the discussion relates directly to police training and the important considerations which lead to program effectiveness, each type of program can be generalized to the rest of the criminal justice system. In other words, the court and correctional subsystems must also concern themselves with each of these programs and their relevant considerations if they are to properly develop their personnel.

Recruit or Preparatory Training*

The most common and by far the most complex type of training undertaken by the police is recruit training. The amount of recruit training provided by most police agencies throughout the country has dramatically increased over the past decade. In the past, the new officer was provided only two or three weeks of training; today, most large police agencies have a recruit-training program lasting at least 10 weeks, with many programs exceeding 15 weeks.

The range of subjects in these programs has expanded to include new courses in human relations, community relations, sociology, psychology, and related social-science skills. Following the lead of the excellent California State standards mechanism, many states have adopted training standards which mandate minimum program length and course content.

While length and content have recently received some attention, there have been only minor changes in the basic format of recruit training and objectives of the training.

In a broad sense, the recruit-training curriculum presently offered throughout the country has aimed at preparation of the "complete officer." That is, over a limited time span, a substantial amount of information aimed at providing the newly-hired employee with a basic level of competency has been given so that, it was supposed, the employee would be able immediately to perform effectively on the street.

The amount of information transmitted to the recruit officer during the average recruit-training program is staggering. In addition to extensive exposure to the law, the recruit receives large amounts of information on structure and organization of the department, self-defense and physical education tactics, a multitude of patrol procedures, investigation techniques, crime-scene search techniques, and sociology and psychology relating to human behavior. The emphasis of present-day recruit-training programs seems to be to provide the recruit officer with a large base of knowledge upon which the subsequent field experiences will be built. In this context, field experience is seen as an important part of the training program.

However, most recruit-training programs have a wide cleavage between the classroom training and the initial field experience. As many observers have noted, the recruit's first experience in the field after the

*Source: Robert Wasserman and David Couper, "Training and Education," in *Police Personnel Administration,* O. Glenn Stahl and Richard A. Staufenberger, (eds.), (Washington, D.C.: © Police Foundation, 1974), pp. 130-141. Some deletions have been made. Reprinted with permission.

academy training often involves an older officer's order to "forget that academy stuff; here is how you must operate."

Making classroom training relevant to field practice has been a complex, continuing problem. The challenge of the recruit-training program is to provide for the new officer a base of skills that will be relevant to field activities which have not been well-defined. In order to provide meaningful recruit training, a police training staff must deal with basic course objectives, re-evaluate the "complete officer" concept, consider both skill training and socialization, and provide for a number of administrative activities, such as student counseling and course standards.

Recruit-Training Objectives. As with all training programs, the recruit-training program must have clear objectives directed toward clearly-defined goals. Generally, there should be three primary objectives in any recruit-training program. The first is to create an understanding of the internal police semi-military system and the community in which the recruit will work. These may be called "environmental concerns."

The second objective is the development of specific skills that will permit the recruit to handle automatically a wide range of problems which he or she will have to resolve. The development of skills in this sense does not directly concern the recruits judgments; rather, the objective is to provide the recruit with "natural skills," such as firearms use, patrol car operation, and related police procedures.

The third objective is the development of judgment in the officer; that is, the ability to apply skills in a manner responsive to the particular characteristics of a problem, people, or neighborhood while being effective and efficient. Judgment is basically the combination of experience and practice that reflects an understanding of the many faceted parts of a given position.

The attainment of these objectives cannot be achieved through a set classroom training experience alone. Police administrators who have come to understand the significance of these objectives have come to recognize that sometimes drastic restructuring of the recruit-training process is required.

Program Structure. While there is not general agreement on the direction that this restructuring should take, police departments such as those in Washington, D.C.; Oakland, California; Madison, Wisconsin; and Boston, Massachusetts, have specifically addressed these concerns in the development of their training programs.

A number of these departments have moved beyond the concept of a single recruit-training program being conducted over a specific number of weeks. The first, and most common, change has been the introduction of several weeks of field experience [called a "practicum"] into the training curriculum. Those departments that have adopted this structure have found that by providing the recruit officer with a chance to practice newly acquired skills while still under the general supervision of the academy, there is an effective, although not sufficient, link between academy training and actual field practice.

These structural changes have often been implemented as a way of dealing with the variation in educational and cultural backgrounds among recruit officers. Under the Equal Employment Opportunity guidelines and stepped-up recruitment procedures of recent years, police agencies throughout the country have found that the composition of their recruit-training classes have drastically changed. No longer is the class homogeneous; there is more variation in sex, race, ethnic origins, abilities, and other background features.

Departments have found it important to have training programs able to respond effectively to these student differences. It is now recognized that when the standard structure of one class for all students is used, some students find the material too easy and boring while others find it extremely difficult. A few departments have attempted to separate trainees according to educational backgrounds but have found that such an artificial division often fell along racial lines. Also, instructional staff often had difficulty in adjusting material to groups having separate abilities.

A few departments have made drastic alterations in the previously accepted structure of having a set period of instruction as classroom time. The police-training program in Boston, for example, has stretched the recruit-training program out over the period of a year. By doing this, the department has moved the time required for developing the "complete officer" to the end of the first year of service from the original 16 weeks. The department has also integrated a large number of field-practice sessions into the course curriculum.

The Socialization Process. While the structure of recruit-training programs is important to determining overall program effectiveness, within the structure the process of socialization determines the understanding the new police officer has of the working environment. Although it exists as a part of every police recruit-training program, the socialization process is rarely recognized, nor is the process usually planned in advance as an integral part of the training program.

A number of police agencies, however, have developed formal integral parts of their recruit-training curriculum to deal with these concepts. They have shown that a formal *internal* and *external* socialization for the recruit is preparation for the realities of the police job.

Socialization has two primary facets: departmental organization and community or neighborhood orientation. Both are very important in determining how the recruit officer will respond to situations within and outside the police organization. Neither is dealt with adequately in most academies.

The internal socialization process deals primarily with the peculiar environment of the police organization. Recruits must fully understand the complex dynamics of the police bureaucracy and the issues which set the tone under which the police do their job. The recruit often has difficulty adapting to the new culture, standards of performance, and morality supported by the police bureaucracy. Some minority-group recruits, for example, may have different time concepts, and adherences to the type of discipline put forth by a training staff may be new to them.

The same is true concerning the command structure and politics of the police organization. If the concept of bureaucratic power and influence is not specifically dealt with during the recruit-socialization process, the new officer will too readily unquestioningly accede to the "survival" advice of older officers. The recruit must be prepared to deal with this advice as well as with the cynicism so commonly found among large numbers of middle-aged police officers in our larger cities.

Other issues are equally important to recruit socialization. For example, in dense, multi-ethnic cities, the potential is great for corruption to be a debilitating pressure on the new recruit who must fully understand the complex dynamics of integrity, community responsiveness, and urban morality. In general, police agencies have failed adequately to confront sensitive issues such as corruption at the recruit-training level; thus, the recruit has been self-taught and greatly influenced by many less-than-desirable situations during his or her first field exposure.

The same is true of the socialization to the community. The great variances among urban neighborhoods in community expectations of police performance makes it imperative that the new police officer understand the cultural and ethnic composition of the area to be policed. Policing is more than just a skill; it is sensitivity to and understanding of neighborhood dynamics and urban sociology. Police training, especially at the recruit level, must provide the bases of such an understanding or the recruit will have to learn slowly and often at great cost from experience.

A significant amount of experimentation has been undertaken in providing community socialization, and some positive results have been obtained. Most of these experimental socialization efforts have been based on the belief that a recruit officer should have a thorough understanding of the community to be policed before assuming responsibility for actions in the field.

One of the pioneers in this area is Dayton, Ohio. As a major element of Dayton's recruit-training program, the recruit officer spends time in a number of selected community social agencies throughout the city as a means to better understand the community service role and the role social agencies can play in assisting law enforcement. During these experiences the recruit officer works briefly alongside an active agency worker, learning about the community being served as well as the agency itself.

The importance of socialization—both internal and external—cannot be over-stressed. The great amount of discretion given the police officer requires a full understanding of the consequences of actions upon the department, the community, and the recruit's own career or life. Recruit training must provide much of that understanding.

Individual Differences. Improved training program structure and more meaningful recruit-officer socialization processes cannot alone provide adequate training for all new recruits, especially given the recently changing composition of the police labor force. With more people from different ethnic and cultural backgrounds being recruited into the police service, police recruit training has had to provide individualized assistance for recruit officers who do not have pre-service skills equal to the group norm.

There are many different types of deficiencies involved. Some recruits may be weak in basic educational skills, such as writing and reading comprehension. Others may have unusual difficulty in learning new languages, such as Spanish. Still other recruits may have physical strength deficiencies.

Police-training administrators must recognize that present classes of trainees are generally not homogeneous, but rather consist of a wide variety of people with differing backgrounds and basic skills. It is the responsibility of the police training staff to assist these recruits in developing additional skills in their individual areas of deficiency. To do so is not easy and represents one of the more important challenges to present-day police training programs.

Washington, D.C., has probably advanced most in this area. Through its structure, it has provided a tailor-made program for each recruit officer, permitting advancement in skill learning at the recruit's own speed. The program stresses the abilities of the individual recruits and permits progress through the training sequence at their optimum learning speed. Heavy remedial assistance in most learning areas is provided as an integral part of the training program.

There is a tendency for this type of approach, however, to become so encompassing that the police job is relegated to being little more than a series of mechanical behaviors rather than the application of skills with understanding, compassion, and discretion. The increase in minority employment has brought into the police service some people with different communication skills. The challenge for the police trainer is to provide the mechanical skills of policing (and the needed remedial skills assistance) in a manner that corrects deficiencies but also provides the understanding of those environmental issues and concerns so central to the recruits' role and performance.

Certainly the definition of the training program in terms of identifiable skills makes it easier to establish minimum standards, and thus to deal with the current perception among so many police officers that minority employment programs lower entrance standards. To base a training program on these beliefs, however, is only self-defeating. Policing is not a series of simple mechanical procedures, and training standards must center on the realistic complexities of the job.

Thus, the development of training standards must be an ever-increasing concern. Police academies with the most successful recruit-training programs have developed behavioral, academic, and skill standards and have applied them equally to all recruits. By establishing these standards in advance, there can be no challenge to the training staff that standards are being lowered. However, the training staff must then provide a series of remedial programs for recruits having skill deficiencies. Subjects often appropriate for remedial assistance include basic English, writing skills, physical agility, self-defense, Spanish, and firearms.

Counseling. There is a great need in recruit training for psychological counseling services during the entire training sequence. While many police departments use psychological screening as a part of their employment process, few departments have established an adequate psychological counseling capacity as a part of the recruit-training program.

The need for such counseling is great, especially with the types of multiethnic classes entering police academies. The stresses common to police work are magnified during the first experiences in the police academy, where the recruit is confronted with a strange and new bureaucratic structure. The pressure of performance is usually intense, and the recruit often finds that problems experienced away from the job, such as marital and family conflicts, tend to become magnified during the training period. This is an excellent time to identify and deal with various personality and behavior problems in recruits.

To meet this need, police-training programs should have a provision for either full-time or consulting psychological services. The provision of psychological counseling services must include recognition of the diverse nature of the recruit population. Where a significant number of women, black, or Spanish-speaking officers are undergoing training, these groups should be represented among the counseling staff.

In the establishment of a counseling capability, training administrators should be careful to distinguish counseling from psychological assessment. If the objective of the counseling program is really assessment of the psychological well-being of the recruit officer, the program will fail, since recruits will fear seeking help. Generally, basic psychological assessment is a part of the selection process; in the training process, it is the responsibility of the training staff to observe behavior and note potential problems. The training counseling staff then serves as a referral resource.

In-Service Training

In-service training programs have generally received less attention than recruit training, primarily because the administrative necessity for this type of training is less intense and less affected by the types of pressures present when newcomers are accepted into the organization. In-service training has often been viewed as a task of secondary importance, to be undertaken only when sufficient time and personnel are available. Even those jurisdictions which have placed priorities on in-service training have found a number of issues that complicate the in-service training process.

Conflicting Purposes. One of these issues is the conflicting purpose of the in-service training program itself. An in-service training program serves two basic needs. The first is the need for a *regular up-grading* for all members of the department in a wide variety of subjects of common applicability. The second need is for *specialized training* relating to a specific area of assignment or responsibility of a particular officer at a particular time.

. Regular up-grading has been the most common type of in-service training program. Aimed at providing the same information to all members of the department, this training is based on the premise that all police officers in a given department must be kept abreast of standard issues, such as changes in the law, new first-aid techniques, recently developed procedures, and new policies.

Few departments have been able to combine this type of up-grading training with the more complex training directed toward an officer's particular job. Specific assignment training is not only important but necessary, if officers are to become proficient at the specialized area of assignment they are in. Policing is not a universal skill adapted to all jobs; there are different skills and kinds of knowledge required in different jobs within the organization. Training must be provided for each of these areas.

The accomplishment of specific assignment training is a complex and logistically difficult task. If a police-training program desires to keep class size to a maximum of 20 students at a time, to facilitate group discussion, it is necessary to conduct a large number of separate classes to accommodate even a medium-size police department's needs. For example, there are needs for specialized training for field patrol officers, investigative personnel, crime-scene search personnel, administrative personnel, and planning and training personnel. To provide this training alone has often meant that the officer is prevented from attending the uniform, standardized up-grading training which is also an important need.

Meeting this dual need requires both commitment on the part of the police administration and the development of detailed training schedules. To a limited degree, Boston and Dayton have implemented such a program. In these cases the department offers a standard course of up-grading training to all members of the police force. Then, at the conclusion of this training, the officer is eligible to enroll in a course module directly relating to his or her particular area of assignment.

Multiple Backgrounds. The provision of in-service training for an entire police department program, even with the aforementioned format, is made more difficult because of the multiple backgrounds of the employees in a large police department. Officers have usually entered the police service at many different stages of the organization's development; thus, they have received greatly varying amounts and types of entry training. When a cross-section of officers are placed in the same classroom, the abilities, knowledge, and expectations of the students often are widely divergent.

The same situation exists with specialized in-service training. Detectives, for example, often have great variations in experience and skill, as do officers assigned to any of the other common police specialties. Either the classroom situation must provide for these individual differences (so that individual student learning is maximized), or individual training programs for each group must be provided.

The Logistics. There are logistical problems in designing and implementing a dual-purpose training program at the in-service level. While difficult to achieve, there should be little duplication between the up-grading training and the specialized training. And the materials covered in the up-grading training must be of somewhat uniform interest and relevance to each member of the department.

The development of a dual-track in-service training program can lay the groundwork for substantially linking training and personnel assignment. Assuming that most assignments require some specialized level of skill, police agencies can begin to require specialized training before transfers are made into new assignments. In this way, a police department can mandate specialized training before an employee assumes a new position, thereby preparing the employee for new duties and raising overall job skills.

When a department is too small to provide enough specialized courses, it should participate in joint courses with other departments on a regional basis. California implemented such a system on a statewide basis by offering specialized training courses as a means for qualifying personnel at various levels of competency. The state offers basic, intermediate, and advanced certificates to officers who have successfully completed courses at those respective levels. The success of the California model indicates that police agencies should consider adopting such a system and making it the basis of pay and a requirement for promotion. Through such systems training can be closely linked to other parts of personnel policy and become an important part of a meaningful career development system.

Management and Supervisory Training

Management and supervisory training, coupled with other personnel programs, can be a major factor in shaping the future of a given police agency. Training provided for supervisors and managers falls into three basic categories: pre-promotion, post promotion, and management seminars. Each is important, but few police agencies have developed and implemented adequate programs for training at all these levels.

Pre-Promotion Supervisory Training. Training immediately provided newly promoted officers before they assume the duties of their new assignment is becoming increasingly accepted as a part of the training requirement. Recognizing that the newly promoted police officer will have a far different set of responsibilities than previously experienced, a growing number of police agencies have institutionalized training prior to assumption of duties. This type of training can have a significant effect on certain personnel practices, especially the promotional examination content.

It has been common for some police agencies to view the promotional examination as a method of up-grading each officer on the police force in the hope that the officer will be promoted. In these cases, it is believed that the entire department will benefit from massive study. In other departments, the examination itself has been seen as the means for the police officer to prepare for the duties of higher office and thus be ready to assume the position, if the examination is passed. In these latter instances, which are clearly the most common, there has been an underlying belief that the officer who came out on top in a promotional examination would be the officer who had best prepared for the new position.

More recently there has been a movement away from such beliefs. Administrators have come to see the promotional examination more as a device to select those personnel who have the ability to be good supervisors, as opposed to having the knowledge required for supervisory duty. There is a significant difference between the two qualifications.

When the promotional examination is directed toward determination of those officers who have the ability to supervise, one implicitly accepts the need for training after the examination to provide the new officer with the required supervisory skills and knowledge. Oral boards and testing techniques are increasingly utilized as a part of the final selection process, especially if there is a probationary period for new supervisory personnel.

The training required at the pre-promotion level is quite different from the recruit or in-service training at lower levels. Starting with sergeants, and more important, as training is provided up the chain of command, there must be an atmosphere which reinforces the new responsibilities placed upon the officers. The overall aim of this type of management training must be to provide an atmosphere that indicates and reviews thoroughly the difference in the new assignment and its added responsibilities. To design such a training program properly, and in preparation of the promotional examination, a comprehensive job description should be developed which clearly defines the duties and responsibilities of the new position, gives relevant examples of duties, and provides the basis for the development of individual training objectives.

As with recruit training, pre-promotion training is the main orientation mechanism through which the newly promoted officer can prepare for new assignments. It is an important vehicle of the department to set the tone upon which supervision and management will rest in the future.

Post-Promotion Supervisory Training. Where training is undertaken for supervisory and management personnel, it is usually as an after thought or to meet a specific need. Only a handful of departments have developed adequate programs for such training.

Training programs for supervisory personnel can serve two purposes. First, they can provide a forum for discussion of issues important to the department. And second, they can provide a vehicle through which the supervisor can become an important part of the overall departmental training effort. It is probably in this second area that the most important gains through training can be achieved.

An important part of every supervisor's role is training; yet it is one of the most neglected. Few police agencies provide the type of reinforcement and assistance which would help to develop the supervisory training role. Without such reinforcement, the police administrator cannot expect the supervisor to be effective in a training role.

One major reason police supervisors are not good trainers may be because they are unsure as to what they are expected to train in. It is the responsibility of the police-training program to provide each supervisor with various materials and information that can be passed on to the officers. For example, a sergeant's training program may train the sergeant in new methods of patrol; the sergeant would then have the responsibility for training officers in these new techniques and observe the officers at work to insure that they have learned the material presented. This type of "training trainers" can have a major impact on changing and clarifying the supervisor's role.

Just as patrol officers need regular in-service training, it is important that sergeants have a dual system of training—one part related to up-grading their knowledge of issues and new procedures, and the other providing them with skill in their particular area of assignment. If the training is relevant and training skills are provided, the supervisors can be expected to undertake training on a regular basis with the officers.

General Management Training. In only the largest police agencies, such as New York's, has any large-scale management training effort been undertaken. Smaller departments have often found that their number of management personnel does not justify such programs. The smaller departments should consider regional efforts, like those implemented on a wide scale in California through the Peace Officer's Training Council.

The skills required of the police manager are even more complex than those required of the first-line supervisor. And the types of skills required of the police manager are far more distant from those at police entrance levels than are those of lower-level supervisors. There is, however, a tendency for management-level police personnel to continue to act as police officers, at worst, and immediate supervisors, at best. Thus, there is a need for management-level training to clarify the management role and to provide vital skills.

One of the more effective management-training programs seems to be the *management-seminar project*. As utilized in a number of cities, such as Dayton and Madison, training is provided through the problem-solving or project-oriented seminar. Rather than simply providing knowledge about management techniques, training is accomplished around some problem or series of studies that directly affect the management responsibilities of top-level personnel. In Madison, for example, a series of high-level task forces were formed to work on department-wide problems, such as policy development, training conceptionalizations, and resource allocation. Through participation in these activities, the police manager has been able to learn, in a "real" setting, the types of planning and implementation skills required in daily responsibilities. Such training is probably far more effective than the normal management lecture.

SUMMARY

Without a proper development and training program, police and other criminal justice personnel cannot effectively serve the needs of a democratic society; superior role performance is unlikely without comprehensive preparatory and continuous in-service training. Consequently, as this chapter has stressed, practicing managers must vigorously pursue adequate departmental resources and support for the developmental process.

The developmental process is defined as those learning experiences, provided by the organization to its members, which produce behavioral changes intended to further the organization's goals. This process should be perceived in a constructive way; that is, to improve both individual and organizational goal attainment. Several examples were cited which indicate that police development and training, and indeed, developmental programs throughout the criminal justice system, is rather meager in terms of the preparation required for adequate role performance. To meet training demands, an agency must design a developmental program which "fits" its particular needs, by using the contingency approach.

Since the primary determinant in moulding human behavior is learning, a basic understanding of learning theory and teaching philosophy is needed to properly design a developmental program. There are two broad families of learning theories, stimulus-response theories of the behavioristic family, and cognitive theories of the Gestalt-field family. The S-R theories explain behavioral changes in terms of environmental stimuli and specific acts of behavior known as responses. According to Gestalt-field theories, learning is cognitive in nature and involves one's total personality; learning may occur simply by thinking about a problem or through insight, rather than through a step-by-step series of S-R connections. Gestalt theorists place a far greater emphasis on analytical processes such as reasoning and problem solving than do behaviorists. Subsequently, Gestalt theories appear to be more appropriate for the major portion of police development and training programs, which involves analytical kinds of learning. The andragogical teaching method uses a Gestalt-field orientation, while the pedagogical method is more closely aligned with the behaviorists. The technological implications of andragogy, based on mutual responsibilities between learner and teacher, are therefore more useful where problem-solving activities are emphasized.

With respect to program development, a useful model was put forth which allows the training program to be constantly improved and modified to meet changing organizational needs and demands. Training is viewed not only as a continuous process, but also as a self-correcting one. If each component of the model is properly developed, the training program will satisfactorily prepare organizational members for their complex roles. Once more, the formal evaluation phase should provide practicing managers with sufficient evidence to provide adequate departmental resources for the developmental process.

Finally, there are three primary types of police developmental programs: recruit or preparatory, in-service, and management and supervisory training. Criminal justice organizations should provide all three types of training if they expect to develop and continuously maintain the operating efficiency of their employees throughout their careers.

DISCUSSION QUESTIONS

1. Discuss several reasons why development and training programs should or should not be assigned top priority by criminal justice organizations in general, and police agencies in particular.

2. Development and training in police and other criminal justice organizations appears to need some improvement. On the basis of your dealings with such agencies, list several areas which you feel require the most attention.

3. Contrast behavioral and Gestalt-field theories of learning, and discuss under what conditions each is of the most value.

4. Contrast andragogy and pedagogy teaching philosophies; give several reasons why you would prefer one philosophy over the other.

5. Discuss the ethical considerations which should be considered before B Mod is used as a management tool.

6. Differentiate between "controlled" and "quasi" experimental designs used in measuring training results; provide an example of a "time series experiment."

7. Discuss why it is important to recognize the socialization process, individual differences, and counseling as effective aspects of police recruit-training.

ANNOTATED BIBLIOGRAPHY

Bass, Bernard M., and James A. Vaughn, *Training in Industry: The Management of Learning,* (Belmont, Calif.: Wadsworth, 1966). The authors maintain that to discuss training without considering the learning process is meaningless. This book was written to show how learning is related to training and vice versa; discusses basic principles of human learning, conditions of learning, learning and training, assessing training needs, designing training programs, and evaluating training programs.

Bigge, Morris L., *Learning Theories for Teachers,* (New York: Harper & Row, 1971). The book describes learning theories so as to guide readers in critically constructing and evaluating their own outlooks concerning the nature of the learning process and formulating their own roles in its promotion; it should provide excellent background materials for instructors in training and development programs.

Knowles, Malcolm S., *The Modern Practice of Adult Education: Andragogy Versus Pedagogy,* (New York: Association Press, 1970). This is a pioneering book in its field, as it introduces the teaching methodology of andragogy and contrasts it with the traditional teaching methodology known as pedagogy. Important technological implications and possible directions of adult education practice are stressed.

MacKinney, Arthur C., "Progressive Levels in the Evaluation of Training Programs," *Personnel*, 34, 1957, pp. 72-77. This article discusses the criteria for judging the validity of training evaluations and suggests various levels of evaluation.

Mager, Robert F., *Preparing Instructional Objectives*, (Palo Alto, Calif.: Fearon, 1962). This short and easily read essay on the preparation of objectives suggests that a useful objective must identify the expected behavioral change, define the important conditions under which the change is to occur, and define the related criteria for measuring the change requirement.

This, Leslie E., and Gordon L. Lippitt, "Learning Theories and Training," *Training and Development Journal*, April, 1966, pp. 2-11 and May, 1966, pp. 10-18. A concise discussion of learning theory schools and their application to the developmental process; emphasizes fitting different learning techniques and conditions to specific kinds of training and learning programs.

Tracey, William R., *Managing Training and Development Systems*, (New York: AMACOM, 1974). The aim of the book is to describe critical elements of the training management process in all types of organizations; includes training and development in the 1970's and the 1980's, planning for training and development, organizing the training department, and controlling training.

Planning for Organizational Change and Development

LEARNING OBJECTIVES

The study of this chapter should enable you to:

☑ Define the concept of planning and list the components of the planning process.

☑ Define equifinality and serendipity.

☑ Describe at least four sources of information which are particularly useful to police planners in collecting and analyzing data.

☑ Discuss several guidelines which may be useful in evaluating planning alternatives.

☑ Differentiate between overcoming resistance and reducing resistance.

☑ Explain why contingency factors play an important role in determining the pace for organizational change.

☑ List several objectives of organization development programs focusing on both organizational outcomes and individual change.

☑ Define the five pure styles of the Managerial Grid, and explain why this strategy may not be the most appropriate for all organizations.

☑ List several objectives of T-groups and discuss the two major problems associated with them.

☑ Describe those critical issues confronting the field of organization development which must be adequately dealt with if OD is to be effective.

ELEVEN

The research presented in the previous chapters leads to two general conclusions: (1) many internal and external environmental variables affect organizational behavior, and (2) there is no one "best" way to structure and manage diverse criminal justice agencies. Thus the variables which have been discussed throughout this text (such as individual differences, group infleunces, leadership style, organization and job design, performance evaluation, and training and development) must be considered and adequately resolved through proper management if a high quality work environment is to be developed or maintained. This is accomplished through the process of planning. Accordingly, this chapter examines how police managers might plan for timely organizational change and still allow for the integration of individual and organization needs. The discussion focuses on: the planning process and types of plans, why change is resisted and ways to overcome such resistance, methods of organization development, and critical issues facing organization development.

THE PLANNING PROCESS

Planning may be broadly defined as "the specification of means necessary to achieve a prescribed end, before action toward the end takes place."[1] Filley, House and Kerr analyze their definition:

Note what this simple definition says. First a plan specifies an end or goal. ... Second, it includes the statement of a series of activities which will result in achievement of the goal. We have *not* said that the *best* course of action is necessarily selected, merely that the acts chosen must make goal attainment possible. ... Finally, we have said that planning precedes action. Humans are unique animals in that we are able to plan because we can visualize the future.

The specification of the means to an end in the form of a plan has certain values in itself ... it makes the goal and the path to that goal unambiguous. Moreover, specifying the means provides measurements for control. If the prescribed means are followed, the plan is said to be in control.[2]

Planning is considered to be a formal process which directs the organization in order to maximize goal attainment in as efficient and effective a manner as possible. Although most police organizations practice a certain amount of planning, few agencies have actually developed and/or utilized

---

1. Alan C. Filley, Robert J. House and Steven Kerr, *Managerial Process and Organizational Behavior,* 2nd ed. (Glenview, Ill.: Scott, Foresman, 1976), p. 429.

2. Ibid., p. 429.

the process to the extent necessary to eliminate the "fire-fighting" approach to management. Many managers still spend a significant amount of their time attempting to solve problems after they have developed (a "reactive" process), instead of anticipating and taking corrective action before such problems occur (a "proactive" process).

Like the program development model discussed in the the previous chapter, the process of planning, shown in Figure 11-1, should be viewed from a systems perspective and regarded as continuous. By considering the relationship between the total criminal justice system and its environment, planning allows the organization to adapt to internal as well as to external changes and demands. Each stage of the planning process is briefly discussed below.

Figure 11-1

Planning Process

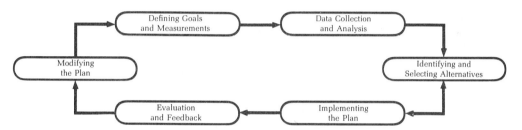

Defining Goals and Measurements: The initial stage of the planning process is concerned with defining goals as well as how they are to be measured or assessed. Goals serve as directional indicators for both organizational and individual performance, and must be understood before strategies for attaining them can be identified. Some form of agreement about what constitutes goal accomplishment is necessary; goals must be explicit enough to allow some form of measurement (Chapter 4). However, goals may be made too specific, therefore smothering individual creativity, as Kast and Rosenzweig have recognized:

Amid the clamor for clarity in organizational goals, it might be wise to consider the possible virtues of vagueness. Clear-cut goals and mechanistic programs for achieving them may discount the human element and lead to a sterile environment which stifles individual initiative and results in underutilization of human resources. Ultrapurposeful action proceeding according to blueprint and schedule may be unpalatable to organizational participants.

If goals are stated in general terms, there is room for organizational participants to fill in details according to their own perception and to modify the pattern to their own liking. Ultra-precision can destroy flexibility and make it more difficult for individuals and organizations to adapt to changing conditions. Vagueness makes it possible to work toward goals by many different means. The concept of *equifinality*—achieving the same end via different means—is an important consideration in viable systems. Vagueness may also foster *serendipity*—the achievement of a particular worthwhile goal by accident. Such results may be an unexpected by-product of organizational activity. The probability of such a happening is increased when objectives are relatively vague and there is room for initiative with regard to the means used to achieve them (emphasis added).[3]

Data Collection and Analysis: The collection and analysis of relevant data is crucial to the planning process, for a plan can only be as good as the information upon which it is based. Much of this phase is related to the discussion in Chapter 3 concerning the significance of developing a spirit of scientific inquiry within the field of criminal justice. As long as a void exists in the research and evaluation area, criminal justice organizations will not be able to collect and properly analyze the types of information which will be the most beneficial to them. Galvin and LeGrande, writing for the International City Management Association, have identified the following sources of information as especially useful to police planners.[4]

1. Review of the Literature: Reviewing pertinent literature (books, journals, reports) within the field, as well as within other disciplines, will usually be an effective first step in data collection.

2. Records, Reports, and Documents: Statistical and analytical interpretations of internal records and reports are necessary to predict the operational needs of a department and to develop a systematic plan. External documents and reports can also provide valuable information and direction for planning activities. Such documents include federal and/or state legislation, city or county council meetings, consultant surveys, annual reports of other departments, studies completed by other criminal justice agencies, and material prepared by business and industrial organizations.

3. Personal Data Collection: The opinions, ideas, and suggestions of organizational members directly involved with a specific problem may be valuable to a planner. Potential outside interview sources should not be overlooked; frequently business organizations have experienced managerial problems similar to of those police agencies. Local college and univesity faculty members may be able to serve as resource persons, either directly—by sharing personal knowledge, or indirectly—by guiding the planner to valuable reference materials. A planner may further need to observe a situation or operation firsthand in order to acquire information not otherwise availble.

4. Questionnaires: When a quantity of information is needed from numerous sources, either internal or external, a formal questionnaire should be an effective means of data collection. When developing a questionnaire, the planner should make sure that it can be answered with reasonable

---

3. Fremont E. Kast and James E. Rosenzweig, *Organization and Management: A Systems Approach*, 2nd ed. (New York: McGraw-Hill, 1974), pp. 442-443.

4. Raymond T. Galvin and J. L. LeGrande, "Department Goals and Planning," in *Municipal Police Administration*, 7th ed., George D. Eastman and Esther M. Eastman (eds.) (Washington, D.C.: International City Management Association, 1971), pp. 211-213.

convenience, that it is not vague or ambiguous, and that it will obtain efficiently all the data needed to accomplish its purposes.

5. Experimentation: Experimentation is the most advanced method of data collection because it creates new information. Because experimental designs offer the greatest degree of control in the collection of data, they offer the planner the most significant and potentially useful information. This method is used to gather data when other means are inadequate.[5] Hopefully, experimentation will become an integral part of the planning process in all criminal justice agencies.

Once the data are collected, they must be analyzed for interpretation. Because a manager frequently determines the relative weight (or importance) assigned to interpretation of the data related to the selection of a plan, the manager should make sure that the data are properly analyzed and interpreted. If the analysis is sophisticated, the manager should consult with someone who has a proper background in statistical analysis. Few criminal justice organizations have employees with such a background, so a manager will probably need to go outside of the department to find such expertise. This may provide an opportunity for developing closer relationships between researchers in academic centers and practitioners in the field.

Identifying and Selecting Alternatives: Once the data have been analyzed, the next step is to take the information and decide on as many practical alternatives as possible. This difficult procedure normally requires a good deal of creative thought, and the planner should seek out as many diverse opinions on the subject as time will allow. "Deviant" or contrary views are often of great benefit in this phase, and thus should not be dismissed from consideration.

Because there are usually several feasible courses of action, the alternatives must be evaluated and the most appropriate selected. A number of guidelines may be used to evaluate each of the alternatives:

1. Which alternative best accomplishes the specific objectives of the plan?
2. Which alternative is most practical when the available resources (manpower and equipment), both present and future, are realistically appraised?
3. Which alternative may be most effectively implemented, considering the time available before action must be taken?
4. Which alternative will be the most acceptable to the political leadership and the various segments of the community?
5. Considering all factors, which alternative has the best chance of successfully solving the problem?[6]

Implementing the Plan: In this stage, the plan is actually put into operation; that is, making sure the various activities of the plan are properly carried out. To do this, practicing managers need to create support for the

---

5. Preston P. LeBreton and Dale A. Henning, *Planning Theory* (Englewood Cliffs, N.J.: Prentice-Hall, 1961), pp. 120-121.

6. Galvin and LeGrande, *op. cit.*, p. 213.

plan; they should make sure that organizational members do not feel that the plan is being "crammed down our throats." The proper implementation of a plan is actually developed in the earlier stages, through active employee participation. If organizational members understand the reasoning behind the plan, where they fit in the plan, and how they will be affected by it (it is important to emphasize how the plan will benefit each employee), resistance should be greatly reduced, thus making implementation less difficult.

Evaluation and Feedback: Evaluating the effectiveness of the plan once implemented is an integral part of the planning process. Indicators which can accurately measure the progress of the planning activities must be developed and continually monitored. Because planning is an open systems process, indicators which measure the effects of the plan on the external environment must also be developed and monitored.

After the plan has operated long enough for valid measurements to be taken, the results should then be fed back to all interested parties—both within and outside of the organization—so that the overall impact or "big picture" of the plan may be understood.

Modification of the Plan: The final stage of the planning process is concerned with modifying the original plan, on the basis of information gathered in the preceding stages. An original plan is seldom effective without some modification, which is best accomplished when planning is viewed as a continuous process, and plans are thus modified to meet current as well as future conditions.

Types of Plans

Two major types of plans and planning processes may be distinguished, standing and single-use plans.

Standing Plans. These are designed to deal with the variety of routine and recurring situations encountered by most organizations. Standing plans provide a major coordinating device for organizational activity, and stem from policies established by the organization. Although complex organizations use standing plans to some degree, they are more appropriate in stable situations. For example, Harvey studied the relationship between "technological complexity" and "program specification" (the latter term refers to the extent to which standing plans are used).[7] He concluded that an organization's structure, particularly its program specification, was directly related to the stability of the organization's task.

There are many organizational advantages to the use of standing plans. Once a policy decision has been reached, a standing plan provides guidelines for decision making and leads to uniformity of operations throughout the organization. Delegation of authority from the top of the hierarchy is thus made easier. By applying the "exception principle" (Chapter 2), organizational members carry out their functions as long as they are covered by

---

7. E. Harvey, "Technology and Structure in Organizations," *American Sociological Review,* 33, 1968, pp. 247-249.

standing plans, and managers can focus on difficulties which may arise and yet maintain adequate control over operations. Also, standing plans—because they are formalized—reduce the degree to which management may act in an arbitrary manner toward employees, and provide for a better understanding of personal freedoms because employees are more aware of what is expected of them.

Although standing plans are necessary for the coordination of organizational activities, they may produce dysfunctional results. Merton discovered that (1) rules and procedures may take on positive values and become ends, rather than means to ends (means-ends inversion), and (2) decision-making tends to become a routine application of precedents with little attention paid to alternatives, which are ruled out by the stated rules and procedures.[8] Consequently such plans, strictly interpreted and followed, can lead to organizational stagnation. Standing plans are thus not as useful in turbulent environments, in which plans cannot adapt to changing conditions.

Single-Use Plans. While standing plans are appropriate for repetitive actions, single-use plans are for single, unrepetitive situations. A single-use plan fits a specific situation and may even be obsolete by the time the goal is attained. Because of its very nature, this type of plan is appropriate, even necessary, for dynamic and unstable situations. Because police organizations operate in environments which are constantly changing, single-use plans are appropriate for most of their planning activities. When such agencies attempt to use standing plans in unstable conditions, repercussions resulting from a lack of timely change will follow. An obvious example of this situation occurred in certain police departments which failed to adjust to the Miranda decision; by failing to retrain their personnel to advise arrested persons of their constitutional rights, many cases were subsequently thrown out by the courts. Such "unforseen" consequences can be greatly reduced through the use of planning and research units, organic structures, frequent reviewing of plans, less reliance on specific goals and detailed policies, and greater emphasis on broader goals and general policies.

CONTINGENCY APPROACH TO PLANNING

Obviously, the planning process should be fitted to the situation. While the basic stages depicted in Figure 11-1 will always be used in planning, the emphasis will vary depending on the conditions under which the organization operates. The practicing manager must determine which type of plan is the most appropriate for the particular situation. Using the common themes and characteristics of organic and mechanistic structures described in Chapter 8, some contingency views of planning are summarized in Table 11-1. This table shows that, when mechanistic structures prevail (closed and stable in nature), single clear-cut goals sent from the top, specific policies,

---

8. Robert Merton, *Social Theory and Social Structure,* rev. ed. (Glencoe, Ill.: Free Press, 1957).

and repetitive plans are appropriate. When organic structures are present (open and adaptive in nature), the organization is a searching, learning system which is continually adapting to multiple goals determined through wide participation; general policies with highly flexible, changing plans are stressed. It should be noted that while either standing or single-use plans may predominate, according to certain organizational characteristics as shown in Table 11-1, both types of plans should be used to some degree by all organizations.

Table 11-1
Contingency Views of Planning

Planning Factor	Organizational Characteristics	
	Mechanistic Structure	**Organic Structure**
Goal Structure	Organization as a single goal maximizer	Organization as a searching, learning system which continually adapts its multiple goals and aspirations
Goal Set	Single, clear-cut	Multiple, determined by necessity to satisfy a variety of constraints
Involvement in Goal Setting Process	Managerial hierarchy primarily (top down)	Widespread participation (bottom up as well as top down)
Types of Plans	Standing plans, specific policies	Single-use plans, general policies
Planning Process	Repetitive, fixed, and specific	Changing, flexible, and general

Source: Adapted from Fremont E. Kast and James E. Rosenzweig (eds.), *Contingency Views of Organization and Management* (Chicago: Science Research Associates, 1973), pp. 315-318.

CHANGE

The process of planning involves programs for change in what an organization does or how it operates. Planning is thus a way of dealing with the future or, as Ewing states, "a technique of so guiding people in the organization that their actions will affect the future in a consistent and desired way."[9]

---

9. David W. Ewing, *The Human Side of Planning: Tool or Tyrant?* (London: Macmillan, 1969), pp. 195-196.

Consequently, the planning process is used to adapt to external environmental demands by introducing internal organizational changes which allow the organization to be more effective. The success of any organizational change effort depends on how well the organization can alter its members behavioral patterns, which are influenced by factors such as managerial leadership practices, how the reward system is used to motivate behavior, and informal group relationships. Any change in the organization, regardless of whether it is introduced through a new organization or job design, or a new training program, involves an attempt to persuade employees to change their behavior and their relationships with one another.

Finally, when planning for organizational change, the practicing manager needs to consider how behavioral changes in employees are most effectively brought about. Depending on the leader's ability to choose the most appropriate leader style, change can be introduced with relative ease or be totally rejected by the membership. In order to bring about timely change in the organization, managers need to consider why people resist change, how resistance can be overcome, and the effects of pace on change.

Resistance to Change

There are many reasons why people do not want the status quo disturbed, as Watson notes: "All of the forces which contribute to stability in personality or in social systems can be perceived as resisting change."[10] These reasons can be grouped in several categories: sunk costs, misunderstandings, group norms, and balance of power.[11]

Sunk Costs: "Sunk costs," broadly interpreted, include time, energy, experience, and money; sunk costs are an extremely influential force in resisting change. An individual or group with many such "investments" sunk into a particular organization or job may not want changes to occur, regardless of their merit. For example, many police agencies are currently attempting to eliminate seniority from the promotional process, in order to base promotions solely on those activities and skills required for a particular position. Resistance to such changes is usually strongest from the older, more experienced employees, who feel that their vested interests in the organization are threatened. This may also account for the reason why "older" people tend to resist change most strongly; they simply have more invested in the system as it exists.

Misunderstandings: Resistance to change is likely when organizational members do not clearly understand the purpose, mechanics, or potential consequences of a planned change, because of inadequate or misperceived communication about change. A critical problem which frequently develops in this area is the uncertainty about consequences of change. If the manner

10. Goodwin Watson, "Resistance to Change," in *The Planning of Change,* 2nd ed. Warren G. Bennis, Kenneth D. Benne, and Robert Chin (eds.) (New York: Holt, Rinehart and Winston, 1969), p. 488.

11. Stephen Kerr and Elaine B. Kerr, "Why Your Employees Resist Perfectly 'Rational' Changes," *Hospital Financial Management,* 26, 1972, pp. 4-6.

in which change will affect employees is not properly communicated, rumors and speculation will surely follow, and the resulting resistance may be strong enough to severely limit the change process.

Group Norms: Groups have a tremendous impact on the behavior and attitudes of organizational members. Group norms (expected behavior from group members) may be a powerful factor in resistance to change. If one follows the norms strictly, one may not easily perceive the need for adaptation or change. If significant organizational changes are to occur, practicing managers must consider group norms and influences, and thus involve group consensus in the planning process.

Balance of Power: One source of equilibrium in organizations is the balance of power among individuals, groups and organizational units. Changes which are perceived to threaten the autonomy, status, or prestige of a group or division will probably encounter strong resistance, regardless of their merit. Such resistance is documented by the case study presented in the following section. A police organization attempted to decentralize its operations by using a neighborhood or team policing concept. Because this approach provides more control and autonomy for lower level management (sergeants), middle level management (lieutenants) originally resisted any changes because of their perceived loss in authority and prestige. The department's detectives also felt that the new system demeaned them by forcing them to work alongside patrol officers in a team effort.

Reducing Resistance

The following discussion focuses on methods by which police and other criminal justice managers can lessen resistance and institute change in a beneficial and constructive fashion. Because of individual differences, the same method(s) will not reduce resistance in every organizational member. Several methods, however, are valuable in reducing resistance: sharing expectations, avoiding coercive tactics, using group decision-making, and making changes tentative.

Sharing Expectations: As indicated at the beginning of this text, a mutual sharing of expectations between the organization and the indivdual greatly facilitates understanding and reduces dysfunctional conflicts. Much of the misunderstanding which may precede organizational change results from too little open communication between the two parties. A lack of trust-worthiness builds up from both directions and the change process becomes a traumatic experience, strongly resisted by rank-and-file members. The organization must maintain two-way commuication and shared expectations, in order to meet specific reasons for resistance and to provide corrective action or further explanation before severe problems develop.

Avoiding Coercive Tactics: Those who resist change are sometimes coerced into accepting the change. Strauss and Sayles accurately interpret the use of coercive tactics as *overcoming* resistance, in contrast to *reducing* resistance.[12] Because of their para-military design, many police organizations assume that whatever is communicated from the top of the pyramid will be readily accepted and put into practice. When questions arise or policies are not carried out enthusiastically, the organization may threaten "uncooperative" members with such sanctions as transfers from an immediate peer group, suspensions, demotions, and even termination.

Such coercive tactics will only worsen the situation. Although this approach may be effective, and lead to immediate compliance with the change, the long range results will certainly be harmful. Resistance may actually become stronger over time, followed by resentment and possibly by sabotage. The related decrease in morale will most likely result in lowered levels of performance and increased employee turnover. Thus, while coercive tactics may intitally suppress resistance, the long term effects for both the organization and the individual will be inflammatory and counterproductive.

Using Group Decision-Making: Kurt Lewin's initial studies on the development of group methods in decision-making revealed that behavioral change is more likely to occur and persist when based on a group, rather than individual, decision.[13] This is especially true (see Chapter 6) when the group is important to an individual, who will change attitudes as well as behavior in order to conform with the group. Lewin further stated that the basis for successful change involves: (1) *unfreezing* existing habits and stereotypes, (2) *changing* to new behavioral patterns and attitudes, and (3) *freezing* or reinforcing the new patterns and attitudes to ensure future conformity. The key to this method is group pressure, which will be especially strong if the participants feel they "own" the decision and are responsible for it.

According to the above analysis, it would appear that a participative management style can reduce much of the conflict and resistance to change which may otherwise occur. Through the use of task forces, committees, group seminars and other participatory techniques, organizational employees can become directly involved in planning for change. By thoroughly discussing the issues, a more accurate understanding and unbiased analysis of the true situation is likely to result. While the group may reject a particular decision, resistance based on misunderstanding will nevertheless be reduced.

Tentative Changes. Changes should often take place on a tentative or trial basis, especially in those organizations which are highly tradition-bound. If employees do not perceive changes as irreversible, they will feel less threatened by any change and their resistance will be reduced. Strauss and Sayles suggest two distinct advantages to this method:

---

12. George Strauss and Leonard R. Sayles, *Personnel: The Human Problems of Management,* 3rd ed. (Englewood Cliffs, N.J.: Prentice-Hall, 1972), p. 251.

13. Kurt Lewin, "Group Decision and Social Change," in *Readings in Social Psychology,* 3rd ed., Theodore M. Newcomb and L. Hartley (eds.) (New York: Holt, Rinehart and Winston, 1958), pp. 197-211.

1. It enables employees to test their own reactions to the new situation, and provides them with more facts on which to base their decision.

2. It helps to "unfreeze" their attitudes and encourages them to think objectively about the proposed changes.[14]

Rapid or Gradual Change?

Planned organizational change should occur at an appropriate pace, neither too rapid nor too gradual. The pace is critical; if change is forced through abruptly and rapidly, severe resistance will be encountered and the results will disrupt the entire organization over a long period of time. On the other hand, if change is so gradual and slow that the employees cannot really see anything "happening," they may return to the more familiar and comfortable ways of the past. Change should thus be introduced quickly enough to show that something is happening and yet, slowly enough to prevent if from totally disrupting the status quo and thus being rejected.

Contingency factors play an important role in determining the pace for organizational change, for organic organizations can withstand more rapid change than mechanistic organizations. Because most police agencies are mechanistic, a gradual or "medium" pace would be the least disruptive route to change, and therefore the most beneficial. The organization should explain the intended changes and consequences to all those concerned. In this way, employees will know what is happening, and fears based on misunderstandings will be reduced or eliminated. For police agencies (or particular subunits) which are more organic in design, where employees may be more amenable to change, there is little reason why change should not be introduced rapidly. Quick change reduces the need for the series of adjustments required by slow change, and which may leave the organization in a continual state of confusion.

Organizational Change: An Example

Because it is difficult to grasp the difficulties and "unforseen" problems which frequently accompany organizational change, a case study is presented below. A large police agency attempted a radical change—from a highly structured, mechnaistic system to a more flexible, organic one. A brief analysis discussing the implementation of planned change follows the study.

Historical Background*. New York City has one of the most tradition-bound police departments in the country. Its organizational problems are serious and enormous and crusted over with a time-hardened protective shell. When the then new Police Commissioner arrived on the scene in 1971, he took the job with the aim of inducing major change in the Department. He knew the Department very well and decided that one of the major needs

---

14. Strauss and Sayles, *op. cit.,* p. 257.

**Source: Morton Bard and Robert Shellow, "Neighborhood Police Teams," in *Issues in Law Enforcement: Essays and Case Studies,* Robert Shallow and Morton Bard (eds.), (Reston, Virginia: Reston Publishing, 1976), pp. 171-182. Some deletions have been made.

was for some kind of transitional model for delivering better services to the unique neighborhoods that constitute New York City. For example, within a two-square block area, there may be an enclave of Greeks; then one of Mohawk Indians in another three- or four-square block area; and of Syrians in still another. Nevertheless, the NYPD policy had traditionally served these diverse areas uniformly. Regardless of the numerous special qualitites In these culturally different neighborhoods, operating procedural orders read as if written by a single mimeograh machine. They were applied literally everywhere, despite the differing problems encountered increasingly in different neighborhoods. The Commissioner thought this was wrong. He felt that there must be some way to relate the unique character of each "Little Italy" or Chinatown or whatever without enfeebling the police or disturbing the general order of the city as a whole.

Introduction of the Plan. The new Commissioner now introduced a plan somewhat like the British in policing style since it was oriented towards service to neighborhoods. The Department's response was at first primarily negative because of normal resistance to change and because the Department had not been consulted. But the public's response was enthusiastic. Suddenly every effective community organization began to put political pressure on the Commissioner to implement the neighborhood team plan in their neighborhoods. So the Commissioner had to move more rapidly than originally planned. While speedy organization was politically expedient, it was organizationally dangerous to proceed before the groundwork had been carefully laid. Both the men in the ranks and the department executives had to understand and participate in the decision if it were to work. In addition, the proper organizational structure and training had to be set up to support the operation.

Even before any team training began, some changes were made in the organizational structure. The Commissioner himself directed the work of "decentralizing" some police functions in the command structure. The initial plan called for establishment of small police departments within each precinct. Certain sergeants were to be designated "team commanders" with responsibilities similar to that of the chief of a small town police force. In that way, each team commander had a force of 35 police officers, and each team would cover one neighborhood. Roughly, that meant five neighborhood teams per precinct.

In effect, this restructuring eliminated the traditional patrol sergeants who, strictly speaking, were accountable to no one on a day-to-day basis. It also re-involved the precinct C.O.'s who had generally been remote from the daily operational problems in the various neighborhoods of their areas.

Under the Commissioner's plan, the newly designated team sergeants were given great flexibility. They could assign manpower according to the priorities they judged that problems had in their areas. They could also assign officers to work in uniform or in plain clothes, whatever suited the developing needs of the neighborhood. The sergeant's new flexibility strengthened his authority, but above all it acknowledged responsibility and his accountability to the people in his neighborhood.

Where in the past everything had been done uniformly, sergeants were now given freedom to make decisions. Depending on the type of relationship he had worked out with the community, the sergeant could set up a neighborhood office, develop ways of getting information from the community people, and supervise his men in a way that permitted both individual freedom and team participation. It was meant to be a marked departure procedurally from the highly mobile, centrally dispatched, controlled police force which had until then been organized in precincts for administrative simplicity and efficiency.

Seen from a broad perspective, this team concept was a shift away from the highly centralized and remote management of police services that had developed in large cities. It was also an effort to decentralize certain functions rationally and shift the point of accountability from the captains to sergeants at the line level.

Initially, one neighborhood in each section of the city was chosen, quietly and without fanfare for the experiment. But word soon got out, and a wholly unexpected public clamor for neighborhood police teams spread throughout the city. It was as if the general public hungered for a return to that closer relationship with police that was virtually impossible so long as unit mobility remained a primary concern of headquarters. As a partial response to the pressure, the words "Neighborhood Police Team" were quickly lettered on patrol cars. Launching this program in this manner before it was thoroughly understood gave it a public relations quality that was potentially destructive. Initially five neighborhoods were designated as team areas but before very long there were over 45. The authors joined in an effort to put the brakes on before the expectations of citizens far out-stripped the Department's ability to deliver the new type of service that everyone was eager to get.

Preparation for Training. After the first teams had been in existence for some time, the Commissioner turned to the problems at hand: the men didn't know what their roles were supposed to be and the organizational structure was vague. The authors were brought in during the early stage to help put together the training program and to serve as general advisors on development of the program itself. They made two inputs: one was to get them to hold off on proliferating the program; the other was to gain a commitment to move toward establishing precinct-wide conversion to the neighborhood program.

Responding to public demand for Neighborhood Police Teams, the Department originally set up approximately forty-five teams in almost as many precincts. In other words, in more than half of the city's seventy-seven precincts, there was only one neighborhood team operating while the rest of the precinct operated as usual. So the competition, the rivalry, the who-takes-calls and who-doesn't confusion were predictably unsatisfactory and irresponsible. The authors suggested the establishment of neighborhood teams entirely in five precincts. They were concerned that sector men and sector squads in the same precincts but outside the teams might sabotage or otherwise undermine the efforts of any "foreign" neighborhood teams in their midst. Indeed, it was seen that it would be extremely difficult to preserve the integrity of those neighborhood teams and give the program a real test unless whole precincts were fully converted to the new system.

A parallel development during this reorganization was the creation of an "Operations Lieutenant" in each of the five precincts. Traditionally in the NYPD a lieutenant occupied what was basically a more-or-less honorific position. It was wasteful; they were virtually high-class clerks. The new operations lieutenant was sent back out on the street and given responsibility for shift supervision. With the team commanders fully responsible for their area and the operations lieutenant responsible for the whole precinct during a given shift, there was not only a potential, but a very real probability, that horns would be locked, particularly on tactical issues. To head off trouble the operations lieutenant was converted into a neighborhood team coordinator. He oversaw the operations of the teams in his precinct. The theory was he would no longer need to vie with the team commanders, but become a vital part of the team program.

Operational Phase. The first neighborhood team was operating by early September 1971. By late December and early January, forty teams were operating. During this two-month period, two things became increasingly evident; first, the men did not know what was expected of them; and secondly, there was highly variable performance on the street.

In response to a profound policy shift, the implementation now followed almost a classic course. The first news came in a TOP (temporary operating procedure) memo which was distributed to all commands. In three single-spaced pages the disturbingly vague TOP was to serve only as a guideline. Using his discretion in setting policy, the Police Commissioner held that in order to deliver services more meaningfully to the many and varied neighborhoods of the city the normal precinct structure would have to change.

Very quickly, the issue of interpreting policy through a training program of some sort became crucial. Should the bulk of training be directed at the brass, the sergeants, or the men? Several of those involved believed that the sergeants had the greatest need to understand neighborhood policing concepts because they were the ones who were to serve as models for the men. It was decided to devote intensive training time to the sergeants and then assist them in training their team members, but to also provide some kind of training for the precinct commanders, their executive officers, and the lieutenants. While the sergeants may have known very well what they were supposed to do and how they were to do it, and while their men may also have understood their roles clearly, the lieutenants could disrupt the entire organization by jerking men from shifts, giving them special assignments, and floating them off here and there.

The training plan evolved from a joint effort of the Police Department and some doctoral candidates who attended one of the authors' seminars in 1972. The seminar group consisted of ten students and ten police officers. Ranging from sergeant to captain and representing three divisions in the

New York Police Department, the officers were there to keep the social scientists informed of the realities of police work. The graduate students were there to contribute their insights and knowledge of human behavior, of changing social systems, and of educational methodology.

The seminar agreed at the outset that the Neighborhood Police Team Concept had several profound implications:

1. it acknowledged the importance of community participation in crime control,
2. it acknowledged the need for new skills and competencies in the delivery of police services, and
3. it acknowledged the need for change in organizational behavior from authoritarian military uniformity to democratic team flexibility.

The planning group concerned with the reorganized approach now decided that the most effective strategy would call for a period of intensive training for approximately thirty team commanders in the experimental precincts. Beginning with a brief orientation with patrol personnel and experimental teams, one of the team commanders together with civilian and police trainers conducted field training over a one-year period. One each of five pairs of trainees (a civilian and an officer) were assigned to the five experimental precincts. Along with the five or six team commanders, the civilian and police trainees would serve as a resident field training faculty within each precinct.

Such assignments were a world shaking opportunity for many team commanders. It is a kind of freedom that can be mind-boggling to those who have been operating in a very tight, authoritarian organization. Some of those selected for training couldn't really handle it. From those who could, we hoped to learn a lot. Certain of those team commanders have done fantastically innovative and unusual things particularly relevant to their areas. Others were not able to rise to the occasion. From them we did learn what kind of person makes a good team commander.

After the basic concepts were decided, we held training sessions for personnel from the planning division and the Police Academy. Together we designed a consecutive five-day training program for the team commanders. It was calculated to project a new concept of supervision. It was hoped that we could thus expose the men to a range of options for use in their on-going educational role in those precincts. Each one of the precincts was planned to become what a teaching hospital is to a medical student. Further, each of those precincts would be related to the Police Academy. In addition, the team commanders, whose roles are at least partly educational, would be part-time training faculty.

To promote continuous training sessions, we encouraged team commanders to hold them not only on unusual subject matter and in unusual ways, but also at unusual times and places. If Sunday morning is quiet, a team commander should be able to pull everybody off the street. With modern communication and response capability, why not? If the public doesn't see officers on the street and gets upset, then the public has to be educated too. That's another police responsibility. If you are doing relevant work and delivering service, the public will buy your approach. Communitites will support efforts that are relevant and effective in the service they provide.

The neighborhood approach collided, of course, with the traditionalists both in the precincts and in the Department as a whole. As mentioned earlier the lieutenants were orignially jealous of the new authority given to the team commanders. The detective division and special squads needed reorientation too. In precincts where the neighborhood model was operative, many detective and special squad functions were already performed by the neighborhood teams. As a result, the team commander had to be consulted before any officers external to his team were brought into the neighborhood. If a special unit did go in, the team responsible for that area had to go right along with them and serve as a guide, thus heading off a possible sabotage of the team effort.

In general, there is a very serious clash between the mobile patrol philosophy and the neighborhood police philosophy in most departments. Mobile patrol emphasizes rapidity of response and rapidity of return to service. In effect: get to the assignment, get it over fast, get back to service ready for the next assignment. On the contrary, with the neighborhood team approach: try to increase contact between police and citizen, and provide a higher quality of service, perhaps spend more time on some problems, get to know people better, be available within the neighborhood. The team commander was expected to monitor reactions of people in the areas he serviced and to identify those who might be considered spokesmen for the various factions of the community. Such spokesmen were (and are) not formally designated. For example, gang leaders can be as important as administration or block captains. The team commanders had to discover those people and relate to them in such a way as to get their input. Then the stage was (and is) set for providing police services adjusted to the needs and problems of each neighborhood.

None of these basic organizational changes were accomplished simply by the Commissioner's original decision to implement a neighborhood police program. Training and retraining and training again was necessary to accomplish changes of the scope contemplated by the neighborhood approach. But even before training could start, it had to be funded. A proposal for funding was submitted in 1971 to the Law Enforcement Assistance Administration, a federal agency. After months of delay, it was approved for eighteen months. The grant was for a one-shot study with provision for possible extension, and it was to be augmented by Police Academy funds. The Academy was also to oversee the performance of the contract. By the time training began and civilian staff was hired, three full precincts and a number of scattered teams had been trying to operate on the neighborhood model without any training at all.

The fate of the training teams differed greatly within each precinct. In only two of the five precincts did the training really got off ground. Even then, it was often not under optimal conditions. The single most critical factor was, of course, the attitude of the precinct commanding officer. For example, in the 24th Precinct only two men from each team were allowed to leave street patrol for training during the same hours. This attacked the very heart of the team training concept since it prevented the trainees from organizing a well-coordinated, smooth-functioning groups. Eighty percent of this same precinct was comprised of rookie policemen who were transferred there during the training. While those coincidental transfers were an attempt to reduce corruption in the precinct, they produced a rapid turnover that directly opposed the Neighborhood Police Team concept of fostering neighborhood police ties. Add to this the fact that all training sessions were held early on Sunday morning and you can begin to get the feel of some of the obstacles to training in a precinct where the NPT program was given low priority.

In the two precincts which understood and supported the NPT concept, the commanding officers were responsible for the positive reception. In fact, even before the arrival of the trainers, one precinct was operating according to the commanding officer's conception of the spirit of the NPT concept. The C. O. held a forum for the men in his command to explain the kinds of innovation that would be introduced. The precinct sergeants also made contacts with 140 block associations and then assigned particular policemen to deal with the various problems brought to light. The C.O. also met with heads of the Parks Department, the Sanitation Department and other local service agencies so as to coordinate their efforts with the police in serving the community. When we pressed this commanding officer for his opinion of the value NPT trainers had been to his precinct, he conceded that they had made some contributions, such as suggestions for rumor control and improved understanding of varying reactions to standard police procedures. Among ethnic groups the Hispanics react particularly negatively to being touched by a policeman when being questioned, for instance. Also the NPT trainers had helped in pointing out the paternalistic attitude of many police toward the people whom they serve. The necessity of treating fellow citizens as adults was stressed.

Even in those instances where training seemed to proceed fairly effectively, many problems were not resolved. For example, during training one team examined a problem in their neighborhood that involved public reaction to police handling of robbery investigations. Often citizens were annoyed when patrolmen completed robbery reports without taking clearly evident fingerprints. After some brainstorming, the trainees suggested that one of the team pairs could carry a fingerprint kit so that this pair could be sent over to take prints when the next such robbery report was being made. A simple enought plan, it was an outcome of team work that would certainly have improved police/community relations—and might have aided in crime solving as well. But the plan was squelched at higher precinct levels and the team was told that the $12.00 purchase price for the kit was not available.

Throughout the field training there was ongoing conflict between the Neighborhood Police Team trainers and their supervisors at the Police

Academy. While both the civilian and police trainers as staff members were, in effect, in the para-military structure of the Police Academy, they operated semi-autonomously. Because most of their funding was external they were not accountable to the Police Academy in the traditional sense. Thus, their very existence was viewed as a threat to the authority of the Academy. In addition to this, the Police Project Director was changed ten or more times in the course of two years. This accentuated the sense of isolation within the Academy structure. Also, the cooperative joint decision-making style of the training team was antithetical to the traditional bureaucratic chain of command of the Police Academy personnel and the Department in general. This stylistic difference and its implications resulted in various disagreements. From the beginning the training team was criticized for its casual dress and flexible hours. Police trainers among the NPT (who were detailed to the project) wore civilian clothes, not uniforms.

By the spring of 1972 the conflict between the police training team and the Police Academy supervisors was intense. The NPT training team was not keeping up with the initial quota set for training hours and was under pressure to proceed with training so as to justify its existence. So the Police Academy initiated an investigation of the training team's progress. That included the sending of evaluation forms on the trainers to the five NPT precincts without the trainers being informed. The Police Academy also demanded a strict account of the hours worked. At first the NPT trainers refused to comply because they resented the imposition of traditional structures. Later they agreed to comply, although they viewed stringent requirements for time and activity reports as harassment. Their morale was at an all-time low.

It became clear that the Police Department would not request that the training grant be refunded. A new administrator was appointed to take charge of all training programs including NPT training. He came with the avowed purpose of "shaping up" the NPT training team, and there were several hostile confrontations. The Police Project Director was released shortly afterwards when his initial contract ran out. Then the trainers were pulled out of the precincts and given training assignments within the Academy. Some members of the team left; the team ceased to function as a team at that point.

Program Evaluation. In evaluating the NPT training program as innovative change, we must first use the goal of the program as a criterion. The goal was to set up a training program in each NPT Precinct, that, first could continue after the trainer had moved on and, second, that could meet the needs of the specific teams involved. Obviously, this also meant that as these teams, their neighborhoods, and their problems changed the programs had to be flexible so as to change with them. Measured against this criterion, the NPT training cannot be considered a success. Only a few precincts have any program at all at this point; the one precinct with both an ongoing program and training had it underway before the NPT trainers arrived on the scene.

It is clear to us from this review of the NYPD experiment that innovation which originates at the top, as was the case with the NPT training program, tends to lose its innovative character as it filters down to the lowest levels of the organization. Two NPT police officers in the precincts that favored the program said that they did not feel that their ways of carrying out their duties had been much affected by the NPT program. When pressed, one admitted that in certain ways his performance had been facilitated. He appreciates the flexible duty hours and the fact that he can now wait to see a case through to the end rather than have to rush on to the next call. He said that not much has changed in his work time away from the stationhouse, but that the atmosphere at headquarters is more open to the public. For others, the training may even have had a negative effect to the extent that it increased some patrolmen's already cynical attitude toward training programs in particular and change in general.

Prospects are not totally bleak, however. There have been a number of innovations as a result of the training program, although they are not necessarily those that were delineated in the goals of the specific training program. First, the introduction of civilians in the institutional police department was a radical change from previous policy; and some of them are still working there. Second, some of the training techniques developed by the NPT trainers have been incorporated into the curriculum at the Police Academy and into the functional management training. This might be considered the institutionalization of some of the innovative aspects of the NPT training program. Third, the even temporary toleration by the police structure of the group decision-making style of the trainers can only be viewed as an innovation when seen in the context of the traditional, military style decision-making of the police. The fact that some civilian trainers are still employed by the Police Department also indicates some degree of acceptance. The fact that the NPT Trainers were evaluated fairly favorably by the precincts when the Police Academy conducted the evaluations also indicates that some attitudinal changes had occurred.

Analysis. In the above study, management did not alter employee behavior to the extent necessary for effective implementation of the planned change. Similar results can be expected in other criminal justice organizations when radical changes are attempted over such a short period of time. While the Commissioner was undoubtedly correct in assuming that traditional patrol operations were not serving the unique needs of many neighborhoods, the desired changes were unfortunately not communicated to the department as a whole. When employees are not consulted in the planning for change, resistance is likely to be high. This frequently happens when top management attempts to introduce change rapidly; employees feel that they are being forced into something which may not be to their advantage.

If the organization's membership had been involved in the planning process from the beginning, the results would probably have been more favorable. The tremendous amount of employee resistance could have been substantially reduced by applying the methods described earlier: sharing expectations, avoiding coercive tactics, using group-decision making, and making changes tentative. Through shared expectations, the anticipated advantages (to both the individual officer and the community) could have been communicated, along with possible disadvantages perceived by the officers who had to carry out the program. Perceived problems and misunderstandings could have been dealt with openly. In spite of initial turbulence, it is better to meet resistance head on and deal with it, than to allow resistance to become uncontrollable.

Participatory management devices such as task forces and group seminars, used early in the planning process, would most likely have reduced resistance to team policing by allowing discussion on exactly what the program involved and what was needed for its implementation. This is not meant to suggest that all departmental members would have been suddenly converted, but much resistance can be overcome through discussions based on facts rather than misperceptions. Members from the community should also have been invited to participate in making decisions which would affect policing in their neighborhoods. Had this been done, the tremendous public pressure for this program could have been anticipated. Also, departmental members would then have been aware of the public's desire for such change (and the reasons for it); this could have affected resistance.

Finally, although the program was to have been tentative, because of the "unforseen problem" of public acceptance it was implemented quickly, before the concept was totally understood, giving it a public relations quality which was potentially destructive. It might have been wiser to introduce team policing only in the experimental districts (as originally intended), evaluate the results, and implement the program organization-wide only if the results indicated that the program was more effective than traditional patrol. In this way, the change would have been tentative, and all departmental members would have had a chance to objectively evaluate the proposed change. In short, the NPT case study offers an excellent example of what can happen when organizational change is not properly planned and is introduced too rapidly, especially in an organization which is relatively mechanistic.

ORGANIZATIONAL DEVELOPMENT

Specific techniques or strategies which have been used for bringing about organizational change in non-threatening and constructive ways will now be considered. *Organization development* or OD is an emerging discipline which uses the behavioral sciences to assist organizations in adjusting to environmental changes. This section will include a definition of organization development; a typology of OD techniques, along with a review of several of the more popular methods and their applicability to the NPT study; and finally, a discussion concerning some of the critical issues facing the field of organization development.

What Is Organizational Development?

While many writers have attempted to define organization development, perhaps the most influential definition is Beckhard's:

Organization development is an effort (1) planned, (2) organizationwide, and (3) managed from the top to (4) increase organization effectiveness and health through (5) planned interventions in the organization's "processes," using behavioral science knowledge.[15]

Organization development, then, is a program for introducing planned and systematic change in an organization. Typically, organizational members must interact and collaborate with one another in the introduction of change; this normally occurs under the direction of a professional change agent—the OD consultant. The consultant uses behavioral science techniques, such as questionnaires, interviews, group discussions, and experimentation (e.g., pilot studies), to diagnose problems and design appropriate change strategies.

Beckhard also lists several characteristics which underlie the concept of organizational development and which guide most OD consultants in their choices of interventions or change strategies:

1. The basic building blocks of an organization are groups (teams). Therefore, the basic units of change are groups, not individuals.

2. An always relevant change goal is the reduction of inappropriate competition between parts of an organization and the development of a more collaborative condition.

3. Decision-making in a healthy organization is located where the information sources are, rather than in a particular role or level of hierarchy.

4. One goal of a healthy organization is to develop generally open communication, mutual trust, and confidence between and across levels.

5. "People support what they help create." People affected by a change must be allowed active participation and a sense of ownership in the planning and conduct of the change.[16]

Objectives of OD. The following objectives are closely associated with organizational development programs. Compiled by Filley, House and Kerr, the first list is primarily concerned with objectives which focus on organizational outcomes; the second list, although ultimately concerned with organizational change, particularly involves individual change in attitudes, beliefs, and behaviors.[17]

Organizational Objectives.

Increasing Effectiveness. This broad and self-evident objective is included . . . as a reminder that OD efforts ultimately "must be justified in terms of the organization's objectives."

Improving Problem Solving. This objective . . . is primarily concerned with programs aimed at conflict reduction and conflict resolution within and between organizational units. Sub-goals in this area would include building trust among groups,

---

15. Richard Beckhard, *Organization Development: Strategies and Models* (Reading, Mass: Addison, Wesley, 1969).

16. *Ibid.*, pp. 26-27.

17. Filley, House and Kerr, *op. cit.*, pp. 489-490.

creating an open climate throughout the organization, and achieving greater collaboration among groups.

Increasing Adaptability. OD efforts are often concerned with increasing flexibility so the organization "can adapt better to the accelerated rate of change in technology . . . and society in general."

Substitution of Systematic Concepts for Outmoded Precedents. A common barrier to commitment, creativity, and involvement is the existence of outmoded traditions and precedents. Many OD efforts seek to replace these with systematic management concepts and up-to-date standards and values.

Individual Objectives.

Providing Opportunities to be "Human." Stated most broadly, this includes "providing opportunities for people to function as human beings rather than as resources in the productive process." Subgoals within this area could include such things as allowing organization members to develop to their full potentials, treating them as people with complex sets of needs which are important to their work, and attempting to create an environment where they can find exciting and challenging work.

Increasing Awareness. Many OD efforts have as a major objective the development of self-awareness among participants, as well as awareness of the mechanics and consequences of various group processes.

Increasing Participation and Influence. There is widespread agreement that "providing opportunities for people in organizations to influence the way in which they relate to work, the organization and the environment" is a critically important component of many organization development programs, and that successful attainment of this objective can ease the path toward attainment of most of the others.

Integration of Individual and Organization Objectives. This "composite" objective focuses upon both the organization and its members, and is viewed by many authors as a particularly important concern of organization development.

Typology of OD Interventions

Although OD techniques or interventions may be classified in many ways, the various types of interventions are summarized below in terms of their depth, from relatively impersonal to highly personal.

According to Burke, interventions occur when an organization: "(a) responds to a felt need for change on the part of the 'client,' (b) involves the client in the activity of planning and implementing a change event, and (c) leads to a normative change in the organization's culture."[18] Burke defines *organizational culture* as a set of shared assumptions about the norms and rules to which the members conform.

If each point is analyzed separately, it becomes clear that OD interventions are a response to a problem(s) perceived by the agency or client. The intervention is a mutual involvement of both the change agent and the client system; the consultant does not do something to the client, but rather does something with the client. It should also be noted that the change agent can

---

18. W. Warren Burke (ed.), *Contemporary Organization Development: Conceptual Organizations and Interventions* (Washington, D.C.: NTL Institute for Applied Behavioral Sciences, 1977), p. 6.

be based inside the organization; therefore, the organization is not precluded from doing something for itself. Finally, the intervention strives for a "normative change" in the organizational culture. The term does not suggest how the culture is to be changed, only that a change should occur.

Roger Harrison has developed a typology which differentiates intervention techniques or strategies in a way which allows rational matching of strategies designed to deal with different organizational change problems. This differentiation is based on the dimension of *depth,* which is defined as the extent of the individual's emotional involvement in the change process.[19] While emotional involvement is present at any level of intervention, the typology is concerned with the degree to which the intervention is related to the involvement. "In focusing on this dimension," Harrison states, "we are concerned with the extent to which core areas of personality or self are the focus of the change attempt." He elaborates:

Strategies which touch the more deep, personal, private, and central aspects of the individual or his relationships with others fall toward the deeper end of this continuum. Strategies which deal with more external aspects of the individual and which focus upon the more formal and public aspects of role behavior tend to fall toward the surface of the depth dimension. This dimension has the advantage that it is relatively easy to rank change strategies upon it and get fairly close consensus as to the ranking.[20]

Discussed below are five common intervention strategies, each of which calls for a successively deeper level of emotional involvement. [21]

1. *Operations Analysis:* The first level is concerned with the roles and functions which are to be performed in the organization, rather than with individual motivation, values, and attitudes. The change strategy focuses on specifying the power, resources, and tasks to be performed, as well as on defining jobs for individuals and groups in the organization.

This level, which is of very modest depth, depends on the structural design of the organization. By basing the interventions on the contingency approach to organization design, the structure can properly conform with the environment. When this is the case, there is a proper organization-task "fit," and individuals are more likely to achieve a sense of satisfaction and competence from their jobs.

2. *Evaluating and Controlling Individual Performance:* The second level is concerned with the selection, placement, training, and evaluation of individuals in accord with job design and other structural characteristics. While this strategy is deeper than the preceding one, "the intervener is concerned with what the individual is able and likely to do and achieve

---

19. Roger Harrison, "Choosing the Depth of Organizational Intervention," *Journal of Applied Behavioral Science,* 6, 1970, pp. 181-202.

20. *Ibid.,* p. 183.

21. The five intervention strategies and much of their discussion is drawn from Harrison, *ibid.,* pp. 184-187.

rather than with processes internal to the individual."[22] Although individuals and groups have "feelings" about training and performance evaluation, the focus is on observable performance, rather than on the individual's personal characteristics. Attempts to facilitate change at this level can include both external rewards and punishments (salary increases, promotions, demotions, and transfers), as well as internal rewards (greater satisfaction and feelings of accomplishment).

Two frequently used change strategies at this level are job enrichment and management by objectives (Chapter 9). For example, MBO permits the supervisor to avoid focusing on personal characteristics of the subordinate, especially those deeper characteristics which managers generally have difficulty in discussing with those who work under them. This process is limited to information which is public and observable, such as setting performance goals and the success or failure of the individual to attain them.

3. *Concern with Work Style:* This level is concerned not only with observable performance but also with the processes by which that performance is achieved. However, this strategy is primarily concerned with styles and processes of work rather than with the processes of interpersonal relationships, which have a deeper dimension. The strategy involves such factors as how the individual perceives his or her role, what is or is not valued, and how the individual acts towards others (delegating authority or reserving decisions for oneself, communicating or withholding information, collaborating or competing with others on work-related issues).

Intervention at this level is oriented toward attempts to structure work behavior and working relationships among individuals and/or groups. The satisfactions or dissatisfactions which organizational members derive from one another's work behavior are diagnosed. This change strategy frequently involves interpersonal or intergroup bargaining and negotiation which may lead to changes in group norms about communications, behaviors, and methods for resolving present and future conflicts. Much of the intervention strategy which has been developed according to Blake and Mouton's concept of the Managerial Grid® is used at this level; the concept involves bargaining and negotiation of role behavior as an important change process.[23]

The Grid OD approach focuses change efforts on two basic leadership dimensions: *concern for people* and *concern for production.* Each orientation is conceptually similar to the consideration and initiating structure leader dimensions of the LBDQ (Chapter 7). The "managerial grid" itself, shown in Figure 11-2, represents several possible leadership "styles." Concern for people is expressed along the vertical axis and concern for production is expressed along the horizontal axis. Each dimension is considered to be independent of the other; a manager's styles may rank high (9) or low (1)

22. *Ibid.,* p. 184.

23. Robert R. Blake and Jane S. Mouton, *The Managerial Grid* (Houston: Gulf Publishing Company, 1964); Blake and Mouton, *Building a Dynamic Corporation Through Grid Organizational Development* (Reading, Mass.: Addison-Wesley, 1969).

on both aspects. Blake and Mouton identify five styles which they consider to be pure, although many other possibilities lie between: 1, 9 - *country club management*, which emphasizes a high concern for people but a low concern for production; 9, 1 - *authority-obedience management*, which emphasizes maximum concern for production and minimum concern for people; 5, 5 - *organization man management*, which reflects a moderate concern for both people and production; 1,1 - *Impoverished management*, which reflects a minimal concern for both people and production; 9,9 - *team management*, which emphasizes a high concern for people combined with a high concern for production.

Figure 11-2

The Managerial Grid

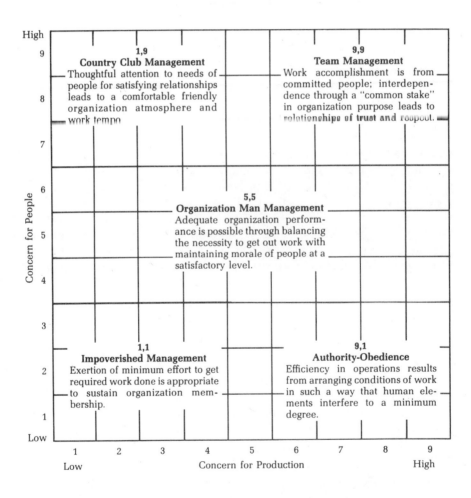

Source: Robert R. Blake and Jane Srygley Mouton, *The New Managerial Grid*, (Houston: Gulf, Copyright 1978, p. 11. Reproduced by permission.)

The managerial grid program assumes that the team style is the most appropraite, and that managers can and should work toward the development of a 9, 9 grid score. The program consists of six phases which usually last three to five years:[24]

Phase 1. Involves studying the "managerial grid" as a theoretical framework for understanding managerial effectiveness; starting with the top management group.

Phase 2. Involves studying the actual behavioral dynamics of the organization; includes testing team development activities against the Grid model for the perfection of problem-solving methods.

Phase 3. Experiences of Phase 2 are extended to include intergroup relationships within the organization; interventions are made in those areas in which coordination among groups can be improved.

Phase 4. Top management works in close cooperation with other groups to develop an ideal "model" for the future management of the organization.

Phase 5. Temporary task forces are formed and begin converting the organization from what it has been to the ideal model developed in Phase 4.

Phase 6. Involves measuring the changes which have occurred from Phase 1 through Phase 5, stabilizing the organization's achievements, and establishing new goals and objectives for the future.

Although the Grid strategy has been widely employed for organizational revitalization in the private sector, there is little rigorous empirical evidence to suggest that the "prepackaged" six phase program necessarily represents the single best change intervention (toward a 9, 9 style) for all organizations. It might be more appropriate to initially study and diagnose the particular problems impeding organizational goal attainment, rather than to begin the change process with a study of the managerial grid. Nevertheless, many of the techniques at this level are useful in developing a more cooperative and conflict free work environment.

4. *Interpersonal Relationships:* The fourth level focuses on the feelings, attitudes, and perceptions which organizational members have about one another. These interventions deal with the quality of human relationships within the organization; feelings like warmth and coldness, acceptance and rejection, love and hate, and trust and suspicion among individuals and groups are included. The consultant attempts to elicit normally hidden feelings and attitudes in order to create more open relationships, which, in turn, should help to develop mutual understandings of one another as persons.

The basic intervention strategy at this level is sensitivity training or T-groups (T for training). A typical training or "laboratory" program lasts from three days to two weeks, involves 10-15 members, and is normally conducted at some secluded location away from the organization. Participants may include organizational "cousins" (people from different work groups in the same organization), members from the same organizational "family" (people from the same work group), or "strangers" (people from outside of

---

24. See: Blake and Mouton, *Building a Dynamic Corporation, op. cit.,* p. 16.

the organization). Police departments, for example, have used strangers in T-groups designed to improve police-community relations, especially with respect to minorities. Sensitivity training has the following objectives:

1. To increase self-insight concerning one's behavior in a social context—to learn how others see and interpret one's own behavior and to gain insight into why one acts the way he does in different interpersonal situations.
2. To increase sensitivity to the behavior of others . . . and the development of the ability to infer accurately the emotional bases for interpersonal communications.
3. To increase awareness of the types of processes that facilitate or inhibit group functioning. For example, why do some members participate actively while others do not? Why do different groups, who may actually share the same goals, sometimes create seemingly insoluble conflict situations?
4. To increase diagnostic and action oriented skills in social, interpersonal, and intergroup situations.
5. To teach a person to learn how to learn—continually to analyze his own interpersonal behavior in order to reach and engage in more effective interpersonal interactions with others.[25]

To fulfill these objectives, the actual phases of a T-group experience generally include the following:

1. In the beginning, there is a purposeful lack of directive leadership, formal agenda, and recognized power and status. This creates a behavioral vacuum which the participants fill with . . . projections of traditional behavior.
2. In the second phase, the trainer becomes open, non-defensive, and empathetic, and he expresses his own feelings in a minimally evaluative way. However, the major impact on each participant comes from the feedback received from the here-and-now behavior of the other group members.
3. In the third phase, interpersonal relationships develop. The members serve as resources to one another and facilitate experimentation with new personal, interpersonal, and collaborative behavior.
4. The last phase attempts to explore the relevance of the experience in terms of "back home" situations and problems.[26]

Because of the highly personal nature of T-groups, they are extremely controversial in the managerial field. While both advocates and critics of sensitivity training emotionally defend their positions, more research must be conducted before this technique can be fully evaluated. At present, there appears to be enough evidence to support its continued use as a developmental strategy. Two problems remain clear, however; the first involves the difficulty of transferring learning which occurred during the T-group program to the organizational setting and actual performance on the job (this

---

25. John P. Campbell and Marvin D. Dunnette, "Effectiveness of T-group Experience in Managerial Training and Development," *Psychological Bulletin,* 70, 1968, pp. 73-104.

26. Andre L. Delbecq, "Sensitivity Training," *Training and Development Journal,* January, 1970, p. 33.

problem has been addressed in previous chapters and can be solved through the proper use of organizational rewards). Second, with respect to the contingency approach, the emphasis on openness, participation, and flexibility may be dysfunctional to the overall needs of highly mechanistic organizations.

5. *Intrapersonal Analysis:* This is the deepest level of intervention, in which the consultant attempts to discover the individual's deeper attitudes, values, and conflicts regarding his or her own functioning, identity, and existence. This strategy emphasizes "increasing the range of experiences which the individual can bring into focus and cope with. ... Those approaches all tend to bring into focus very deep and intense feelings about one's own identity and one's relationships with significant others."[27] An example of this strategy is the use of "marathon" labs, which are similar to the T-group process described above but are longer and even more intense.

In this typology, the deeper the level of intervention, the more significant the impact, either positive or negative, on organizational members. For this reason, Harrison suggests two criteria for choosing the appropriate intervention: (1) it should intervene at a level no deeper than that required to produce lasting solutions to the problems at hand, and (2) it should intervene at a level no deeper than that at which the energy and resources of the client can be committed to problem solving and to change.[28]

CONTINGENCY APPROACH TO OD INTERVENTIONS

With respect to the above criteria for selecting a proper level of OD intervention, the contingency approach offers much to practicing managers as they attempt to determine the usefulness of different change techniques. Figure 11-3 shows Harrison's intervention strategies superimposed over a continuum of organizational characteristics, with mechanistic and organic structures at the two extremes. An organization or unit whose structural characteristics lie toward the right hand side of the continuum will benefit most, at least initially, from intervention strategies whose depth is relatively superficial. Therefore, sensitivity training may not be appropriate at this stage. As one moves steadily across the continuum, deeper levels of intervention (such as job enrichment and the managerial grid program) are appropriate. At the extreme left of the continuum, the deepest and most emotionally involved strategies of change (such as sensitivity training) are most beneficial.

---

27. Harrison, *op. cit.*, p. 187.

28. *Ibid.*, p. 201.

Figure 11-3

Contingency View of Intervention Depth and Change Strategy

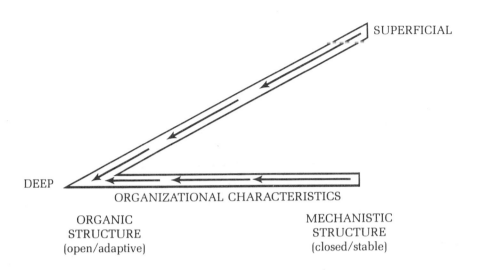

Source: Adapted from Edgar F. Huse and James L. Bowditch, *Behavior in Organizations: A Systems Approach to Managing,* 2nd ed. (Reading, Mass.: Addison-Wesley, 1977), p. 400.

The need to recognize individual differences cannot be stressed too greatly. Although a particular criminal justice organization may be highly mechanistic, there may well be specific units which could benefit from deeper levels of intervention than would be the case for the organization as a whole. Practicing managers must continually be aware of such differences, and plan accordingly.

Several OD strategies might have helped the New York Police Department in managing organizational change. Because the NYPD is highly mechanistic, the most superficial strategy, operations analysis, could have been useful in determining which design would conform to the environment. The second strategy (in terms of depth), evaluating and controlling individual performance, was used to a certain extent. Training, the only form of intervention used to help guide organizational change, could have had a significant impact in New York, had it been introduced prior to and not after implementation of the program. If a team policing style would turn out to be the most profitable for the organization and its environment, the third strategy, concern with work, would eventually become necessary. Because team policing requires a team management approach, several phrases of the managerial grid program might have been valuable.

If Grid OD is to realize its full potential, it cannot be rushed; the entire six phase program generally requires three to five years for proper development (40 teams in the NYPD program were operating within approximately

3 months). Important aspects of this program include the stress placed on intergroup relationships and on coordination among team members (such as between patrol officers and detectives or between sergeants and lieutenants), the close association of groups with top management (what is the chief really thinking?), the temporary use of task forces in converting the organization to the planned model, and measuring the changes which should have occurred. Further development might use the strategy of interpersonal relationships. T-groups made up of participants from all parts of the organization, as well as members from the community, could increase interpersonal communication and awareness of those processes which make team management easier. Both departmental and community members could increase their understanding of one another and of their society.

In conclusion, each of these OD strategies, beginning with the most superficial in terms of depth, can assist the organizational change process. However, as the NPT study suggested, if change is rushed in mechanistic organizations, the results can be more destructive than productive.

ISSUES FACING OD

A number of critical issues directly confront the use of OD. Although these potential problems can usually be corrected, they must be adequately considered if OD is to be effective.

Tendency to use one "best" approach for all situations: In the past, OD practitioners have tended to regard the approach with which they are the most familiar as the single best strategy, regardless of the situation or what the preliminary "diagnosis" revealed. For example, in the middle and the late 1960's, sensitivity training was used widely as the primary OD method and considered to be a cure-all for any organization's ills. More recently, the use of job enlargement/enrichment and management by objectives in police departments has been regarded as a panacea for all of the organization's problems. Although each strategy has merit, none can be applied to all organizations in all situations. As Strauss has bluntly suggested, "For my taste, OD has been plagued by too much evangelical hucksterism. As an academician, I am repelled by the cloying emotionalism and unsubstantiated claims that appear in some of the literature and much of the advertising."[29]

Lack of scientific evaluation: Because it is difficult to measure precisely the effects of OD interventions, rigorous scientific evaluation of OD is lacking. Measuring difficulty is particularly troublesome when the intervention requires several months or even years, during which time the consultant introduces many changes throughout the organization. While it is difficult to pinpoint and measure changes throughout the organization, how else can one know whether or not improvements would have occurred without the OD Intervention? Subsequently, practicing managers cannot be sure

---

29. George Strauss, "Organizational Development: Credits and Debits," *Organizational Dynamics*, 1, 1973, p. 13.

whether the time, effort, and money spent on OD is worthwhile. As mentioned earlier, the managerial grid program is an example of a highly popular strategy which has little empirical justification. This second problem may be related to the first; OD consultants frequently are not sure of the success and impact of their "pet" strategy, so they continually use the same intervention technique in all circumstances.

Ethics and Values: Because OD interventions require employees to be open and candid when they assess organizational problems, they must be assured that their remarks will not be used against them. This is important, because while consultants view themselves as responsible to the total organization, they are paid by management, and the question of where their loyalties lie is often raised. Consultants must be careful about using information which has been supplied through an honest and trustworthy relationship with organizational members. The information exchange should be viewed as similar to the doctor-patient relationship, and held in confidence unless the employee specifies otherwise. If such information is used for other than OD purposes, the change process can be set back enormously and any relationship with management may be destroyed.

Another problem develops when the consultant attempts to apply his or her personal values and norms to the organization, rather than dealing with the self-articulated needs ("felt needs") of the client. This does not imply that the consultant should view the current organizational climate as the proper one, but the intervention should start where the clients are, not where the consultant feels they should be. Otherwise the clients may feel pressured into changing too rapidly, which could lead to greater resistance and detrimental results.

Finally, the consultant and the organization must have a mutual understanding concerning who has access to the data collected and how that data will be used. Because of past abuses, police personnel are often suspicious that data collected by behavioral scientists will be used against them in some way or another. In order to assure full cooperation, organizational members must be guaranteed that the information collected will be used solely for the purpose of organizational improvement and that it will remain anonymous. If these issues are properly handled, and if mutual trust is established between the consultant and the client organization, OD interventions can be of immense value to criminal justice organizations.

SUMMARY

The planning process is vital to all criminal justice organizations if they are to adapt to environmental changes and integrate individual and organizational needs. Practicing managers must devote sufficient time to developing the six primary stages of this process: defining goals and measurements, data collection and analysis, identifying and selecting alternatives, implementing the plan, evaluation and feedback, and modifying the plan. Employee participation throughout the entire process can help create support for the plan, which, in turn, should make implementation easier. Two major types of plans exist: standing plans and single-use plans. The former are designed for routine and recurring events and are more appropriate under relatively stable conditions, while the latter are designed for non-repetitive events and are more appropriate under relatively unstable conditions. The contingency approach to planning considers the characteristics of the organization (mechanistic or organic in nature).

Factors which both inhibit and promote resistance to planned change were discussed. People tend to resist change because of sunk costs or investments in the status quo, misunderstandings with respect to a planned change, the impact of group norms on individual attitudes and behavior, and the balance of power among individuals, groups, and organizational divisions or units. Such resistance may be reduced by the sharing of expectations between the organization and the individual, avoiding coercive tactics so that resistance can be reduced rather than overcome, using group decision techniques so that the participants feel that they "own" the decision and are responsible for it, and allowing for tentative change in agencies which are highly bureaucratic and tradition-bound. A case study of organizational change provided a good indication of the degree of resistance which can occur when major changes are introduced too rapidly into mechanistic structures, especially when the above methods for reducing resistance are not considered during the planning process.

An emerging discipline known as organizational development or simply OD involves five levels of interventions, which are differentiated according to their dimension of depth or emotional involvement of the individual in the change process. The five levels, each successively "deeper" in emotional involvement, include: (1) operations analysis, (2) evaluating and controlling of individual performance, (3) concern with work style, (4) interpersonal relationships, and (5) intrapersonal analysis. The contingency approach helps in properly selecting the level of intervention for a particular organization or subunit. Deeper levels are more appropriate for those agencies or units which are relatively organic, while the surface levels are more appropriate, at least initially, for mechanistic designs. Finally, if those critical issues which currently confront OD can be overcome (tendency to use a single "best" appproach in all situations, lack of rigorous evaluation, and potential problems of ethics and values), then OD can greatly benefit police and other criminal justice agencies during their transition and adaptation to change.

DISCUSSION QUESTIONS

1. Discuss why the process of planning should be regarded as continuous, and how this process can help eliminate the "fire-fighting" approach to management.
2. Contrast standing and single-use plans and discuss under what conditions each is most appropriate.
3. Discuss several reasons why people tend to resist change and several methods you feel would be the most effective in reducing resistance.

4. Describe the advantages of both rapid and gradual change; provide an example of either type, as witnessed by you in an organization.

5. Discuss what you think were the primary reasons for the resistance encountered in the NPT case study, and why you do or do not believe that such resistance was legitimate.

6. Describe the five common OD strategies according to their dimension of depth; describe change techniques which could be used for each.

7. Discuss why the level of OD intervention should be no deeper than that which the energy and resources of the organization can commit to problem solving and change.

ANNOTATED BIBLIOGRAPHY

Bennis, Warren G., Kenneth D. Benne, and Robert Chin (eds.). *The Planning of Change,* 2nd ed. New York: Holt, Rinehart, and Winston, 1969. A comprehensive anthology on adapting theories of social and personal dynamics to the process of planned organizational change; contents include four major parts: the evolution of planned change, elements of planned change, dynamics of planned change, and values and goals.

Gibbons, Don C., Joseph L. Thimm, Florence Yospe, and Gerald F. Blake, Jr. *Criminal Justice Planning: An Introduction.* Englewood Cliffs, New Jersey: Prentice-Hall, 1977. The book represents an attempt at an introductory, yet comprehensive, discussion of justice system planning; it reviews the existing literature on planning and identifies some of the major directions that criminal justice planning ought to pursue.

Harrison, Roger, "Choosing the Depth of Organizational Intervention," *Journal of Applied Behavioral Science,* 6, 1970, pp. 181-202. In this article, organization intervention strategies are differentiated from one another in a way which permits rational matching of strategies to differing organizational change problems; the differentiation is based on "depth" of individual emotional involvement in the change process.

Harvey, Donald F., and Donald R. Brown. *An Experiential Approach to Organization Development.* Englewood Cliffs, N.J.: Prentice-Hall, 1976. This book thoroughly discusses most current OD techniques and whether empirical findings exist on the results; an experiential learning approach is used—the concepts are practiced by using the techniques in a simulated organizational setting.

Huse, Edgar F. *Organization Development and Change.* St. Paul, Minn.: West, 1975. This book describes underlying concepts and assumptions of the rapidly growing field of organization development as well as the better-known OD strategies, ranging from those techniques which are relatively impersonal in nature through those which are highly personal.

O'Neill, Michael E., Ronald F. Bykowski and Robert S. Blair. *Criminal Justice Planning: A Practical Approach.* San Jose, Calif: Justice Systems Development, 1976. This book attempts to combine the various "bits and pieces" of criminal justice planning in a logical, practical and usable framework; resource sections added at the end of selected chapters provide examples which clarify and illustrate specific planning techniques.

TWELVE

Police Management: Challenges of the Future

LEARNING OBJECTIVES

The study of this chapter should enable you to:

☑ Describe the two prevailing conditions in police systems which call for the decline of highly bureaucratic structures and managerial styles.

☑ List the fundamental changes in the basic philosophy which underlies managerial behavior.

☑ Describe the five core problems confronting future organizations.

☑ Describe each of the "cooperative" goals set forth for the improvement of the quality of police work environments.

☑ List several advantages which may be derived from collaboration.

☑ List four recommendations for management practice which are in need of immediate attention if police organizations are to reach desirable levels of competency.

☑ Differentiate between basic and applied research and discuss why each is important to management practice.

☑ Discuss what is meant by the "linking" role for practicing managers.

☑ Describe the concept of a "skill hierarchy" and discuss why it is of importance to lower level employees.

☑ Discuss the advantages of a "personal profit plan" for all organizational employees.

TWELVE

The preceding chapters have covered a wide variety of subject matter. This final chapter draws things together by incorporating the presented information and making some predictions about the future challenges and orientations of police management. Although this text has concentrated on analysis and description, using empirical research to summarize what is, the focus now shifts to one of prescription, or concern with what should occur if police management is to be improved. Although the following recommendations and conclusions are subjective and necessarily speculative, they are based on the findings presented previously. If a majority of these suggestions is adopted, it is believed that police working environments can be substantially improved, and organizational efficiency and effectiveness increased. And, although the prescriptions in this chapter focus on police management, they can be applied to the proper management of all criminal justice organizations. Consequently, the following goals and recommendations could significantly affect criminal justice management *per se*.

THE DECLINE OF BUREAUCRACY

Two prevailing conditions in police systems necessitate, at least to some degree, the decline of highly bureaucratic structures and managerial styles: (1) the realization that police organizations function within turbulent environments, and (2) the attraction of young, highly educated, and demanding individuals into the police field. With respect to the former condition, in the past many police agencies have not responded well to the changing societal demands made on them, chiefly because of an improper "fit" between the organization and its environment; unstable environments require more flexible, organic structures which can readily adapt to changing situations. With respect to the second consideration, it is doubtful that the current mechanistic structures will be able to provide a stimulating atmosphere which will develop and utilize the full potential of the "new breed" entering the field today. Here there may be an improper "fit" between the individual and the organization. If police organizations wish to maintain high quality personnel, their managerial styles should become more flexible and humanitarian.

The above conditions suggest that police management must be decisively transformed if it is to adequately meet the internal needs of the organization as well as the external demands placed on it. Warren Bennis has observed a fundamental change in the basic philosophy which underlies managerial behavior, reflected most of all in:

A new concept of *Man,* based on increased knowledge of his complex and shifting needs, which replaces an oversimplified, innocent push-button idea of man.

A new concept of *power,* based on collaboration and reason, which replaces a model of power based on coercion and threat.

A new concept of *organization values,* based on humanistic-democratic ideals, which replaces the depersonalized mechanistic value system of bureaucracy.[1]

Bennis further suggests that the primary cause of this shift in management philosophy stems "not from the bookshelf but from the manager himself." He believes that the success of McGregor's *The Human Side of Enterprise*[2] was based on:

[A] rare empathy for a vast audience of managers who were wistful for an alternative to a mechanistic conception of authority. It foresaw a vivid utopia of more authentic human relationships than most organizational practices allow . . . The real push for these changes stems from some powerful needs, not only to humanize the organization, but to use the organization as a crucible of personal growth and development, for self-realization.[3]

While contemporary management philosophy, in either the public or private sector, may not provide grounds for such optimism, there does appear to be "movement" in this direction. Even within the police field, known for its authoritarian management philosophy, many organizations are attempting to adapt a more humanitarian style. The NTP case study presented in the previous chapter provides an excellent example of just such an attempt to change, even though the results were less than spectacular, largely because of the way in which the change process was initiated and carried out.

Core Organization Problems of the Future

Considering these changing conditions, Bennis perceives five core problems affecting organizations of the future. These are also critical to the future development and success of all criminal justice organizations, and each will be briefly discussed below.[4]

1. *Integration* contains the entire range of issues having to do with the incentives, rewards, and motivation of the individual and how the organization succeeds or fails in adjusting to these needs. Integration may be thought of as that ratio between individual needs and organizational demands which creates the transaction most satisfactory to both. The problem of integration stems from our "consensual society," in which personal attachments play a great part and the individual is appreciated as a moral, integrated personality.

---

1. Warren Bennis, "Organizations of the Future," *Personal Administration,* 30 (September-October, 1967), p. 8.

2. Douglas McGregor, *The Human Side of Enterprise* (New York: McGraw-Hill, 1960).

3. Bennis, *op. cit.,* p. 8.

4. The discussion of the five core problems is drawn from Bennis, *ibid.,* pp. 9-10.

2. *Social Influence* essentially involves the problem of power and its distribution within the organization. As demonstrated in Chapters 6 and 7, power distribution and leadership behavior are complex issues. Studies produce varying interpretations, and almost always in ways which coincide with the researcher's biases (which may include a cultural leaning toward democracy). Nevertheless, in contemporary police organizations, the problem of power must be seriously reconsidered in recognition of highly diverse and complex role responsibilities, which make the one-man authoritarian rule (from the top) obsolete.

3. *Collaboration* is a problem which grows out of the same social processes which lead to conflict and stereotyping, and out of those centrifugal forces which divide nations and communities. There are too many fruitless and often crippling mechanisms for conflict resolution: avoidance or suppression, annihilation of the weaker party by the stronger, sterile compromises, and unstable collusions and coalitions. As organizations become more complex they fragment and divide, developing group patterns and information codes which frequently exclude others and on occasion exploit differences for inward harmony. Ways must be discovered which can deal with conflicts of this type and minimize the suspicion and mistrust which inevitably arise. However, this does not mean that conflict is always avoidable or necessarily harmful; a certain amount of conflict is healthy for an organization and can produce creative and productive ends.

4. *Adaptation* is a problem created by a turbulent environment. The pyramidal structure of bureaucracy is suitable for organizations whose tasks are highly routine and repetitive. However, because *all* police systems operate in environments which are dynamic and uncertain rather than placid and predictable, these systems must be directed toward more flexible orientations which can adapt to changing external demands. Although this statement may at first appear to be an overgeneralization, it is argued that while not all external police environments are as turbulent as others, the distinction is mainly one of *degree*. For example, although the environment of a police department in a large city may be more turbulent than that of a department in a small city, each organization must continually adapt to changing external stimuli (such as public opinion, special interest and/or minority group interests, political influences, and new laws and ordinances,), if it is to adequately serve the community. Because their environments are turbulent and not placid, police agencies cannot function effectively by using a highly mechanistic approach.

5. *Revitalization,* another problem which will confront organizations of the future, is of extreme importance to police agencies. According to Bennis, the elements of revitalization are:

   a. An ability to learn from experience and to codify, store, and retrieve the relevant knowledge.

   b. An ability to "learn how to learn," that is, to develop methodologies for improving the learning process.

c. An ability to acquire and use feedback mechanisms in performance, to develop a "process orientation;" in short, to be self-analytical.

d. An ability to direct one's own destiny.

These qualities have a good deal in common with what John Gardner calls "self-renewal." For the organization, this means paying careful attention to its own evolution. Without a planned methodology and explicit direction, the organization cannot realize its full potential.

Figure 12-1 summarizes the core problems confronting contemporary organizations, and the emerging conditions (20th century) which appear necessary if criminal justice agencies are to resolve these problems and meet their prevailing internal and external needs.

IMPROVING THE QUALITY OF WORK ENVIRONMENTS

The preceding discussion about the decline of bureaucracy and the core problems confronting contemporary organizations provides a basis for an expanded discussion on how police management must evolve if working environments are to be noticeably improved. To this end, a set of "cooperative" goals will be prescribed which are designed to increase the integration of individual and organizational needs, thus establishing a foundation for a high quality work environment.

Figure 12-2 presents hypothesized and sequential relationships among the "cooperative" goals. This set of goals strives to build a high degree of cooperation *between* the organization and all organizational members, as well as *among* all organizational members, in the belief that *cooperation* is the key to developing an enjoyable and rewarding work environment. Each goal is based on the two major premises advocated in Chapter 1: (1) the quality of individual and organization interactions can be improved to the benefit of both parties, and (2) the responsibility for improving the quality of individual and organization interactions lies with both the employee and the organization.

If the five goals shown in Figure 12-2 are to be achieved, approximately equal contributions must be made by both the individual and the organization. However, because organizations are "organized," the initial impetus toward establishing an atmosphere of cooperation may need to originate from the organization itself. Furthermore, while each goal is considered to be a valuable end in itself, it is believed that before the ultimate goal of adaptation and revitalization can occur, each of the preceding goals must reach high degrees of attainment. Also, each of the goals develops and depends on the others, but if the first goal of sharing expectations is not realized, the others will probably not be fulfilled to the degree necessary to have a substantial impact on improving the work environment. Below, each goal is considered in sequential order.

Table 12-1
Core Problems Confronting Contemporary Organizations

Problem	Bureaucratic Solutions	New 20th Century Conditions
Integration The problem of how to integrate individual needs and organizational goals.	No solution because of no problem. Individual vastly over-simplified, regarded as passive instrument or disregarded.	Emergence of human sciences and understanding of man's complexity. Rising aspirations. Humanistic democratic ethos.
Social Influence The problem of the distribution of power and sources of power and authority.	An explicit reliance on legal-rational power, but an implicit usage of coercive power. In any case, a confused, ambiguous shifting complex of competence, coercion, and legal code.	Emergence of self-reliance and power sharing. Leadership too complex for one-man rule.
Collaboration The problem of producing mechanisms for the control of conflict.	The "rule of hierarchy" to resolve conflicts between ranks and the "rule of coordination" to resolve conflict between horizontal groups. "Loyalty."	Increased needs for independence and minimization of mistrust and suspicion.
Adaptation The problem of responding appropriately to changes induced by the environment.	Environment stable, simple, and predictable; tasks routine. Adapting to change occurs in haphazard and adventitious ways. Unanticipated consequences abound.	External environment of organization more "turbulent," less predictable. Unprecedented rate of technnological change. Increased need for flexible orientation which allows for adaptation.
"Revitalization" The problem of growth and decay.	Underlying assumption that the future will be certain and basically similar, if not more so, to the past.	Rapid changes in technologies, tasks, manpower, norms and values of society, goals of organization and society all make constant attention to the process of revision imperative.

Source: Adapted from Warren Bennis, "Organizations in the Future," *Personnel Administration*, 30 (September-October, 1967), p. 18.

Figure 12-2

**Cooperative Goals for the Improvement
of Police Work Environments**

Initial Sharing of Expectations

This all important first goal is related to the expectation-integration model proposed in the first chapter. If the individual and the organization are to truly complement one another in achieving mutually desirable and beneficial ends, they must initially share their expectations about one another (expectation-integration). The individual asks: Why is the organization interested in me; what does the organization perceive my role to be once inside the organization; what types of objectives and goals does the organization expect me to pursue; what does the organization expect from me in the future? Conversely, the organization asks: Why is the individual interested in this organization; what does the individual perceive his or her role to be once inside the organization; what types of objectives and goals does the individual expect to pursue; what does the individual expect from this organization in the future? Questions such as these must be dealt with by both parties, if a satisfactory relationship is to develop.

This expectation-sharing process should begin during the employee recruitment phase prior to hiring (during the initial employment interview), and continue through recruit or preparatory training. This makes it possible for both parties to accurately assess one another and determine if each feels comfortable enough with the other to establish an ongoing association.

Expectations should be mutually shared, so that each party knows what to expect from the other. Individual and organization expectations will seldom be exactly the same before the individual decides to go to work for a particular agency, or a particular agency decides to hire the individual. In most situations there will be differences, some of them substantial. However, if these differences are known, each party can work constructively toward "bridging the gap" and establishing a high quality work environment. If, on the other hand, such differences are not shared, each party may work against the other in an attempt to satisfy selfish ends. Subsequently, both the individual and the organization are discontent with each other, which produces dysfunctional consequences and a low quality work environment.

Chapter 1 listed turnover as one of the more serious problems concerning individual and organization interactions. In the example provided, a young college recruit (anxious to be innovative) could not cope with a tradition-bound agency and resigned within a short period of time. Such a situation could most likely have been avoided if expectations had initially been shared; the individual would have realized that the organization was highly traditional, and the organization would have realized that the individual would not simply accept the status quo. Initially then, each party would have known what to expect from the other, and an attempt could have been made to determine whether or not a mutually satisfying relationship would be possible.

Even under conditions where substantial differences between the parties are apparent, a profitable relationship can often be established. Each party, however, must be willing to make some compromises, to give and take to a certain degree. In the example cited above, the individual and the organization may conclude that, although some changes would be desirable, their implementation will take a sustained and conscientious effort. Therefore, the organization knows that the individual will pursue constructive change, and the individual knows that the change process may take considerably more effort than anticipated. Each party is aware of the adjustments which must be made to accommodate the other.

The importance of this first step toward improving the quality of the work environment cannot be overstated. By rigorously promoting expectation-integration, both the individual and the organization start off in step with one another and clear the path for fulfilling each of the remaining goals.

Humane Relationships

This goal follows naturally from the first and is a vital ingredient to the definition of management provided in Chapter 1. Because of the preoccupation with hierarchical status and power in many police organizations ("don't ask questions, simply follow orders"), humane and trusting relationships frequently are not established between the organization and the individual. Humane relations are possible, however, if each party is willing to share their expectations from the beginning of their association. In this way, sources of discontentment can be mutually worked out and a sufficient level of humane dealings can be reached. Although it is difficult to specify exactly what this level should be, it will involve a climate of trust; neither party will take advantage of the other.

This second goal transcends individual-organization interactions, for humane relationships should be built throughout the organization. In other words, individual reactions to the ideas of other organizational members should be compassionate and charitable.

Establishing humane relationships throughout the organization is an extremely difficult task. As discussed in the last chapter, this is one of the primary aims of most OD strategies, and it may take several years or longer to accomplish. The problem stems from the nature of complex organizations; the number of differentiated functions works against high levels of humane and trusting relationships being developed among all organizational members and units. Because not everyone is equally concerned with the operation of certain units (those inside are more concerned than those outside), it is difficult to establish humane relationships over wide areas. Also, it takes only a few instances of inhumane behavior (such as deception, animosity, or "backstabbing,") to reduce painfully built up positive relations to negative ones. Nevertheless, if the remaining cooperative goals are to be achieved, at least a moderate level of humaneness must be developed throughout the organization.

Open Communication

The achievement of a moderate level of humane relationships should also help to create open communication throughout the organization. This basically means that individual-organization and individual-individual communications should be straight-forward and "above board;" facts are not distorted for personal or other purposes. People can "say what they mean" accurately and forthrightly, without fear of damaging and vengeful reprisals.

An organization can be judged to have a high degree of openness when neither party to a communication is afraid to send or receive information which may be negative, provided that it is sincere. In turn, such information is internalized constructively and used for purposes of improvement. This does not imply that positive information is not communicated; it is, but the main problem in cultivating openness usually concerns the communication of negative but accurate information. Consequently, open communication means that information which is critical can be dealt with maturely. If an individual or group is considered deficient in certain areas of work, they can be approached openly about the subject, and methods for improving performance can be discussed. Conversely, if the organization is perceived to have certain policies which are too rigid and thus confine the individual or group, the policies can be openly discussed and suggstions offered for their revision.

If open communication is to be developed throughout the organization, the lessening of bureaucracy once again becomes an important goal. The preoccupation with hierarchial status and power severely inhibits open communication, which may be impossible in those police agencies which strictly follow a rigid, para-military design and all the sanctions which accompany it. In such agencies, the degree of fear felt by a person in a low status position when approaching a person in a high status position is a monumental roadblock to open communication. Under such circumstances, simple dialogue between the two parties is often difficult, while open communication is practically unheard of. It is clear, therefore, that much less emphasis should be placed on hierarchical status and power if this goal is to be realized.

Channels of communication must not only be opened in the formal sense, but informally as well; the informal organization plays a crucial role toward the achievement of open communication. Consequently, the honest opinions of informal leaders should be actively solicited in an attempt to avert potential problems and conflicts. For example, because *unions* are playing an ever-increasing role in the lives of organizational members, frank discussions should take place between management and union leaders, in an effort to prevent conflicts which could prove harmful to union and non-union members alike. The stifling of open communication may lead to severe conflict and even hostility in the long run, thus producing a climate of "working against" rather than "working for" one another. Such an attitude can lower employee morale and motivation, which leads to decreased levels of initiative and performance.

The inability to bring conflict "out into the open" where it can be confronted is one of the major problems facing practicing managers. Since conflicts are an inevitable part of organizational life, they should be recognized and dealt with early so that they do not reach crisis levels and undermine individual and organizational performance. If conflicts are openly confronted early enough, the prospects for preventing harmful consequences are substantially improved.

The goal of open communication is similar in many respects to the second goal of establishing humane relationships, for it is not realistic to believe that individuals and units throughout the organization can be equally affected. Openness also can be destroyed by only a few instances in which individuals or groups are treated unfairly or punished after communicating in an accurate and honest way. The organization can help assure open communication by giving positive rewards for this desired behavior. Once organizational members realize that open communication is really desired, the attainment of this goal is possible.

Collaboration in Decision-Making and Conflict Resolution

The fourth goal focuses on utilizing the individual strengths of organizational members, in collaboration with one another, to help make relevant decisions and resolve conflicts. The extent to which a teamwork approach can be useful in these areas stems directly from each of the preceding goals (especially that of open communication); failure to achieve them sufficiently will greatly inhibit the potential benefits of collaboration.

Collaboration seeks to obtain high levels of participation and "pulling-together" by organizational members as part of an attempt to maximize individual, group, and organizational effectiveness. This "pulling-together" concept is precisely what the team policing style of management attempts to maximize, although simply implementing this particular style in an organization will not accomplish this purpose. The pros and cons of participation in the decision-making process have been sufficiently debated elsewhere; the "new breed" of individual entering the police field will probably not only benefit from participatory management, but will demand it.

If collaboration in decision-making can be increased throughout the organization, both the individual and the organization should profit. Some of the anticipated advantages of collaboration are:

1. A more thorough understanding of what the organization is, where it is going, and how it will get there.
2. A more thorough understanding of how the individual fits into the organization and contributes to it, and vice versa.
3. A greater understanding of the "worth" of other organizational members.
4. An increased emphasis on cooperation between organizational members and groups, leading to decreased levels of dysfunctional competition.
5. Increased control by the individual over his or her own destiny within the organization, leading to greater "ego" involvement and commitment.
6. Higher levels of motivation, leading to increased effort and performance.

Collaboration should also be useful in resolving conflicts. Although a certain amount of conflict is necessary in order to initiate organizational change, too much can severely damage an organization and substantially lower its performance levels. As discussed in Chapter 6, conflict can be both functional and dysfunctional; it is also judged as either good or bad according to some value system. Conflict may thus be perceived as helpful by one group or individual, and at the same time, perceived as harmful by another group or individual. If such conflict can be dealt with through collaboration of the parties involved, and each side comes to better understand the viewpoint of the other, they are not as likely to use one another to accomplish selfish ends.

By emphasizing the "pulling-together" concept, the teamwork method stresses that all members are a part of the same organization and should be working toward the overall effectiveness of that organization, and not just toward the attainment of special interests. Through the use of collaboration in resolving conflicts, negative and self-defeating outcomes become more apparent. Conflict can thus assume a positive role by calling attention to changes which must be made in order to correct deficiencies and unfair practices. This means, of course, that each party must be willing to give and take to a certain degree, if the organization and its members are to achieve common goals.

Capability for Adaptation and Revitalization

The other cooperative goals culminate in the development of the capability for adaptation or self-renewal. The achievement of this ultimate goal depends, as have the others, on the mutual contributions of both the individual and the organization.

While organizational adaptation and revitalization cannot take place without the cooperation of the individual, the importance of this goal to the individual is frequently underestimated. Because police organizations operate in dynamic environments, individuals must become willing to accept a certain amount of change if they are to remain vital to the organization. If individuals cannot adapt to change, revitalization (as described earlier by Bennis) will not occur, leading to stagnation on the job and other unhealthy outcomes (such as being put "out to pasture" because one's skills and abilities are no longer needed). This goal is as crucial to the individual as it is to the organization.

As discussed in the last chapter, the organization can do much to encourage greater receptivity to change by reducing the threatening aspects often associated with the change process. However, while the organization can make allowances for the development of this goal, it is up to the individual or group to carry through and actually permit the processes of adaptation and revitalization to take place.

This capability, then, is significant because of the decay which will inevitably occur without it. As Bennis puts it: "Growth and decay emerge as the penultimate conditions of contemporary society. Organizations, as well as societies, must be concerned with those social structures that engender buoyancy, resilience, and a 'fearlessness of revision'."[5] While police organizations have not generally been known for their "fearlessness of revision," they will need to move in this direction if they are to keep pace with their unpredictable environments.

In sum, by moving toward the accomplishment of the cooperative goals described above, even though they may not be completely attainable, police management can significantly improve the quality of work environments. As a result, individual and group performance levels should increase, thus improving the overall effectiveness of the organization.

DEALING WITH CHANGE: THE CONTINGENCY APPROACH

By now it should be apparent that the future success and well being of police organizations depend on their ability to effectively deal with change. In order to prevent stagnation and decay, organizations must be able to adapt to changing environmental demands, and over the long haul, be able to revitalize themselves. The contingency approach, which involves the application of appropriate managerial concepts and strategies to specific organizational circumstances, allows for the introduction of timely change and subsequent revitalization. Consequently, it is the most suitable for the management of meaningful change.

Most important to the implementation of timely and constructive change in organizations is the ability to lead and coordinate activities relevant to the change process. Future managers, therefore, must act as effective change agents in their leadership roles and be able to skillfully guide their organizations in new directions. Subsequently, because the contingency approach allows for the introduction of change according to changing circumstances, managers should understand contingency theory and its application.

---

5. Bennis, *ibid.,* p. 10.

The previous chapters have made numerous recommendations for management practice, based on contingency theory. Below are suggested four final recommendations which are in need of immediate attention if police organizations are to reach desirable levels of competency according to community expectations. While each is considered critical, without effective implementation of the first, the others will not have much meaning.

The *first* recommendation calls for *increased emphasis on rigorous empirical research.* Only scientifically validated research findings can discover management practices which are appropriate for specific organization circumstances. Most of the managerial concepts and practices now in use in police organizations are based on tradition and familiarity; they have seldom been tested empirically. How then, can practicing managers know if their practices are sound and the best available? The answer is simple; they cannot. Although traditional practices may be perceived as "working well," the question must be posed: Relative to what? Hopefully, this text has helped both the student and the practitioner of management to realize the importance of developing a spirit of scientific inquiry. Only through rigorous research can one determine which managerial practices are the most efficient and effective for overall goal attainment. Without research, the manager operates in a vacuum, continually repeating the mistakes of the past.

Many of the research findings presented in the book have involved organizations other than those within the criminal justice field, simply because the majority of sound empirical studies on management have been conducted in the private sector. Relatively little rigorous empirical research has been attempted in the area of police and criminal justice management. Police managers, however, are beginning to realize that research is just as important to the well being of their organizations as it is to those in private industry. Because the contingency approach is research-oriented, future managers will need to have at least a rudimentary understanding of research methods and how research results can be applied to their organizations. Police managers should not be afraid to encourage researchers to study their organizations, with the mutual aim of improving the work environment. This does not preclude the notion that police agencies may wish to hire and use their own researchers, for most agencies could readily profit from improved, or newly created, research and planning units.

Both *basic* research and *applied* field research are essential to contingency management. While basic research is needed to develop the theoretical aspects of contingency management, applied field research is currently of greater importance to police organizations as they attempt to discover and incorporate appropriate managerial practices. Luthans has addressed this situation:

Although there is little agreement in the terminology that is used to differentiate the various types of research methods, basic research is used here to mean the systematic investigation of theoretical problems inherent in contingency management. The more needed field research is applied and includes both field studies and field experiments. A field study would systematically investigate environment-management relationships as they exist in a real, field setting without attempting to influence the variables. In this way, meaningful contingency relationships could be identified for management practice. One major advantage of a field study is that there is little or no disruption and hence no "Hawthorne effect" problem with the results. Secondly, because the study is conducted in the actual setting, the problems of generalization are minimized. The results of a field study can be directly applied to management practice. The major disadvantages are controlling the variables and drawing any generalizations about cause and effect. The field experiment, on the other hand, overcomes these disadvantages but has the problem of disrupting the situation, and generalizations are less confident. In a field experiment changes are introduced in order to test a hypothesis or evaluate the effectiveness of some intervention. For example, the environmental situation may be changed to see what impact this will have on the effectiveness of various management concepts and techniques. In the future, existing contingency relationships must be continually tested and new contingency relationships must be determined through such field research techniques.[6]

The *second* recommendation calls for *police organizations to move toward more flexible, organic structures.* This does not mean that contemporary designs need to be completely restructured; as Chapter 8 indicated, mechanistic designs for organizations and/or specific subunits are appropriate under certain conditions. However, because these organizations do operate in unstable environments (although differing in their degree of instability), the classic bureaucratic designs require some changes if they are to avoid substantial decay.

Because of the differentiation in the turbulence in their environments, some police agencies will need to become more flexible than others. To illustrate, imagine a continuum with the most mechanistic structure at one end and the most organic at the other; a municipal police organization operating in a highly turbulent, heterogenous community will probably need to move further along the continuum—toward the organic end—than would a county police organization whose environment is more stable and homogeneous.

In helping police agencies move toward the organic end of the continuum, varying degrees of the "matrix" structure appear useful. From the discussion in Chapter 4, the reader may recall that matrix designs use "task" forces which capitalize on individual strengths in a participatory and collaborative manner. Gradations of this design could easily be applied to contemporary agencies. For example, temporary and/or permanent task forces, composed of members from separate organizational units (regardless of rank), may be used to respond to developing problems and conflicts. It is also highly desirable, and in many instances mandatory, to have community members become a part of these teams. The Dayton Police Department, which pioneered the use of police-civilian task forces, uses a series of task forces, each composed of, for instance, four police officers and four citizens who meet over a series of weeks and establish guidelines for the department

---

6. Fred Luthans, *Introduction to Management: A Contingency Approach,* (New York: McGraw-Hill Book Company, Inc., 1976), p. 431.

in such areas as the use of force, high speed chases, and domestic squabbles.[7] In this way, the organization continually interacts with its environment, and can more readily adapt to changing conditions and influences.

If the organization incorporates both temporary and permanent task forces, there should be some overlapping membership between the groups so their efforts may be "in sync" with one another and not disjointed. Also, if an agency were to progress this far toward the matrix form, the police manager would become a "linking pin" or coordinator between the various teams.[8] In such a linking role, the practicing manager must be able to direct research (help members to gather and evaluate information which may be useful to them in solving problems and reaching decisions), mediate between groups in a "pulling-together" fashion, and make recommendations which are for the common good of the organization (the most profitable for all organizational members).

The potential benefits of such a matrix design can be illustrated by the team policing concept. Under a team policing structure, decision-making is decentralized down to the team level, where local needs and expectations can be accomodated; the public has easy access and input into the planning process through intimate contact with team members. Patrol officers are viewed as *generalists*, responsible for managing their assigned areas in the manner they consider most appropriate. While some *specialists* will always be needed in situations which require extraordinary skills or diligence (as in a perplexing homicide investigation), team members will handle practically all matters and problems concerning their district. When specialists are required, they will work at the discretion of the team manager, who will coordinate their activities with other team members, to ensure a more cooperative and effective effort can take place. When unusual circumstances develop, *ad hoc* committees or task forces, as described above, can be used. If properly implemented, team policing reestablishes the importance of patrol work, and patrol becomes the real backbone of policing.

Although most police organizations need to become more flexible in order to adapt to their environments, it is unlikely that any one design is going to be effective for all parts of the organization. Police management in the future, therefore, must apply the most effective mix of organic and mechanistic characteristics to their organizations and units, in accord with prevailing conditions.

The *third* recommendation calls for *increased recognition of the significance of work at lower organizational levels*. If motivational and performance levels of employees who work at the bottom of the organization's hierarchy, particularly patrol personnel, are to be improved, increased rewards and status must be provided. The only avenue through which these

---

7. John G. Rogers, "Top Cop Is a Specialist in Helping People," *Parade*, September 26, 1976, pp. 20, 22.

8. For an in-depth discussion of the "linking pin" concept, see: Rensis Likert, *New Patterns of Management* (New York: McGraw-Hill, 1961), and *The Human Organization* (New York: McGraw-Hill, 1967).

employees can now obtain higher pay and status after their first few years of service is through promotion (Chapter 5). This literally forces outstanding performers to compete for a limited number of supervisory positions, even though they may be completely satisfied with their present positions. Consequently, those outstanding performers who are most vital to the successful operation of the organization feel compelled to seek promotion in order to be properly rewarded for their efforts.

Worsening the severity of this problem is the long-held assumption that an excellent lower level performer will automatically become an excellent supervisor (e.g. a good patrol officer will make a good sergeant). Experience has indicated that this is not necessarily the case, and may even result in decreased motivation and performance. Nevertheless, as long as excellent performers at the lower levels are required to seek promotion for rewards, this situation will not change.

One reasonable alternative for contemporary police organizations would be the creation of new career paths for lower level employees. Swanson has suggested that the establishment of a "skill hierarchy" would enable those working at the bottom of an organization to earn additional pay and recognition as they progress up each skill level:

Paralleling the rank hierarchy, this scheme would allow a person to remain at the bottom of the organizational structure—where significant satisfaction may be obtained from the work—yet earn as much or more than those supervising or managing them. Each skill level might contain a cluster of skills that are deemed important by the organization. In Miami, Florida, for example, skill level I might consist of: (1) maintaining a ninety percent proficiency in speaking Spanish, and (2) continued certification as a lifeguard. (The choice of these factors represents a hypothetical organizational evaluation of the importance of these skills considering the large Cuban population and emergencies in the ocean and attending waterway systems) . . . The skill hierarchy might be termed a professional police officer track in contrast to the traditional management path.

The rank and skill hierarchies have both real and implied terminal points. An officer could not rise beyond being chief, or, for example, skill level V, as both are pinnacles. The implied cap in the rank hierarchy is the level beyond which one's ability will not carry him or her; personal aptitude and industry have a similar effect in the skill hierarchy. What inducements would there be to tap the creativity of persons who have reached the terminal points in their careers? One solution—which would be applicable to all persons in the organization—would be to create a "personal profit plan." Individuals who made significant contributions, e.g., designed new methods to improve services or cut costs, would receive credits toward early retirement. By accumulating credits over a period of years, retirement at fifty percent pay at eighteen years would be possible instead of the normal fifty percent at twenty years. To stimulate continuous, but less important contributions, bonus vacation days could also be awarded. These might be applicable to one year only, or be a permanent annual supplement to the normal number of vacation days.[9]

---

9. Charles R. Swanson, "An Uneasy Look at College Education and the Police Organization," *Journal of Criminal Justice,* 5 (1977), p. 318.

It should be noted that the terminal point in the skill hierarchy should be difficult enough to attain that it is a motivational factor well into the individual's career. This type of career path, combined with a "personal profit plan" would allow the employee to remain highly motivated throughout his or her entire career in the organization.

The reader should also be aware that such a skill hierarchy is based on merit rather than seniority or longevity. This concept is crucial if the motivational and performance levels of the newer employee, as well as of the more seasoned, conscientious employee, are to be maintained or increased. High motivational and performance levels lead to organizational change and revitalization rather than stagnation and decay. Police managers, especially those at the upper levels, should vigorously pursue changes in the reward structure which allow the organization to reward its employees for actual performance on the job rather than seniority.

The *fourth* and final recommendation calls for *increased initiative and imagination on the part of practicing managers*. Simple observation suggests that many police managers have fallen into a "complacency rut," or a "doing things as they have always been done before" attitude. If work environments are to be improved, these patterns will need to be altered. Previous examples of managerial complacency are not difficult to find. In the past, for instance, most departments distributed an equal number of officers into three shifts around the clock (e.g., 8 a.m. to 4 p.m., 4 p.m. to midnight, midnight to 8 a.m.), long after statistics indicated that crime rates were not so evenly divided. Today, it is common knowledge that manpower should be allocated according to need and not to the clock; some shifts may have a greater number of officers than others, or overlapping shifts (e.g., 8 p.m. to 4 a.m.) may be created. Another example lies in the area of random patrol, the effectiveness of which was not seriously questioned before the Kansas City study. While many other examples could be cited, the point is that whenever traditional management concepts are thought to be "cast in bronze" and thus unchangeable, inertia sets in and the decaying process begins.

To break free of the complacency rut, the future manager will need to thoroughly question the effectiveness of time honored concepts. He or she will need the initiative and knowledge to conduct research which questions traditional practices, and if the results indicate that changes are required, the imagination to develop new procedures. Furthermore, the future manager must have the courage to follow through and attempt to implement new procedures once they are successfully tested. This does not suggest that all traditional concepts and practices are obsolete and ineffective, but practicing managers must be willing to look to the future for new ways of adapting to change, rather than to the past or the status quo.

CONCLUDING COMMENTS

This final chapter has provided some suggestions, based on contingency theory, designed to integrate the future needs of police organizations and their members. If practicing managers can guide their agencies toward attaining the goals, and follow the recommendations outlined above, higher quality work environments will result and organizational efficiency and effectiveness will substantially improve.

When utilizing the contingency approach to management practice, however, the doctrine of *no one best way* must be continually emphasized. The above suggestions cannot be thought of as cure-alls; they are not equally feasible and/or necessary for all police agencies. Although each suggestion is consistent with the research findings presented in the book, each must ultimately be adapted to "fit" the current needs and goals of individual members and the organization itself; contingency relationships which are valid today may not be valid tomorrow. There is one logical conclusion in contingency management: "Existing contingency relationships must be continuously tested and new contingency relationships must be determined."

Finally, police management is entering a new, more sophisticated era. Those in the field are rapidly recognizing the difficulty of properly managing organizations in dynamic and unstable environments, and traditional concepts and practices are being challenged. Strategies are being used which consider group processes and decisions, and which recognize individual worth as well as the importance of individual differences. However, the era is just beginning, and there is much room for improvement. The future role for police managers will be both exciting and challenging. By using the contingency approach, practicing managers should be able to contribute significantly to the future progress and development of their organization and its members. Only time can tell how significant that contribution will be.

SUMMARY

This chapter was prescriptive, predicting what should occur if police management is to substantially improve work environments and overall organizational efficiency and effectiveness. The recommendations, although subjective and speculative, are based on the research findings which have been presented in the previous chapters.

Two prevailing conditions call for the decline of highly bureaucratic structures and managerial styles: (1) the realization that police organizations function within turbulent environments, and (2) the influx of young, highly educated, and demanding individuals into the police field. Police management must undergo some decisive transformations if it is to adequately meet the internal needs of the organization as well as the external demands placed on it. Five core problems will affect the future development of criminal justice organizations: integration, social influence, collaboration, adaption, and revitalization.

A set of "cooperative" goals, each aimed at enhancing individual-organization integration, could establish a foundation for a high quality work environment. The achievement of each goal depends on the equal contributions of both the individual and the organization. The set of goals, listed in sequential order, includes: initial sharing of expectations, humane relationships, open communication, collaboration in decision-making and conflict resolution, and the capability for adaption and revitilization. Each goal is a valuable end in itself, but if the ultimate goal of adaptation and revitilization is to be achieved, each of the preceding goals will need to reach high degrees of attainment. By moving toward the accomplishment of these cooperative goals, even though they may not be completely attainable, police can significantly improve the quality of work environments.

The future success and well being of police organizations depend on their ability to effectively deal with change, and the contingency approach is the most suitable for the management of meaningful change. Also, if timely change and adaptation are to take place, future managers will need to act as change agents in their leadership roles and skillfully guide their organizations in new directions. Finally, four recommendations need immediate attention if police organizations are to reach a desired level of competency. The first calls for an increased emphasis on rigorous research, the second calls for a move toward more flexible organic structures, the third calls for increased rewards and status for lower level employees, and the fourth calls for practicing managers to use initiative and imagination in discovering and implementing improved management practices.

DISCUSSION QUESTIONS

1. Discuss the five core problems confronting contemporary organizations (as described by Bennis).
2. Discuss the sequential relationships among the "cooperative" goals and how their accomplishment can improve police work environments.
3. Provide several examples of why collaboration in decision-making and conflict-resolution may be useful to practicing managers.
4. Explain why increased emphasis on empirical research should be of immediate concern to police managers.
5. Discuss the potential benefits of the matrix design as applied to contemporary police organizations.
6. What degree of importance do you attach to the recommendation which calls for the increased recognition of the significance of work at lower organizational levels?
7. Discuss what you perceive as the role for future police managers, as well as the primary problems they must confront.

ANNOTATED BIBLIOGRAPHY

Bennis, Warren G., *Changing Organizations.* New York: McGraw-Hill, 1966. This collection of essays addresses the cause and consequence of change in organizational behavior, and is divided into two parts: the first identifies some important evolutionary trends in organizational development, and the second focuses on the ways behavioral scientists can illuminate and direct processes of change.

Bennis, Warren G., "Organizations of the Future," *Personnel Administration,* 30 (September-October, 1967), pp. 1-19. The decline of the bureaucracy as the most efficient organizational structure in contemporary society is emphasized; five core organization problems of the future are discussed, along with the importance of training managers to handle change.

Cohn, Alvin W., ed., *The Future of Policing*, Beverly Hills, Calif.: Sage Publications, 1978. Many of the important implications facing police managers in the future are addressed in this series of essays; topics for discussion include: future directions for managers, the changing nature of police management, measuring productivity, the future of women, collective bargaining, and policy improvement.

Goldstein, Hermann, *Policing a Free Society*. Cambridge, Mass.: Ballinger, 1977. This timely work critically reexamines many of the traditional issues which have been problematic in the past; the book begins by examining the basic problems endemic to the police and concludes with a discussion of how changes might best be brought about.

Murphy, Patrick V., and David S. Brown. *The Changing Nature of Police Organization*. Washington, D.C.: Leadership Resources, 1973. A concise monograph which focuses on some of the future requirements and demands facing police organizations and their management; six broad generalizations, which require constant action and initiative on the part of police leaders, and some leading examples of organizational change are provided.

Roberg, Roy R., ed., *The Changing Police Role: New Dimensions and New Issues*, San Jose, Calif.: Justice Systems Development, 1976. The work focuses on the changing nature of the police role in contemporary society and the resulting implications for police organizations; personnel practices, organizational characteristics, and current programs and techniques are highlighted.

Subject Index

A

Achievement Motivation, 114
Achievement-Oriented Leadership, 174, `176
Adaptation, 316
  capability for, 323-324
Ad Hoc Committees, 327
Administration, 27
Administrative Management, 25-29, 32-33
All-Channel Network, 134-135
American Telephone & Telegraph (AT&T) Studies, 218-219
Andragogy, 257-259
Applied Research, 325
Art, 9, 10
Authority, 26, 148-149
  acceptance theory of, 37
  commensurate with responsibility, 28-29
  obedience management, 304
Autonomy, 221, 225
Available Data, 66

B

Bankwiring Room Experiment, 31
Basic Research, 325
Behavior, 106-107
  individual differences, 107-109
  Model of, 107
Behavior Modification (B Mod), 255-256
Behavioral Science, 34
  levels of analysis, 35-37
  research, 30-31, 34-37
Behavioral Theories, 254-256
Bethlehem Steel Company, 23
Boston Police Department, 267, 268, 272
Budget, 8, 267

Bureau of Business Research, 161
Bureaucracy, 24-25, 32-33, 195
  decline of, 314-315
Burns-Stalker Study, 195-196
Business Organizations, 192

C

Causal Relationships, 63
Central Tendency Error, 233
Centralization, 203-205, 292
  situational influences of, 205
Chain Network, 134-135
Chain of Command, 94
  See also:
    hierarchy, 25-26
    sclar chain, 26-27
Change, 286-290
  case study of, 290-299
  rapid or gradual, 290
  reducing resistance to, 288-290
  resistance to, 287-288
  strategies, 194
Chicago Police Department, 66
Circle Network, 134-135
Classical Management Theory, 22-29, 32-34
  Principles of, 25-29
Closed Systems, 33, 40
Coercive Organizations, 192
Coercive Tactics, 288-289
Cognition, 109-110, 256
Cognitive Dissonance, 123, 137
Cognitive Theories, 254, 256-257
Collaboration, 316
  in conflict resolution, 322-323
  in decision-making, 322-323
Commanding, 27

Commonwealth Organizations, 193
Communication, 130, 150
  networks of, 134-135
  open, 300, 321-322
  overlay, 149-150
Competition, 140
  intergroup, 140
  intragroup, 140
Concern For People/Production, 303-305
Conflict, 6, 139-140
  episode, 139
  feet, 139
  latent, 139
  manifest, 139
  perceived, 139
  resolution, 322-323
Consensual Society, 315
Consideration, 161-162
Constant Errors, 232-233
Construct Validity, 229-231
  error reduction approach, 231-233
  judgmental approach, 231
Content Theories, 109, 116-124
Contingency Approach/Theory, 15-17, 23,
    43-47
  in relation to:
    change, 324
    communication, 135
    development, 253
    framework for, 35-37
    job design, 228-229
    leadership, 165-177
    motivation, 124-125
    od interventions, 307-309
    organization design, 203-211
    organizational characteristics, 102
    performance evaluation, 244-245
    planning, 285-286
    program development, 253, 259
Contingent Relationships, 43
Continuous Production Firms, 196
Continuum Model/Leadership, 165-169
Control Beats, 72-73
Control Groups, 63-64
Controlling, 6, 27
Cooperative Goals, 317, 319-324
Coordinating, 7, 27
Coordinative Principle, 27
Core Job Dimensions, 219-220
Corrections, 3, 14, 16, 39, 41, 44
Counseling, 271
Country Club Management, 304
Courts 3, 13, 16, 39, 41, 44
  organization chart of, 86
Criminal Justice System, 3, 10-11, 14-16,
    39, 41, 44

D

Dayton Police Department, 269, 272, 275
  police-civilian task forces, 326-327

Decentralization, 203-205, 207, 291-292
  situational influences of, 205
Decision-Making, 4, 203-204, 285, 300, 327
  collaboration in, 322-323
  participation in, 240, 289
Decision Overlay, 146-147
Decision Process/Point, 147
Deductive Reasoning, 58
Deductive Theory, 55
Defense, 11, 13
Departmentalization, 28-29
Dependent Variables, 45, 57-58
Descriptive Theory, 56, 314
Development/Training Programs 265-275
Developmental Process, 250-251
Differentiated Functions, 93-94
  horizontal, 95-97
  vertical, 94-95
Differentiation, 42
Direct Instruction, 138
Directive Leadership, 174-176
Discipline, 26
Discretionary Stimuli, 135
  affecting individual attitudes and val-
    ues, 137
  beliefs, 136-137
  job knowledge and skills, 138-139
Displacement (of Goals), 92
Division of Labor 25, 26, 93
Dynamic Equilibrium, 40

E

Economic Organizations, 192
Education, 251
Effectiveness, 8
Efficiency, 7
Empirical Reference, 57
Empirical Research/Quality of, 59-60
  increased emphasis on, 325-326
Energy Transformation, 40-42
Entropic Process, 42
Environment, 16, 40-45
  influences of, 88-89
Environmental Simplicity-Complexity,
    197-200, 284
Environmental Suprasystem, 43,45
Equal Employment Opportunity, 268
Equifinality, 42, 281
Equity Theory, 123-124
  equity, 27
Espirit de Corps, 27
Esteem Needs, 110
Ethics/Values, 310
Evaluation/Measurement, 63-64, 263-265,
    284, 297-298
  and control of individual performance,
    302-303
  lack of, 52-53, 309-310
Exception Principle, 28-29, 284

Exchange Theory, 132
Expanding Jobs, 217
Expectancy Theory, 117
  expectancy, 117
  Porter-Lawler model, 119-123
  Vroom model, 117-119
Expectation—Integration Model, 5, 7
  expectations (sharing of), 4-6, 288, 319-320
Experimental Groups, 63-64
Experiments, 63-65, 283
  field, 64-65
  laboratory, 64
  simulations, 65
External Consistency, 57
External Socialization, 268-269
External Validity, 62-63

F

Federal Government, 52
Feedback, 42, 106, 138, 221, 240, 265, 284
Felt Conflict, 139
Fiedler Model, 170-173
Field Studies, 62-63
Flat Organizational Hierarchies, 205-207
Focal Person, 120-121
Forced Distribution Evaluation Procedure, 238-239
Formal Organization, 30, 37
  characteristics of, 80-81
  examples of, 85-87
  synthesis with informal organization, 37-38
Functional Overlay, 145-146
Functional Principle, 27
  authority, 96
Functional Relationships, 43-45
Functional Supervision, 84, 145
Fusion Process, 38

G

General Management Training, 275
Generality/Generalizable, 57, 63
  generalists, 327
Gestalt-Field Theories, 256-257
Goals, 7
  changes in, 92
  cooperative, 317, 319-324
  corrections, 14-15
  courts, 13
  criminal justice system, 11, 14-15, 88
  displacement, 92
  measurement of, 90, 281-282
  operational, 91
  operative, 91
  organization-individual, 89-91
  planning, 281-282

  police, 11-13, 89
  setting of, 90, 240
  succession, 92
Graphic Rating Scale, 233-236
Groups, 83, 130
  characteristics, 131
  formal, 83, 133
  formation, 131-132
  informal, 83, 133
  influences on individuals, 135-139
  interest, 90
  norms, 131, 288
  social elements, 131-132
  task objectives, 132

H

Halo Error, 232-233
Hawthorne Effect, 30, 330
Hawthorne Studies, 30-32
Hierarchy, 25-26, 94
  See also:
    chain of command, 94
    sclar chain, 26-27
  flat, 207-209
  tall, 207-209
Higher Order Needs, 110, 113, 115, 226
Homeostasis, 42
Horizontal Differentiation, 95-97
Human Relations Theory, 23, 29-34
Human Resources, 7
  development of, 250
  effective use of, 9
  needs & personality traits of, 200-203
  skills & abilities of, 198-200
Humane, 8, 301
  relationships, 320-321
Hygiene Factors, 115-116
Hypothesis, 57-59

I

If-Then Contingencies, 45-46
  propositions, 57
Illumination Study, 30
Impoverished Management, 304
Incarceration, 11, 14
Independent Variables, 45, 57-58
Individual, 83, 106
  differences, 107, 216-217, 270-271
  expectations, 5-6
  influences, 89
  input/outcomes, 123-124
  needs & personality traits, 200-203
  perceptions, 117
    rewards, 120, 122
    role, 119-120
  skills & abilities, 198-200
Inductive Theory, 55

Informal Organization, 30, 142
  case study of, 150-153
  open communication, 325-326
  overlays, 142-150
  synthesis with formal organization, 37-38
Informal Overlays, 142-150
Initiating Structure, 161-162
Initiative, 27
Inputs, 40-42
In-Service Training, 271-273, 275-277
Instrumentality, 117
Integration (Individual/Organization), 1-5, 301, 315
  See also:
    interactions, 3-5, 321
Integrative Organizations, 192
Intended Rational Coordination, 97-98
  administrative system, 97
  hierarchical, 97
  roles, 98
  subgoal specification, 98
  voluntary, 98
Interdisciplinary Orientation, 3, 80
Interest Groups, 90
Intergroup Competition, 140
Interindividual Error, 232-233
Internal Consistency, 57
Internal Socialization, 268-269
Internal Validity, 62-63
International Association of Chiefs of Police (IACP) 56, 234-235
  rating scale of, 235
International City Management Association (ICMA), 67, 141, 282
Interpersonal Relationships, 305-307
Intervention Strategies (of OD), 306-311
  concern with work style, 306
  evaluating/controlling individual performance, 306-307
  interpersonal analysis, 311
  interpersonal relationships, 309-311
  operations analysis, 306
Interviews, 31, 65
Intragroup Competition, 140
Intraindividual Error, 232-233
Intrapersonal Analysis, 307

J

Job Characteristics Model of Work Motivation, 219-221
Job Content/Context Factors, 116
Job Descriptive Index, 226
Job Design, 4, 216
  and motivation, 218-222
Job Diagnostic Survey (JDS), 221-222
Job Enlargement/Enrichment, 217-218, 303
  case study of, 224-228
  implementation of, 222-224

Job-Task Pyramid, 143, 148
  pyramid of authority, 142

K

Kansas City Police Department, 68,70
Kansas City Preventive Patrol Experiment, 66-76
  conclusions, 74-75
  description, 70-74
  hypotheses, 68
  major findings, 68-69

L

Latent Conflict, 139
Law of Effect, 254-255
Law Enforcement, 11
Law Enforcement Assistance Administration (LEAA), 52, 53, 295
Leadership, 158-159
  behavioral theory of, 160-165
  contingency theory of, 165-177
  formal/informal, 32, 151-153
  trait theory of, 159-160
Leadership Behavior Description Questionnaire (LBDQ), 161-163, 303
Learning, 253
  behavioral theories of, 254-256
  Gestalt-Field theories of, 256-257
Least Preferred Co-worker, (LPC), 170
Legalistic Style of Policing, 193
Leniency Error, 233
Lincoln Police Department, 203
Line-Staff Concept, 96
Linking Pin Concept, 327
Love Needs, 110
Lower Order Needs, 110, 113, 115, 132

M

MacGregor, 178
Macro Analysis, 56-57
Madison Police Department, 267, 275
Management, 6-8
  art or science, 9-10
  levels of, 7, 94, 205-206
  principles of, 25
  seminar project, 275
  styles of, 307-309
  training, 273-276
Management by Objectives (MBO), 91, 98, 114, 239-241, 303
Managerial Grid, 303-305
Manifest Conflict, 139
Marathon Labs, 311
Mass Production/Large Batch Firms, 196

Material Resources, 8
Matrix Organization, 98-99, 326-327
  example of, 100
Means-ends chain, 91
  inversion, 92, 285
Measurement Contamination/Deficiency, 230
Mechanistic Systems, 195-196, 326-327
  design characteristics of, 208-210
  in reference to:
    job design, 230-231
    od interventions, 311-312
    performance evaluation, 247
    planning, 290
Metropolitan Police Department, 262, 267, 270
Micro Analysis, 56-57
Midvale Steel Company, 23
Milo Company, 151
Modeling, 138
Modern Management Theory, 23, 34-43, 47-48
Motivating Potential Score (MPS), 221-222
Motivation, 109
  content theories of, 109-116
  and job design, 218-222
  process theories of, 109, 116-124
Motivation—Hygiene Theory, 114-116
  in reference to:
    job design, 218-219
Multivariate Approach, 119
Mutual-Benefit Organizations, 192

N

Need Hierarchy, 110
Negative Entropy, 42
Neighborhood Police Teams, 290-299, 309, 315
  See also:
    team policing, 171-172, 218-219, 331
Neo-Classical Theory, 23, 29-34
Network Influences, 146-147
New York Police Department, 203, 275, 290-299, 308
Normative Change, 302
Normative Organizations, 192
Normative Theory, 56
Norms, 32, 81
  group, 131, 288
  organizational, 301
  ouput, 31

O

Oakland Police Department, 267
Objectives, 7

in reference to:
  recruit training, 267
  task, 132
  training, 261-262
Official Goals, 90-91
Ohio State Leadership Studies, 161-163
Open Systems, 16, 40-44
Operant Behavior, 254-255
Operational Goals, 91
Operational Theory, 57
Operations Analysis, 302
Operative Goals, 91
Order, 26
Order Maintenance, 11
Organic Systems, 195-196, 326-327
  design characteristics of, 208-210
  in reference to:
    job design, 230-231
    od interventions, 311-312
    performance evaluation, 247
    planning, 290
Organization, 2, 80
  charts, 85-87, 100, 151-152
  classical pyramid, 191
  classifications of, 191-194
  fundamental characteristics, 81-82
  goals, 90-93
  the "how" of, 93-98
  influences, 89
  informal, 30, 142-153
  matrix, 98-100, 326-327
  the "when" of, 99-101
  the "who" of, 81-84
  the "why" of, 84-89
Organization charts, 84
  formal examples:
    milo, 151
    penitentiary, 87
    police, 85, 100
    superior court, 86
  informal examples:
    milo, 152
    overlays, 142-150
Organization Design, 190
  external influences, 195-198
  internal influences, 198-203
Organization Man Management, 304
Organizational Behavior (Theory of), 36-37
Organizational Behavior Modification (OB Mod), 255-256
Organizational Culture, 301
Organizational Development, 299-300
  depth of, 302
  interventions of, 302-307
  issues of, 309-310
  objectives of, 300-301
Organizing, 27

Outputs, 40-42

P

Paired Comparison Evaluation Procedure, 236, 238-239
Parole, 11, 14
Parsimony, 57
Partial Inclusion, 83
Participative Leadership, 174, 176-177, 289, 299
    case study of, 178-186
Path-Goal Model, 173-177
Pattern-Maintenance Organizations, 192
Peace Officer's Training Council, 275
Pedagogy, 257-259
Peer Evaluation, 242-243
Penitentiary (see Prison)
Perceived Conflict, 139
Perception, 107-108
Performance Evaluation, 229
    methods of, 233-243
        employee comparisons, 236, 238-239
        graphic rating scales, 233-236
        mbo, 239-241
    who evaluates, 242-243
    rewards, 243-244
Person-Role Conflict, 121
Personal Profit Plan, 328-329
Personalizing Process, 38
Physiological Needs, 110
Planning, 27, 280
    process of, 281-284
    type of, 284-285
Pleasure-Pain Principle, 254
Police, 3, 11, 16, 39, 41, 44
    brutality, study of, 62
    organization charts of, 85, 100
    role of, 11-13
    styles of operation, 193
Police Foundation, 68, 71
Political Organizations, 192
Porter-Lawler Theory of Motivation, 119-123
POSDCORB, 28
Positive Theory, 56
Post Promotion Supervisory Training, 274-275
Power, 148-149, 319
    balance of, 288
    overlay, 147
Practicum, 271
Preparatory Training, 266-271
Pre-Promotion Supervisory Training, 273-274
Prescriptive Theory, 56, 314
Preventive Patrol, 71
Prison/Penitentiary, 14, 88, 210
    organization chart of, 87
    simulated study of, 65

typologies of, 194
Proactive Beats, 72-73
Probation, 11, 14
Process Theories, 109-116
Program Development, 259-265
Program Evaluation, 263-265
Program Management, 99
Program Specification, 284
Project Management, 99
Propositions (testable), 57
Prosecution, 11, 13
Psychological States, 219-220
    counseling, 275
Public Services, 12
Purex Corporation, 244

Q

Quasi Experimental Design, 264-265
Questionnaires, 65, 282-283

R

Random Sampling, 63
Rank Hierarchy, 328-329
Ranking Evaluation Procedure, 236
Reactive Beats, 72-73
Reciprocation, 90
Recruit Training, 266-271
Relay Assembly Experiment, 30-31
Reliability, 58
Remuneration of Staff, 26
Research Design, 60-61
    choices and constraints, 62
    major designs:
        available data, 66
        experiments, 63-65
        Field studies, 62-63
        surveys, 65-66
Resistance, 287-288
    example of, 290-299
    reduction of, 288-290
Respondant Behavior, 254-255
Response-Stimulus (R-S) Model, 255
Responsibiltiy, 26
Revitalization, 316-317
    capability for, 323-324
Rewards, 4, 123, 327-329
    cost outcomes, 132
    expectations, 9
    extrinsic, 121-122
    intrinsic, 121-122
    performance 243-244
Role Conflict, 121
Role Episode, 120
    received role, 120
    role behavior, 120
    role expectations, 120
    sent role, 120

Role Perception, 119-120
Role Playing, 138
Role Senders, 120-121
Rule of Thumb Management, 24

S

Safety Needs, 110
Salary Structure, 122, 124
Science, 9-10
  behavioral, 34
  social, 34
Scientific Management, 22-24, 32-33
Scientific Method, 57-59
  manner, 34
Sclar Chain/Principle, 26-27
  See also:
    chain of command, 94
    hierarchy, 25-26
Sears Roebuck Company, 209
Secondary Analysis, 66
Self-Actualization Needs, 110, 132
Self-Evaluation, 243
Sensitivity Training, 305-307
Serendipity, 281
Service Organizations, 192
Service Style of Policing, 193
Single-Use Plans, 285-286
Situational Determinants, 23, 45
Skill Hierarchy, 328-329
Skill Variety, 221,225
Smith & Cranny Model of Motivation, 54
Social Influence, 316
Social Reality, 136
Social Sciences, 34
Social Services, 11-12
Social System, 16, 39
Socialization Process, 38, 268-269
Sociograms, 145
Sociometric Overlay, 144-145
Span of Control, 28-29, 32, 205-206
  for business success, 197-198
Specialization, 26-27
  specialists, 327
Staff Principle, 27
  authority, 96
Standing Plans, 284-286
Steady State, 40, 42
Stimulus-Response (S-R) Theories, 254-256
Strictness Error, 233
Subordinate Evaluation, 242-243
Succession (of Goals), 92
Sunk Costs, 287
Supervisory Evaluation, 242
Supervisory Training, 273-278
Supportive Leadership, 174, 176
Surveys, 62, 65-66
Synergy, 43, 131
Systems Approach/Theory, 3, 15-16, 37-43,
  46-47

for planning process, 285-289
for program development, 259-265
Systems Management, 11, 99
Systems Training and Recruitment
  (STAR), 262

T

Tall Organizational Hierarchies, 205-207
Target, 141
Task Forces, 70-71, 99, 299, 326-327
  police-civilian, 326-327
Task Identity, 221
Task Significance, 221, 225
Task Specialization, 93
Team Management, 304
Team Policing, 171-172, 218-219, 327
  neighborhood police teams, 290-299
Temporary Operating Procedure (TOP),
  293
T-Groups, 305-307
Theories X and Y, 111
  assumptions of, 111-113
  leadership, 160-161
Theory, 52-55
  criteria to evaluate, 57
  differentiation of:
    development, 55-56
    level of analysis, 56-57
    primary purpose, 56-57
Throughputs, 40-42
Time and Motion Studies, 23
Time Series Experiment, 264-265
Traditional Management Theory, 22-29,
  32-34
Training, 251-252, 265-275, 292-293
  in-service, 271-273
  management/supervisory, 273-275
  objective, 261-262
  recruit/preparatory, 266-271
  specialized, 272-273
Transformation Process, 40
Two Factor Theory, 115-116

U

Unions, 322
Unit/Small Batch Firms, 196
Unity of Command, 26, 28
Unity of Management, 26
Utilitarian Organizations, 192

V

Valence, 117
Validity, 58
  external, 62-63

internal, 62-63
Variable, 54
  dependent, 45, 57, 63
  errors, 232
  independent, 45, 57, 63
Vertical Differentiation, 94-95
Vroom's Theory of Motivation, 117-119

W

Watchman Style of Policing, 193
Western Electric Company, 30
Wheel Network, 134-135
Woodward Studies, 196-198

Work Design, 216
Work Environment, 9, 323-328
Work Motivators, 115-116

Y

Y Network, 134-135
Yale Job Inventory, 225

Z

Zone of Indifference, 38

Name Index

Adams, J. Stacy, 123, 127
Adams, Thomas F., 251
Albers, Henry H., 204
Albright, Ellen, 77
Alcabes, Abraham, 252
Aldag, Ramon J., 224
Allport, Floyd H., 83, 176
Alvares, Kenneth M., 173
American Bar Association, 260
Applewhite, Philip B., 135
Argyris, Chris, 38
Ary, Donald, 44, 58, 77
Ashour, Ahmed S., 173
Atkinson, John W., 114
Astin, Alexander W., 200
Azumi, Koya, 102
Baker, Thomas J., 218
Bakke, E. Wight, 38
Ballachey, Egerton L., 109
Banks, W. Curtis, 65
Bard, Morton, 290
Barnard, Chester I., 10, 37, 89, 158
Barrett, R. S., 243
Bass, Bernard M., 251, 263, 277
Beckhard, Richard, 300
Bell, Cecil H., Jr., 210
Benne, Kenneth D., 55, 287, 312
Bennis, Warren G., 55, 287, 312, 315, 318, 324, 331
Bercall, Thomas E., 12
Berelson, Bernard, 34
Bigge, Morris L., 254, 257, 277
Biglan, Anthony, 173
Bird, Charles, 159
Black, James A., 61, 77
Blair, Robert S., 312
Blake, Gerald F., Jr., 312
Blake, Robert R., 303, 304, 305
Blalock, Herbert M., Jr., 77

Blanchard, Kenneth H., 162, 163
Blau, Peter M., 133, 134, 193, 213
Blood, Milton R., 217
Bobbitt, H. Randolph, 102
Bordua, David J., 213
Brayfield, Arthur H., 35
Breinholt, Robert H., 102
Bridwell, Lawrence G., 111
Brief, Arthur P., 224
Brown, Charles E., 55, 66
Brown, David S., 332
Brown, Donald R., 312
Brownrigg, William, 144
Buck, Gerald, 251
Burke, W. Warren, 301
Burns, Tom, 195, 208, 213
Bykowski, Ronald F., 312
Campbell, Donald T., 63, 77, 264
Campbell, John P., 109, 114, 251, 306
Carlisle, Arthur Elliott, 178
Carroll, Stephen J., 240, 241, 248
Cartwright, Dorwin, 131, 132, 155
Chaiken, Jan M., 202
Champion, Dean J., 61, 77
Chandler, Alfred, 204
Chemers, Martin M., 173
Chester Jacobs, Lucy, 44
Chin, Robert, 55, 287, 312
Cline, James L., 11
Cohen, Bernard, 202
Cohn, Alvin W., 332
Cole, George F., 11, 16
Coons, Alvin E., 161, 188
Coser, Lewis, 139
Coubrough, J. A., 25
Couper, David, 262, 266
Craig, Henry W., 65
Cranny, C. J., 54
Cribben, James J., 188

Crockett, Walter M., 35
Crutchfield, Richard S., 109
Cumming, Elaine, 12
Cumming, Ian, 12
Cummings, Larry L., 116, 123, 229, 240, 242, 243, 247
Cyert, Richard M., 90
Dalton, Melville, 19, 150, 151
Davis, Keith, 155, 158
Delbeca, Andre L., 306
Deneault, Henry N., 259
Dessler, Gary, 205
DeVitt, H. William, 116
Dickson, W. J., 31
Dieckman, David, 55, 66
Doktor, Robert H., 102
Donnelly, Martin, 201
Dorsey, John T., Jr., 143, 149, 150
Drabeck, Thomas E., 103
Drucker, Peter F., 6
Dubin, Robert, 149
Duffee, David, 194
Dunnette, Marvin D., 109, 251, 306
Eastman, Esther M., 8, 282
Eastman, George D., 8, 282
Edell, Laura, 12
Etzioni, Amitai, 24, 31, 32, 33, 84, 92, 103, 192
Evans, Martin G., 173
Evans, W., 208
Ewing, David W., 286
Fayol, Henri, 25
Feldman, Kenneth A., 200
Fenster, Abe, 201
Festinger, Leon, 123, 137, 150
Fiedler, Fred E., 170-173, 188, 209
Filley, Alan C., 33, 34, 35, 54, 57, 96, 280, 300
Finnigan, James C., 202
Flippo, Edwin B., 204
Follet, Mary Parker, 147
Ford, Robert N., 218, 247
French, Wendell L., 210
Funk, Charles Earle, 8
Galvin, Raymond T., 282, 283
Gardner, Burleigh B., 150
Gardner, John, 317
Geary, David Patrick, 202
George, Claude S., Jr., 22, 49
Gerth, H.H., 25
Ghiselli, Edwin E., 159, 160, 188
Gibbons, Don C., 312
Golden, M. Patricia, 58, 61, 77
Goldstein, Herman, 12, 332
Goodin, Carl V., 247
Graen, George, 173
Guion, Robert M., 234
Gulick, Luther, 28
Guller, Irving, B., 201
Haas, J. Eugene, 103

Hackman, J. Richard, 3, 56, 80, 82, 94, 97, 98, 101, 118, 127, 135, 136, 198, 217, 219, 220, 221, 224, 225, 228, 247
Hage, Jerald, 102
Haimann, Theo, 10
Hall, Douglas T., 19
Hall, Richard H., 208, 213
Hallstrom, Don, 251
Halpin, Andrew W., 161
Hardyck, Curtis, 77
Hare, A. Paul, 131, 155
Harrison, Roger, 302, 307, 312
Hartley, L., 289
Harvey, Donald F., 312
Harvey, E., 284
Henderson, A. M., 25
Heneman, Herbert G., 243
Henning, Dale A., 283
Hershey, Paul, 162, 163
Herzberg, Frederick, 115-116, 127, 218, 248
Hickson, D. J., 209
Hilleory, Joseph M., 243
Hinings, C. R., 209
Hodgetts, Richard M., 117, 124
Homans, George C., 131, 155
House, Robert J., 19, 33, 34, 35, 54, 57, 96, 173, 188, 280, 300
Hower, Ralph M., 208
Hulin, Charles L., 217, 226
Hunt, Raymond G., 209
Huse, Edgar F., 312
Indik, Bernard P., 36
Jacobs, Lucy Chester, 44, 58, 77
Janson, Robert, 219
Jenkins, William O., 159
Johnson, Richard A., 39, 49
Kahane, Murray, 145
Kahn, Robert L., 39, 49, 83, 120, 158, 159
Kast, Fremont E., 15, 28, 39, 43, 45, 46, 49, 91, 96, 97, 99, 107, 208, 209, 282, 290
Katz, Daniel, 39, 49, 83, 120, 158, 159
Kelley, Clarence M., 70, 74
Kelling, George L., 55, 66
Kendall, Lorne M., 226
Kerlinger, Fred N., 78
Kerr, Elaine B., 287
Kerr, Stephen, 33, 34, 35, 54, 57, 96, 163, 164, 188, 244, 280, 287, 300
Klimoski, Richard H., 243
Knowles, Henry P., 209
Knowles, Malcolm S., 258, 277
Koontz, Harold, 26, 49
Kowalewski, Victor, 201
Krech, David, 109
Landy, Frank J., 247
Lawler, Edward E., 3, 9, 56, 80, 82, 94, 97, 98, 101, 109, 121, 122, 127, 135, 136, 198, 207, 217, 224, 228, 251
Lawrence, Paul R., 94, 97, 191, 208
Leavitt, Harold J., 106, 209
LeBreton, Preston P., 283
LeGrande, J. L., 282, 283

Leonard, V. A., 29
Lepawsky, Albert, 145
Levinson, Harry, 89, 90
Lewin, Kurt, 52, 106, 289
Lewis, Joseph H., 77
Likert, Rensis, 113, 327
Lippitt, Gordon L., 253, 278
Lipton, Douglas, 78
Litterer, Joseph A., 97, 103
Locke, Bernard, 201
Lombard, George F. F., 209
London, Manuel, 243
Lorsch, Jay W., 94, 97, 191, 208, 209
Lupton, Tom, 24
Luthans, Fred, 15, 17, 39, 43, 45, 47, 49,
   133, 197, 207, 256, 326
MacKinney, Arthur C., 264, 278
Macy, Barry A., 8, 9
Mager, Robert F., 261, 278
Malm, F. T., 123
Maltz, Michael D., 78
March, James G., 8, 90, 103, 127
Marcus, Joan, 201
Martinson, Robert, 78
Maslow, Abraham H., 110, 127
Massarik, Fred, 145
Massie, Joseph L., 32, 33, 49
Mausner, Bernard, 115
Mayo, Elton, 30
McClelland, David C., 114
McConkie, Mark L., 247
McGregor, Douglas, 19, 89, 111, 127, 315
McNaul, James P., 102
Medsker, Leland L., 200
Merton, Robert, 285
Metcalf, Henry C., 147
Miles, R. E., 199
Miller, Delbert C., 78
Mills, C. Wright, 25
Miner, John B., 50, 242, 248
Mintzberg, Henry, 19
Mirvis, Phillip M., 8, 9
Mitchell, Terence R., 37, 173, 176
Mooney, James D., 27
More, David G., 150
Moreno, J. L., 145
Morse, John J., 90
Mouton, Jane S., 303, 304, 305
Munro, Jim L., 16, 223
Murphy, Charles J., 163, 188
Murphy, Patrick V., 332
Myers, Charles A., 123
National Advisory Commission, 83, 252
National Criminal Justice Reference Ser-
   vice, 78
Newcomb, Theodore M., 200, 289
Newman, Donald J., 88, 90
Odiorne, George S., 91
O'Donnel, Cyril, 26
Oldham, Greg. R., 219, 220, 221, 247
Oncken, Gerald, 173
O'Neill, Michael E., 312

Orris, James B., 173
Parker, L. Craig, Jr., 201
Parnas, Raymond, 12
Parsons, Talcott, 25, 84, 191, 213
Pate, Tony, 55, 66
Paul, William J., Jr., 248
Perrow, Charles, 91, 209
Petrinovich, Lewis F., 77
Pfiffner, John M., 131, 142
Piven, Herman, 252
Pondy, Louis R., 139, 155
Porter, Lyman W., 3, 35, 56, 80, 82, 94, 97,
   98, 101, 118, 121, 122, 127, 135, 136,
   198, 200, 207, 217, 228
President's Crime Commission, 15, 116,
   227
Pugh, D. S., 209
Purdy, Kenneth, 219
Raia, Anthony P., 241
Razavieh, Asghar, 44, 58, 77
Redfield, Charles, 150
Reiley, Alan C., 27
Reiss, Albert J., 62, 213
Rigors, Paul, 123
Rizzo, John R., 241
Robbins, Stephen P., 44, 45, 203, 218
Roberg, Roy R., 11, 13, 201, 202, 332
Robertson, Keith B., 248
Roethlisberger, F. J., 31
Rogers, John G., 327
Rosenzweig, James E., 15, 28, 39, 43, 45,
   46, 49, 91, 96, 97, 99, 107, 208, 209,
   282, 286
Ruch, Floyd L., 257
Runcie, John F., 59, 77
Saxberg, Borje O., 209
Sayles, Leonard R., 190, 289, 290
Schein, Edgar H., 130, 133, 155
Schmidt, Warren H., 165, 168, 178, 188
Schriesheim, Chester A., 163, 188
Schwab, Donald P., 116, 123, 229, 240, 242,
   243, 247
Scott, William G., 10, 37
Scott, W. Richard., 133, 134, 193, 213
Seiler, John A., 208
Serpico, Frank, 121
Shagory, George E., 259
Shaw, Marvin E., 155
Shellow, Robert, 290
Sherwood, Frank P., 131, 142
Simon, Herbert A., 8, 32, 89, 127, 146, 209
Skinner, B. F., 254
Skrzypek, George J., 173
Smith, Alexander B., 201
Smith, Bruce, 67
Smith, Patricia Cain, 54, 226
Snyderman, Barbara, 115
Stahl, O. Glenn, 247, 266
Stalker, G. M., 195, 208, 213
Stanley, Julian C., 63, 77, 264
Staugenberger, Richard S., 247, 266
Steiner, Gary A., 34, 130

Stieglitz, Harold, 204
Stogdill, Ralph M., 145, 159, 161, 163, 188
Strauss, George, 190, 289, 290, 309
Swanson, Charles R., 328
Taft, Ronald, 233
Tannenbaum, Robert, 145, 165, 168, 178, 188
Tannenbaun, Arnold S., 176
Taylor, Frederick W., 22, 24, 145
Terkel, Studs, 3
Thimm, Joseph L., 312
This, Leslie E., 253, 278
Thompson, James D., 22, 209, 213
Thorndike, Edward L., 254
Tolman, Edward C., 257
Tosi, Henry L., 240, 241, 248
Tracey, William R., 278
Trent, James W., 200
Urwick, Lyndall, 28, 29, 147
Vaughn, James A., 251, 263, 277
Vroom, Victor H., 116, 117, 127, 176
Wahba, Mahmoud A., 111

Walker, William F., 201
Wallach, Irving A., 12
Wasserman, Robert, 262, 266
Watson, Goodwin, 287
Weber, Max, 24, 25
Weick, Karl E., Jr., 109, 251
Weschler, Irving, 145
Wexley, Kenneth N., 173, 243
Whisenand, Paul M., 11, 140
White, William F., 103
Wilks, Judith, 78
Wilson, James Q., 12, 193
Wilson, O. W., 29, 66, 67
Witte, Raymond P., 202
Woodward, Joan, 196, 208, 213
Work, Charles P., 53
Worthy, James Z., 207
Wren, Daniel A., 2, 50
Yospe, Florence, 312
Yukl, Gary A., 173
Zander, Alvin, 131, 132
Zimbardo, Philip G., 65, 257

Criminal Justice and Law Enforcement Books

of

WEST PUBLISHING COMPANY

St. Paul, Minnesota 55102

January, 1979

CONSTITUTIONAL LAW

Maddex's Cases and Comments on Constitutional Law 2nd Edition by James L. Maddex, Professor of Criminal Justice, Georgia State University, 486 pages, 1979.

CORRECTIONS

Burns' Corrections—Organization and Administration by Henry Burns, Jr., Professor of Criminal Justice, University of Missouri–St. Louis, 578 pages, 1975.

Kerper and Kerper's Legal Rights of the Convicted by Hazel B. Kerper, Late Professor of Sociology and Criminal Law, Sam Houston State University and Janeen Kerper, Attorney, San Diego, Calif., 677 pages, 1974.

Killinger and Cromwell's Selected Readings on Corrections in the Community, 2nd Edition by George G. Killinger, Member, Board of Pardons and Paroles, Texas and Paul F. Cromwell, Jr., Director of Juvenile Services, Tarrant County, Texas, 357 pages, 1978.

Killinger, Cromwell, and Wood's Readings on Penology—The Evolution of Corrections in America 2nd Edition by George G. Killinger, Paul F. Cromwell, Jr., and Jerry M. Wood, about 350 pages, 1979.

Killinger and Cromwell's Selected Readings on Introduction to Corrections by George G. Killinger and Paul F. Cromwell, Jr., 417 pages, 1978.

Killinger, Cromwell and Cromwell's Selected Readings on Issues in Corrections and Administration by George G. Killinger, Paul F. Cromwell, Jr. and Bonnie J. Cromwell, San Antonio College, 644 pages, 1976.

Killinger, Kerper and Cromwell's Probation and Parole in the Criminal Justice System by George G. Killinger, Hazel B. Kerper and Paul F. Cromwell, Jr., 374 pages, 1976.

Krantz' The Law of Corrections and Prisoners' Rights in a Nutshell by Sheldon Krantz, Professor of Law and Director, Center for Criminal Justice, Boston University, 353 pages, 1976.

Rubin's Law of Criminal Correction, 2nd Edition (Student Edition) by Sol Rubin, Counsel Emeritus, Council on Crime and Delinquency, 873 pages, 1973.

Rubin's 1977 Supplement.

CORRECTIONS—Continued

Smith & Berlin's Introduction to Probation and Parole 2nd Edition by Alexander B. Smith, Professor of Sociology, John Jay College of Criminal Justice and Louis Berlin, Formerly Chief of Training Branch, New York City Dept. of Probation, 270 pages, 1979.

CRIMINAL JUSTICE SYSTEM

Kerper's Introduction to the Criminal Justice System 2nd Edition by Hazel B. Kerper as revised by Jerold H. Israel, 520 pages, 1979.

Senna and Siegel's Introduction to Criminal Justice by Joseph J. Senna and Larry J. Siegel, both Professors of Criminal Justice, Northeastern University, 540 pages, 1978.

Study Guide to accompany Senna and Siegel's Introduction to Criminal Justice by Roy R. Roberg, Professor of Criminal Justice, University of Nebraska-Lincoln, 187 pages, 1978.

Wrobleski and Hess' Introduction to Law Enforcement and Criminal Justice by Henry M. Wrobleski and Karen M. Hess, both Professors at Normandale Community College, Bloomington, Minnesota, 525 pages, 1979.

CRIMINAL LAW

Dix and Sharlot's Cases and Materials on Basic Criminal Law by George E. Dix, Professor of Law, University of Texas and M. Michael Sharlot, Professor of Law, University of Texas, 649 pages, 1974.

Ferguson's Readings on Concepts of Criminal Law by Robert W. Ferguson, Administration of Justice Dept. Director, Saddleback College, 560 pages, 1975.

Gardner and Manian's Principles, Cases and Readings on Criminal Law by Thomas J. Gardner, Professor of Criminal Justice, Milwaukee Area Technical College and Victor Manian, Milwaukee County Judge, 782 pages, 1975.

Heymann and Kenety—The Murder Trial of Wilbur Jackson: A Homicide in the Family by Philip Heymann, Professor of Law, Harvard University and William Kenety, Instructor, Catholic University Law School, 340 pages, 1975.

LaFave's Principles of Criminal Law by Wayne R. LaFave, Professor of Law, University of Illinois, about 600 pages, 1978.

Loewy's Criminal Law in a Nutshell by Arnold H. Loewy, Professor of Law University of North Carolina, 302 pages, 1975.

CRIMINAL PROCEDURE

Davis' Police Discretion by Kenneth Culp Davis, Professor of Law, University of Chicago, 176 pages, 1975.

Dowling's Teaching Materials on Criminal Procedure by Jerry L. Dowling, Professor of Criminal Justice, Sam Houston State University, 544 pages, 1976.

Ferdico's Criminal Procedure for the Law Enforcement Officer 2nd Edition by John N. Ferdico, Assistant Attorney General, State of Maine, 409 pages, 1979.

Israel and LaFave's Criminal Procedure in a Nutshell, 2nd Edition by Jerold H. Israel and Wayne R. LaFave, 372 pages, 1975.

CRIMINAL PROCEDURE—Continued

Johnson's Cases, Materials and Text on The Elements of Criminal Due Process by Phillip E. Johnson, Professor of Law, University of California, Berkeley, 324 pages, 1975.

Kamisar, LaFave and Israel's Cases, Comments and Questions on Basic Criminal Procedure, 4th Edition by Yale Kamisar, Professor of Law, University of Michigan, Wayne R. LaFave, Professor of Law, University of Illinois and Jerold H. Israel, Professor of Law, University of Michigan, 790 pages, 1974. Supplement Annually.

EVIDENCE

Gardner's Criminal Evidence by Thomas J. Gardner, Professor of Criminal Justice, Milwaukee Area Technical College, 694 pages, 1978.

Klein's Law of Evidence for Police, 2nd Edition by Irving J. Klein, Professor of Law and Police Science, John Jay College of Criminal Justice, 632 pages, 1978.

Markle's Criminal Investigation and Presentation of Evidence by Arnold Markle, The State's Attorney, New Haven County, Connecticut, 344 pages, 1976.

INTRODUCTION TO LAW ENFORCEMENT

More's The American Police—Text and Readings by Harry W. More, Jr., Professor of Administration of Justice, California State University at San Jose, 278 pages, 1976.

Police Tactics in Hazardous Situations by the San Diego, California Police Department, 228 pages, 1976.

Schwartz and Goldstein's Law Enforcement Handbook for Police by Louis B. Schwartz, Professor of Law, University of Pennsylvania and Stephen R. Goldstein, Professor of Law, University of Pennsylvania, 333 pages, 1970.

Sutor's Police Operations—Tactical Approaches to Crimes in Progress by Inspector Andrew Sutor, Philadelphia, Pennsylvania Police Department, 329 pages, 1976.

Wrobleski and Hess' Introduction to Law Enforcement and Criminal Justice by Henry Wrobleski and Karen M. Hess, both Professors at Normandale Community College, Bloomington, Minnesota, 525 pages, 1979.

JUVENILE JUSTICE

Cromwell, Killinger, Sarri and Solomon's Text and Selected Readings on Introduction to Juvenile Delinquency by Paul F. Cromwell, Jr., George G Killinger, Rosemary C. Sarri, Professor, School of Social Work, The University of Michigan and H. N. Solomon, Professor of Criminal Justice, Nova University, 502 pages, 1978.

Faust and Brantingham's Juvenile Justice Philosophy: Readings, Cases and Comments, Second Edition, by Frederic L. Faust, Professor of Criminology, Florida State University and Paul J. Brantingham, Department of Criminology, Simon Fraser University, 467 pages, 1979.

Fox's Law of Juvenile Courts in a Nutshell by Sanford J. Fox, Professor of Law, Boston College, 286 pages, 1971.

Johnson's Introduction to the Juvenile Justice System by Thomas A. Johnson, Professor of Criminal Justice, Washington State University, 492 pages, 1975.

Senna and Siegel's Cases and Comments on Juvenile Law by Joseph J. Senna, Professor of Criminal Justice, Northeastern University and Larry J. Siegel, Professor of Criminal Justice, Northeastern University, 543 pages, 1976.

MANAGEMENT AND SUPERVISION

Gaines and Ricks' Selected Readings on Managing the Police Organization by Larry K. Gaines and Truett A. Ricks, both Professors of Criminal Justice, Eastern Kentucky University, 527 pages, 1978.

More's Criminal Justice Management: Text and Readings, by Harry W. More, Jr., 377 pages, 1977.

More's Effective Police Administration: A Behavioral Approach, 2nd Edition by Harry W. More, Jr., Professor, San Jose State University, about 350 pages, 1979.

Roberg's Police Management and Organizational Behavior: A Contingency Approach by Roy R. Roberg, Professor of Criminal Justice, University of Nebraska at Omaha, 350 pages, 1979.

Souryal's Police Administration and Management by Sam S. Souryal, Professor of Criminal Justice, Sam Houston State University, 462 pages, 1977.

Wadman, Paxman and Bentley's Law Enforcement Supervision—A Case Study Approach by Robert C. Wadman, Rio Hondo Community College, Monroe J. Paxman, Brigham Young University and Marion T. Bentley, Utah State University, 224 pages, 1975.

POLICE–COMMUNITY RELATIONS

Cromwell and Keefer's Readings on Police-Community Relations, 2nd Edition by Paul F. Cromwell, Jr., and George Keefer, Professor of Criminal Justice, Southwest Texas State University, 506 pages, 1978.

PSYCHOLOGY

Parker and Meier's Interpersonal Psychology for Law Enforcement and Corrections by L. Craig Parker, Jr., Criminal Justice Dept. Director, University of New Haven and Robert D. Meier, Professor of Criminal Justice, University of New Haven, 290 pages, 1975.

VICE CONTROL

Ferguson's the Nature of Vice Control in the Administration of Justice by Robert W. Ferguson, 509 pages, 1974.

Uelman and Haddox' Cases, Text and Materials on Drug Abuse Law by Gerald F. Uelman, Professor of Law, Loyola University, Los Angeles and Victor G. Haddox, Professor of Criminology, California State University at Long Beach and Clinical Professor of Psychiatry, Law and Behavioral Sciences, University of Southern California School of Medicine, 564 pages, 1974.

N7223—4z